SHAPERS OF
JAPANESE BUDDHISM

SHAPERS OF
JAPANESE BUDDHISM

edited by
Yūsen Kashiwahara
and
Kōyū Sonoda

translated by
Gaynor Sekimori

KŌSEI PUBLISHING CO. • *Tokyo*

This book was originally published in Japanese by Shakai Shisō-sha under the title *Nihon Meisō Retsuden* © 1968 by Yūsen Kashiwahara, Kōyū Sonoda, et al.

The five Japanese priests whose portraits appear on the cover are Kūkai (center, reproduced courtesy of Tō-ji temple, Kyoto) and (counter-clockwise from top right) Nichiren (courtesy of Kuon-ji, Yamanashi); Saichō (courtesy of Ichijō-ji, Hyōgo); Dōgen (courtesy of Hōkyō-ji, Fukui); Shinran (courtesy of the Nara National Museum, Nara).

Editing by Jiho Sargent and Joy S. Sobeck. Typography by Morio Takanashi. Cover design and layout of illustrations by NOBU. The text of this book is set in a computer version of Baskerville with a computer version of Optima for display.

First English edition, 1994

Published by Kōsei Publishing Co., Kōsei Building, 2-7-1 Wada, Suginami-ku, Tokyo 166, Japan. Copyright © 1994 by Kōsei Publishing Co.; all rights reserved. Printed in Japan.

ISBN 4-333-01630-4   LCC Card No. applied for

Contents

Photographs follow page 100

Preface to the English Edition

We welcome this opportunity to contribute to the understanding of Japanese Buddhism among people of other nations. The biographies presented here are the same as those in the Japanese edition, but discussions of Japanese history have been simplified to make the central information more accessible to non-Japanese readers. Our emphasis remains, however, on the ways in which the subjects' religious understanding and activities interacted with the social conditions of their times.

We have sought to maintain a balance between accessibility and scholastic usefulness by eliminating Japanese terms, Japanese document names, and alternative names for persons from the main text, while providing these in appendixes. In the case of Chinese persons and documents, the names are also given in Chinese and, for Indian documents, in Sanskrit as well.

Some explanation is needed of the handling of personal names in this edition. The Meiji Restoration of 1868 led to extensive changes in Japan's use of names. Before that time, ordinary people did not have family names; these were reserved for the nobility and those who had been specially granted names. Soon after the Restoration, however, all citizens registered family names for use from that time forward. English-language usage often follows the

Japanese form of family name before personal name (e.g., Toku-gawa Ieyasu) for figures of pre-Restoration times and the English form of personal name before family name (e.g., Yūsen Kashiwa-hara and Kōyū Sonoda) for those of post-Restoration times. Be-cause the biographies presented here span the point of change but fall mostly in the pre-Restoration period, all names are given in the text and glossary with family name first. (Authors' names, however, follow the Western order, surname last.)

At the same time, a change occurred in the usage concerning priests' names. Buddhist priests were, and are, given dharma names when they enter the clergy. The dharma name corresponds to a personal name, and an additional name may be given for use in place of a family name. There may also be suffixes to the dharma name, such as "ni" to designate a woman's name or "bō" to designate a man's. Actual family names have been used for clerics only since the Meiji Restoration. Before that time, the dharma name was used, generally without any additional name. Honorary titles, however, were often used in place of the dharma name. For simplicity, this book uses only the dharma names of early clerics (in a few cases, an additional name, such as "Shaku," is also given) and uses dharma names for repeated references to post-Restoration priests, giving the family name only in the initial men-tion.

Geographic names also changed substantially. The early prov-inces and domains were replaced in 1871 by today's prefectures. "Edo" became "Tokyo," and other changes occurred. Maps in an appendix show the correspondence between old and modern names for places cited in the text.

Finally, for those who wish to learn more about the subjects of the biographies, there is a reading list.

We hope in this way to be of service both to general readers and to those with academic interest in the religious leaders that have played so important a role in Japanese history.

Preface to the Japanese Edition

More than fourteen hundred years have passed since Buddhism was brought to Japan. During that time it has so deeply influenced Japanese culture, both tangibly and intangibly, that it is now impossible to talk of that culture without mentioning Buddhism. With the reappraisal of traditional Japanese culture in recent years, the time is ripe for a reevaluation of Buddhism as well.

Though Japanese Buddhism is composed of a large number of sects, each with its own distinctive sutras and teachings, all are similar in their objective of freeing humanity through the teachings of Shakyamuni. Their differences stem only from the diverse ways in which those teachings have been experienced through the ages. Buddhist history consists of many heroic confrontations with human suffering by unique individuals at particular times and places.

The twenty people selected for main entries in this book are all great Buddhists who represent the ages in which they lived. Nearly half are persons that we consider today to be the founders of various sects and branches, but they were not selected for that reason alone. The basis for inclusion was, in all cases, the extent to which each person is representative of Japanese Buddhism at a certain historical moment. To put it another way, we asked ourselves how much the person actually understood the teachings of the Buddha under the moderating conditions of a particular society and time, and to what degree those teachings were witnessed in the person's own life. The reader reflecting upon the lives of these twenty figures will gain a clearer view of the long history of Japanese Buddhism and a better perspective on the role Buddhism has played in various historical periods.

History has been called a dialogue between past and present. We can do nothing to hasten its conclusions. The twenty biographies presented here give the basic patterns of the subjects' lives, as understood by the authors, and so provide the raw material for such a dialogue. As you read the book you will be able to enter directly into dialogue with each priest or scholar, unhindered by the constraints of period or sect, to study their teachings. The authors are foremost scholars in the field of Buddhist history, experts with many years' experience in their respective areas of study. They have written with the interests of the nonspecialist, and especially the younger reader, in mind, but they have not deviated in the slightest from the highest standards of modern scholarship. Seventy-five brief biographies, the second part of this book, have been appended to cover the broad sweep of Japanese Buddhism. It is our hope as editors that the reader will find this small book useful in a variety of ways.

PART ONE
Twenty Major Biographies

Gyōgi
(668–749)

by Ryū Sakuma

The *Continued Chronicles of Japan* provides obituary biographies of six clerics: Dōshō, Dōji, Gembō, Gyōgi, Ganjin, and Dōkyō. The compilers must therefore have considered these six to be representative of the Buddhist clergy in the Nara period (710–784). Even today, with the perspective offered by the intervening twelve hundred years, we could hardly better that selection.

Birth

When Gyōgi's grave, within the grounds of Chikurin-ji at Ikoma in the present Nara Prefecture, was opened in 1235, a biographic epitaph was discovered engraved on the copper container protecting the silver reliquary holding his ashes. The reliquary was subsequently taken to Kyoto and displayed to believers. Now, only a fragment remains, on which are engraved some eighteen characters from the epitaph. Official correspondence concerning the discovery, which a priest named Jakumetsu sent to Nara's Tōshō-dai-ji where it is still preserved, incorporates a copy of the full epitaph, made at the time of the discovery.

According to the epitaph, Gyōgi was born in 668 at his mother's house in the Ōtori district of Kawachi Province, entered the

priesthood in 682, and, obtaining the favor of the emperor, was
the first person to be given the title of senior high priest, heading
the government's Bureau of Clergy, in 745. He died at Sugawara-
dera near Nara in 749, aged eighty-one. The epitaph was written
in the month after his death, so it constitutes the oldest biography
we have of Gyōgi; from internal evidence, it is highly reliable.

Gyōgi's family was a branch of a family said to be descended
from the Korean scholar Wani, who came to Japan in 404 and introduced Confucianism to the country. His descendants settled in
Kawachi and Yamato provinces. Like other immigrant families,
Gyōgi's family no doubt preserved traditional technical skills and a
receptivity toward continental culture. In 659 they sponsored the
founding of a temple called Sairin-ji. Other families in the same
area who also traced their descent from Wani were notable for
producing central figures in Nara Buddhism, including Dōshō (see
biography in part 2), Jikun, and Kyōshun.

Gyōgi entered the priesthood at fifteen, possibly at Yakushi-ji,
although the records are not clear on this point. His ordination
master is thought to have been Dōshō, known as the founder of
Japan's Hossō sect. Gyōgi's biography as recorded in the *Continued
Chronicles of Japan* states that he read and immediately mastered the
basic Hossō texts: the *Treatise on the Stages of Yoga Practice* and *Treatise on the Establishment of the Doctrine of Consciousness Only*. Gyōgi's
later interest in social welfare projects may reflect the strength of
Dōshō's influence.

Ordinary Cleric

When Dōshō died in 700, Gyōgi was in the prime of life at thirty-
two and well able to strike out on the path his life was to follow. It
is from this time that records attest to his long and arduous efforts.
The *Continued Chronicles of Japan* summarizes this period as follows:

> Gyōgi traveled around the capital and countryside preaching to
> and converting the masses. He had a thousand followers, both
> laity and clergy. Wherever he went, when people knew he was

coming the villages would empty and men and women would vie to show him reverence. He led all according to their ability and made them incline to good. With his followers, he built bridges and erected dikes in strategic places. Wherever news of him spread, people came and provided their labor, so that the structure was soon finished.

The *Biographical Chronology of Gyōgi,* compiled in 1175, amplifies the account. This record tends to some of the overstatement common in traditional clerical biographies, but in statements about the forty-nine chapels he built in the region surrounding the capital, his social welfare projects, and his promotion of Buddhism, it appears to be largely based on contemporary records and can therefore be trusted. There is little mentioned prior to 702, but after 704, when he converted his own home into a temple, he built chapels almost every year. It should be emphasized that his chapels were not full-blown temples but rather places where people could gather and hear the dharma. Activities such as canal and bridge building centered largely in Settsu, Kawachi, and Izumi provinces. His social welfare projects included the construction of six bridges, one main road, fifteen ponds, six drainage channels, three aqueducts, two ferry depots, four canals, and nine charity houses.

To appreciate the reasons for both Gyōgi's activities and his initial rejection by the government, we must consider the economic conditions of the time. Japan's central government first asserted its authority to own and allot all land and to collect taxes, following the *ritsuryō* legal system based on the contemporary Chinese legal system, during the first phase of reforms in 646. In 702, the Taihō Code was promulgated. This code incorporated a full-scale revision of the existing codes, strengthening the position of provincial and district officials regarding collection of taxes and allotment of land. Under this system, rice land was allotted to each household in an amount corresponding to the number of household members, with adjustments made every six years. In return, the household was liable to a rice tax, which was a form of rent, plus a produce tax on output other than rice and a labor tax, payable as military or public works service or in goods at a fixed conversion rate between labor and goods.

The produce and labor taxes, especially, placed an increasingly heavy burden on small farmers. To make matters worse, the country suffered a string of epidemics and freak weather conditions between 704 and 708. Construction of a new capital at Nara began in 708, and central control intensified after 715 under the growing power of Fujiwara no Fuhito, the leader of a major clan. As the burdens borne by the farming population grew, increasing numbers of farmers deserted their land, prompting a decree in 715 that required all persons who had resided in a district for even as little as three months to pay the district produce and labor taxes. A further edict in 717 deplored the loss of tax revenue by the actions of absconding farmers. Clearly large numbers of people were leaving their land allotments to avoid the tax liabilities.

These were the conditions, then, under which Gyōgi persisted in his religious activities. He employed primitive magic and Taoist practices within his Buddhist teaching and encouraged good through atonement. People flocked to hear him, leaving villages deserted. Some people donated money to him, others provided labor. His followers, laity and clergy, totalled more than a thousand. The description of a popular religious teacher in the *Continued Chronicles of Japan* closely resembles Gyōgi:

> Great crowds of people would gather on the outskirts of the capital, and he led them astray with his bewitching words. At times there were ten thousand people, but even the smallest numbers amounted to several thousand.

For such a band, the building of the forty-nine chapels and the construction of bridges, roads, and so on would not have imposed great difficulties. Such work must have contributed greatly to increasing the productivity of ordinary farmers. In a time of food shortages, the existence of charity houses, offering meals and lodging, must have earned the gratitude of the destitute "starving by the roadsides, dying in the ditches," to whom the houses seemed a buddha encountered while they were in hell. What did cause problems, though, was that Gyōgi's followers included large numbers both of absconding farmers and of priests ordained without government permission. (Permission was required for ordination because priests were considered to be protectors of the nation and its prosperity, so they were expected to live in government-supported temples.) For such people, working under Gyōgi's protection may have been the best method of earning their daily sustenance.

In 717, the government issued an edict condemning certain religious activities and clearly naming Gyōgi:

1. Farmers, disregarding the law, shave their heads of their own accord, don priests' robes, and, becoming privately ordained priests, evade their responsibilities. This is strictly forbidden.

2. Male and female priests should remain quietly within their temples and residences, studying and teaching the Buddhist Way. The ordinary priest Gyōgi and his followers, however, are irresponsibly preaching karmic retribution of good and evil to the people as a whole, enticing farmers to abandon their calling. They are not only violating the teachings of Shakyamuni but also breaking the nation's laws.

3. It is forbidden for male and female priests to go in and out of houses of the sick, practicing suspicious rites. The treatment of illness shall be carried out within the limits prescribed by the law.

The brunt of the edict was against those male and female priests who moved among the masses using magical practices and against the privately ordained priests and absconding farmers that Gyōgi's band admitted into its protection. An added impetus to the issuance of the edict was the need to make a thoroughgoing effort to control priests through the Clerical Code.

This was confirmed in ongoing policy after 717. First a stratagem was devised to commend exemplary priests. In the early winter of 718, the Great Council of State notified the Bureau of Clergy that it should encourage learning and commend those who were models of Buddhism, those who were considered leaders of junior clerics, and those who were considered masters of particular teachings. Consequently, in the following year, Dharma Masters Shin'ei and Dōji (see biography in part 2) were officially recognized and given the income from fifty households. The policy was clearly a conscious reaction to religious activists among the population, including Gyōgi.

Another means by which the government attempted to increase its control over the Buddhist clergy was by reinstituting the official certification system for clergy, first mentioned in 703, demanding the official recording of all ordination details. In this way, privately ordained priests and official priests could be sharply differentiated and more thoroughgoing supervision accomplished. In an entry for the New Year, 720, the *Continued Chronicles of Japan* recorded that "male and female priests have been officially certified for the first time." By reviving the practice, the government hoped to exclude from the Buddhist organization all those who had assumed the garb of priests without authority. As a result of the renovation and clarification of hitherto defective methods of control, all ordained members of the clergy became government officials. This policy continued without change even after government authority shifted from the Fujiwaras to Prince Nagaya.

Results of the new policies were recorded in government documents. In 721, for example, Hōren was commended for his knowledge of the medical arts; Gyōzen, for his mastery of the Consciousness Only doctrine; and a Korean priest known in Japan as Dōzō, for his leadership in Buddhism. Similarly, in 727, the high priest heading the Bureau of Clergy, Gien, was commended for his care in following tradition.

Government regulations for clergy extended as far as the reciting of sutras and other chanting rituals in 720, and in 722 the Bureau of Clergy was based at Yakushi-ji for smoother policy formulation. At the same time, "male and female priests of shallow learning" were criticized for preaching in the capital about karmic retribution of good and evil and for breaking the Buddhist precepts, and were forbidden to forcibly ordain members of the general populace in the capital region. We can assume from this that Gyōgi and others were still subject to control without any change. Further, we are reminded that the policy of differentiating between the officially and the unofficially ordained was still in effect in 724, when the Ministry of Civil Administration, which was in charge of Buddhist affairs among other things, announced that there were

1,122 cases of irregularity in clerical registers around the country.

In 731, when the Fujiwara family was gaining renewed power, a new policy came into effect regarding Gyōgi and his band: "At this time, *ubasoku* and *ubai* [male and female lay Buddhists] that are followers of the dharma master Gyōgi, and that have trained themselves according to the Buddhist teachings, will be permitted to be officially ordained in the case of men sixty-one or older and women fifty-five or older." According to the centrally administered land allocation and taxation system of that time, "old men" aged sixty-one or older were exempt from taxation. Even while the government was intent on maintaining its taxable population, the new policy represented the beginning of an amelioration in the government's attitude to Gyōgi compared with the severe suppression he and others like him suffered during the Yōrō era (717–724). It is interesting to note that the *Continued Chronicles of Japan* entry just quoted refers to Gyōgi not as an "ordinary priest" but as a "dharma master."

Priest of Yakushi-ji

A document composed in 738 refers to Gyōgi as "most venerable," a designation given only to a limited number of priests in that period. This emphasizes the change in government policy and in the official attitude toward Gyōgi that took place within the decade. The *Biographical Chronology of Gyōgi* contains a document that suggests a connection with the imperial court in 733. In addition, we should note that in 734 the Great Council of State stipulated the basic requisites for ordination as at least three years of religious training apart from secular life and the ability to chant the *Golden Light* or *Lotus* sutra. Ordination was permitted for anyone who could meet these conditions. In this, too, we can see a broadening of tolerance for Gyōgi's followers.

Among the documents stored in Nara's Shōso-in treasure house is a letter of recommendation for ordination of a lay practitioner in which Gyōgi, "a master priest of Yakushi-ji," is mentioned as instructor. Though not dated, the document is considered from internal evidence to have been written some time after 740 and prior to

Gyōgi's appointment in 745 as senior assistant high priest of the Bureau of Clergy.

What concerns us here is the reference to Gyōgi as "master priest." Under the official certification system for clergy of 720, an aspirant to the priesthood first had to receive a recommendation for initial ordination. After ordination, he or she was given an ordination certificate stamped with the seal of the Ministry of Civil Administration, and was then called a *shami* (male novice) or *shamini* (female novice). Only those with an ordination certificate could receive the full clerical precepts. The system became further regulated when the Chinese priest Ganjin arrived in Japan in 753. Before that, full precepts ceremonies were conducted at a number of temples, including Daian-ji, Asuka-dera, and, after 721, Yakushi-ji, the headquarters of the Bureau of Clergy, with no insistence on the presence of ten priests who had been properly ordained themselves. After the full precepts ceremony, the ordainee received a precepts certificate with the seal of the Ministry of Civil Administration and was then called a *biku* or *bikuni* (male or female cleric). The third and final rank, that of master priest, was given to selected people who had already achieved the first two ranks, though we do not know the details of how selection took place. It can also be conjectured from documents of the period that high-ranking official priests were equivalent to government officials of the fifth rank and above.

As we have seen, Gyōgi was already being referred to as "most venerable" in 738, and at some point before 745 he achieved the rank of master priest. How was it that the former "ordinary priest" came to enter Yakushi-ji and achieve such high rank? The question seems even to have been raised at the time, according to a story recorded in the *Miraculous Stories from the Japanese Buddhist Tradition* about the priest Shaku Chikō:

Shaku Chikō was a man of Kawachi Province and priest of Sukita-dera in the Asukabe district in the same province. He was innately intelligent and unexcelled in knowledge. He composed commentaries on the *Ullambana Sutra, Great Perfection of*

Wisdom Sutra, and *Heart Sutra* among others and lectured on the Buddhist teachings to many students.

There was at that time a *shami* called Gyōgi. Emperor Shōmu was impressed with his dignity and virtue and deeply respected and believed in him. Out of reverence and praise for him, people of the time called him a bodhisattva. In the winter of 744, he was appointed senior high priest [of the Bureau of Clergy]. At this, Dharma Master Chikō became envious and abused him, saying, "It is I who am wise, and Gyōgi is no more than a *shami.* Why therefore does the emperor ignore my wisdom and praise and use one who is a mere *shami?*" Resenting the situation, he retired to live at Sukita-dera.

If we ignore the year of the appointment (744), this is a deeply interesting statement. First, Gyōgi was not referred to as a practicing priest of an official temple but as a *shami* of shallow understanding. Second, there was something extraordinary in his appointment as senior high priest of the Bureau of Clergy that aroused the opposition of the official priests. His connection with Yakushi-ji should have followed his appointment as an official priest, and his direct promotion to the rank of master priest must have ignored the normal course.

The specialness of the situation resembles that of a privately ordained priest, Maruko no Muraji Miyamaro, who succeeded in finding gold in Mutsu Province, was given the Buddhist name of Ōhō (which can be interpreted as "supplier of treasure"), and was raised directly to the rank of master priest.

In Gyōgi's case, what brought about a change in the government's attitude toward him were his Buddhist teaching activities among the people, his great influence among the masses, and his ability to mobilize his followers for civil engineering projects. It would therefore be natural to suspect that his promotion was chiefly a reward for his efforts involving various projects between 741 and 745, from the construction of the new capital of Kunikyō in Yamashiro Province to that of the Great Buddha of Tōdai-ji in Nara (first proposed in 743).

Senior High Priest

About the time when it is thought that Gyōgi began to be wooed by the authorities, Japan was beset with a succession of natural calamities, famines, and the spread of epidemics. The government sponsored Shinto prayers to the native deities and Buddhist rites of propitiation, but they seemed to have no effect, for in 737 all four sons of Fujiwara no Fuhito died of smallpox. Tachibana no Moroe then came into power, and under him a priest named Gembō and Kibi no Makibi, both recently returned from China, became influential figures in the government. The Fujiwara family, however, strongly criticized how these men were running affairs, and in 740 Fujiwara no Hirotsugu, a grandson of Fujiwara no Fuhito, who was an official in the military and administrative headquarters at Dazaifu on Kyushu, cited the prevailing calamities in pointing out the deficiencies of the government, requested that Gembō and Kibi no Makibi be removed from office, and raised an army in rebellion. Though the rebellion was put down and Hirotsugu was executed the same year, the affair destroyed Emperor Shōmu's peace of mind.

Believing that disturbing elements had risen in the capital, Nara, the emperor decided at the end of 740 to abandon Nara and erect a new capital, to be called Kunikyō, in Yamashiro Province. Work commenced early the following year, and progressed rapidly. Early in 741, the emperor issued an edict concerning the erection of a pair of official temples called Kokubun-ji, one for men and one for women, in each province.

For such construction, not only draft labor but also the cooperation of the landed gentry class was necessary. The strength of those who followed Gyōgi began to be appreciated for the first time. On the occasion of a bridge being built over the Sawada River, not far from the new capital, *ubasoku* from all over the country rendered their services. Gyōgi was doubtless behind this.

Further, late in 743 the emperor issued an edict commanding the erection of a Great Buddha. Perhaps behind the plan was a wish during a time of distress to unite the people in a great undertaking. The work can be seen as contributing to the maintenance and restoration of the Chinese-style *ritsuryō* government. Four days later, Emperor Shōmu went to Shigaraki Palace for the start of work on the image of Vairocana Buddha. Gyōgi and his followers canvassed the people for their support and contributions toward the undertaking. Here we can clearly see the plan of the government to use Gyōgi's organizational abilities and can keenly appreciate one aspect of Gyōgi's greatness regarding his long efforts at spreading Buddhism among the common people. Late in 744 the framework for the great statue was set up at Kōga-ji in Shigaraki. The emperor himself took part in pulling the ropes. Early in the following year, Gyōgi was appointed senior high priest. The appointment possibly was on the one hand a reward for his efforts toward construction of the Great Buddha, and on the other a recognition that he had the stature and influence to oppose the high priest, Gembō, who was beginning to deviate from his responsibilities in the Bureau of Clergy. As we saw in the excerpt from the *Miraculous Stories* quoted earlier, this was an appointment that had to be forced on the clerical world.

The construction of the Great Buddha took on new life after the capital was transferred back to Nara. Work was resumed in the grounds of Konshō-ji (now Tōdai-ji), east of the capital. We can conjecture that again Gyōgi played an important role in the work. We do not know, however, whether he stood at the head of the common people as before. In the first weeks of 749, Gyōgi conferred the bodhisattva precepts on the emperor. Soon afterward, Gyōgi became ill at Sugawara-dera and died after entrusting his temples to his dharma successor Kōshin. So ended, at the age of eighty-one, a life of many fluctuations.

Ganjin
(688–763)

by Ryū Sakuma

Seeking a Precepts Transmitter

In 732 the Japanese government decided once more to send an embassy to the T'ang court in China after an interval of seventeen years. They appointed an ambassador and deputy ambassador, four magistrates, and four official recorders. That autumn the court ordered the building of four ships for the embassy. The following summer, 733, the four ships left port together. On board were two priests of Kōfuku-ji: Eiei and Fushō. According to accounts such as the *Records of Tōdai-ji*, their dispatch was the work of Ryūson, a priest of Gangō-ji, who was concerned that there was no truly qualified precepts transmitter in Japan, and of Prince Toneri, who gave practical help in finding one.

This account as it stands is unsatisfactory and unconvincing. Why only now was it thought necessary to invite a precepts transmitter to come from China? Two hundred years had passed since the official transmission of Buddhism to Japan. Receiving the precepts must already have become an indispensable ritual for male and female clergy. Although the formality of having three ordination masters and seven attesters who were themselves properly

14

ordained was not followed, there is no doubt that granting the precepts had become customary practice. Furthermore, what with the arrival in Japan of highly qualified Chinese priests and the return of Japanese scholar-priests from the continent, there was ample opportunity to follow the letter of the ritual if that had been desired.

The fact that no plan to invite a Chinese precepts transmitter had been put forward previously suggests another dimension to the invitation. Some scholars are of the opinion that bringing such a qualified Chinese priest would have established formal ritual and thus given strength to the measures being taken against Gyōgi's band. The official attitude toward Gyōgi had already ameliorated, however, so that cannot be the whole answer. Another possibility that should be considered is that the introduction of the formal precepts in Japan was part of a plan to create a better clergy. Late in 734 a directive from the Great Council of State announced that "the transmission of Buddhism lies with the male and female priests," and set forth minimum requirements for candidates for ordination. After the Yōrō era (717–724) the government had taken to encouraging scholarship among the clergy as a means of control, which lends weight to the control hypothesis.

The central role ascribed to Ryūson also needs examination. In 732 he was not yet thirty, and though he was later to become a preceptor in the Bureau of Clergy and a priest of great erudition, it is scarcely conceivable that he then had the influence to make such a request of Prince Toneri. It is more likely that the plan emanated from a member of the Bureau of Clergy, someone like Benjō or Shin'ei, who played a large role in recommending and planning policy concerning Buddhist affairs, or Dōji (see biography in part 2), who had been appointed to the Bureau of Clergy as a preceptor in 729. Dōji had returned to Japan in 718 after spending seventeen years in China. From that time he was considered, with Shin'ei, an outstanding leader in the Buddhist world and a source of hope for the future. He wrote some sections of the *Chronicles of Japan* under the direction of Prince Toneri and later established Daian-ji and participated in establishing the system of a pair of temples in each province. Following his return from China, Dōji wrote a treatise called *A Fool's Idea* in which he deplored the inadequacies of the Japanese Buddhist clergy as compared with the Chinese. It is very likely that he devised the scheme to bring a Chinese master to Japan to establish an organization emulating the Chinese, which could foster well-qualified priests for "the protection of the nation and the good of the people."

Ganjin Comes to Japan

The four ships of the embassy took the southern route to China via the East China Sea and arrived near the estuary of the Yangtze four months after leaving Japan. The Chinese emperor, Hsüan-tsung, and his court were at that time in Lo-yang. Chinese records attest that the Japanese mission arrived at the capital in the summer of 734. Eiei and Fushō doubtlessly also arrived then, as members of the embassy. Once there, they were assigned by the T'ang government to a temple, where they received the orthodox ordination, with the 250 precepts in the *Vinaya of Four Categories,* from Ting-pin. Ting-pin, like Chien-chen (in Japanese, Ganjin), was an eminent master of the Vinaya (precepts) sect and was the author of *Commentary on Fa Li's Annotations on the Vinaya of Four Categories.*

While in residence at that temple, Eiei and Fushō made the acquaintance of Tao-hsüan (in Japanese, Dōsen), a priest well-versed in the Vinaya and a scholar of Hua-yen (Kegon) and T'ien-t'ai (Tendai) doctrines. They invited Dōsen to go to Japan. The embassy left for Japan in the winter of 734. On the ambassador's ship were Gembō and Kibi no Makibi, returning to Japan after several years in China (and bringing the art of embroidery, the game of Go, and a form of four-stringed lute). On the deputy ambassador's ship were Dōsen, the Indian priest Bodhisena, and the Vietnamese priest Fo-che. The former ship did not reach Japan until the following year; the latter, blown south toward Indonesia, did not arrive until 736. After reaching Japan, Dōsen lived mainly at Daian-ji in Nara. It was he who presented the ideological basis for the building of the Great Buddha. In 751 he was appointed preceptor in the Bureau of Clergy, and the following year he chanted mantras at the dedication of the Great Buddha under the direction of Bodhisena. His students included Saichō's master, Gyōhyō. Dōsen also had a close relationship with Kibi no Makibi.

Meanwhile, Eiei and Fushō pursued their studies in Lo-yang and Ch'ang-an. Soon nine years had passed, and they still had not found a precepts transmitter willing to travel to Japan. Not wanting to return to Japan with their mission unaccomplished, they conferred with the priest of a temple in Ch'ang-an, who was a student of Ganjin. Perhaps at his recommendation, they traveled to Yang-chou in the winter of 742, where they succeeded in meeting Ganjin for the first time. Ganjin, then fifty-four, was a master of the Nan-shan school of Vinaya interpretation and was also versed in T'ien-t'ai doctrines. His fame was widespread in China. An account of Ganjin, *The Journey of the T'ang Great Master to the East,* written in 779, describes that meeting:

Eiei and Fushō arrived at Ta-ming temple, prostrated themselves at the feet of the Great Priest, and described their mission in detail. "The Buddha-Dharma in its eastward flow has reached the country of Japan, but although the dharma is being propagated, there is no one able to transmit it. . . . We ask whether any priest would be willing to cross to the east and cause the dharma to flourish there." The Great Priest replied, "That is a country where Buddhism is destined to flourish. Who among my followers will respond to that invitation and set out for the land of Japan, there to transmit the dharma?" There was silence among the followers. No one made any answer. At length a priest named Hsiang-yen spoke. "That country is exceedingly far away, and it is difficult to arrive there safely. In a hundred sailings, less than one is successful. The human body is hard to acquire, and to be born in China is even more difficult. We have not yet acquired training, and the fruits of our practice have not yet appeared. Therefore all the followers remain silent and do not answer.'' The Great Priest then said, "This is for the good of the dharma. A Buddhist should not care about risking his life. Since none of you will go, I will go myself.''

With Ganjin's powerful statement, the decision was made. That, though, was but the beginning of many years fraught with difficulties and troubles as the priests attempted to make the arduous journey back to Japan. The first attempt in the summer of 743 was foiled when the party was arrested on a trumped-up charge of piracy and their ship was seized. Two more attempts were made, but the ship was in both cases driven ashore by adverse winds. The fourth try, early in 745, was confounded by official action at the behest of various concerned priests and Ganjin's followers, to prevent him from leaving China. Plans for the crossing were resumed in 748. This time again the ship encountered heavy winds and was blown off course, far to the south. *The Journey of the T'ang Great Master to the East* says:

> There was no water on board. They could not swallow even a grain of rice, so parched were their throats, and could not spit either. When they drank sea water their stomachs immediately swelled. Never in all their lives had they experienced such torture.

Perhaps as a result of this experience, Eiei became sick and died after the survivors of the shipwreck had been rescued. It was late in 749. Ganjin's eyes began to fail around this time, and eventually he lost his sight completely.

In 750 the Japanese government again decided to send an embassy to China and appointed an ambassador plus Kibi no Makibi as one of two deputy ambassadors. Arriving in China in 752, they negotiated with the T'ang government to allow Ganjin to return with them, but did not meet with success. They therefore pledged to welcome him aboard unofficially. Finally, near the end of 753, Ganjin and his party set sail aboard the deputy ambassador's ship. Shortly before the end of the year, the ship touched land at a bay in southern Kyushu. They reached the Kyushu government headquarters at Dazaifu a week later and arrived safely at Naniwa, the port from which the ship had departed, about a month after that. Eleven years had passed since the first attempt to sail to Japan. In the interval, thirty-six of Ganjin's companions, including Eiei, had lost their lives. Ganjin was already sixty-six. Twenty-four Chinese clerics accompanied him to Japan.

Ganjin's Influence

Ganjin and his party received a great welcome from the government and the people. They arrived at the capital early in 754 and, guided by Rōben, the founder and first administrator of Tōdai-ji (see biography in part 2), went to bow before the Great Buddha. They were assigned lodgings at Tōdai-ji, where they were visited by Dōsen, Bodhisena, and government leaders who congratulated them on their arrival. Kibi no Makibi later came to Tōdai-ji as an imperial messenger, bearing this pronouncement:

> Great and exalted priest, you have come to this land from far across the blue waves. Truly my desires have been answered and my happiness knows no bounds. More than ten years have passed since the building of Tōdai-ji, and it has always been my wish to see an ordination platform installed here and the precepts transmitted. This wish has been constantly in my heart. Now many venerable priests have come from afar to transmit the precepts, and my heart truly rejoices. From henceforth I entrust to you the administering of the precepts and the transmission of the clerical regulations.

In summer, an ordination platform was set up in front of the Great Buddha Hall at Tōdai-ji. The retired emperor Shōmu ascended the platform and received the bodhisattva precepts, as did the empress dowager Kōmyō, the reigning empress Kōken, and 440 members of the clergy. In addition, it is recorded that high-ranking priests abandoned their previous precepts and were ordained anew. Soon an edict was issued ordering construction of a precepts hall, and this was completed in the autumn of the following year (755). Living quarters for Ganjin and his party were built in the grounds of Tōdai-ji and named Tōzen-in (T'ang Meditation Hall). All seemed to be going well, but in fact problems were mounting.

Ganjin's designation as administrator of the precepts and transmitter of clerical regulations naturally involved a conflict between the old and the new. The Vinaya school already existed in Japan as the Ritsu sect, a study group concerned with the clerical regulations, and its exponents were to be found at all the capital's major temples. There is a record of a debate at Kōfuku-ji between one of Ganjin's Chinese clerics and two Japanese clerics, and other writings also hint at dissension. Though Japanese priests submitted to the new requirements, the resignations from the Bureau of Clergy of Dōsen (who was Chinese himself) and Ryūson (who had been instrumental in bringing Ganjin in the first place) stemmed from their incompatibility, as representatives of the old order, with Ganjin.

Problems also arose over the precepts transmission itself. Japan already had a history of precepts conferral, though it was not done according to the orthodox ritual requiring three ordination masters and seven attesters. Also no formal ordination platform was used. Records refer to the existence of ordination ceremonies at Daian-ji, Asuka-dera, Yakushi-ji, and Kōfuku-ji. Unlike China, Japan did not allow all applicants to obtain official ordination. Buddhism was considered to bear an important responsibility for protecting the nation. Male and female priests of the period received special rights from the government as people appointed to work for national prosperity and protection. Consequently, control of ordination and conferring of the precepts was also held by the government. Upon initial ordination, novice priests received an ordination certificate stamped with the seal of the Ministry of Civil Administration, and only those who possessed such certificates were permitted to receive the full precepts. Furthermore, not all novice priests could receive the precepts, even though they had ordination certificates. Each temple is thought to have notified the Bureau of Clergy of the results of its investigation of the aspirant's character and other things. The minimum requirements for those who wished to become priests, whether men or women, had been stipulated in 734 as the ability to chant either the *Lotus Sutra* or the *Golden Light Sutra,* to perform Buddhist rituals, and to have performed religious training apart from secular life for at least three years. In fact, judging from contemporary records, the actual requirements for ordination were a lot stiffer than that. After precepts ordination, the male or female priest received a precepts certificate, again stamped with the seal of the Ministry of Civil Administration.

As we have already seen, after Ganjin arrived from China, he established a new precepts hall and assumed full responsibility for all ordinations. According to an entry in the *Later Chronicles of Japan* for early 813, "Since the Tempyō-Shōhō era [749–757], when someone received the precepts any previous ordination certificate was voided and the name removed from the official register. The name was restored to the official register only after ordination in the orthodox way with ten qualified priests in attendance." Thus, in place of the previous precepts certificate, one with the signatures of all ten masters had to be obtained. But even though there had been a change in the issuing of the precepts certificate and in the jurisdiction of ordination as a whole, because the jurisdiction of the presiding priests as individuals was not recognized, there had been no essential alteration of the system. An ordination certificate was still required to receive the precepts, and all precepts ordinations had to take place in the precepts hall at Tōdai-ji. After 761, ordination centers were also established at Yakushi-ji in Shimotsuke Province and Kanzeon-ji in Tsukushi (in the north of Kyushu). When we consider that precepts ordinations were conducted annually and only at designated regional temples, we have to agree that Ganjin's reforms did not go beyond ritual.

The retired emperor Shōmu finally died in 756. Three weeks later, the Bureau of Clergy was reconstituted; Ganjin and Rōben were appointed senior assistant high priests, Jikun junior assistant high priest, and Hosshin (one of Ganjin's Chinese followers) and Kyōshun, preceptors. These appointments were partly a reward for services rendered during the retired emperor's illness and partly a political act on the part of government officials. It is known that many priests of this period were skilled physicians. Whereas Rōben and Jikun recited sutras dedicated to the emperor's health, Ganjin, to whom is ascribed a work called *Master Ganjin's Secret Method,* probably had specialized medical knowledge. From a political point of view, Jikun had been master lecturer to the court, and not only had he been deeply respected by the retired emperor Shōmu and empress dowager Kōmyō, but, appointed as administrator of Kōfuku-ji, he also was close to Fujiwara no Nakamaro, the most prominent figure in the government at the time. The empress dowager also greatly relied on Kyōshun, the head of Hokke-ji. That Ganjin and Hosshin, whose Japanese cannot have been very proficient, were appointed to the Bureau of Clergy in the company of people like Jikun and Kyōshun, means that there must have been great hopes for their ability in other areas—their great learning and their purity of practice, which were sufficient to preserve and protect the nation, and their leadership of the male and female clergy.

The Tōdai-ji register of the possessions of Emperor Shōmu that Kōmyō dedicated to Tōdai-ji records that the arrival in Japan of Bodhisena and Ganjin had been unprecedented events in Japanese Buddhist circles. In 757 an edict was published that stated that "for the protection and maintenance of Buddhism, nothing is more important than the precepts and regulations. To practice the precepts is to offer true worship. Therefore rice fields have long been bestowed upon precepts transmitters in the official temples. Henceforth, whenever temples hold twice-monthly community ceremonies [which included handling of precepts violations among the clergy], rice donations will always be measured out and augmented. We hope that indolent priests will be spurred in their efforts and that masters with deep training will continue with their training." Late in the same year, new rice fields in Bizen Province were bestowed upon Tōdai-ji's Tōzen-in for the support of those who had come from all over the country to study the Vinaya. Such were the hopes placed in Ganjin and his company.

Establishment of Tōshōdai-ji

In the autumn of 758, Empress Kōken abdicated in favor of Prince Ōi, the son of Prince Toneri, who thus became Emperor Junnin. The assembled ministers and members of the Bureau of Clergy gave honorific titles to retiring empress Kōken and her mother, the empress dowager. Kōken referred to Ganjin in her edict:

> This priest Ganjin, senior assistant high priest [of the Bureau of Clergy], is indeed pure in his practice of the precepts and does not change though his hair becomes white with age. He came from afar, crossing the blue waves, and arrived here at our court. I command that he be given the title of Great Priest and be esteemed and venerated. Government affairs are demanding and troublesome and should not make demands on one so advanced in years. I therefore give him leave to retire from the Bureau of Clergy. Those priests from various temples who wish to learn the Vinaya should go and study under him.

As a result, Ganjin left his position in the Bureau of Clergy, gave up politics, and devoted himself to the training of priests, both male and female.

Exactly a year later, in the autumn of 759, a temple was finished on land that Ganjin had been awarded, which previously belonged to an imperial prince. It was called Tōritsu Shōdai-ji, and its income came from the rice fields in Bizen Province he had received earlier. Tōritsu Shōdai-ji (known later as Tōshōdai-ji) was clearly a private, as opposed to an official, temple. It was doubtless considerably smaller than it is today, probably being no more than a remodeling of the prince's former residence.

There Ganjin and his followers moved. Tōdai-ji's Tōzen-in was conferred upon Hosshin, with the honorary title of Priest of the Precepts. Only the priests essential for precepts ordination and Hosshin's direct followers remained there. During Ganjin's lifetime, Tōshōdai-ji received the donation of an assembly hall from the imperial palace, which was dismantled during renovations from 760 to 761 and rebuilt at Tōshōdai-ji as the lecture hall. The dining hall was donated by Fujiwara no Nakamaro at about the same time. The main hall appears not to have been built yet. As a private temple, its economic base was not strong enough to afford massive building.

The biography of Ssu-t'o, one of Ganjin's Chinese followers, in *A Record of Clergy in the Enryaku Era* says that Ganjin was criticized for moving to Tōshōdai-ji. We do not know the details, but it is possible that it was because he was beating out a path in an entirely new direction in attempting to build a temple devoted solely to the teaching and transmission of the Vinaya. The idea of one temple housing only the priests of a particular school was quite foreign to the thinking of the time. Another possible cause for criticism was his transfer from Tōzen-in to Tōshōdai-ji of the income from the Bizen Province rice fields.

Ganjin's Death

The death of Empress Dowager Kōmyō in 760 had resounding political repercussions. Fujiwara no Nakamaro, having lost his patron, found his influence steadily dwindling and faced growing opposition from people averse to his power and from the priest Dōkyō, who was then associated with the retired empress, Kōken. Now far away from political affairs, Ganjin devoted himself to building his temple and training priests in the Vinaya. Around the spring of 763 his health began to decline. His successor, Ninki, realizing that Ganjin's death was not far away, called the other followers together and they had a portrait statue made of him. This is the statue now kept in the Founder's Hall at Tōshōdai-ji. On June 22, 763, Ganjin assumed the full lotus meditation position, and, facing west, quietly closed his seventy-five years of life.

His ten years in Japan cannot have been entirely pleasant. Despite the great welcome he had received on all sides when he came, his work involving the establishment of the precepts had been fraught with difficulties. Nevertheless, his nobility of character, his indomitable spirit, and his profound knowledge made a deep impression on many people, and his influence as a true teacher of Buddhism was extensive.

Of all Ganjin's followers, the one to achieve the greatest fame was Hosshin. He had become a preceptor in 756 and remained in the Bureau of Clergy after Ganjin's retirement, residing at Tōzen-in as Priest of the Precepts. In 760, he helped Rōben and Jikun to set up a system of ranks for priests and in the following year was instrumental in extending ordination platforms to eastern Japan and Kyushu, thereby playing an important role in the expansion of the precepts system in the country. Ssu-t'o, who had been insep-arable from Ganjin ever since they first tried to cross to Japan, devoted his efforts to eulogizing his dead master. He wrote a biog-raphy of him in three volumes (*Life of the Great Priest*), and in 779 commissioned the writing of the other biography quoted earlier, *The Journey of the T'ang Great Master to the East*. Another Chinese follower, Ju-pao, who could not have been older than ten when he arrived in Japan with Ganjin, contributed most to the completion of Tōshōdai-ji after Ganjin's death. To his efforts are attributed the building of the main hall around 780, the construction of the Kenjaku-dō (a building originally belonging to a Fujiwara), the priests' quarters, and the pagoda. The small private temple had become a great complex of majestic appearance.

Saichō

(767–822)

by Kōyū Sonoda

Saichō and Mount Hiei

Almost every Japanese associates Mount Hiei, northeast of Kyoto, with Saichō, who spent the greater part of his life there. In fact, it is impossible to talk of Saichō's life without mentioning Mount Hiei and equally difficult to discuss his thought and religion without taking the mountain into consideration.

Mount Hiei rises some eight hundred meters above sea level in a graceful shape beloved by the people of Kyoto. Today a scenic road cuts through along the north-south ridge, and it is possible to reach the summit from the city's center in a little less than an hour. Visitors throng there in summer to escape the heat and to enjoy their leisure, but even then it is rare for the weather on the mountain to be clear and sunny. Though the sun might be shining on the world below, once you reach the top of the mountain you find fog settling before you realize it, and it is quite common to be unable to take advantage of the superb view. Clouds and fog envelop the mountain. Walking among the fog-enshrouded cedars, you find your clothing damp with the cold droplets. Even inside buildings, the fog creeps like smoke from under the eaves, making everything damp and moldy.

It is even worse in winter. To spend a whole winter up on the deserted summit is to experience nights of extreme cold when the temperature falls below $-10°C$. So cold is it that the ridgepoles and ceiling beams creak. It is far more grueling than you would ever expect. To make matters worse, you have only to take a step outdoors to see the dazzling brilliance of Kyoto lying at your feet. To have a center of prosperity and comfort so close, yet have to endure the terrible environment on the mountain, is another face of religious practice on Mount Hiei.

For many centuries, life on Mount Hiei has been summed up as a life of learning, humidity, cold, and poverty. Humidity and cold clearly refer to the demanding climatic conditions on the mountain; learning and poverty, on the other hand, are the subjective human element, the conditions necessary for a practitioner to concentrate on seeking enlightenment.

Life on the mountain must, above all things, be simplicity itself. Saichō said that life is at its best when one wears clothing made of rags discarded by the roadside, lives in a thatched hut of bamboo, and sleeps at night upon straw. Clerics should eat only what is unsought and freely given, he said. Saichō imposed on his dharma heirs the same twelve-year period of strict training on the mountain that he himself had undertaken. His advocacy of secluded training and learning should not be interpreted as mere asceticism. His life of extreme frugality was backed by an intense religious spirit. Saichō called this spirit "aspiration for enlightenment," and asked, "What is the treasure of the nation? The treasure is a mind that aspires to enlightenment. A person possessing an enlightenment-seeking mind is a treasure of the nation" (*Regulations for the Annual Quota Students of the Tendai Lotus Sect*).

A person who is truly useful to the nation and society is one who aspires to enlightenment. Saichō hoped that twelve years of religious training on the mountain would help cultivate that aspiration. The frugal style of life and demanding training were not ends in themselves. They were only the means by which the aspiration for enlightenment could be realized. Another quotation brings out this aspect even more clearly: "Within the aspiration for enlightenment there are food and clothing, but within food and clothing there is not the aspiration for enlightenment'' (*Precepts for Perfect and Sudden Enlightenment*).

Saichō was saying that to achieve the liberation to be gained from religion, one must first discard the freedoms of the secular life. It was this outlook of a single-minded pursuit of enlightenment that gave birth to the tradition of learning, humidity, cold, and poverty that characterized religious life on Mount Hiei. Saichō selected Mount Hiei as a place where religious freedom could be realized. "Forgetting hunger, taking pleasure in the mountain; enduring the cold, dwelling in the valleys": these words from his *Treatise on the Mahayana Precepts* reveal no trace of strained endurance.

Cleric and Hermit

Saichō was born in 767 in Ōmi Province, to the east of Mount Hiei. His birth name was Mitsu no Obito Hirono. He died at the age of fifty-five, in 822.

His father was from a Chinese immigrant family said to have been descended from the last emperor of the Later Han dynasty. His mother's family is not known. An interesting episode has been transmitted concerning Saichō's birth. His father was a devout Buddhist, who even converted his house into a temple, but he grieved because he had no children. One day he climbed Mount Hiei seeking an auspicious place to supplicate the deity of the mountain. After several days, he came across such a site, balmy with sweet fragrance, "on the left flank of Mount Hiei, to the right of the shrine." There he built a hut and acknowledged his faults with great sincerity. On the fourth night, just as dawn was breaking, he was shown in a dream the birth of a son, blessed with marks of goodness and virtue. Legend says that the dream child was the boy that was to become Saichō. Though this story is not of the order of the Buddha's birth or of Christ's virgin birth, it illustrates how miraculous tales naturally accrue to the birth of great religious figures. Saichō, then, was the child sent in answer to a supplication to Hie Sannō, the deity of Mount Hiei. Here began the fate that would eventually link him with the mountain.

When Saichō was eleven, he entered the Ōmi Provincial Temple and studied under Gyōhyō, a dharma heir of Dōsen, the Vinaya master who arrived in Japan in 736. Before going to that temple, Gyōhyō had long been associated with Daian-ji in Nara. Saichō was officially ordained as a novice in 780, when he was thirteen, filling a vacancy in the temple's clergy quota left by the death of a priest named Saijaku. The "sai" in Saichō's name may have been chosen out of respect for that dead priest. In the summer of 785, at the age of eighteen, he received full ordination at the ordination platform of Tōdai-ji in Nara, according to the regulations of the time. Since 754 the government had controlled all ordinations, and since 761 only three temples in the whole country were allowed to perform them. Upon completion of the precepts ordination, Saichō possessed qualifications that made him a full-fledged priest in the eyes of the world. Up until this time his life had gone smoothly, but three months after the precepts ordination he was suddenly assailed by feelings about the transience of worldly things. He took refuge in the mountains, away from settled areas, to lead a life of meditation "sitting under trees and upon rocks." The place he went was Mount Hiei.

Saichō entered the clergy in a period of social turbulence. In 780 the indigenous Ezo people mounted a great rebellion in the north, and weaknesses in the centrally dominated *ritsuryō* system of land allocation and taxation were becoming apparent. Emperor Kammu moved the capital to Nagaoka in 784, attempting to ameliorate the situation. Perhaps it was these unsettled conditions that induced the eighteen-year-old Saichō to despair at the thought of the world's fragility. The Ōmi Provincial Temple he had entered overlooked the main east-west highway. Saichō must have seen bands of landless and homeless vagrants and companies of soldiers setting off in the morning on their way east to put down the rebellion, plus long columns arriving in the evening from the east, bearing heavy consignments of tribute. Also, in the very year Saichō was ordained at Tōdai-ji, the temple where he had trained was burned down.

Saichō lived in a small hermitage on Mount Hiei from 785 to 797, devoting himself quietly to meditation. His spiritual condition of this time is plainly reflected in the vow he made when he went to Mount Hiei: "The three realms, floating in boundless time, are filled with suffering from which there is no respite. Living beings, their existence tumultuous, can only lament, for there is nothing that is joyful."

This opening sentence holds the keynote of the vow—a strong sense of impermanence. Even more attention is drawn by the words he uses to describe his own insight about himself: "I, Saichō, of fools the most foolish, of the deluded the most deluded, unworthy, desolate, lowest of the low."

A modern scholar has suggested that four hundred years later, when Shinran (see biography in part 1) adopted the sobriquet "desolate fool," he was influenced by Saichō's expression of misery. Whatever the truth of the matter, Shinran took the name when he was thirty-four, the year that he was exiled to Echigo during the Jōdo sect's persecution. When we remember that Saichō was only eighteen when he wrote those words of deep personal insight, we have to acknowledge his uncommon and precocious religious spirit. He did not seek to dissolve his feeling of transience in ideas of the impermanence of the secular world, but took it upon himself personally as a sense of guilt.

Study in China and Establishment of the Tendai Sect in Japan

In his vow, Saichō pledged five things, after which he stated: "I vow that not I alone will taste release and that not I alone will realize calm. I vow that all beings of the world will together reach the wonderful enlightenment."

How did he come to such a statement, filled as it is with Mahayana spirit? Under Gyōhyō's tutelage he had already studied the orthodox teachings of the Hossō sect, the doctrine of Consciousness Only, so it is fairly safe to conclude that this was his own doctrinal position at the time he went to Mount Hiei. That sect, though, stated firmly that the potential for buddhahood (buddha-nature) differed according to the inherent capacities of living beings and that for some, buddhahood was impossible. One cannot, therefore, interpret the vow and its "I vow that not I alone will taste release" in terms of the Hossō teachings. It is not at all strange that Saichō should have become more and more attracted to Kegon teachings as found in Fa-tsang's *Discussion of the Five Teachings and the Ten Sects* and other works.

Saichō's autobiography indicates that his interest in Chinese T'ien-t'ai doctrine grew out of references to it in works such as these. His joy when he was at last able to get hold of T'ien-t'ai writings can well be imagined. What was so appealing about T'ien-t'ai thought was its concept that all beings have the potential for buddhahood, a theory that was to be clarified through religious practice and training. The far-reaching T'ien-t'ai philosophy of the reality of phenomena even taught that vegetable life, such as trees and grass, is capable of buddhahood. The encounter with T'ien-t'ai writings decisively affected not only Saichō's life but also the whole future development of Japanese Buddhism. First Kūkai's Shingon sect and later the Pure Land, Zen, and Nichiren sects that developed in the Kamakura period (1185–1336), though their direction of practice differed, were all based on this premise of the universal potential for buddhahood.

Emperor Kammu moved the capital to Kyoto in 794. At last Saichō's meditative existence on Mount Hiei, northeast of the new capital, became known to the court. In 797, he was appointed as one of the priests serving the court, and five years later, in 802, he was invited to be one of the lecturers at a Lotus Sutra Meeting for the study of T'ien-t'ai works at Takaosan-ji (now Jingo-ji) in the northern suburbs of Kyoto. As a result of this meeting, Saichō was given an opportunity to visit China.

In the autumn of 804, four official diplomatic ships set sail with a favorable wind from a port of Kyushu. Saichō, aboard the second ship, reached Ming-chou in northern Chekiang Province in autumn. His purpose being formal training in T'ien-t'ai doctrine, Saichō set off immediately for Mount T'ien-t'ai, also in Chekiang. The restorer of the T'ien-t'ai sect, sixth patriarch Chan-jan, had already died, but the sect was flourishing as a result of the revival. Saichō studied under two of Chan-jan's leading dharma heirs, Tao-sui and Hsing-man. The prefectural governor had just invited Tao-sui to lecture on *Great Concentration and Insight* (a collection of lectures on meditation by Chih-i, the T'ien-t'ai sect founder) at another temple. Saichō, his visit to Mount T'ien-t'ai completed, attended the lecture and received from Tao-sui the formal T'ien-t'ai dharma transmission and bodhisattva ordination with the Mahayana precepts. Chinese ordination at the time consisted of both the *Vinaya of Four Categories* (for men, 250 precepts; for women, 348), the "three pure precepts" from the *Treatise on the Stages of Yoga Practice,* and the Brahmajala precepts (ten grave, and forty-eight minor, prohibitions) from the *Sutra of the Perfect Net.* The combination of the latter two sets of precepts was called the "Mahayana precepts." In Japan, however, only the *Vinaya of Four Categories* precepts were then in use.

Saichō spent that winter studying and copying sutras and religious works; he also received dharma transmission from Hsingman. His period of study abroad had been circumscribed from the first, for he had been sent abroad as a short-term student, and in all he stayed in China only eight and a half months. Nevertheless, his purpose had been amply fulfilled, and he brought back with him 230 Buddhist works in 460 volumes.

When Saichō returned to Japan in the summer of 805, Emperor Kammu was critically ill and Saichō was immediately invited to the palace to recite sutras dedicated to his recovery. In early 806, Tendai, the Japanese offshoot of the Chinese T'ien-t'ai sect, was granted its first two official ordainees in the annual quota, effectively marking the start of the sect in Japan. (At the time, the government authorized ordination of only about ten trainees each year, assigning specific numbers to individual temples and sets of teachings.) The appointments, however, had a strong appearance of being a reward for Saichō's efforts during the emperor's illness. They did not go so far as to establish the true religious organization that Saichō wanted. He was to spend the rest of his life striving to get permission to establish an independent Mahayana ordination platform on Mount Hiei.

Emperor Kammu died in the spring of 806. He was succeeded by Emperor Heizei. The era name was changed, and there was a flurry of changes in government policy. The new reign signaled a

long period of dormancy for Saichō, bereft of his patron, and for
his sect.

Religious Study and Practice on Mount Hiei

Saichō, whose spiritual quest developed from an extreme sense of
being "unworthy, desolate, and lowest of the low," had met
the One Vehicle doctrine of Chinese T'ien-t'ai, which emphasizes the enlightenment of all beings, not of oneself alone. He
succeeded in receiving formal transmission of those teachings and
gained imperial sanction to disseminate them in Japan. The feeling of isolation that enveloped Mount Hiei in the next few years
cannot be attributed only to the loss of Emperor Kammu's patronage but must also have reflected Saichō's own personal sense
of discontent. The apprehensions of the master were reflected in
the susceptibility of his students, and very few among the annual
appointees stayed on the mountain. The next few years were a
time of groping for Saichō.

In the spring of 810, Saichō instituted a series of lectures on
Mount Hiei concerning the *Golden Light Sutra, Sutra on Benevolent
Kings,* and *Lotus Sutra.* This marked the beginning of the discussions on Buddhist teachings for which the mountain became
famous. During the tenth century, Ryōgen (see biography in part
2) organized them into a series of annual debates centering on the
Lotus Sutra, sometimes called the "Discussions on the Mountain."

With the completion of the Lotus Meditation Hall in 812, the
practice of the Lotus Samadhi (one of the four meditation practices
of Tendai, known also as the "half-sitting and half-walking" practice) began. It is clear that in this period Saichō was pouring his
energy into establishing Tendai training practices on the mountain. As already mentioned, Tendai is based upon the great philosophy of the reality of phenomena. Realization of that principle
was to be gained through the form of meditation known as Concentration and Insight. Saichō seems to have thought that this
could be done through study and discussion. He never established
a particular institute of learning like Kūkai's Shugei Shuchi-in, a
school of Buddhism and Confucianism, but rather made the whole

of the mountain into an instrument for teaching. In the same way that medieval Christian scholasticism became the fountainhead for European culture, Mount Hiei was the wellspring of medieval Japanese culture. The period of dormancy that marks Saichō's middle years was on the surface a time of quiet, but in fact it was then that the groundwork was laid that would determine the constitution and nature of the Tendai center on Mount Hiei.

Saichō's relationship with the Shingon master Kūkai (who had spent two and a half years in China studying the esoteric teachings) dates from this period. Kūkai was seven years Saichō's junior, and Saichō sought his acquaintance by writing to him, asking to borrow some of the esoteric texts that he had brought back to Japan and requesting instruction in those teachings. In the winter of 812, Saichō and three of his students, Taihan, Enchō, and Kōjō, went to Takaosan-ji, where Kūkai was residing, to receive the primary initiation into esoteric Buddhism. According to one historian, the *Memorial Presenting a Record of Newly Imported Sutras and Other Items* now held by Tō-ji, the Shingon center in Kyoto, is definitely in Saichō's hand and must have originated on Mount Hiei. Saichō might have borrowed the memorial and copied it for his own use, and it seems at some point to have been returned by mistake to the archives at Tō-ji. Thus Saichō had at his side Kūkai's list, from which he selected works he had not yet seen and wrote asking Kūkai to lend them. Late in 813, however, Kūkai curtly rebuffed Saichō's request to borrow a commentary on the esoteric *Sutra of the Principle of Wisdom*. With that, their relationship rapidly soured.

Though the refusal of Saichō's student Taihan to return to Mount Hiei after having been sent to study with Kūkai had its effect on the deteriorating relationship between Saichō and Kūkai, the ultimate reason was their differences in character and religious outlook. Kūkai had written in answer to Saichō's final request that "the innermost purport of the secret storehouse cannot be achieved through writings, but only transmitted from mind to mind. Writings are the dregs, the rubble." The profoundest teachings of Shingon, he stated, could only be attained through mysticism, not study. There is no way of knowing how Saichō felt when he received the refusal, but in the preface to his *Basics of Tendai*, written in 816, he wrote, "The followers of the newly arrived Shingon teachings reject succession through the written word," indirectly censuring Kūkai's stance. The incident regarding the sutra commentary demonstrates the basic differences in their positions. Saichō was a proponent of the virtues of study and learning, whereas Kūkai undoubtedly valued mysticism. The eight-year relationship revealed the strong personalities and individual religious outlooks of both; it could only end in a parting of the ways.

Debate with Tokuitsu
and the Question of Mahayana Ordination

In 816, with the severance of relations with Kūkai, Saichō departed for the eastern plains area. His activities there centered around the temples of Mitono-dera and Ono-dera, both under the control of dharma descendants of Chinese Vinaya master Ganjin. Here Saichō erected pagodas housing a thousand copies of the *Lotus Sutra* and lectured to the people of the grassy plains on the powerful message of the One Vehicle doctrine. More important in terms of Saichō's own life, though, was his contact there with ordinary, uncultured people, leading him to put an end to the long period of dormancy. It is usual to consider that people of religion bring others to enlightenment through their teaching, but in reality, often they are themselves enlightened by those they teach. This is amply so in the case of Saichō.

In the depths of this backwater there unexpectedly dwelled a brilliant scholar, Tokuitsu of Iwashiro Province, a Hossō priest who early in his life had left the region of the capital and come to the eastern plains. Tokuitsu conducted his religious work from Enichi-ji in Iwashiro Province and Tsukubasan-ji in Hitachi Province. The local people called him a bodhisattva. It was with this man that Saichō debated on the three vehicles versus the one and on the provisional teachings versus the true, a debate that continued for the rest of Saichō's life and that is one of the high points of Japanese intellectual history.

Tokuitsu had written a work entitled *On the Buddha-nature*, attacking the Tendai position. Saichō, while still in the east, refuted it with *A Mirror Illuminating the Provisional and the Real.* The debate continued, with Tokuitsu contributing *Winged Feet of Enichi Temple, A Mirror of the Orthodox and the Heterodox, Essentials of the Lotus,* and more. Saichō upheld his position in *Eliminating Errors Concerning the Lotus, Essays on Protecting the Nation, Treatise on Discerning the Real and the Provisional,* and others. Finally a pause came with Saichō's publication of *Excellent Words About the Lotus* in 821. The subject of the debate was the merit of the Tendai concept of the one vehicle over the Hossō three vehicles. It was an academic debate pure and simple, but it revived Saichō's inherently uncompromising spirit and deepened his conviction regarding the superiority of his own Tendai doctrine. Already past fifty and knowing his days were numbered, he felt that the time had come for him to fulfill his life's vow.

On his return to Mount Hiei, he worked on putting together the *Regulations for the Annual Quota Students of the Tendai Lotus Sect,* which appeared in 818. In the regulations he announced his intention to abandon the 250 precepts that he had received as a youth of eighteen at Tōdai-ji and to gain imperial sanction for an independent Mahayana ordination platform based on the *Sutra of the Perfect Net.* According to clerical leaders in Nara, who dominated the official Buddhism of the time, these Mahayana precepts were the bodhisattva precepts for lay practitioners, not the regulations for the ordained. The bodhisattva precepts were considered a form of commitment to Buddhism on the part of lay followers especially, and thus ranked lower than those of the *Vinaya of Four Categories* which testified to one and all that a cleric was qualified in the eyes of the world. For Saichō to assert that these bodhisattva precepts should take the place of the *Vinaya of Four Categories* precepts seemed, from the viewpoint of contemporary Japanese Buddhism, to be highly eccentric. Religious history, however, often shows unorthodox beliefs gaining eventual orthodoxy. Saichō's movement for independent Mahayana ordination was an exercise of the same order as Shinran's decisions to eat meat and to marry.

What spurred the aging Saichō in his quest was his own rigorous aspiration for enlightenment, which made him understand that religious organizations needed autonomy. In doctrinal terms the question was merely one of the respective merits of the Mahayana and *Vinaya of Four Categories* precepts. In terms of institutional history, though, it was a question of who had the authority to ordain clerics and to administer the precepts. Saichō stressed the necessity of liberating the clerical precepts, administered for the government by the Nara sects, from the coils of national authority and of returning to the original autonomy of the religious organizations themselves.

In reply to the opposition of the Bureau of Clergy, Saichō wrote, in the *Treatise on the Mahayana Precepts:* "I respectfully beg that the two official quota students of Tendai, a Lotus sect, be permitted to remain on Mount Hiei for study and practice there, according to the law of the Buddha's land [India], without having to enter their names in the clerical register or being under any kind of [outside] regulation" (Article 52).

Here Saichō was stressing the necessity of abolishing all official control over religious organizations. In Article 51, he quoted from the regulations concerning clerics that applied in China: "Under the system prevailing in China, names of clerics are submitted to the authorities only after their ordination. This method is not intended to deceive. . . . I respectfully ask you to consider the system prevailing in China and to make a thorough investigation of its merits. There can be no consent to any deception of the government. I am only seeking satisfactory results regarding religious training; I do not question the registration itself."

What he wanted was an end to the system whereby the government controlled who would be ordained. In its place he advocated a system whereby the temple itself voluntarily submitted to the government the names of those clerics it decided to ordain.

It is apparent that the question of the Mahayana precepts was inseparable from that of the annual quota students. The origin of Saichō's deep sense of inadequacy and of his period of withdrawal on Mount Hiei after Emperor Kammu's death can be found in the new sect's lack of autonomy. His organization was based on both strict religious beliefs and a denial of the status quo. Though it was given official sanction in the wake of the existing Nara sects, out of imperial gratitude for Saichō's prayers for the emperor's recovery, its morale was naturally low. It was only through Saichō's strenuous efforts at the end of his life that Japan's first truly independent Buddhist sect came into being.

Unfortunately, Saichō died before the independence of his Mahayana ordination platform was approved. He drew his last breath at the Chūdō-in on Mount Hiei on June 27, 822. Through the good offices of his dharma heirs and of two court officials, the petition was finally granted seven days after his death. Thenceforth, the annual quota students were ordained and given the precepts on Mount Hiei and were able to carry out the official requirements concerning their registration without leaving the mountain to report in person. As a result of the independence of the Mahayana precepts, the national system of control over male and female priests virtually lost all meaning. We must therefore consider Saichō's cause as a reform movement for sectarian autonomy. Though Japanese Tendai marks as its foundation Emperor Kammu's sanction, it was the establishment of the Mahayana precepts that first gave it autonomy. It was from that point that it truly began, with the basis laid down for trainees to spend twelve years in practice on the mountain, pursuing a pure aspiration for enlightenment.

Today, Kyoto has a population of 1.5 million, augmented over the year by several million visitors. I wonder how many people, among the residents and visitors looking up at Mount Hiei, give a thought to the ideal of religious freedom, the "pleasure in the mountain," that Saichō extolled all his life. The Japanese cedars on the mountain are perhaps even now enshrouded in mist, but the lamp of the dharma that Saichō held aloft more than a thousand years ago will never be extinguished.

Kūkai
(774–835)

by Kōyū Sonoda

Kūkai: Fact and Legend

There are few figures in Japanese history about whom such abundant biographies have been written as Kūkai, popularly known by his posthumous title, Kōbō Daishi. The *Collected Biographies of Kōbō Daishi,* compiled in 1934 to mark the eleven hundredth anniversary of his death, or entry into eternal samadhi, contains all the biographical works written before 1868 and totals 93 works in 194 volumes. Adding those published since 1868 would probably double the number. In addition, there are the "unwritten biographies," the vast oral tradition and folklore that still exist in every part of Japan. Though it would be virtually impossible to gather them together, they would doubtless fill an enormous set of volumes rivaling the *Collected Biographies* in size. In strictly historical terms, Kūkai's activities were limited to western Japan, particularly the region of today's Osaka and Kyoto and the island of Shikoku. In the world of folklore, though, his traces are to be found in the eastern and northern regions as well, and legends concerning his travels, and his wells and springs, are to be found throughout Japan.

Usually studies of traditional biographies are plagued by a

paucity of materials, but in Kūkai's case the opposite is true; there are difficulties deciding what to accept and what to reject. The traditional biographies contain, in addition to verifiable historical fact, a surprisingly voluminous mixture of absurd nonsense, and it is often difficult to separate the two. Nevertheless the miraculous and mystical legends that pervade the biographies derive from the special relationship that grew up between Kūkai and the common people, so it is wrong to discard them unconditionally in the name of historical accuracy.

Most ubiquitous are the tales about wells and springs associated with Kūkai. A typical story is that in a certain village there was not sufficient water for irrigation, so the villagers had to be sparing in use of the water they drew from a far-off well. One day, there came passing through the village a traveling priest, who asked for a drink. The villagers willingly brought him one, whereupon the traveler, in thanks, struck the ground with his staff, and a spring of water came gushing up. The traveler was in fact Kūkai. In such tales he appears as a figure with mystical, supernatural powers, who can answer the pressing needs of the common people. At the core of such legends is the historical fact of Kūkai's multifaceted social undertakings.

The best known of such activities is his direction of the reconstruction of the reservoir called Mannōike in Sanuki Province on Shikoku. It was, and is, the area's largest reservoir, formed by damming a river and surrounded on three sides by hills. It is eight kilometers in circumference and covers 3,600 hectares of land. The reservoir was originally constructed by a provincial administrator around 703, but it broke its retaining wall during a great flood in 818. In 820, the government sent an official to take charge of reconstruction. He and the provincial governor strove to complete the repairs, but the work made little progress. The governor therefore requested that Kūkai, a native of the area and extremely popular with the local people, be sent to accomplish the task. An 821 entry in the *Abbreviated Chronicles of Japan* reads:

The [provincial governor of] Sanuki says: . . . "The priest

Kūkai is a native of the district. . . . He has now been long gone from his native place and lives in Kyoto. The farmers yearn for him as they do their parents. If they hear that the master is coming, they will fly to welcome him. I sincerely request that he be made superintendent so that the work might be completed.''

So Kūkai was appointed director of the reconstruction of Mannōike. We do not know how the work progressed subsequently, but in an entry for two months later, the *Abbreviated Chronicles* notes that twenty thousand new coins were given to Kūkai, suggesting a reward for the completion of the work. We can therefore conjecture that the difficult task was completed in a scant two months after Kūkai's appearance on the scene.

Originally the construction and maintenance of irrigation ponds had been the responsibility of the state. According to the *Procedures of the Engi Era* (a collection of supplementary governmental regulations of the tenth century), each province was to provide the resources for such work. Indeed, during the zenith of the *ritsuryō* system, it was, as seen above, a provincial administrator with whom responsibility for building of Mannōike rested. About one hundred years later, the central government assigned a specialist to aid the local officials in the task of reconstructing it, but he was unable to complete the work. The rapid decline in the power of the central government during the intervening century is clearly illustrated. Kūkai's popularity was such that he could bolster the declining influence of the central government.

Popular legend has it that it was Kūkai's supernatural abilities that enabled him to complete the huge job, but reliable historical sources do not bear this out. Kūkai's success rested neither on magical ability nor on engineering skill, but on the confidence the local people had in him, as demonstrated by the governor's words, ''If they hear that the master is coming, they will fly to welcome him.'' Wherever Kūkai went, people swarmed of their own accord to meet him. This charisma was both the fundamental reason that Mannōike was completed successfully and the source of legends concerning Kūkai's magical powers. It was this grip he had on the imagination of the people that national and local power and community controls could not match. Let us now examine Kūkai's life to discover where his special strengths came from.

The Life of Kūkai

Kūkai was born in 774 in Sanuki Province on Shikoku. His birth name was Saeki no Mao. His father's family were local aristocracy whose ancestors were reputed to have been the provincial governors. The clan had produced many administrators and scholars. Kūkai, who from childhood had been regarded as highly gifted, was sent to the capital at fourteen to study under his maternal uncle, the tutor to the crown prince. At seventeen he succeeded in entering the university, where he studied *Tso's Commentary on the Spring and Autumn Annals* and China's Five Classics (the *Classic of Changes, Classic of History, Classic of Poetry, Collection of Rituals,* and *Spring and Autumn Annals*). It was in this period that he undoubtedly accumulated the wealth of knowledge that so astounded Chinese literary circles when he later visited T'ang China.

The turning point in Kūkai's life, set as it was toward an illustrious official career, came during his university studies when he met "a Buddhist priest."

> During that time, a Buddhist priest showed me a text called the *Mantra of Akashagarbha*. . . . Believing what the Great Sage [the Buddha] says of the truth, I hoped for a result, as if rubbing pieces of wood together to make fire. I climbed Mount Ōtaki and meditated at Cape Muroto. The valleys reverberated with the echo of my voice, and the Bright Star [Venus] appeared in the sky. From that time on I despised the fame and wealth of the court and city; I thought only about spending my life in the midst of the precipices and thickets of the mountains (Preface to *Indications of the Goals of the Three Teachings*).

Kūkai wrote this work in his later years, recalling his younger days. He learned a mantra for acquiring a good memory, a man-

tra dedicated to Akashagarbha Bodhisattva, from a certain priest;
cast aside his prospective career with no qualms; and threw
himself into the life of a mountain ascetic, traveling around
Shikoku's quiet, secluded holy places such as Mount Ōtaki and
Cape Muroto. Who was this priest who persuaded him to take the
severe path of an ascetic, to move from the concerns of this world
to those beyond it? Since ancient times there have been various
conjectures as to his identity, and Gonzō of Daian-ji, in Nara, has
been mentioned as well as refuted. The identity does not really
matter, for the key to Kūkai's "conversion" lies not in a chance
meeting with a particular cleric but somewhere else entirely.

Recall that Kūkai came from a family of local gentry. During
this period, locally prominent families acted as district officials and
military officers; they were the final units in local administration,
though at the same time they were also members of their own
village communities. Their lives were complicated in that they
always embodied two sides, the ruler and the ruled, the exploiter
and the producer. With the decline of the *ritsuryō* system, exploitation by the central authorities grew so much that the local gentry
hardly knew whether they were supposed to act as agents of the ex-
ploiters or as protectors of local interests. The reason early Buddhism pervaded this class so widely lies in this basic contradiction
in their lives.

Kūkai's abandonment of his university life in the capital and his
espousal of ascetic practice also seem to originate from the contradictions and troubles faced by local landowners. He would have
fully absorbed the sufferings of the farming community and been
perplexed by the gentry's conflicting stance regarding the common
people. His university education would have been no use at all to
him in resolving those problems. Day after day there would have
been repeated the stereotyped lectures and readings of the Chinese classics that formed the backbone of *ritsuryō* ideology. Bored
with his classes, he had only to meet a Buddhist priest who showed
him the *Mantra of Akashagarbha* to choose unhesitatingly to throw
away everything for a life of asceticism in the mountains. His later
zeal in the reconstruction of Mannōike derived partly from the fact
that he was born not far from there and partly from the great

influence of his family background. There can be no doubt that he was convinced that the repairs were essential if the lives of the farmers were to be preserved. Here is the community awareness of one who was born a member of the local gentry. For a major project like that of Mannōike, however, it was hard to organize labor through individual communities. When the national government was unable to use its authority to bind people together to complete the work, there was nothing to do but look to the influence of a great religious figure, such as Kūkai. What people hoped for from him was an ideology that could bind together the individual farming communities and the local gentry. For Kūkai, this ideology was Shingon esotericism. Let us look now at how he discovered it.

Shingon and Kūkai's Visit to China

The text that was related to Kūkai's decision to become a priest, the *Mantra of Akashagarbha,* was a work of the new, orthodox teachings on esoteric Buddhist meditation translated by Shubhakara-simha, the founder of esoteric Buddhism in China. It is clear from this that the priest who persuaded him to lead an ascetic life was himself an esoteric practitioner. It was only a question of time before the clear-sighted Kūkai discovered and read one of the central texts of Shingon esotericism, the *Great Sun Sutra.*

According to the biographies, Kūkai came across it beneath the eastern pagoda of Kume-dera in Yamato Province. The reliability of this story is problematic, and the date is not clear, yet it must be a fact that he encountered the *Great Sun Sutra* sometime before he went to China in 804. Broadly speaking, esoteric Buddhism is divided into the old and the new. It was thought until recently that esoteric Buddhism in the Nara period had been confined to the old form, but recent studies have shown that sutras and commentaries of the new esotericism were even then relatively widespread. The *Great Sun Sutra* and the *Mantra of Akashagarbha,* which were both known by Kūkai before he went to China, were works of the new school, and Kūkai's understanding of them was considerable.

Esoteric Buddhism emerged during the last period of the development of Buddhism in India, and from relatively early times the eastward movement of Buddhism brought sutras associated with it into China via Central Asia. These early works represented miscellaneous esoteric Buddhism, with their incorporation of magical elements from folk religion or old esotericism. With the development of the southern sea route to China by Muslim traders in the seventh century, texts of pure esoteric Buddhism, or new esotericism, began to be imported to China directly from the center of esoteric Buddhism, southern India. Esoteric Buddhism was initially introduced to China by Vajrabodhi, who arrived by sea at Canton in 720, and by Shubhakarasimha, who had arrived by the inland route four years earlier, in 716. Esoteric Buddhism after the time of these two masters is commonly known as the new stream, and was more organized than the older type. It was, in fact, Shubhakarasimha who translated both the *Great Sun Sutra* and the *Mantra of Akashagarbha* into Chinese. There was nothing strange, therefore, in Kūkai's wish to go to China and receive tuition in the deeper meaning of certain aspects of the *Great Sun Sutra*.

His chance came sooner than expected. In the autumn of 804, the first of the official diplomatic ships, in which Kūkai was traveling, arrived in northeastern Fukien province. Kūkai, in the train of the ambassador, eventually reached the T'ang capital, Ch'ang-an, after a long and arduous journey. Though Ch'ang-an had declined following a rebellion, it was still the greatest city in the world of its time. The Chen-yen (Shingon) school of esoteric Buddhism was the most popular of all the Buddhist schools in the capital, particularly through the efforts of the famed esoteric master, Amoghavajra, who had translated and circulated a large number of esoteric texts, surpassing even Vajrabodhi and Shubhakarasimha, and who had received the Buddhist vows of three successive emperors.

On his arrival in Ch'ang-an, Kūkai went first to study Sanskrit under the north Indian masters Prajna and Munisri. Mastery of Sanskrit was essential for the study of esoteric Buddhism. It was typical of Kūkai's thoroughness that he gave his attention to language before going to study at the Ch'ing-lung temple under Hui-kuo, the true master for whom he had been searching. Kūkai became a student of Hui-kuo in the middle of 805. Kūkai himself records, in the *Memorial Presenting a Record of Newly Imported Sutras and Other Items,* that as soon as Hui-kuo saw him, the latter cried out, "I have long known that you would come. For such a long time I have waited for you! How happy I am, how happy I am today, to look upon you at last. My life is reaching its end, and there has been no one to whom I could transmit the teachings. Go at once to the initiation platform with incense and flowers!" Shortly after this dramatic first meeting, Kūkai received the initiation ritual of the Womb-Store Realm. The next month he was initiated into the Diamond Realm, and in the following month, he received the final ritual, the transmission of the teachings. Thus in just three months, Kūkai received from his master formal transmission of the major esoteric teachings. Hui-kuo, who had said on the first meeting that his life was running out, died near the end of that year, aged fifty-nine, having transmitted the dharma to Kūkai. It was fortunate for Kūkai that he should have received dharma transmission from such an illustrious teacher so close to his death, but Hui-kuo also was lucky in finally being able to meet a suitable dharma heir. Having received the transmission of orthodox Chen-yen from Hui-kuo, Kūkai became the eighth patriarch of Chen-yen, and the direct line of transmission crossed the sea to be passed along in Japan.

In the autumn of 806, Kūkai returned to Japan aboard a diplomatic ship and came ashore in northern Kyushu. With him he had brought 216 works in 451 volumes, of which 142 works in 247 volumes were translations of texts of the new esoteric Buddhism, chiefly those of Amoghavajra. In addition we should note the existence of forty-two Sanskrit works in forty-four volumes. Kūkai also brought back with him various graphic works and ritual implements, which tell of the completeness of the transmission of his dharma lineage.

Kūkai and Saichō

It can be verified that Kūkai remained at Dazaifu on Kyushu from the time of his return to Japan until early 807, but his circumstances over the two and a half years are not clear at all. Recent research suggests that he remained in Kyushu until 809, preparing for the future and making copies of the works he had brought back from China. This was in marked contrast to Saichō, who returned to the capital quickly and received imperial sanction to ordain two annual quota priests. Kūkai remained unflurried, awaiting his chance.

That great spectacle, outstanding in the history of Buddhism in Japan, the association between Saichō and Kūkai, appears to have begun very soon after Kūkai arrived in the capital in 809. At the time, Saichō was forty-two, and he wrote to the thirty-five-year-old Kūkai asking to borrow certain texts. In the winter of 812, Saichō and his students went to Takaosan-ji, where they received the initiation of the Womb-Store Realm from Kūkai. The first communication that can be verified as being sent by Kūkai to Saichō also dates from that time. This is in the famous collection of letters to Saichō written in Kūkai's own hand, which is preserved at Tō-ji and has been designated a National Treasure. The letter is replete with Kūkai's brimming self-confidence:

> You [Saichō] and I and [Shūen of] Murou-ji should meet in one place, to deliberate upon the most important cause for which the Buddha appeared in the world, together raising the banners of the dharma and repaying the Buddha's benevolent provision.

As far as Kūkai was concerned, only three people in Japan were qualified to teach Buddhism. Saichō was widely known as an intellectual who had brought back a new kind of Buddhism from China, and Shūen, a Hossō priest, was among the prominent figures of the traditional Buddhist sects. Compared with these two men, Kūkai was barely known in society at large, but his confidence was obviously strong nevertheless.

Kūkai's dazzling genius is graphically apparent in the calligraphy of that letter, which is considered his greatest masterpiece. A comparison of Kūkai's and Saichō's calligraphy reveals their differences in personality. If Saichō's is like the crystalline water of a mountain stream, Kūkai's is like the resonance of the vast ocean. Despite the warm friendship that throve initially between the two men, their differences in personality contained the seeds for their eventual parting of the ways. It was the personalities of these two that were to shape the development of the Tendai and Shingon sects and to stamp a deep individualism on the Buddhism of their era.

Mount Kōya and Tō-ji

Kūkai's brilliance soon brought him into contact with the court of the new emperor, Saga. In the winter of 809, Kūkai had already answered the emperor's request to write calligraphy on a pair of folding screens. Exchanges between the emperor and Kūkai continued; Kūkai presented the emperor with books of poetry copied in his own hand (811), brushes and writings (812), books on Sanskrit and poetry (814), and screens with calligraphy on them (816). The real friendship between the two is apparent in a poem included in the *Collection of National Polity*, an anthology of prose and verse in Chinese compiled in 827. It includes a poem entitled "A Farewell to Kūkai, Departing for the Mountains":

> Many years have passed
> Since you chose the path of a priest.
> Now come the clear words
> And the good tides of autumn.
> Pour no more the scented tea;
> Evening is falling.
> I bow before you, grieving at our parting,
> Looking up at the clouds and haze.

Saga wrote this poem after he had abdicated in 823 to spend his time in cultural pursuits. There is no sense of ruler and subject here. Kūkai and Saga were renowned, with Tachibana no Hayanari, as the greatest calligraphers of their time, and the three were called collectively the Three Brushes. Historians of calligraphy see a marked influence of Kūkai in the emperor's style of writing.

Kūkai thus gained entry into court circles as the leading exponent of Chinese culture and won the emperor's patronage. Backed by that patronage, he spread the teachings of Shingon esotericism that he had brought back with him. We should note in particular the founding of a temple on Mount Kōya in 816. In the summer of that year, Kūkai had sent a formal message to the emperor asking for the grant of "a flat area deep in the mountains" on Mount Kōya, where he could build a center to establish esoteric training. He was no doubt thinking in particular about the temples on Mount Wu-t'ai administered by Amoghavajra, which he had heard about when he was in China. Though Kūkai was not able to finish the temple during his lifetime, Mount Kōya, as the site of the master's eternal samadhi, became the most hallowed center of the Shingon sect.

Early in 823, Kūkai was granted Tō-ji, a temple situated at the entrance to Kyoto. In the winter of the same year, he received permission to use the temple exclusively for Shingon clerics, as a specialist training center for the esoteric doctrines, similar to Ch'ing-lung temple in Ch'ang-an. Tō-ji and Mount Kōya thus became the bases for Shingon in Japan. With the establishment of Mount Kōya and the grant of Tō-ji, the foundations were laid for the religious organization of the Shingon sect. Both were gifts of Emperor Saga.

In the summer of 823, Saga abdicated in favor of Emperor Junna. During the reign of this emperor Kūkai's glory reached its peak. That summer, he was authorized to have fifty Shingon priests permanently residing at Tō-ji, and in the summer of 825, he received imperial permission to build a lecture hall there. In 827 he performed a ritual for rain and was elevated to the rank of senior assistant high priest in the Bureau of Clergy. Early in 834, he received permission to establish a Shingon chapel within the imperial palace, similar to one in China, and he constructed a mandala altar there. Shingon teachings were already penetrating the court deeply. Here again Kūkai was in startling contrast to Saichō, who feared the court would contaminate student priests and sought an independent ordination platform on Mount Hiei.

Kūkai did not exhibit the belligerence toward the older sects that Saichō did. His attitude was one of temporary compromise, awaiting a time when he could bring others around to his position.

In 822, a Shingon chapel, Nan-in, was established at Tōdai-ji. This became a means of spreading Shingon from within the stronghold of Nara Buddhism. Among the many priests who came under Kūkai's influence through Nan-in was the former crown prince Takaoka, who had lost his position after being implicated in a conspiracy to put the retired emperor, Heizei, back on the throne (810), and had become a priest with the name of Shinnyo at Tōdai-ji in 822. It did not take much time for all the Nara sects to be completely dominated by esoteric Buddhism.

Later Years and Entry into Samadhi

Kūkai's tolerance sprang from his personality and his genius, as well as from the nature of Shingon teachings themselves. In 830 he completed his work on the classification of the teachings and the place of Shingon within them, the *Ten Stages of the Development of Mind* in ten volumes. The classification was performed at the order of Emperor Junna, who had required all the sects to detail the essentials of their teachings. This work is based upon the chapter "The Stages of Mind" in the *Great Sun Sutra*. Kūkai divided the human mind (or religious consciousness) into ten categories and compared each level with various non-Buddhist and Buddhist philosophies and sects in order to show that Shingon is superior to all. Kūkai's *Ten Stages* is more than just a classification of the teachings in the traditional style, for he extends the classification beyond the Buddhist sects to all religions and systems of ethics. From the standpoint of the esoteric teachings, the great and splendid wisdom of Mahavairocana Tathagata dwells profoundly within even the shallowest kinds of thought and religion. Consequently, the One Vehicle thought of esoteric Buddhism (Shingon), unlike the One Vehicle doctrine of exoteric Buddhism (Tendai and Kegon), is not incompatible with the Three Vehicles theory of Hossō. This tolerance inherent in Shingon prevented the Buddhist sects of Nara from coming into direct conflict with Kūkai's Shingon, and allowed them, almost without realizing it, to be absorbed within it. It was not only the Nara sects that were so influenced. The same thing is evident in the teaching program of

Shugei Shuchi-in, the school Kūkai founded next to Tō-ji, which offered Confucian and Taoist as well as Buddhist studies; in social endeavors such as the reconstruction of Mannōike; and even in Kūkai's multifaceted cultural pursuits. As far as Kūkai was concerned, even making tea and writing poems in the company of the emperor and nobles were forms of religious activity. The fact that he was so eminently popular among the people can be considered a further expression of his religious outlook.

Kūkai died on Mount Kōya on April 23, 835, and it is believed that even now he remains in eternal samadhi in his bodily form within the inner shrine on the mountain. This belief also is a legacy of the burning admiration felt for him by the people as a whole.

Kūya
(903–972)

by Yuishin Itō

Patriarch of the Nembutsu

Kūya was one of the first to disseminate the Pure Land devotional practice of intoning Amida Buddha's name (nembutsu) among the common people of Japan. He has therefore been called the Patriarch of the Nembutsu. It was he who took the practice of nembutsu from the temple to the world outside and made it popular among ordinary people. Because he constantly intoned the phrase "I take refuge in Amida Buddha," he was known as Amida's Wandering Sage (Amida Hijiri), and because he lived among people in an urban environment, performing social work and spreading religion, others called him the Wandering Sage of the Marketplace (Ichi no Hijiri).

A distinguished scholar of the time, Yoshishige no Yasutane, who observed Kūya's activities and became a fervent admirer, showed a high regard for the benefits of Kūya's dissemination of nembutsu practice. He wrote, in a collection of tales about those believed to have been reborn in the Pure Land, *Records of Pure Land Rebirth in Japan,* that "before the Tengyō era [938–947] it was rare to find people in religious training halls or assemblies who practiced contemplation of the name of Amida. How much more so was it neglected by men of small caliber and by foolish women! But after the Sage came, he himself intoned the nembutsu and caused others to intone it also. That the nembutsu thereafter became so popular is because of the Sage's power to convert ordinary people." Yoshishige called Kūya "a messenger of the Buddha," believing him to have been sent by Amida Buddha to bring to salvation all those fallen into pollution and evil in this worldly existence.

Another leading scholar of Chinese classics compiled the *Eulogy for Kūya* on the occasion of Kūya's first memorial service, praising his character and religious exploits, and describing him as "a distinguished sage, whose virtues were incalculable and who from the beginning was a practitioner of the bodhisattva way."

Kūya preached to nobles and scholars as well as to thieves and felons, but the main recipients of his teachings were commoners. Among priests who contributed to the development of popular Pure Land practices were many who had been led by Kūya's words and who had held dear his memory. It is said of Senkan, a priest serving the court and the composer of the *Verses in Praise of Amida,* that he entered the life of a nembutsu practitioner inspired by Kūya's admonition to throw all away in the pursuit of the truth. Ippen, founder of the Ji sect (see biography in part 1), likewise revered Kūya as "my guide to the Way." As a religious figure concerned with dissemination among the common people, Ippen is considered the person most resembling Kūya in later times. There later emerged a particular type of religious teacher called *hijiri* whose appearance was suggested by the statue of Kūya at Rokuharamitsu-ji, which was carved in the early thirteenth century. With a staff topped by an antler in one hand, a small hammer in the other, and a gong suspended from his neck, Kūya went around chanting the nembutsu. Such wandering clerics became known popularly as Amida sages, and in their appearance and behavior they were the successors of Kūya.

Kūya held neither rank nor position in the priesthood. He elected to remain among ordinary people, where the Tendai and Shingon priests rarely ventured. He practiced the oral invocation of Amida's name and the bodhisattva way, becoming a worthy recipient of the designations of True Messenger of the Buddha and Patriarch of the Nembutsu. As a pioneer of popular Pure Land belief, he holds a special position in Japanese religious history. The tenth century, in which he lived, was a time of repeated uprisings as the traditional centralized government moved toward collapse. There was a close connection between the tendencies of the age and the kind of religion that Kūya offered.

Early Years

Kūya was born in 903, just after the resurgence of Fujiwara family power in the wake of a failed attempt to shore up the imperial government along the traditional lines of the *ritsuryō* system. His life closed in 972, as the power of the Fujiwara family was approaching its zenith. We do not know where he was born or in what circumstances. Legends sprang up early to account for the deficiency and attributed imperial descent to him; there is, however, no truth to the story that he was the fifth son of Emperor Daigo.

From his youth he led the life of a lay practitioner (*ubasoku*). According to the *Eulogy for Kūya,* he traveled to famous mountains and holy caverns throughout Japan, en route leveling precipitous roads with a plow, divining water courses with his staff, and gathering up and cremating bodies abandoned by the wayside, all the while intoning the name of Amida to console their spirits.

Around the age of twenty he entered the Owari Provincial Temple, becoming a trainee priest. It was at that time that he took the name of Kūya. Kūya was a privately ordained, not an official, priest, as was usual among the clerics of his time who were from the common people. In 948, when he was forty-five, he went to Mount Hiei, where he received precepts ordination from the head of the Tendai sect, Enshō, and was given the new name of Kōshō, marking his new status as a qualified priest. He did not use that name, however, but retained his trainee name of Kūya for the remainder of his life. Since the Nara period, popular religious figures had tended to be either lay practitioners or unordained priests (*shami*), and the fact that Kūya kept his former name underlines his determination to remain a man of the people.

It was during the early part of his life that Kūya probably gave shape to those practices that became the backbone of his religious expression—wandering and begging, asceticism, the seeking of auspicious signs, bodhisattva practice, and urging others toward almsgiving.

After entering the clergy, he embarked on even more severe ascetic training. He went to Mineai-dera in Harima Province and for several years immersed himself in Buddhist sutras and commentaries. He also visited a statue of Kannon, the compassionate bodhisattva, on the island of Yushima, off Shikoku. Hoping to gain a sign, he spent several months there undertaking austerities—not eating grains, burning incense on his arms, and going for a period without moving or sleeping. The burn marks on his arms are reputed to have been made at this time. At last he achieved his goal. Further, he traveled to the northern areas of Honshu, to districts where Buddhism was scarcely known, carrying Buddhist statues and scriptures in a pack on his back, blowing a conch shell, and preaching the dharma. One version says that Kūya made this trip late in life; whatever the truth of the matter, he spent his younger years as an unordained priest wandering the country, performing ascetic practices, and teaching others.

During Kūya's stay in the eastern provinces, a struggle began for control of that area, a conflict that was to break out into open rebellion early in 940. Kūya fled before the turmoil, going toward the central provinces. He entered Kyoto in 938, the year when the name of the era was changed to Tengyō, literally, Heavenly Joy, in the hope that misfortunes, especially earthquakes and wars, would cease. The Kūya that was to remain in people's memories and to claim a place in history was about to come into being. That year, his thirty-fifth, marked a turning point in his life.

Amida's Wandering Sage

At that time, the *ritsuryō* system of government was collapsing. The noble families, who should have been leaders of society, were losing their traditional status and their links with the provincial gentry; many were living in reduced circumstances as a purely urban class. They were thus impotent before insurrection and, tossed by the billows of social change, had lost even their spiritual direction.

The western part of Kyoto, afflicted by repeated flooding, had been virtually abandoned, creating in the eastern part a jumble of dwellings of both the nobility and the poorer classes. So packed were the buildings that it was said if a fire broke out in one house, the neighboring houses could not be saved from destruction, and if a dwelling was attacked by thieves, those surrounding it would not be able to evade the stray arrows. In the marketplaces were crowds of beggars and poor people, and their plight was made worse by the fact that just at that time laborers on public works projects had been released from their duties and were left without any means of support, seeking as best they could enough food to exist for a day at a time. In addition, the townspeople trembled under the fury of epidemics and placed statues at roadsides to appease the malignant spirits thought to be the bringers of plague. Such was the actuality of Kyoto when Kūya came there in 938.

He moved around the city with his begging bowl and used the offerings he received for religious work and to feed the poor. The marketplaces swarming with people were the main sites of his Buddhist teaching. He brought relief to those made outcasts by their trades, and to the recently liberated government slaves, through the practice of nembutsu, bringing the Pure Land teachings to those who wanted an escape from material and mental distress.

Very soon Kūya's name became widely known among the people. *Records of Pure Land Rebirth in Japan* includes the story of a metalworker who was still far from home when the sun set. He was carrying a large amount of money in his robes and was afraid of being robbed. He approached Kūya and asked whether there was anything he could do to ensure his safety. Kūya replied that he should meditate on Amida Buddha. As the metalworker walked on, he did indeed encounter a bandit and intoned the nembutsu as he had been instructed. The robber cried out, "It's the Wandering

Sage of the Marketplace," and went away, without making any
attempt to rob him. Kūya obviously was known and honored even
among bandits.

His religious work was always closely connected to the activities
of the world of the common people. When water was scarce, he
went around all quarters of the city digging wells, known to the
grateful populace as Amida's wells. He cleared impassable roads
and built bridges where there were none. He also built small stone
pagodas at the gates of prisons, so that those inside could worship
the image of the Buddha and hear the sound of the dharma as the
pagoda's bells shook in the wind.

In the summer of 944 he made thirty-three images of Kannon
Bodhisattva and drew pictures of Amida's Pure Land and of
Mount Potalaka, where Kannon was believed to dwell. In the autumn of 951, he made statues of Kannon and other Buddhist figures which he placed in the temple he had founded, Saikō-ji (later
known as Rokuharamitsu-ji). Kyoto had been struck by a plague
that year, and Kūya carved the statues to express compassion for
the sufferers. He led the statue of the eleven-faced Kannon
through the streets of the capital to drive away the disease, and it
is said that the epidemic instantly retreated. Epidemics spread
quickly through the city at that time, originating in the swamps of
the western suburbs. The poor suffered greatly because of them.
The whole city needed relief. Kūya's religious work responded
effectively to the needs of the very poor and those burdened with
anxiety.

In 948 Kūya went to Mount Hiei to receive orthodox precepts
ordination from the head of the Tendai sect, Enshō. This marked
a new departure for him, now an official priest rather than an illegal
unordained priest or a privately ordained popular practitioner. After
that he began to mix more with the nobility. One person who expressed an admiration for him was the minister of the left, Fujiwara no Saneyori, who established a karmic affinity with him at
the dedication of the *Great Perfection of Wisdom Sutra* in 963. Saneyori's brother, the great counselor Morouji, also had connections
with Kūya and became his patron "in this world and the next."
When Morouji died in 970, Kūya had the high-ranking Tendai

priest Yokei, who was later the Tendai sect head, read the formal notification of the death to Emma, the lord of the underworld, in front of the coffin. The brothers were both influential at court, of a different social stratum than Kūya, unless it is considered that the circumstances of his birth were indeed higher than usually thought. In any case, following his precepts ordination, growing numbers of the nobility began to appear on Kūya's horizon.

Connections with the nobility meant that Kūya's stage for religious dissemination was growing larger and larger. With such backing, his religious work began to take on an unprecedented scale. The images carved in 951 are an example of this. As a result of the Mount Hiei ordination, the nobles were added to the common people as recipients of his teachings, so his reception of the precepts from Enshō had deep meaning. Representative of the large-scale religious work undertaken as an official priest with the patronage of the nobility was the dedication of the *Great Perfection of Wisdom Sutra* in 963.

Dedication of the Great Perfection of Wisdom Sutra

A copy of the six hundred volumes of the *Great Perfection of Wisdom Sutra,* written in gold letters, was completed in the autumn of 963. Its dedication ceremony was undertaken on a vast scale. Kūya had been working on the project since making his initial vow to undertake the work in 950, two years after he received precepts ordination from Enshō. It is likely that the undertaking was made with the approval of Enryaku-ji, so it is possible to consider Kūya's ordination as a strategic move to help the work to progress smoothly.

The dedication of the project, written on Kūya's behalf, mentions the way donations were collected from among Kūya's supporters. "I vowed to sell even myself in the marketplace but people everywhere showed signs of their faith through multitudinous karmic linkages. Contributions of the smallest coin or a grain of rice gradually combined their strength, and thus a significant result was attained." Kūya was, as this shows, able to complete his work

of more than thirteen years with the help of the tiny contributions
of the common people. He related at the dedication ceremony that
"formerly I had not even a single bowl but just sang my determination in the ten directions. Then this world and the next worked
together and the distant and the near were astounded. East- and
west-side dwellers, rich and poor, high and low, all came to take
refuge, and the dedication was made possible." The dedication
ceremony was also enabled through the good wishes of rich and
poor, high and low. It is clear that though Kūya received the
patronage of the nobility, at the core of his support were the combined efforts of the commoners.

The *Great Perfection of Wisdom Sutra* had long been regarded as
effective in neutralizing disasters, and it was believed to protect
against epidemics. As a result great numbers of common people
contributed toward the copying of such a powerful sutra. Their
support was undertaken in the simple but vigorous belief that the
miraculous powers of the *Great Perfection of Wisdom Sutra* might
dispel calamity and disease.

When Kūya came to Kyoto, roadside statues believed to prevent evil from going any farther were a common sight. People
acted in a frenzy to expel disease and malignant spirits. These
same people were now the supporters of Kūya's undertaking; his
greatest admirers were those who lived in fear of illness. Kūya won
their hearts by copying the sutra.

On September 14, 963, the dedication ritual took place on the
eastern bank of the Kamo River. Six hundred priests were invited
to the ceremony. The copies of the sutra were on two barges, one
with a prow in the form of a dragon and the other with a prow in
the form of a mythical waterfowl. Music played continuously; during the day priests gave lectures, and at night there was a festival
of ten thousand lanterns. Jōzō, a priest of Yasaka-dera, who was
in the assembly, is said to have astounded people by detecting,
among the mendicant clerics gathered there, Monju the bodhisattva of wisdom, appearing in response to the merit of Kūya's
work.

That day in the palace a religious debate took place between the

Hossō priest Hōzō and the Tendai priest Ryōgen (see biography in part 2) concerning whether all living beings have the potential for buddhahood and whether a human can gain enlightenment in this life, through hearing the dharma or through solitary efforts. The debate would seem to have had social significance, but in actuality was no more than academic, with influence and fame being the attractions. The contrast between debate divorced from practice and the strenuous efforts of Kūya in taking Buddhism to the people became more and more obvious, and the two events, the debate and the dedication of the *Great Perfection of Wisdom Sutra*, were diametrically opposed to each other. The dedication received high praise from the populace and it marked an epoch in Kūya's life.

There are very few traces left of Kūya's later life, though he appears to have based himself at Saikō-ji. It is unclear just when the temple was built, but it was already in existence in the Higashiyama district of Kyoto during the early 960s. There is a strong possibility that there was some connection with the building of a hall at the time of the *Great Perfection of Wisdom Sutra* dedication. The temple was restored in 977, five years after Kūya's death, by his successor, Chūshin, and renamed Rokuharamitsu-ji. The new name was a play on words between the name of the locality, Rokuhara, and the Buddhist term *rokuharamitsu*, the Six Perfections. The Rokuhara district extended to the foot of Higashiyama from the eastern bank of the Kamo River and was synonymous with a cemetery for the lower classes, which occupied most of the area. Rokuhara was the plain where the spirits of the dead were thought to gather and the site of funerals. It was this place that Kūya, who had gathered abandoned corpses from the roadsides and said memorial services over them, selected as the site for Saikō-ji.

Saikō-ji was Kūya's base, a popular temple where commoners could freely gather. People continued to visit the temple after his death, in reverence for his moral influence. Rokuharamitsu-ji soon became closely connected with the legend of Kūya, and lectures on the *Lotus Sutra* and nembutsu services were held there, attracting large numbers of people from all over the city, lay and ordained, men and women. In eight or nine years those who had made karmic connections there numbered in the tens of thousands.

The Western Paradise

Kūya died at Saikō-ji in 972, aged sixty-nine. As his death approached, he sat upright facing the west, wearing a white robe and holding incense in his hands. He told his followers that a great host of buddhas and bodhisattvas had come to welcome him to paradise, and with those words of joy, closed his eyes in death.

Though Kūya was devoted to Kannon Bodhisattva and Amida Buddha and had faith in the *Lotus* and *Great Perfection of Wisdom* sutras, the basis of his religion was Pure Land faith and practice. Both the scene of his death and his vow on undertaking the copying of the *Great Perfection of Wisdom Sutra* to ''practice the bodhisattva precepts, to think constantly upon Amida, and to attain eternal rebirth in the western paradise'' are evidence of his determination to be reborn in Amida's realm.

A poem of Kūya's also speaks of the western paradise. According to the *Eulogy for Kūya,* his first sight of an image of Amida made him wish to see the Pure Land with his own eyes. That night in a dream he saw himself sitting on a lotus, and looking around, he saw that all was as described in the sutras. On awaking, he wrote in his joy, ''Though the western paradise is said to be far away, it is none other than the place we strive to reach.'' Those who heard it praised him. In another poem, reportedly written in the marketplace, Kūya said, ''One who intones 'I take refuge in Amida Buddha' even once will assuredly climb upon the lotus flower.''

As is apparent by the leanings of Kūya's friends, his nembutsu was of the Tendai type. It was a multiple, rather than a single, devotional practice. In his faith in Kannon and Amida and his reliance on the *Lotus* and *Great Perfection of Wisdom* sutras, he emphasized the oral invocation of Amida's name and spread the teachings of the Pure Land among all social classes. Kūya was also a firm believer in keeping the Mahayana precepts that he had received from Enshō. We remember his vow again in this context. Further, Kūya's multifaceted religious and social work and his dissemination efforts among the people were seen as ''bodhisattva practice.'' Kūya also thought of his religious activities as the work of a bodhisattva benefiting others. It is unclear when that concept crystallized in his mind, but it was clearly an idea that continued to develop as his activities among the people of Kyoto progressed. Such consciousness of his mission certainly was related to his spiritual growth, but was also connected to the need to rationalize a religious movement that had such a strong impact on society. In addition, his receiving of the Mahayana precepts from Enshō must certainly have been a factor in characterizing his religious activities as bodhisattva practice. The spirit at the root of his practice was, in Saichō's words, "putting others first and the self last, conferring benefits on others and forgetting the self; this is the greatest compassion." It was this concept of bodhisattva practice that made the regulation of conduct so important.

The copying of the *Great Perfection of Wisdom Sutra* was an act to benefit others, as was encouraging people to practice nembutsu. Kūya's nembutsu had its frenzied, magical side, but nevertheless it was taught for the sake of others. The words in the *Records of Pure Land Rebirth in Japan* "He himself intoned the nembutsu and caused others to intone it also" carry the conviction that this was a bodhisattva act benefiting others. His popularity among both the commoners and the nobility was a result of his nondiscriminating awareness. The joining of religious practice to the bodhisattva way gave Kūya's nembutsu a strongly social character, and Kūya's religion was greatly honored by the intellectuals of his day.

Hōnen

(1133–1212)

by Yuishin Itō

Figure of Controversy

Hōnen offered people a new kind of religious hope, the Pure Land teachings, in the confused times following the war between the Taira and Minamoto families. Like many of his predecessors, Hōnen was forced to walk a thorny path with many ups and downs. The more the number of adherents to his revolutionary exclusive practice of nembutsu increased, the stronger grew the opposition to it from the temples in Nara and on Mount Hiei. They even considered Hōnen a sworn enemy of Buddhism. In his later years there was hardly a time when he was not under a cloud of persecution, and he was finally exiled at the advanced age of seventy-four. His grave was vandalized in 1227, and the wood blocks of his great work, the *Collection of Passages on the Original Vow and the Nembutsu*, were publicly burned. Surely none of the founders of new schools in the Kamakura period was subjected to more animosity and insult than was Hōnen.

Seeking only the way that led to deliverance and abhorring fame and position, Hōnen never wavered in his faith, even in the face of censure and persecution. He was fortunate to have good patrons and sympathizers, who responded to his teachings that "the time is now" and that there must be "a correspondence between the capacity of hearers and what is taught." As those who appreciated his doctrine increased, dharma students and believers grew ever more numerous. Though Hōnen himself never had any intention of founding a separate sect, that is what happened. The faithful regarded Hōnen as a transformation of Amida Buddha and a reincarnation of the Chinese Pure Land practitioner and teacher Shan-tao. The many biographies written after his death attest to the veneration in which he was held.

Hōnen taught that the Pure Land doctrine was the only one suited to those who were poor, stupid, or unable to keep the precepts. He taught that those who believed deeply in Amida's Original Vow and practiced nembutsu (repeatedly chanting the name of Amida Buddha) exclusively could be certain that they would be included in Amida's salvation. Honen's theory of salvation, called the Pure Land teaching, heralded a great revolution in religious thought, becoming a watershed in the history of Buddhism in Japan. Hōnen therefore stands at the divide of Japanese Buddhism.

Early Life

Hōnen was born at the very end of the Heian period, in 1133, into a family of provincial gentry in a village in Mimasaka Province. His father was the constable, and his mother was a daughter of a prominent family in the region, who traced their origins to a legendary Chinese prince of the third century. In 1141, when Hōnen was eight, a tragedy occurred that greatly affected his future. The manager of the nearby imperial estate attacked and mortally wounded Hōnen's father in a night foray. After that Hōnen was placed in the care of his mother's brother, the priest of Bodai-ji, also in Mimasaka Province. There Hōnen remained until 1147, when at the age of fourteen he was sent to Mount Hiei to receive ordination. He studied Tendai doctrine under Genkō and Kōen, who became Hōnen's ordination master. His desire to live a life of seclusion deepened as time went by, and in 1150 he moved to Kurodani, on the western side of the mountain, which had long been a center for nembutsu practice, to study under Eikū, a dharma successor of Ryōnin (see biography in part 2), the founder of the Yūzū Nembutsu sect. Hōnen had already given up all idea of revenge for his father's death. His one concern was to bring a religious attitude to people buffeted by delusory attachments. Eikū, delighted to find such a young person resolved to follow the religious way, gave him the name of Hōnenbō Genkū, saying he had been born a holy man. The name Genkū was made using one character from the name of his first teacher, Genkō, and one from that of his new master, Eikū.

The Tendai organization at that time showed signs of corruption, as scions of the nobility filled the highest ecclesiastical ranks and pursued worldly ambition, and priests delighted in conflict, passing the bounds of lawlessness. As a result, priests serious about their training entered specialized centers far removed from the temptations of fame and wealth, where they could spend their lives seeking the Way. Such men were called *hijiri*. Hōnen became a *hijiri* of the Kurodani training center.

For more than twenty years, Hōnen remained at Kurodani, spending his days in study and religious training. In that time he absented himself only once, when he was twenty-three, to visit Seiryō-ji, near Kyoto, which housed a famous image of Shakyamuni brought from China, and to seek instruction in Nara. Otherwise he never left Kurodani, absorbed as he was in resolving the questions that deeply perplexed him. His starting point being the inner conviction that the threefold training of Buddhism (morality, contemplation, and wisdom) was not for him, he continued along the path of a spiritual pilgrim, doubting the traditional way of liberation. "Is there perhaps another teaching, other than the threefold training, that corresponds to my mind," he asked, "a practice that is sufficient for my body?" During that time he is said to have read through the entire Buddhist canon five times and to have studied over and over again the commentaries of his own Tendai sect and other sects. In so doing he burnished his natural genius; his understanding and wisdom were spoken of in the highest terms. On one occasion, he was involved in a discussion with his teacher, Eikū, concerning the relative merits of nem-

butsu as visualization or as invocation. Hōnen favored the latter
practice and would not yield to Eikū's assertion that invocation
was an inferior practice. Finally Eikū became so angry that he
threw a wooden pillow at Hōnen. The episode typifies Hōnen's un-
willingness to compromise and his unrelenting attitude toward
scholarship.

While Hōnen remained absorbed in his training on Mount
Hiei, the world below was increasingly caught up in turmoil. A
dispute over the imperial succession erupted into open conflict in
1156 with the deep involvement of the rival Minamoto and Taira
clans. Their rivalry continued until 1159, when the Tairas gained
the upper hand and thereafter wielded undisputed power and influence. Political strife caused growing social unrest. Villages were
impoverished, bands of thieves brought terror to the land, and warrior clerics and samurai exercised raw power. Corruption ran rife.
The traditional Buddhist sects of Kyoto and Nara completely ignored the cries of the people. The country's only hope was the
emergence of someone who held forth the promise of salvation. Finally in 1167, Taira no Kiyomori was appointed grand minister of
state, the first member of a military family to receive that honor.

On Mount Hiei, Hōnen's long spiritual journey approached an
end when finally he found the inspiration he was looking for. He
came across a passage in Chinese Pure Land master Shan-tao's
Commentary on the Meditation Sutra that reads: "Think solely upon
Amida's name. Whether walking or standing, sitting or lying
down, do not be concerned with what is long or what is short. Do
not cease thinking upon his name even for a moment. This is an
act that ensures rebirth in the Pure Land, for it is in accordance
with the vow of that Buddha." Immediately Hōnen was enlightened. A place had long been prepared for him by the Buddha.
Hōnen said, "When I read that passage, I was impressed by the
fact that even ignorant beings such as myself, by meditation upon
those words and by practicing invocation of the name, not ceas-
ing for a moment, will unfailingly attain rebirth in Amida's Pure
Land. I was led not only to believe in the teachings bequeathed by
Shan-tao, but also earnestly to follow the vow of Amida. Especially
engraved in my mind was that phrase 'For it is in accordance with

the vow of that buddha.' " He wrote in the *Collection of Passages on the Original Vow and the Nembutsu,* reminiscing about the past, that when he read that work, he "realized its original purpose and immediately threw away all other practices for the sole practice of nembutsu." It was 1175, and Hōnen was forty-two.

The Jōdo (literally, Pure Land) sect considers 1175 as the year it was founded. It should be remembered, though, that 1175 was the year when Hōnen himself turned toward the saving power of Amida; it was not actually the year that the Jōdo sect was formally established.

One night Hōnen dreamed that he met Shan-tao, and his dream persuaded him that he had discovered absolute truth and should disseminate it among the people. With that, he left Mount Hiei.

Hōnen's Influence Grows

Having left Mount Hiei, Hōnen soon settled in a part of Kyoto called Ōtani and built himself a simple dwelling, where he absorbed himself in the practice in which he had put his faith. Although Hōnen enjoyed peace of mind, the city of Kyoto was in turmoil. In the summer of 1177, the city suffered the greatest fire in its history, while the deadlock between Taira no Kiyomori and the retired emperor Go-Shirakawa continued without hope of resolution. Kujō Kanezane, the Fujiwara regent who became Hōnen's principal patron, lamented, "The world has fallen into disarray, with fire, robbery, popular unrest, rebellion, and strife between clergy and laity." Shortly afterward, a conspiracy against Kiyomori was exposed by one of the confederates, and in 1180 the tension erupted in civil war when the Minamotos raised the call to arms against the Tairas. Near the end of that year, a son of Taira no Kiyomori burned Nara's Tōdai-ji and Kōfuku-ji for giving help to the Minamotos.

In 1183, eight years after Hōnen moved to Ōtani, a Minamoto commander attacked and terrorized Kyoto in defiance of Minamoto no Yoritomo's plans. It is said that was the only time Hōnen did not devote himself to the holy teachings. Otherwise his study continued throughout those confused times. If he had visitors, he taught them about the Pure Land and encouraged them to recite the nembutsu. His approach was extremely mild.

Hōnen's recognition among the clergy of the traditional sects in Nara and Kyoto dated from the Ōhara Discussion of 1186 (or 1189, according to another theory). The suggestion for the meeting came from Kenshin, a Tendai scholar, later appointed the head of Tendai, who invited Hōnen to discuss his doctrine. Priests who attended included Myōhen of the Sanron sect; Jōkei, a Hossō scholar (see biography in part 2); Tankyō of Tendai; Chōgen of Tōdai-ji (see biography in part 2); and Nembutsubō of Ōjō-in in Saga. Describing the various practices of the different sects and explaining his reasons why only the Pure Land teachings were suited to the present age, Hōnen deeply impressed his listeners. Thanks to the Ōhara Discussion, Hōnen became well known. He was then in the twelfth year of his life away from Mount Hiei.

In 1190 Hōnen gave a series of lectures at Tōdai-ji on the three Pure Land sutras, at the request of Chōgen, a participant in the Ōhara Discussion. Also, the previous year, he had begun associating with Kujō Kanezane, a Fujiwara regent who became the most influential of Hōnen's patrons. Hōnen's dharma students increased greatly after the Ōhara Discussion, and this was the time when those who were to found the five important subsects of the Jōdo sect came to study under Hōnen: Shōkū, founder of Seizan (see biography in part 2); Benchō, founder of Chinzei (see biography in part 2); Kōsai, founder of Ichinengi; Chōsai, founder of Kuhon-ji; and Ryūkan, founder of Chōraku-ji. His relations with the Kujō family continued to deepen. Kujō's daughter Gishū-mon'in, the consort of Emperor Go-Toba, received the laywomen's precepts from Hōnen in 1191, and Hōnen was again her ordination master when she was ordained as a priest ten years later. Kujō also received the laymen's precepts at various times after 1189, and he was ordained as a priest under Hōnen in 1202. Followers from the military class also appeared, including direct vassals of the Minamoto shogunate.

Thus it was between 1185 and 1190 that the number of Jōdo believers increased remarkably, and a band of followers of nembutsu as an exclusive practice grew up centered on Hōnen. After the disturbances of civil conflict ceased, nembutsu practice flourished, as an atmosphere of reconstruction overtook the capital. It was during this time of burgeoning popularity that Hōnen composed the *Collection of Passages on the Original Vow and the Nembutsu* to clarify Pure Land doctrine in a systematic way.

Collection of Passages on the Original Vow and the Nembutsu

The *Collection of Passages* was written in 1198 at the request of Kujō and set forth the doctrinal structure for Hōnen's personal conversion in 1175, the elements of which were organized by Hōnen to account for his belief.

> If we wish to free ourselves from the round of birth and death, we should lay aside at least for now one of the two excellent teachings, the holy path, and select and enter the way of the Pure Land. If we wish to enter the way of the Pure Land, which advocates two methods of training, the true and the miscellaneous, we should at least for now reject the miscellaneous method and select the true one. If we wish to practice the true method, which includes "essential" and "helpful" practices, we should set aside the helpful practice and select only the essential one. The essential one [which ensures rebirth in the Pure Land] consists of invoking the Buddha's name. This certainly results in rebirth in the Pure Land, for it accords with the Buddha's Original Vow.

Hōnen discarded the holy path, that is, all Early Buddhist and Mahayana teachings other than those of the Pure Land, closed the gate of meditation, sealed up the door of the holy way, abandoned the miscellaneous method, and selected the invocation of the name. It was this nembutsu, selected after all other practices had been "discarded, closed off, sealed up, and abandoned," that was the very act indicated by Amida to ensure rebirth in his Pure Land. The key to salvation had been discovered in the intention of the Buddha. Even the stupid and vile, the poor, and those who broke the precepts, or did not even keep them at all, had only to engage in the exclusive practice of nembutsu to be carried along by the power of Amida's vow to Pure Land rebirth. Therefore all practices other than nembutsu were denied, even aspiration to enlightenment, which is the basis for all Buddhist training, and the threefold training of morality, contemplation, and wisdom. To all those who were ignorant, poor, or immoral, Hōnen showed a new way that might assure them of a lotus seat in Amida's realm.

Because this revolutionary doctrine stigmatized the established sects for not meeting the needs of the era, it was only a matter of time before they counterattacked. Perhaps that is why Hōnen added a postscript to the *Collection of Passages* stating that his doctrine was not to be openly revealed. "I beseech you, that once you have perused this work, you bury it beneath your walls and do not leave it before your window."

Conflict

Hōnen had none of the material resources of the large temples, and he made no attempt to establish an organization that could supervise his dharma students. Nevertheless his band grew until Kyoto was filled with his followers, supporters having come from all parts of the country. The established temples could not overlook such an influential, powerful group.

Late in 1204, the clerics of Enryaku-ji appealed to the head of Tendai, Shinshō, to ban nembutsu. In the following month Hōnen tried to placate them by assuring Shinshō that he was anything but a slanderer of the dharma and handing them a document called the *Seven-Article Injunction,* which he had asked his followers to sign. It may be summarized as follows:

1. Do not criticize Shingon or Tendai, or speak ill of any buddhas or bodhisattvas.

2. Do not dispute with learned people or with followers of practices other than nembutsu.

3. Do not look down with biased minds on people with other beliefs and practices.

4. Do not, while saying that keeping the precepts is not essential

for a nembutsu follower, encourage sexual indulgence, drinking, or meat eating; do not hold that a practitioner of the Vinaya is only following the miscellaneous practices or assert that those who call upon the name of Amida have no fear of doing evil.

5. Do not, being of shallow learning, state personal views without restraint, engage in disputes, or confuse the foolish.

6. Do not use popular and emotional styles of preaching or resort to heresies to convert the ignorant laity.

7. Do not claim that one's own heretical interpretations are correct or that they are the master's.

The injunction highlights the abuses perpetrated by charlatan nembutsu practitioners among Hōnen's dharma students. There were those who delighted in arguing with people of other beliefs; those who indulged in sexual relationships, meat eating, and drinking; and those who actively sought out patrons, wanting fame and position, who liked popular preaching methods and who used the Pure Land teachings as entertainment. Hōnen was seen as their ringleader.

He was largely able to avert trouble over the Enryaku-ji anti-nembutsu movement, but in the autumn of 1205, Kōfuku-ji priests also appealed to the retired emperor Go-Toba to ban nembutsu. The document they presented, known as the *Kōfuku-ji Petition,* was a statement of nine errors that they claimed were perpetrated by nembutsu followers:

1. Establishing a new sect without imperial sanction.

2. Drawing new images, in particular the Sesshu Fusha Mandala, which depicted followers of Tendai and Shingon slightingly.

3. Belittling Shakyamuni.

4. Neglecting good works and slandering Mahayana.

5. Rejecting the Shinto deities.

6. Obscuring the Pure Land, for other practices might also lead to the same goal.

7. Misunderstanding nembutsu, dependence on the Original Vow for Pure Land rebirth being an action of the ignorant.

8. Harming the followers of Shakyamuni. Establishing a sect that does not uphold the Vinaya, resulting in the destruction of Buddhism.

9. Sowing confusion in the land.

The petition also demanded that two of Hōnen's apprentices, Gyōku and Junsai, be punished for heresy. Hōnen responded by expelling Gyōku from the sect for teaching rebirth through the nembutsu of a single calling. Though Kōfuku-ji persisted with its petition, the tension would probably have eased if two of Hōnen's apprentices had not been arrested. While the retired emperor Go-Toba was away on a pilgrimage to Kumano Shrine at the end of 1206, ladies of his court invited Jūren and Junsai to hold a special overnight service at the palace, and misconduct between the ladies and the priests was said to have occurred. The emperor was exceedingly angry and sentenced the two to death. Imperial wrath did not stop at that; their master, Hōnen, was ordered into exile.

Exile and Death

Early in 1207, Hōnen was banished to the island of Shikoku. Even Kujō's campaign to gain him pardon did not succeed. The remaining dharma students felt great anxiety about Hōnen's health and wept bitter tears. Hōnen was then seventy-four years old and had been living since the previous year in the Komatsudani district of Kyoto. Fearing the parting would be forever, his apprentices gathered around him, and he spoke of what was in his heart. "I do not resent this sentence of exile. Although we now live in the same city, I am an old man and the time for my final parting must be approaching. Mountains and seas may divide us, but we are sure to meet again in the Pure Land. I have long taught nembutsu here in Kyoto and have often thought I would like to go into the country and preach it there also. Until now that opportunity had not come. That my wish has been fulfilled is due to the graciousness of His Majesty."

Hōnen then began to speak about the teachings of nembutsu as an exclusive practice. A follower called Sai Amidabutsu interrupted, wanting to protect him. Hōnen stopped him, saying, "Even if it means my execution, I cannot stop speaking of the teachings of the exclusive-practice nembutsu."

Hōnen, returned to lay status under the name of Fujii Moto-hiko, was originally banished to southern Shikoku, but Kujō's efforts resulted in this being changed to the northern part of the island. So great was Kujō's demoralization over Hōnen's exile that he died less than a month later, aged fifty-eight.

Hōnen left the capital in spring, 1207. Traveling through Harima Province, he arrived at the island of Shiaku, off Shikoku, ten days later. He preached about nembutsu in the course of his journey. At one place he converted an old couple who were fishers, at another, a prostitute, and on Shiaku island, an estate steward. From Shiaku, Hōnen crossed to the mainland of Shikoku, but it is uncertain exactly where he spent his exile.

The exile should not be seen so much as a punishment of Hōnen himself as a sop to the anti-nembutsu movement of the established temples. In fact he was pardoned at the end of the same year but was not permitted to enter the capital. For four years he remained at Kachio-dera in Settsu Province. He came back to Kyoto, after a five-year absence, late in 1211. Because his former residence had fallen into disrepair, he was given accommodation in a small hillside temple above Ōtani. Hōnen became ill the day after New Year's Day, 1212, the strains of his exile finally overcoming him, and took to his bed. Nevertheless he continued to chant the nembutsu as tirelessly as before and to lecture to his dharma students on passages in the sutras. One student, knowing that the time for his master's rebirth was approaching, asked about establishing a memorial temple after his death. Hōnen replied that if they erected a memorial to him, the dharma would not be disseminated. He said they should let his memorial fill the land, so wherever nembu-tsu was, there would be his memorial temple also, even if it were only the thatched cottage of a fisherman.

Hōnen's illness continued to worsen. Three weeks from the start of the illness, Hōnen's best apprentice and dharma successor, Genchi, requested something written in his master's own hand. Thereupon Hōnen wrote what has become known as the *One-Page Testament,* setting forth the essentials of nembutsu.

Two days later, Hōnen grew weaker and weaker as the morning

progressed. Hearing the news, followers crowded around his dwelling. Around noon, he slipped peacefully into death, chanting Amida's name. He was seventy-nine years old.

The dwelling in which Hōnen died is the site of the Seishi-dō chapel at Chion-in, the present headquarters of the Jōdo sect. His remains were buried on a hill above it. Until 1227 memorial services were held there on the twenty-fifth of each month. Nembutsu followers thronged to these services, and the area was as busy as a market as they made reverence before his image. Trouble came to a head, however, in 1227. Enryaku-ji clerics decided to destroy Hōnen's tomb, and laborers from Gion Shrine were ordered to do the work. Dharma successors secretly removed Hōnen's body to Nison-in in Saga. Finally, the remains were cremated early in 1228.

Shortly after Hōnen's death, a religious association called the Chion-kō was established to honor the master and to encourage the practice of nembutsu. It praised five virtues of Hōnen: encompassing all sects and teachings, disseminating the Original Vow, teaching the exclusive-practice nembutsu as the central tenet, ensuring Pure Land rebirth, and benefiting beings after death. The eulogy begins: "Our revered master disseminated these teachings and encouraged this practice to bring to the dharma both the laity and the clergy. As grass sways in the wind, they respond, believing and worshipping. Such conversion is not limited to this life, for its virtues increase after death. Our debt of gratitude is as high as a mountain, and his [Hōnen's] virtue is as fathomless as the deep ocean." Hōnen's benefiting of others is explained: "Our revered master showed forth the way to Pure Land rebirth for the common person through his religious teachings. He manifested the select Original Vow to be a mirror for practitioners of nembutsu. Our debt of gratitude only increases, for his bequeathed virtue is as of this world."

Hōnen continued to be vilified after his death, but his teachings remained as widely accepted as ever. For his followers, he gradually took on the image of a savior, and he was called a transformation of Amida, a manifestation of Daiseishi Bodhisattva, a reborn Tao-cho (a Chinese Pure Land master), and a reincarnation of

Shan-tao (another Chinese Pure Land master). Hōnen, who advocated the exclusive practice of nembutsu in the time of change that
marked the end of the age of the aristocracy and the beginning of
the medieval period, admirably fulfilled his historic task and is
even now undergoing transformation into the figure of a religious
founder.

Eisai
(1141–1215)

by Aishin Imaeda

Eisai, known as the founder of Japanese Zen, was born in a family affiliated with Kibitsu Shrine in Bitchū Province at the very end of the Heian period, when fundamental changes had begun to disrupt both religion and society. He was small in stature but endowed with the makings of a man of action, well-suited to living in a disturbed age.

He first studied the basics of Buddhism under his father, who himself had been a student at Mii-dera (the head temple of the Tendai Jimon subsect). Eisai went on to study the Tendai esotericism as transmitted through Mii-dera under Jōshin of An'yō-ji and, in 1158 after Jōshin's death, under his dharma brother Semmyō. He had received preliminary ordination at the Sammon subsect headquarters, Enryaku-ji, on Mount Hiei in 1154, at which time he had been given the Buddhist name Yōjōbō. He was also called Senkō Hōshi, after the subtemple in which he dwelled.

There was constant conflict between the Sammon and Jimon subsects; clerics attacked each other's temples, burned them down, and joined in bloody fights. There could be no reconciliation between them. It was perhaps Eisai's close personal connection with the Mii-dera side that made him increasingly critical of the Buddhism taught on Mount Hiei and later helped him develop a friendship with the Minamotos, themselves supporters of Mii-dera.

Seeking a way to breathe new life into the Tendai teachings, Eisai left Mii-dera around 1162 for Daisen in Hōki Province and attached himself to Shūzenbō Kikō. Kikō seems to have been deeply versed in the Zen component of the fourfold Tendai teachings (Concentration and Insight, esoteric teachings, Mahayana precepts, and Zen). Eisai no doubt was educated in Zen by Kikō and evolved a conviction that this was the path he should pursue. He later returned for a short time to Mount Hiei, where he received the dharma transmission of Tendai esotericism from Ken'i and continued his studies of the most profound Tendai teachings.

Journeys to China

In 1168, Eisai took passage aboard a merchant vessel bound for China, determined to visit the birthplace of his own sect and to seek elements of Chinese T'ien-t'ai that might reinvigorate Tendai in Japan. Landing in China, he chanced to meet a Tōdai-ji priest called Chōgen (see biography in part 2), who had arrived the previous year. Together they visited Mount T'ien-t'ai, where they paid respect at the tomb of Chih-i, the third patriarch of T'ien-t'ai, then reached the famous Rock Bridge, where they saw statues of five hundred disciples of the Buddha. Following in the footsteps of Saichō (see biography in part 1) and Enchin (see biography in part 2), they could not but recall those great men who had preceded them. Next they traveled to Mount A-yu-wang and bowed to the famous Buddha reliquary there. A meeting with the reception priest of a Ch'an temple in Ming-chou benefitted Eisai greatly.

Though Eisai had gone to China to study T'ien-t'ai doctrine, he found when he arrived that the area south of the Yangtze was completely dominated by Ch'an (Zen) Buddhism. Even more astounding was that the very headquarters of the T'ien-t'ai sect, as well as the temple on Mount A-yu-wang, had changed allegiance from T'ien-t'ai to Ch'an. What Eisai saw all around thus was not T'ien-t'ai at all, but the Ch'an of the Southern Sung dynasty. There is no doubt that he was attracted by Ch'an and excited by its newness; he must have wanted to stay and absorb that teaching before returning home. Nevertheless, at Chōgen's urging, Eisai took ship with his companion in autumn of the same year. He had been in China only six months, and there had been no time for him to acquire Ch'an training.

There are very few records about what Eisai did after his return to Japan. His close relationship with Chōgen might be expected to have continued in some form, but there are no documents to bear out that supposition. He is known to have presented some sixty volumes of T'ien-t'ai scriptures to Myōun, Tendai's head, at Enryaku-ji, but he did not return to live on Mount Hiei. Perhaps he was not welcome there, being of the Mii-dera lineage and having witnessed the popularity of Ch'an in China. All we know is that he spent time in his home district in Bitchū Province and at Seigan-ji in northern Kyushu, awaiting a chance to return to China. During this time he must have made persistent efforts to prepare himself intellectually for the second journey, for there are large numbers of writings and copies of sutras said to have been used by Eisai around 1185.

Through his deep study of T'ien-t'ai, he was filled with a burning admiration for Shakyamuni Buddha, and it became his ambition to visit India and pay homage at the eight great pagodas built to commemorate places associated with the Buddha. He was dissuaded from this, probably by a patron and by the warfare continuing in his home district. In 1186, eighteen years after his first voyage, Eisai renewed his attempts to get to China and finally, in the spring of 1187, he sailed to the capital of Chekiang.

Eisai immediately sent a request to the Chinese officials for permission to travel overland to India, but this was refused because of the Mongol domination of Central Asia. Despondent, Eisai boarded ship once more to return to Japan. Here fate intervened: a contrary wind drove Eisai's ship to Wen-chou.

Transmitting the Huang-lung Lineage

Eisai subsequently studied Lin-chi Ch'an (Rinzai Zen) of the Huang-lung school for three years under Hsü-an Huai-ch'ang, first at Wan-nien temple on Mount T'ien-t'ai and then at Ching-te temple on Mount T'ien-t'ung (after Hsü-an was appointed chief priest there), where he inherited the lineage of his master. As a dharma successor of Hsü-an, the grandson of Huang-lung Hui-nan, the eighth patriarch of Lin-chi Ch'an and founder of one of the two Lin-chi lineages of the time, Eisai became a true man of Zen, with a formal seal of transmission, transmission lineage, robes, and ritual articles all bestowed upon him with the good will of his master. It was at this time that he received the Ch'an name of Myōan.

There is a poem in the imperial anthology *Collection of Ancient and Modern [Japanese] Poems Continued,* compiled in 1265, that Eisai is thought to have written during this period for his mother, left behind in Japan:

> The treetops of China are already bare:
> Where my mother is, at the sun's source,
> The autumn leaves would be scattered by now.

Eisai also demonstrated his skill in construction while in China. He assisted with building and renovation of the main gate and corridors of Wan-nien temple, Kuan-yin-yüan and Ta-szu temples, Chih-i's mausoleum on Mount T'ien-t'ai, and the Thousand Buddhas Pagoda on Mount T'ien-t'ung. This reflects the high level of Japanese construction techniques, which Eisai probably learned through his association with Chōgen, who had been in charge of the restoration of Nara's Tōdai-ji since 1181.

Eisai returned to Japan on a Chinese merchant vessel in 1191, after an absence of four years. Landing in Kyushu, he was invited to dwell in a small temple recently established there. The following year, he built a temple named Hōon-ji beside Kashii Shrine in Chikuzen Province. It was there that for the first time in Japan an ordination ceremony was held in which a pure Zen lineage was bestowed.

As his efforts brought growing popularity for the new Zen, Eisai found himself subject to the animosity of Rōben, a priest in the same province. Supported by Mount Hiei, Rōben submitted a complaint to the court. As a result, the court prohibited Eisai's activities and those of another Zen priest, Dainichibō Nōnin, in the autumn of 1194.

By this time Eisai was already in Kyoto teaching Zen, and he had debated doctrine with Nōnin, a priest of China's other Lin-chi lineage, Ta-hui. It seems likely that Eisai suffered by association, for Nōnin ambitiously strove to promote his Zen as an exclusive practice, an anathema to the established sects. Eisai, in contrast, had no intention of setting up Zen as a separate sect; he wanted to use it only to reinvigorate Tendai, replacing the traditional Zen component of the fourfold Tendai teachings with the new Zen of the Huang-lung lineage. The gap between the thinking of the two men was not recognized, and their activities were equally suppressed.

Propagation of Zen as a Defense of the Nation

Eisai was not a man to be daunted by these reversals. It was at this time that he began writing his principal work, *Propagation of Zen as a Defense of the Nation,* in which he argued that the new Chinese Ch'an should be introduced to strengthen the traditional Tendai ideology of Buddhism as a vehicle for the protection of the nation.

In 1195 Eisai received a hearing at court by order of the imperial regent, Kujō Kanezane, who had been Hōnen's patron. This was no doubt an attempt at mediation by Kujō, a Minamoto sympathizer himself and supporter of Eisai, who also had strong Minamoto ties. The connection between the two may have arisen through Chōgen, who had been on close terms with the regent from around 1183. Summoned to repeat his assertions to Kujō's subordinates, Eisai replied that Zen was nothing new, and indeed had been recognized by Saichō himself as a genuine Buddhist teaching introduced by Bodhidharma from India. Rōben, not understanding this, had incited the clergy of Mount Hiei to lodge a complaint at court. If Enryaku-ji rejected Zen, Eisai argued, it would be denying the intentions of Saichō. If Saichō had been censured for his doctrine, Japanese Tendai would never have been established. Surely Saichō's thought has been properly understood, he insisted. Tendai intellectuals are said to have stood silent before his reasoning.

Tendai priests did not have to wait for Eisai to tell them about Zen, for it was already common knowledge among them. The Zen that was an integral part of Tendai practice, though, was that of T'ang China, the Ox Head Ch'an lineage that Saichō had learned on Mount T'ien-t'ai. That taught by Eisai, on the other hand, was of the later Huang-lung lineage. It was no wonder that Mount Hiei's conservative clerics were not altogether satisfied by Eisai's arguments. If Eisai had continued his efforts in the Kyoto area, further confrontations would have been inevitable, so he decided to set off for Kamakura, seeking a new sphere for his activities.

Kamakura

In 1195, the shogun, Minamoto no Yoritomo, traveled to Kyoto on the occasion of dedication ceremonies at Tōdai-ji, just when the controversy over Eisai's religious ideas was creating a public sensation. It would be interesting to know what Yoritomo and his warrior followers made of the rise of the new Zen. The new governing class was seeking some sort of cultural embellishment to set itself apart from the Kyoto aristocracy, traditional patrons of the older Buddhist sects. It is likely that the Kamakura shogunate leaders felt the freshness and attraction of Eisai's Southern Sung Zen and would have liked to bring it to Kamakura. From Eisai's point of view, close relations with the Kamakura shogunate could only be advantageous, given his connection with Mii-dera and its close ties with the Minamotos.

There is no evidence to substantiate these suppositions, but Eisai was never one to let an opportunity slip. Further, Kujō

Kanezane fell from power in 1196; Eisai's journey to Kamakura could well have been made as a result of losing one patron and feeling a need to form a close connection with another.

It is not clear exactly when Eisai went to Kamakura. His name is first mentioned there in 1199 when he conducted a rite to Fudō Myōō, so his arrival must have preceded that. The following year, he was placed in charge of the construction of a temple called Jufuku-ji that Hōjō Masako, the widow of Minamoto no Yoritomo, had vowed to build. The site of the temple had originally been a residence of Yoritomo's father, Minamoto no Yoshitomo, a warrior of the late Heian period. It was later converted into a temple for memorial services for Yoshitomo.

Eisai was the officiating priest at a variety of religious services and meetings on behalf of the shogunate. He was trusted by the third Minamoto shogun, Sanetomo, in particular, and it was for Sanetomo that Eisai wrote the two-volume work *Drink Tea and Prolong Life,* which he presented to the ailing shogun early in 1214. This work recommending tea as a medicine, stressing its healthful qualities and other virtues, may be the reason he has been considered ever since to be the one who introduced tea to Japan. (Actually tea had been introduced by Kūkai about 400 years earlier, but did not become popular at that time.)

What stands out in Eisai's relations with the leadership at Kamakura is that he does not appear as a practitioner of undiluted Zen. This seems paradoxical in light of his character up until the time he produced the *Propagation of Zen as a Defense of the Nation.* When it is considered that the Kamakura warriors were not intellectually ready to cope with the rich Chinese Ch'an tradition, however, it is not surprising that the mainstay of their belief lay in the elaborate rituals and petitions of traditional Japanese Buddhism.

Sand and Pebbles, a compendium of Buddhist traditions completed in 1283, says:

The late founder of Kennin-ji, High Priest Eisai, taught the precepts, respected all the rules of conduct, valued Tendai, Shingon, and Zen teachings, and encouraged the practice of nembutsu among the people. . . . Eisai founded Kennin-ji and Jufuku-ji in Kamakura and Shōfuku-ji on Kyushu. He did not oppose the customs of the provinces, but accommodated himself to Ritsu, Tendai, Shingon, and other teachings, and did not practice Chinese ways to the exclusion of all else, for he was awaiting his time. In the same way, the sutras and commentaries formerly were taught simultaneously in India, and in China the coexistence of the three teachings deepened understanding. His Zen was inwardly Zen, with some Shingon elements on the surface.

Eisai did not consider himself completely estranged from the older sects, but rather felt he was incorporating the new Zen into the existing traditions. Furthermore, he was deeply interested in Tendai-style esoteric practices. Such eclecticism, merging the old and the new, must have been very suitable for the Kamakura leaders. It was therefore as a leader of rituals and petitions in the Tendai tradition that Eisai won the support of the shogunate while he waited for an opportunity to return to Kyoto.

Establishment of Kennin-ji

Finally in 1202 the shogun, Minamoto no Yoriie, founded Kennin-ji in Rokuhara, a Kyoto district under direct jurisdiction of the government, and granted it to Eisai. The new temple set aside special chapels for Shingon esoteric practices and Tendai meditation practices, and it was authorized as a branch temple of Enryaku-ji. This is further evidence that Eisai was not consciously advocating a complete break from Tendai.

In this way Eisai continued to maintain the position that he was introducing innovations to Tendai. Early in 1205, however, he was blamed by the people of Kyoto for a strong wind that brought damage to the capital. They said that Eisai had brought a new religion to Japan and that his followers had stirred up a great wind by walking around the city in their strange, long-sleeved robes. The court, hearing these allegations, wanted to expel him from the city. Eisai, now backed by the powerful Kamakura shogunate, was not the same person as before, however. He replied calmly that wind is a force of nature, not a man-made phenomenon. Obviously the storm had nothing to do with him. Still, he continued, if people really believed that he was responsible, they would have to recognize him as a wind god, whom no wise emperor would dare drive from the city. His argument carried the day and even brought Kennin-ji the status of an official temple. Though this episode, recounted in *Sand and Pebbles* and other sources, probably should not be considered historical fact, it does reflect a movement by envious clerics on Mount Hiei to persuade the court to impose a second ban on Eisai's activities.

With the patronage of the Kamakura shogunate sustaining him, Eisai increasingly established his position among the Kyoto aristocracy. In 1206 he was appointed by the court as supervisor of the Tōdai-ji reconstruction, succeeding Chōgen, who had died that year. An important factor in the appointment must have been the need to employ someone having close contacts with the shogunate, the motivating force behind the project. Another was his obvious skill in building; he had assisted with restoration work in China, had introduced Sung architectural techniques to Japan, and had built the temples of Shōfuku-ji, Jufuku-ji, and Kennin-ji. The time had come when his genius could be exhibited on a large scale. Eisai amply fulfilled the hopes of those who had appointed him and brought work on the Great Buddha Hall to completion in a scant four years.

During this time, Eisai was also given the task of rebuilding the nine-storied Hosshō-ji pagoda, which had been destroyed by lightning. This was completed in six years, and the retired emperor Go-Toba and his son, Emperor Juntoku, attended the great dedication ceremony in 1213.

On that occasion, Eisai presented all of the offerings he had received from those who were taking part in the ceremony to the superintendent of the six imperial temples in Kyoto, Prince Dōhō. Fujiwara no Sadaie, one of the foremost scholars and poets of the time, criticized Eisai's act as being little more than a bribe. Apparently Eisai wanted entree to the court through Dōhō, an uncle of Go-Toba, and to be given the highest of the clerical ranks, high priest. Hearing of this, the Mount Hiei clergy exhibited violent opposition and brought the sacred tree of Hiyoshi Shrine down to the city in protest. For the time being the idea was dropped.

Despite this, Eisai next appealed to the court to be granted the title of Great Master, an honor that had always been given post-humously. Once again, his request brought anger and opposition from Jien, the head of Tendai, and others, and it was refused as being reserved for eminent priests after death. Instead, Eisai was granted the rank of provisional high priest. The courtiers were not pleased with his strategy; Sadaie condemned his actions as not being worthy of an eminent priest, and even Go-Toba was reported to have regretted bestowing the title upon him. Perhaps Eisai's behavior stemmed from the fact that he was a skilled man of action. *Sand and Pebbles* says, ''People look down on Buddhist practitioners of low rank as beggar clerics, and Buddhism in turn becomes underrated,'' and explains Eisai's determination to be given the rank of high priest as being for the sake of the dharma, not for self-aggrandizement. This, though, tends to sophistry.

There is one theory that indicates Eisai was awarded the purple robe, the highest degree of court recognition of a priest, as a reward for his work on the Hosshō-ji pagoda reconstruction. This would have been impossible because Eisai had not even been awarded the rank of high priest, the highest of the court-awarded ranks. Furthermore, such was the opposition to Eisai at the time among courtiers and officials that an honor of that level would not even have been considered.

There is no reason to think that Eisai, though he had brought back Southern Sung Ch'an on his second return from China, had any conscious intention of changing his affiliation from Tendai to Zen as a separate sect. He preferred to maintain a revisionist position, conducting gradual reforms from within Tendai by incorporating in it the practices of the Huang-lung Ch'an lineage. All the same, he has been generally regarded as a Zen master, the founder of Zen in Japan, as well as the person who introduced tea to the country. Eisai died before the title of Zen master was created, and he closed his life not as the Zen priest Myōan Eisai, but as the Tendai priest Yōjōbō Eisai. Furthermore, his followers all tended to have Tendai names, and they were strongly conscious of being Tendai priests. It was only after his teachings later began to flourish as pure Zen that he was called the founder of Japanese Zen.

In any event, Eisai was the first to transplant Southern Sung Ch'an to Japan, despite stiff opposition from the traditional sects and the nobility. His close ties with the Kamakura shogunate allowed him to establish bases for that Zen in Kamakura and Kyoto, from which emerged outstanding followers, especially in the eastern region. Eisai paved the way for the establishment of the pure Zen sects and did much to build a foundation for the later development of Zen.

Two theories exist as to the date of Eisai's death. *Mirror of the East,* recording events between 1180 and 1266, says he died in Kamakura on July 4, 1215, whereas other chronicles, such as *The Genkō Era's History of Buddhism,* completed in 1322, are unanimous in stating he died the same year in Kyoto, on August 2. The latter date should be considered correct.

Shinran

(1173–1262)

by Takehiko Furuta

Shinran, founder of the Jōdo Shin sect of Pure Land Buddhism, defended the Buddhist clergy's abandonment of the precepts on celibacy and diet.

There is an anecdote in the *Notes of Oral Transmissions,* composed in 1331 by Shinran's great-grandson, Kakunyo (see biography in part 2), concerning Shinran's attitude toward eating meat. Hōjō Tokiuji, son of the third Kamakura regent, had vowed to make a copy of the Buddhist canon and had invited a number of priests, including Shinran, to proofread the copy. At mealtimes the priests would remove their Indian-style outer robes, symbols of the Buddha's followers, before unashamedly enjoying fish or fowl. This was believed to violate the precept against killing living things. Shinran alone kept on his outer robe as he ate fish. Tokiuji's son asked Shinran his reason. At first he just replied that he had forgotten to remove it. The son continued to pester him with questions, though, until he finally answered. ''In the period of the Decay of the Dharma there is nothing in the way of precepts that a cleric should keep. So it is that I eat meat the same as a lay person. I only eat wearing my outer robe, the very symbol of a Buddhist follower, so that the fish can acquire some merit.''

There is no way of knowing whether this story is based on fact. We should not reject it outright, perhaps, for Shinran does not appear here as a high-ranking advisor to the Hōjō family but as one among a large number of clerics employed to work on sutra copying and proofreading. The conversation forms a dramatic interlude, but what is of real interest is the underlying attitudes.

At that time meat-eating was already common among the Buddhist clergy and was permitted as long as they removed their outer robes at mealtimes. Shinran, though, was offended by such an easy justification and wanted to examine it in the light of the teachings considered essential in the period of the Decay of the Dharma. The anecdote is faithful to the image of Shinran given by reliable primary sources. He was not the first to violate the rule against eating meat; rather, he tried to understand the meaning of the rule.

It is well known that Shinran married and fathered seven children. At least one source contends that he had had a wife before his marriage to the cleric Eshinni. In *Teaching, Practice, Faith, Attainment,* Shinran wrote, commenting on a passage in the *Sutra of the Perfect Net:* "In a degenerate age it is not unusual for a priest to keep a wife or have children. Therefore, that the authorities should punish this as a violation of the precepts is an atrocity, like spilling the blood of a buddha." Here Shinran speaks of himself at the time of the banishment of Hōnen and his followers in 1207, protesting what had happened. This suggests strongly that even before his exile to Echigo Province at the age of thirty-four, Shinran had a wife.

When Shinran was living in Kyoto as a young man, he wrote some verses, translated here as prose:

When karmic retribution leads the practitioner to violate the precepts of chastity, I will assume the body of a maiden and be the object of that violation.

Having adorned his present life, at the time of his death I will guide him to rebirth in the Pure Land of Utmost Bliss.

These strange and somewhat scandalous verses are quoted by Kakunyo in the *Illustrated Life of the Revered Master of Hongan-ji,* and because they also appear in a transcript that Shinran had one of his dharma students make of his *Record of Shinran's Dreams,* their authenticity is beyond doubt.

"I" refers to the Kannon Bodhisattva statue at Rokkaku-dō temple in Kyoto, which appeared to Shinran in a dream in 1201 or 1203. The verses are reminiscent of Goethe's "Eternal Woman draws us upward" (the last line of *Faust*). His state of mind at the time is suggested by his use twice of the word "violate." The precepts shackled a priest of his day and age. In the face of temptation, Shinran was inspired by the idea that Kannon would take the female form and save him, an idea that was confirmed in a dream.

Condemned in terms of public ideas of morality but holding firm to his own experience, Shinran searched for a higher religious meaning in the depths of that experience. This search was fundamental to his philosophical development.

Shinran was not the first cleric ever to marry. There are many examples of priests' marrying in such collections of religious tales as *Tales of Times Now Past,* an eleventh-century work. He was a pioneer, rather, in terms of religious justification for the fact.

Overcoming Oppression and Exile

Kakunyo's *Illustrated Life* opens with the following statement about Shinran's genealogy: "The revered master was of the Fujiwara clan. His direct ancestor, who was the twenty-first descendant of Amatsu Koyane no Mikoto, was Nakatomi no Kamako, the inner minister."

This extravagant claim, which would have astounded Shinran as much as anyone else, goes on to say that he was the son of Hino Arinori, a member of the declining aristocracy. According to a reliable reference in a letter from Eshinni to her daughter, Shinran was an ordinary temple priest on Mount Hiei, whose duty was perpetual recitation of the nembutsu in a hall there for one of the four Tendai meditation practices, perpetually moving practice. After having spent his life among the lower echelons in temples belonging to the Tendai sect, which was virtually the established religion of the day, in an organization that prided itself on being favored by emperors and princes and on being founded to "protect and preserve Japan," Shinran left Mount Hiei, full of anguish, for a hundred-day retreat at Rokkaku-dō in Kyoto. Eshinni wrote concerning this time, "He visited the temple every day, rain or shine, regardless of obstacles." After the retreat, with the courage of desperation, he decided to join Hōnen. "Wherever the venerable Hōnen goes, even if it be to a hell, I will follow. I give no thought to whatever criticism others offer me."

Thus in 1201, at the age of twenty-eight, Shinran became a member of Hōnen's band. He records his action in *Teaching, Practice, Faith, Attainment* as follows: "In the first year of the Kennin era, I abandoned the miscellaneous practices and took refuge in the Original Vow." Behind this factual statement lay a determination that made him leave the officially recognized Tendai sect for a group whose exclusive practice of nembutsu made it only a matter of time before the group would be suppressed.

Hōnen's followers came from all classes, from the nobility to commoners, so they were a mass of contradictions. It was Hōnen's tolerance that made him welcome everyone equally. Then sixty-eight, he valued Shinran's fervent determination to seek the Way. In 1205 he let Shinran copy his *Collection of Passages on the Original Vow and the Nembutsu* and inscribed the copy with its title; the words, "I take refuge in Amida Buddha; nembutsu is the fundamental practice ensuring rebirth in the Pure Land," the maxim of the Pure Land movement; and "Shakkū," the name Shinran received when he joined Hōnen. Hōnen also wrote out a Chinese verse for Shinran that expresses an aging master's solicitude for a keen young apprentice, and the apprentice's deep emotional response. The spirit Hōnen imparted to Shinran is well illustrated in a letter Shinran wrote near the end of his life (in 1260, at the age of eighty-seven):

I well recall how the venerable Hōnen would often smile pleasantly in his undiscriminating and simple way when he saw humble people, saying, "They are assured of rebirth in the Pure Land." In contrast, when he met people who were proud of their learning he would say, "What sort of thing will this man's Pure Land rebirth amount to?'' Though a long time has passed since then and I am nearly ninety years of age, I remember those things vividly.

The period with Hōnen, which remained in Shinran's thoughts like a warm, undying flame, was brought to a sudden end by the storm of persecution in the spring of 1207, when he was thirty-four. Jūren and Junsai, famous for their appealing voices and preaching abilities, were executed. Hōnen and his six apprentices were exiled, each to a different area. Records of the nobles of the time state that Jūren and Junsai had adulterous relations with the ladies of the retired emperor Go-Toba's palace under the pretext of conducting a nembutsu service, inviting Go-Toba's wrath. The root of the problem lay in the immorality and lack of discipline among some of Hōnen's followers, and the incident rocked the whole movement. All his life Shinran himself held to the view that Hōnen had been the victim of calumny in appeals to the court by Kōfuku-ji and other traditional temples.

Hōnen was exiled to southern Shikoku, though the records state he remained in a northern area of Shikoku for the period. Shinran was sent far away from his master, to Echigo Province in northwestern Honshu. Life in this northern region was difficult for an exile, as the *Procedures of the Engi Era,* an early tenth-century work, details that exiles, regardless of social class, sex, or age, were to receive 1.8 liters of rice and one small spoonful of salt per day. The following spring they would be given seed to plant. From the next autumn, all supply of food would cease.

Such hardship strengthened Shinran's character. This is evident in a petition he submitted to the secretary of the council of state around 1210. After referring to the retired emperor Go-Toba and the current emperor, he wrote: ''The lords and their retainers [i.e., the emperor and nobility], violating the dharma and acting contrary to righteousness, have given rise to unreasonable anger and resentment.'' He went on to accuse the authorities of ''illegal behavior'' in the execution of Jūren and Junsai. Such spirit is rare in Japanese intellectual history. This strong spirit was to remain undimmed to the end of his life. Compared with the verses he wrote as a young man discussed earlier, his style in the petition is robust and direct. A decade of hardship had forged a strength of spirit.

Following the accession of a new emperor, at a time of tense relations between the court in Kyoto and the shogunate in Kamakura, Hōnen and Shinran were pardoned. In 1212, soon after his return to Kyoto, worn out from the stress of exile, Hōnen died at the age of seventy-nine in Ōtani, eastern Kyoto. We can sense Shinran's anguish in the lines he wrote on Hōnen's death in the epilogue to *Teaching, Practice, Faith, Attainment.* He had been separated from his master throughout five years of exile and now by death.

Bereft of his master, he did not return to Kyoto, but set off for the eastern provinces. Without Hōnen to turn to, Shinran had to confront his doubts and problems alone. It was from these difficulties and gropings that his philosophy and his greatest work, *Teaching, Practice, Faith, Attainment,* took shape.

Three Stages of Conversion

The basis of *Teaching, Practice, Faith, Attainment* is Shinran's concept of three stages of conversion. He describes his spiritual life, dividing it into three periods corresponding to the nineteenth, twentieth, and eighteenth vows of the *Sutra of Infinite Life.*

The first stage he called "the temporary gate of the myriad practices and good deeds," to describe rebirth through the power of accumulated roots of goodness from the perspective of traditional Buddhism, by such actions as selfless giving, keeping the precepts, building temples, making images, and engaging in ascetic practices. Shinran's spiritual life remained at this stage until he went to Hōnen. His personal experience as a lower-class priest on Mount Hiei convinced him that those were not suitable means for the poor to seek rebirth, for the poor had no wealth and little leisure.

The second stage, "the true gate of the roots of virtue and goodness," was one in which practitioners are unable to give up attachment to training that depends on no outside power, as practiced so far, though now they are given to the exclusive practice of nembutsu. Despite holding to nembutsu, practitioners are unable to prevent a selfish pride in their own abilities, intellectual understanding, and merits. Shinran's description of this stage reflects his anguish at his inability to avert his gaze from himself even after he joined Hōnen's band.

The third stage, the final one, Shinran called the "sea of the selected vow." Now he had wakened to the need for absolute dependence on the power of Amida. He had thrown away the self full of discrimination and pride and had accepted nembutsu itself as having been bestowed completely by Amida. Self and others, without difference, could all then appear, impure and evil as they might be, within the radiance of true equality. Such radiance would then illumine all differences and discriminations of society and show forth the true character of those who acted outwardly as if they were wise and good. It is a mistake to assert, as some did later, that the power of Amida's vow meant the weak depending on the strong. On the contrary, the power of that vow is the wellspring of a strength that will not submit either to unreasonable authority or to systematic indifference, coming as it does from the realization that one is in the presence of the absolute.

The third stage is not something that one can announce as attained through one's own power on a specific date. Having decided to walk the way of exclusive practice of nembutsu, the practitioner is eventually led without contrivance or calculation to understanding. It appears that Shinran experienced a deepening of this kind of awareness when he was in his forties. He recorded the three stages of conversion in 1224, when he was fifty-one.

It would be a mistake to consider the stages only in terms of the development of Shinran's philosophy on a personal level. They also served notice that the anti-establishment exclusive-practice nembutsu movement would prevail over the established schools and sects. The first stage was when established religion flourished, centered on the pre-Kamakura sects; the second signaled the beginning of the exclusive-practice movement, in its period of agitation; and the third indicated the ultimate point of unshakable realization of "other power," the true heart and mind given by Amida, the diamond-like mind that is indestructible. Even those who persecuted and suppressed the nembutsu movement could have a change of heart, turn to the teachings, and be purified.

Starting at this time, several laws forbidding the exclusive-practice nembutsu movement were issued in succession. In 1221 the shogunate and court in tandem strengthened their control over the farming population and increased their efforts to exploit it. The lower echelons of the system—townspeople, lower-class warriors, and merchants—were filled with discontent, and it was from such people that the nembutsu movement gained much of its support. It was against these, therefore, that the onslaught of the authorities fell.

This was the situation when Shinran returned from the eastern provinces to his Kyoto birthplace around 1235, when he was sixty-two. Even after his return, though, Shinran maintained strong links with his followers in the east.

The severest persecution of the followers in the eastern provinces occurred between 1249 and 1256, between Shinran's seventy-sixth and eighty-third years. In the context of the *ritsuryō* system, the movement there represented a threat to the nation, being contemptuous of the native deities and the buddhas and deliberately misleading the country people. Official severity was exacerbated by the fact that Shinran had himself been exiled as a young man.

It was at this time that Shinran wrote to a central figure in the congregations of the eastern provinces, "The present judgment is not your responsibility alone. It belongs to all Pure Land nembutsu followers. I was spoken of by others in similar fashion when in my youth I was with the late venerable Hōnen. You do not have to cope with this alone, for it is something that all those who recite the nembutsu should face with solidarity."

Here Shinran was firm in his opinion, as he had been at the time of the conviction of Jūren and Junsai and the exile of Hōnen and other members of his band, that the persecution was not the fault of any one individual but a question of a conflict of belief between the exclusive-practice nembutsu movement and the authorities. He was to maintain this belief throughout his life.

Tragic Later Years

A painful incident marred the later years of this iron-willed man. From 1249 to 1256, Shinran's son Zenran remained in the eastern region to confront the situation there during the persecution. As time went by, he began informing Shinran in Kyoto that some leaders there were following a false faith. At first Shinran was inclined to believe his son's reports, but as the situation became clearer, it grew apparent beyond all doubt that it was Zenran himself who was subverting the faith and causing dissension among Shinran's followers.

Zenran, in pursuing a policy of dissemination by establishing ties with the powerful and their followers, had discarded the central tenet of Shinran's faith, Amida's eighteenth vow, comparing it to a "wilted flower." He justified his stance by asserting that what he taught had been secretly transmitted to him by Shinran.

Three factors seem to be behind Zenran's attempt to establish his own movement. First, he sought the patronage of the powerful in order to legitimize his own position and to withstand the pressure exerted by the Kamakura shogunate. Second, he abandoned the unadulterated faith of Shinran and attempted to reach a compromise with the established religious order. Third, he tried to seize control of Shinran's congregations, already in the process of economic union, by abusing his father's trust in him. These were the "skillful means" devised by the young Zenran. Conscientious followers in the east refused to accept his offers, however, faced as they were with the danger of a schism in their ranks.

Acquainted with the facts, Shinran wrote to Zenran in 1256: "The baseness of what you have done is beyond all bounds. I have resolved that no more may you call me father, nor I think of you as son. I have declared this before the Three Treasures and the deities. What a pitiful thing this is!" Here is the lament of an aging father who has had to cast away a beloved son, in the face of the power and seduction of a new social order. This was the bitterest price that Shinran ever had to pay in defending the course of action that he believed in.

At the age of eighty-two, in 1255, in the midst of the persecution, Shinran wrote *Verses in Praise of Prince Shōtoku,* in which he quoted from the prince's Seventeen-Article Constitution (composed in 604): "The claims of the rich are like a stone flung into water, but the disputes of the poor are like water cast onto a stone." He wrote of the bitterness of the charges against his nembutsu movement and the helplessness of the Japanese people in general.

After the Zenran affair, Shinran wrote, "It has been a good thing that, as a result, people's lapses of faith have been revealed." Here we catch a glimpse of the optimism and boundless affirmation on which Shinran could draw in the midst of tragedy.

His turbulent life drew to a close in Kyoto, near the end of 1262, when he was eighty-nine. Kakunyo, in his *Essay to Correct False Faith,* states that Shinran wrote a will stating that he wanted his body flung into the Kamo River as food for the fish. This reveals the impulse of a natural poet, along with his refusal even in death to entrust himself to the establishment, funerals and cemeteries being still administered by the established sects at that time. Today his remains are entombed in an imposing cemetery at Ōtani, in the Higashiyama district of Kyoto.

Dōgen
(1200–1253)

by Aishin Imaeda

Prodded by a Temple Cook

During the Kamakura period, many founders of sects were concerned with the exigencies of what they believed was the age of degeneration (the period of the Decay of the Dharma) and therefore employed simple methods, such as nembutsu or chanting the title of the *Lotus Sutra,* as a means of release. Dōgen, however, was satisfied with neither the old nor the new Japanese Buddhism. He discovered a new path in the Zen of Shakyamuni's true dharma.

A famous anecdote related by Dōgen in his *Instructions for the Zen Cook* tells how, soon after Dōgen arrived in a Chinese harbor in 1223, an old priest came to the ship to buy Japanese mushrooms. He told Dōgen that he was the cook at the temple on Mount A-yu-wang. Deeply interested in Ch'an temples, Dōgen rained questions on the elderly priest. As their conversation continued and nightfall approached, Dōgen invited him to spend the night aboard the ship. The priest declined, however, saying that if he were not at the temple there would be difficulties about the meals the following day. Dōgen responded, "Surely there is at least one person there who can cook! Why don't you, a senior priest, advanced in years, give up your position as cook and give all your

97

attention to the practice of zazen?'' The old priest gave a great laugh. ''You still do not understand what the words mean, what real training is. Come to Mount A-yu-wang someday and train there.'' Dōgen was not yet able to understand that devoting oneself to cooking was Buddhist training just as much as devoting oneself to zazen.

The lightning impact of the priest's words spurred Dōgen, making him feel, however vaguely, that a new world had opened up before him. His aspiration for enlightenment was renewed.

Tendai Cleric

Dōgen was born in a mountain villa on the outskirts of Kyoto early in 1200, the year after the sudden death of Minamoto no Yoritomo, the first Minamoto shogun. He is said to have been the son of the inner minister, Koga Michichika, and a daughter of a Fujiwara regent. Both parents were of the high nobility, and Dōgen's success in life was ensured. By the age of four he had read a book by a famous Chinese poet, and at six he studied Chinese classics: the *Classic of Poetry* (one of the Five Classics) and *Tso's Commentary on the Spring and Autumn Annals*. His father died when he was two, however, and his mother, when he was seven. The double loss must have deepened his sense of life's impermanence.

The young Dōgen seems to have determined early to become a priest. By the age of eight he was already reading Vasubandhu's *Abhidharma Storehouse Treatise*. Around the time of his coming-of-age ceremony he was formally adopted by a maternal uncle, who had perceived his ability and wanted to train Dōgen as a successor in the government. Dōgen, having ever since his mother's death set his heart on becoming a priest, broke the relationship with his uncle in 1212, when he was twelve. Late one night in spring, he secretly left home and went to the foot of Mount Hiei where another maternal uncle, the priest Ryōken, was living. Dōgen spoke of his determination and asked for help in the necessary procedures. Ryōken, knowing of his brother's hopes for the boy, did all he could to dissuade Dōgen from the plan, but to no avail. Dōgen's sincerity convinced him. Ryōken sent his nephew to

Shuryōgon-in training center on Mount Hiei. The following year he was ordained at Enryaku-ji by the Tendai sect's head, Kōen, and given the name Buppōbō Dōgen. (He later changed his name to Kigen Dōgen.) Thus it was that Dōgen took his first steps in Buddhist training as a Tendai cleric.

Under Kōen, Dōgen absorbed himself in the study of the fundamentals of Tendai doctrine. At that time, however, Mount Hiei was no longer worthy of being called Japan's foremost Buddhist training center. It was a hotbed of corruption where clerics lusted after fame and profit, a fortified center that sent out cleric-soldiers to do battle with Kōfuku-ji, Mii-dera, and other temples. It was hardly a suitable environment for religious training. As Dōgen's learning increased, he was assailed by intense doubt. Tendai taught that living beings originally possess the potential for buddhahood, so why did the buddhas of the three worlds of the past, present, and future teach the need for religious training? Confronted by this fundamental question, Dōgen found his way blocked.

Realizing that he would not find an answer as long as he remained on Mount Hiei, he went to visit Kōin, the head of Mii-dera. Unable to resolve Dōgen's doubt, Kōin recommended that he go to China and study the new type of Ch'an that was dominant there.

Priests such as Eisai had already brought Japan news of Southern Sung Ch'an. In 1217, therefore, Dōgen went to Kennin-ji, the temple Eisai had founded, and studied the Huang-lung lineage Rinzai under Eisai's successor, Myōzen. It is commonly thought that Dōgen met Eisai, but this seems hardly possible considering Eisai died in 1215. The critical attitude toward Tendai doctrine that Dōgen acquired from Kōin and Myōzen was extremely influential in setting the later direction of his thought. It was in the company of Myōzen that Dōgen finally set foot in China in 1223.

Meeting Ju-ching

The decisive encounter with the old temple cook led Dōgen to visit the five major Lin-chi (Rinzai) Ch'an temples, and he studied

Ch'an under the greatest masters of the Ta-hui lineage, then dominant in Southern Sung Buddhism, including Wu-chi Liao-p'ai of
Mount T'ien-t'ung and Che-weng Ju-wen of Wan-shou temple on
Mount Ching. He became greatly disillusioned with the Ch'an he
found there, contaminated as it was by worldly concerns stemming
from the close connections between the Ta-hui lineage and the
governing classes.

Still with a genuine urge to seek enlightenment, Dōgen finally
met Ju-ching, the new head of T'ien-t'ung temple, a priest of
Ts'ao-tung (Sōtō) Ch'an. Under the strict guidance of this priest,
known and revered for his unrelenting Ch'an, Dōgen studied for
three years, eventually coming to understand the true dharma
transmitted directly by the Buddha and the patriarchs. He returned to Japan in 1227, after five years abroad, having received
from Ju-ching documents setting out the lineage of the dharma
transmission as the seal of approval of his apprentice's accomplishments.

Upon his return, Dōgen immediately went back to Kennin-ji
and began disseminating Zen, the dharma of Shakyamuni's transmission as he had come to understand it. Zazen alone was the true
gate of Buddhism. He reiterated his conviction that absorption
in only zazen was the supreme Buddhist path. From the time of
Shakyamuni, the patriarchs had all achieved supreme enlightenment through zazen, and although other practices led to enlightenment, Dōgen believed that they deviated from true, correct
Buddha-Dharma. Furthermore, he said that zazen was by no
means a difficult or ascetic practice; rather, because it was the
"dharma gate of the easy and pleasant practice," it could be
recommended for all people everywhere. Late in 1227, Dōgen
therefore set out the meaning and practice of zazen in his *General
Advice on the Principles of Zazen*. His famous *Eye Treasury of the Right
Dharma* is a collection of later lectures in which he energetically
expressed his most heartfelt beliefs.

Just Sitting

Dōgen's practice of "just sitting" quietly in zazen, not depending

Wooden statue of Gyōgi in meditation, owned by Tōshōdai-ji in Nara Prefecture. 13th century. Important Cultural Property.

Gyōgi oversees the building of a ferry depot. Detail from Gyōgi bosatsu gyōjō eden, *painted by Kose no Kanaoka, 14th century. Important Cultural Property. Owned by Ebara-ji, Osaka. Photo courtesy of Ebara-ji.*

Right: Hollow dry-lacquer statue of Ganjin in meditation, owned by Tōshōdai-ji, Nara Prefecture. 8th century. National Treasure.

Below: Scene from Tōsei-den emaki, *depicting Ganjin's journey to Japan. Owned by Tōshōdai-ji, Nara Prefecture. Painted by Rengyō in 1298. Important Cultural Property.*

Portrait of Saichō, owned by Ichijō-ji, Hyōgo Prefecture. Late Heian period. National Treasure.

Below: Main hall of Enryaku-ji, on Mount Hiei, near Kyoto, once the site of a small temple built by the young Saichō in 788.

Kyoto National Museum

*Portrait of Kūkai, owned by Tō-ji, Kyoto. Donated to Tō-ji by the retired emperor
Go-Uda in 1313. Important Cultural Property.*

*Mannōike, the irrigation reservoir at Mannō, Kagawa Prefecture, the rapid repair of which was ac-
complished under Kūkai's supervision.*

Wooden statue of Kūya owned by Rokuharamitsu-ji, Kyoto, by the 13th-century sculptor Kōshō. The tiny figures coming from its mouth represent Kūya's repeated invocations of the name of Amida Buddha. Important Cultural Property.

Opposite, above: Portrait of Hō-nen, owned by Chion-in, Kyoto. Kamakura period. Important Cultural Property.

Opposite, below: On his way to exile, Hōnen teaches a harlot at Muro-no-tomari that salvation is in invoking Amida Buddha. Detail from Hōnen shōnin eden, *owned by Chion-in. Kamakura period. National Treasure.*

Portrait of Shinran, owned by the Nara National Museum. Kamakura period. Important Cultural Property.

After inscribing it, Hōnen returns to Shinran the copy Shinran made of Hōnen's Collection of Passages on the Original Vow and the Nembutsu. *Detail from* Zenshin shōnin den'e. *Owned by Senjū-ji, Mie Prefecture. Painted in 1295.*

Portrait of Dōgen, at Hōkyō-ji, Fukui Prefecture. Courtesy of Hōkyō-ji.

Wooden statue of Eisai, owned by Ju-fuku-ji, Kamakura. Late Kamakura period. Courtesy of Jufuku-ji.

Eihei-ji, in Fukui Prefecture, founded by Dōgen in 1244, and one of two head temples of the Sōtō sect.

Opposite, below: Nichiren expecting to be beheaded at Tatsu-no-kuchi. Detail from Nichiren shōnin chu ga san, painted by Kubota Tōtai in 1536. Owned by Honkoku-ji, Kyoto.

Portrait of Nichiren painted by Fujiwara Chikayasu in 1282, owned by Kuon-ji, Yamanashi Prefecture. Courtesy of Kuon-ji.

Portrait of Rennyo, owned by Nishi Hongan-ji, Kyoto. Muromachi period.

Left: Copy of the wooden image of Ippen at Muryōkō-ji, Kanagawa Prefecture. The original was carved in 1475. Courtesy of Muryōkō-ji.

National Museum of Japanese History

Portait of Ikkyū, painted by Bokusai, owned by the Tokyo National Museum. Late 15th century. Important Cultural Property.

Below: Portrait of Takuan, owned by Shōun-ji, Osaka. Painted in 1639. Courtesy of Shōun-ji.

Below: Ippen and his band perform the dancing nembutsu at Ichinoya, Kyoto. Detail from Ippen shōnin eden, painted in 1299 by En'i. Owned by the Tokyo National Museum. National Treasure.

Above: Self-portrait of Ryōkan, owned by Chūōkōron Bijutsu Shuppan.

Portrait of Shimaji Mokurai in his mid-50s, when he was chief priest of Gangyō-ji, Morioka. Owned by and courtesy of Gangyō-ji.

Above: Gesshō's last work, an unfinished mandala, in gold paint on deep blue paper. Owned by Jōju-in, Kyoto.

Statue of Gesshō, owned by Jōju-in, Kyoto.

Above: Middle, Shaku Sōen; standing, left, Suzuki Daisetz; and other Japanese in San Francisco, 1905. Courtesy of Tōkei-ji, Kamakura.

Below: Shaku Sōen and other clerics with Mr. and Mrs. Alexander Russell at the Karamon gate of Engaku-ji, Kamakura. Courtesy of Tōkei-ji.

Portrait of Kiyozawa Manshi five months before his death, in 1903 at the age of 41. Owned by Ōtani University, Kyoto. Courtesy of the library of Ōtani University.

Fourth from right, middle row, Kiyozawa Manshi; with followers who lived together in a house in Tokyo called the Lively Wide Cavern. Courtesy of Myōtatsu-ji, Ishikawa Prefecture.

Above: Suzuki Daisetz in 1965.

Below: Suzuki Daisetz studying at the Shōden-an of Engaku-ji, Kamakura, in 1949.

on the use of koans as subjects for meditation, might be thought of as just another version of "silent illumination" Zen, and indeed he spoke repeatedly of Ju-ching's teachings that enlightenment would be attained not by offering incense or bowing or reciting the sutras, but by zazen alone.

Throughout the *Eye Treasury of the Right Dharma*, though, Dōgen interprets koan stories, and nowhere in it does he explicitly deny their use. His "just sitting" is therefore not a rejection of koan records but rather an affirmation of his own understanding of the Buddha-Dharma and a strong criticism of the codified type of koan Zen practice that had become stultifying. He even dismissed as "laughable" the formulas employed in training Zen students, such as the "three mysteries and the three essentials" and the "four kinds of attitude to subject and object" of Lin-chi I-hsüan, founder of Lin-chi Ch'an, and the five ranks of Tung-shan, founder of Ts'ao-tung Ch'an.

Dōgen also criticized the *Regulations for Ch'an Temples*, by Chang-lu Tsung-tse, as leaving much to be desired, and recommended a return to the *Regulations of Pai-chang*, the oldest of the books of regulations, dating from the T'ang dynasty, which had become highly revered. In this we can discern Dōgen's yearning for the Zen communities of the classical period and his pure idealism. Dōgen, the "Old Buddha," was devoted to the truth.

He wrote a number of manuals concerning religious practice in daily life, beginning with *Instructions for the Zen Cook*, to put his own ideas into practice. Six of these, later collected as the *Regulations for Life at Eihei-ji*, clearly tell of Dōgen's meticulous attention to methods of religious practice. He vigorously rejected the sectarianism of the Zen lineages that called themselves the Five Sects and the Seven Schools or that called the true dharma transmitted from the Buddha such things as the Zen sect, the Bodhidharma school, or the School of the Buddha Mind. Here is a graphic reminder of Dōgen's purity of purpose.

In his transmission of the true teachings of Shakyamuni, Dōgen harshly criticized other sects. Along with his denunciations of Zen practice linked with nembutsu or esoteric rituals, he asserted that the theory of "the unity of the three religions" (Confucianism,

Taoism, Buddhism) was the greatest heresy of all. In contrast to Eisai, who had provided special chapels for Shingon esoteric practices and Tendai meditation practices at Kennin-ji, Dōgen displayed a stern conviction and an uncompromising stance. It is hardly surprising that he was equally contemptuous of current beliefs about the period of the Decay of the Dharma; no one else seems to have rejected that belief as flatly as Dōgen.

Though Dōgen thus rejected sectarianism, he greatly valued the *Lotus Sutra,* the principal scripture of the Tendai sect. Calling it the "monarch of sutras," he taught that of all the sutras it most faithfully conveyed the "true dharma transmitted directly by the Buddha and the patriarchs." Here we have a skillful blending of Dōgen's own thought on the true dharma and the *Lotus Sutra.* We should perhaps consider this as his inheritance of the Tendai teaching that the *Lotus Sutra* alone is the truth and all others are merely "skillful means."

It was inevitable that Dōgen should eventually draw enmity on himself. Around 1230 the priests of Mount Hiei decided to destroy Dōgen's residence at Kennin-ji and expel him from Kyoto. Perhaps to avoid conflict, he moved out of Kennin-ji to an abandoned temple called Gokuraku-ji, on the outskirts of the capital. Here he built Kōshō Hōrin-ji as his residence and maintained his teaching efforts, never relenting in his single-minded criticism of Tendai and the other sects. During this time, former apprentices of Dainichibō Nōnin joined him following their master's death, adding impetus to the already vigorous band. Why they came is not clear, but they, like Dōgen, prized the "pure Ch'an" of Southern Sung China over the "mixed Zen" of Eisai and others; had suffered persecution by priests from Mount Hiei; and had been forced to leave Kyoto. Further, Dōgen had studied in China with the same priests of the Ta-hui lineage studied by Nōnin and may have shared a closeness as a result.

It is important to note, however, that though Dōgen's basic thinking did not change dramatically before or after his period at Kōshō Hōrin-ji, he began harshly criticizing Ta-hui and his lineage. He may have learned from his new apprentices about shortcomings in the Ta-hui teachings and seen the need to reeducate those apprentices. It cannot be an accident that Ta-hui's main work and Dōgen's *Eye Treasury of the Right Dharma* have the same title. That title expresses Dōgen's confidence that his Buddha-Dharma was identical with the true dharma of Shakyamuni.

Founding Eihei-ji

Dōgen's increasing popularity only served further to irritate Mount Hiei's clerics, and pressure on him continued to grow. Refusing to submit, he published *Significance of the Right Dharma for the Protection of the Nation,* in which he emphasized that Zen itself is the true Buddhism capable of defending the nation. This work further angered priests on Mount Hiei, and a complaint was made to the court that its conclusions were only Dōgen's personal (and mistaken) interpretations. Those at court who shared this view added to the growing vehemence of anti-Dōgen pressure.

A further reason for Dōgen's departure from Kyoto may have been the unexpected advent of a powerful rival in the neighborhood. A little while before, in 1241, Enni Bennen had returned from study in China, bearing a seal of dharma transmission from Wu-chun, a leading figure in the influential Hu-ch'iu lineage, which had now surpassed the Ta-hui in importance. In early 1243, with the patronage of the head of the Kujō family and on land donated by him, Enni founded Tōfuku-ji, a temple in the mixed Tendai-Shingon-Zen tradition, on a scale not yet seen in Japan. Thus ironically there were, in the same outlying district of Kyoto, two Zen establishments diametrically opposed to each other in outlook. Tōfuku-ji, furthermore, had cordial relations with Mount Hiei, and having erupted so suddenly on the scene with massive financial support from a branch of the Fujiwaras, it must have posed a considerable threat to Dōgen and his followers.

It was clear that if Dōgen stayed where he was he would face a two-pronged attack, from Mount Hiei on one side and Tōfuku-ji on the other. In the autumn of 1243, therefore, he left his Kyoto training center in the care of an apprentice and went to a secluded valley in Echizen Province, the property of one of Dōgen's lay followers. Why Dōgen chose such an out-of-the-way place has been a matter of conjecture for centuries. Perhaps Kōshō Hōrin-ji had not been conducive to Zen training, being too near the city, or perhaps he had been influenced by Ju-ching's instructions to dwell deep in the mountains, in secluded valleys, teaching only a few especially able apprentices, and to avoid close relations with kings and ministers. Yet he had made no effort to follow these principles on his return to Japan, when he settled first in Kennin-ji and then in Kōshō Hōrin-ji. The most convincing theory seems to be that he moved to Echizen because his lay follower in Kyoto had land there and invited him to use some of it.

Still, it cannot have been easy for the purist Dōgen to move, simply because he had been invited to do so, to a district that was a Tendai stronghold with powerful temples. There must have been a compelling reason. Perhaps it was because a number of Nōnin's apprentices who had joined Dōgen were from Echizen, in particular from one Tendai temple, Hajaku-ji. It is very likely that they were the ones who promoted the shift. This temple was close to the offered site, and the abandoned Yoshimine-dera, which Dōgen first used, may have been a branch of the Tendai lineage to which Hajaku-ji belonged. It seems very likely, therefore, that Dōgen's invitation to a Tendai-dominated area reflected an intra-sectarian rivalry of the kind existing between Mount Hiei and Mii-dera. That would explain why people connected with Hajaku-ji flocked to Nōnin and later to Dōgen. It is easy to conjecture that Dōgen, forced away by Mount Hiei, would conversely be made welcome if such were the conditions within the competing Tendai lineage.

After about a year at Yoshimine-dera, Dōgen moved to the newly established Eihei-ji in the autumn of 1244. Here he embarked upon a routine of strict training according to his ideas about the true dharma, in a community of like-minded followers. His thought likewise became clearer and more far-reaching.

Rejection of Lay Buddhism

Long before, Dōgen had awakened, through the words of the temple cook of Mount A-yu-wang, to the realization that every facet of life, including the special work each person has been assigned, and not zazen alone, is part of Zen training. In consequence, there remains the question of why zazen is considered so important in the Zen sects.

Dōgen himself wrote that of all the actions of daily life, zazen in particular is the gateway to true enlightenment, and that all the patriarchs had attained enlightenment through it. If, though, all actions can be considered religious training, lay practice as well as clerical training must be admitted. On this point, Dōgen's views changed considerably over the years.

When we look at the *General Advice on the Principles of Zazen,* which Dōgen wrote soon after his return from China, it is clear from his use of the term "general advice" that he intended Zen to apply equally to laity and clergy. The ability to attain enlightenment, moreover, was a matter of individual determination, so secular life and work were not automatically a deterrent to Buddhist training, and whether a person was a cleric was not ultimately the question. Dōgen here shows a broad tolerance, admitting that the laity, both men and women, could achieve buddhahood.

Toward the end of his time in Kyoto and at the beginning of the Echizen period, Dōgen engaged in an increasingly acrimonious criticism of the Ta-hui lineage of Rinzai and was involved in the writing of the *Significance of the Right Dharma for the Protection of the Nation,* in both cases asserting the purity of the true dharma transmitted directly by the Buddha and the patriarchs. He emphasized the superiority of a secluded, ordained life, saying that Zen training necessitated rejection of the hindrances of secular life and the embracing of a secluded life in the mountains. Likewise he made an about-face from his previous stance that the capable and the untalented, rich and poor, men and women, could alike aspire to Buddhist training, now denying that lay persons of either sex could achieve buddhahood. Naturally he did not concern himself with the question of worldly benefits. Here we may discern Dōgen's esteem for the purity of religion and his hatred of easy compromise.

In 1247 the fifth Kamakura regent, Hōjō Tokiyori, invited

Dōgen to Kamakura. There Dōgen spent some seven months but returned to Eihei-ji, having declined the regent's offer to build a temple for him. He also refused the regent's proposed donation of land in Echizen. There is a famous anecdote concerning his apprentice Gemmyō, who later brought back to Eihei-ji a document setting forth the land donation. He was reprimanded severely and expelled from the temple, and not only was his place in the priests' quarters removed, but the ground beneath his seat was also dug out to a depth of more than two meters. It is an example of Dōgen's characteristic fastidiousness. The story of Dōgen's grateful acceptance of the retired emperor Go-Saga's offer of a purple robe is no more than a later legend.

Some ten years after he moved to Echizen, Dōgen realized that the end of his life was approaching and gave a last message to his followers in the manner of Shakyamuni, which later became a chapter of the *Eye Treasury of the Right Dharma*, "The Eight Aspects of Enlightenment." Here he wrote, "Expounding these points to all living beings, we are no different from the Buddha Shakyamuni." Appointing Koun Ejō to be his successor at Eihei-ji, Dōgen left Echizen for Kyoto in August 1253, wearing no more than the simple black robe of an ordinary cleric. He died in the capital on September 23, 1253.

Nichiren
(1222-1282)

by Manabu Fujii

In 1222, when Nichiren was born, Japan was still feeling the repercussions of the momentous events of the previous year, known to history as the Jōkyū Disturbance, when the retired emperor Go-Toba attempted to overthrow the Kamakura shogunate. His decree to chastise the Kamakura regent came to nothing, and he found himself exiled. People's attention had turned to the attempts of the shogunate, now consolidated on the Kamakura regent, to end the strife.

Nichiren was born in a little fishing village called Kominato, far from the capital, in Awa Province. In later years he spoke of himself as "a son of an outcast who lived near the sea," as "the son of a poor fisherman," and as "a child of a humble commoner."

The term "outcast" that he used was a contemptuous epithet commonly applied at that time to fishermen and hunters, those who made their living by taking life. By this it can be seen that Nichiren was not favored by birth. He thus differed from the other founders of sects during the Kamakura period in that his origins were far lower. Hōnen, for example, was the son of a member of the provincial gentry who was the constable. Similarly, Shinran belonged to a noble family, Eisai to descendants of the founders of a province, Dōgen to a noble family, and Ippen to a high-ranking warrior family. These were no children of obscure commoners, but rather sons of the Kyoto nobility or provincial gentry. Furthermore, they came from the capital or its immediate region, not from the culturally and economically backward eastern provinces. Of all the sect founders, Nichiren alone was born in the remote east, of unimportant fisherfolk. His humble origins were to become his starting point as a religious figure and a chance element in how he formulated his ideas.

To anticipate my conclusion, I would assert that Nichiren skillfully turned around those adverse conditions. He continued all his life to love the poor people living in his remote home district, unblessed though they were by the benefits of the advanced culture of the capital. At the same time, it is a distinct likelihood that the intensity of his abrupt and impulsive character was formed by the geography of the Bōsō Peninsula, washed by the turbulent Pacific and seared by intense sunlight.

When, as a result of his study tour of the great temples of the Kyoto region, Nichiren became convinced that he should found a new sect, he chose as his sacred ground not one of those powerful temples, but a small country temple on Mount Kiyosumi in Awa Province. There is no doubt that he was supported in his early endeavors by local people rather than rich patrons. His teaching activities and powerful method of conversion were also centered on the eastern provinces, between Kamakura and the Bōsō Peninsula, and he never again took a step in the direction of the central provinces. Even in his later years, when he retired to Mount Minobu to live in a small hermitage far from human habitation, he revealed in letters to followers his fond memories of the fishing village where he grew up, those who worked there, and the smell of the seaweed on the windswept shore. In this way Nichiren remained the son of a fisherman of the eastern seaboard, born and raised among the common people.

Son of an Outcast

Nichiren tried neither to hide nor to apologize for his lowly birth. Rather he did not let it worry him. During his time, the governing classes supported the doctrines of the dominant Nara and Heian sects of Buddhism, in particular Tendai and Shingon, which taught self-reliance in religious practice. These sects constituted what became known as Court Buddhism, and their chief temples were all in the central provinces. They possessed great numbers of large manorial estates all over the country and were the source of the authority and ideas of the nobility. As proprietors of tax-exempt lands, they occupied a position of control over the common people as secular administrators, collecting the basic land tax from cultivators and administering the labor tax. In their dealings with commoners, their view of religious ethics also lent weight to traditional authority.

People were considered to be either good or evil. Good works consisted of building temples, having Buddha-images made, erecting pagodas, sponsoring ceremonies, and copying and chanting sutras. Those who did good works like these could hope to be reborn in the Pure Land. Obviously, they had to be rich, educated members of the nobility. By contrast, sins included the taking of life in battle and all unenlightened acts that went against the precepts. Warriors, merchants, farmers, and women in general, therefore, were termed evil and could not achieve Pure Land rebirth. In particular, outcasts such as hunters and fishermen, who made their living by the heinous evil of taking life, were thought to be virtually beyond all release. Such views imposed an intolerable spiritual burden on the people, depriving them of hope in both this world and the next.

Nichiren's parents, by his own description, must have made their living either directly or indirectly from fishing. Within the context of the small seashore community, they could have been anything from simple fisherfolk, scratching a livelihood from the take of a single rod, to entrepreneurs with a large number of fishermen and boatmen in their employ. To the manorial estate proprietor, though, such distinctions were meaningless: anyone who lived and worked by the sea was automatically considered an outcast. However eminent the family that Nichiren came from in comparison with the community, its sons would still have been called "sons of outcasts."

When Nichiren undertook his study tour of the temples of Nara and Kyoto, Mount Hiei, Mii-dera, and Mount Kōya, which were the very seedbed of Court Buddhism, how would he have been regarded by the other student clerics, sons of the nobility or local gentry? Speaking with a broad country accent, this "son of outcasts" could hardly have found himself in a situation where advancement was at all possible. Seeing the contemptuous eyes of those around him, he must have confronted for the first time, as a person of religion, the questions of the nature of evil and the ability of an outcast to gain rebirth.

It was not Nichiren alone who was concerned with settling this problem. Behind him stood the poor and ignorant people of the eastern seaboard, suffering from the same fate but unable even to raise the question in their minds. The answer could only lie in releasing the people from the bonds of the unjustifiable religious ethics of the governing classes and giving meaning to their lives. Herein lay the success of Nichiren and those who followed him in developing a true religion of the people.

Birth of a New Religion

When he was twelve, Nichiren entered Kiyosumi-dera, a temple near his home, to study Buddhism. At that time it belonged to the Tendai sect and had strong ties with the Mount Hiei nembutsu tradition. Nichiren's master, Dōzen, was a nembutsu practitioner. Nichiren was formally ordained at sixteen and given the name Zeshōbō Renchō. Later he said that he decided to become a priest to discover how to escape the round of birth and death and to seek that which had permanence. This was a common quest among Pure Land practitioners of the time. Nichiren, then, as a young student priest, aspired to Pure Land teachings.

In 1239 the young Nichiren decided to undertake a study tour of the central provinces. Studying first in Kamakura, he went in 1242 to Kyoto, where he stayed on Mount Hiei, from there visiting Mii-dera, Mount Kōya, and Shitennō-ji. He may have been distressed and alienated by what he saw there of Court Buddhism with all its authority of magnificence and tradition. Nevertheless, Nichiren continued to delve into the sacred texts, seeking enlightenment. At some point, Nichiren discovered discrepancies in the Pure Land doctrine as transmitted in the sutras. Groping, he was able to allay his doubts when he read in the *Nirvana Sutra,* "Follow the dharma, not man; follow those sutras that reveal the whole meaning of the dharma, not those that reveal only a part." This he interpreted as meaning that all truth could be found in the Buddha's teachings, and that people should not depend on scriptures that did not transmit the teachings of the Buddha. This conviction led to his belief in the *Lotus Sutra* as the one ultimate teaching of the Buddha, the reason for his birth in this world. At this point Nichiren abandoned Pure Land practice and became a devotee of the *Lotus Sutra.* His ten years of study in the Kyoto region had clarified his future course. At that point he saw it as his true mission to work within Tendai to return the sect to its original stance of advocating the supremacy of the *Lotus Sutra,* as Saichō had taught, a stance that had been undermined by the incursion of Pure Land and esoteric teachings.

Nichiren returned to Kiyosumi-dera in May 1253. Standing in his master Dōzen's temple, he attacked Pure Land teachings and expounded the *Lotus Sutra* as the one and only truth leading to attainment of enlightenment and fortunate rebirth. He also changed his name to Nichiren at this time. This is regarded as Nichiren's initial statement of his teachings, when he established his sect. Dōzen and the priests at Kiyosumi-dera were taken aback by Nichiren's outlook, and Nichiren soon felt the animosity of the local steward, a nembutsu follower. Pressure from the steward forced Nichiren to leave his old temple.

Persecution

Nichiren then spent many years in a small hermitage on the

southern outskirts of Kamakura. There, according to traditional accounts of the time, he continued to disseminate his teachings, publicly attacking both Pure Land teachings and Zen on street corners. Between 1257 and 1260 a series of unprecedented calamities struck the eastern provinces in the form of earthquakes, drought, typhoons, famine, and epidemics. The peasants trembled with fear. To Nichiren these disasters were not merely unfortunate natural occurrences or the happenings of fate, but a warning. There was, therefore, a way to stop them. The cause of the catastrophes and the means to prevent them were linked to the governing authorities. Nichiren confronted the shogunate squarely and found the cause of the disasters in the scriptures. They were caused principally, he said, by the growing popularity of evil sects, such as Hōnen's Jōdo and the Ritsu sect, causing the deities protecting Japan to return to heaven, leaving the country to its fate. To save the country, all people, from the governing classes down, should return to the true dharma and pay homage to the One Vehicle of the *Lotus Sutra*. Unless this happened, the calamities would continue unabated, and the nation eventually would collapse because of insurrection and foreign invasion. Nichiren set out these convictions in his *Treatise on the Establishment of the True Dharma and the Peace of the Nation*, which he presented in 1260 to the former regent and real power-holder, Hōjō Tokiyori, under the name of "Nichiren, a Tendai priest."

Regardless of whether the calamities could have been prevented by a return to exclusive faith in the *Lotus Sutra*, the important point is that Shinran, in Kyoto at the same time, could console the peasants of the east, whose lives were threatened, only in terms of the doctrine of the impermanence of birth and death. Nichiren, in contrast, advocated not sitting and waiting for death but rather acting bravely to save the situation. In doing so, he naturally came up against the power of the government, for saving of the masses had to be a thing of this world, not of the next. In this sense, the *Treatise on the Establishment of the True Dharma and the Peace of the Nation* was a seminal work in Nichiren's life.

At first Hōjō Tokiyori ignored Nichiren's treatise. Nembutsu followers in Kamakura, however, could not overlook it. In 1261 they attacked Nichiren's hermitage and then brought a petition before the shogunate, resulting in Nichiren's being exiled to Izu. In 1263 he received a pardon and returned to Kamakura. He went to the Bōsō Peninsula for a visit home in 1264. There he found the steward's antipathy toward him as strong as ever; he and his party were ambushed by the steward near the estate. Nichiren himself escaped serious injury and returned to Kamakura.

There the oppression continued, but its effect was only to inspire Nichiren with increased confidence in his mission. He had read in the scriptures that those who taught the *Lotus Sutra* in the period of the Decay of the Dharma would be persecuted, and he felt that this prophecy corresponded with his own experience. He felt confident, therefore, that he was a true practitioner of the *Lotus Sutra* in the time of the Decay of the Dharma.

It was during this period that Nichiren's teaching became increasingly intemperate and his rejection of other sects, more and more violent. He preached the complete abandonment of the self and absolute homage to the *Lotus Sutra;* the priority of faith; the merit of the five syllables in the title of the *Lotus Sutra,* in which the essence of the whole sutra was contained; and the necessity of chanting the title with devotion.

Gradually Nichiren attracted followers and apprentices in Kamakura. The small band of ordained and lay followers who gathered around him included the future six senior dharma successors, Nisshō, Nichirō, Nikkō, Nikō, Nitchō, and Nichiji. Their exclusive devotion to Shakyamuni, their reliance on the *Lotus Sutra* alone, and their rejection of other sects caused great unease among the established schools.

In 1268 an envoy arrived in Kamakura bearing a letter from Kublai Khan, the Mongol leader, demanding tribute. Nichiren and his followers took this to prove the accuracy of the *Treatise*'s prediction of foreign invasion, so they stepped up their attacks against other sects. Fearing a Mongol attack and anxious about a suitable policy, the shogunate could not ignore such behavior in its own capital. In the autumn of 1271, Nichiren was arrested near

Kamakura and secretly sentenced to death, but he was reprieved and only sent into exile on Sado Island. The persecution, however, extended to his apprentices and supporters, then numbering some 260. Some were imprisoned or deprived of their holdings, and others gave up their faith. It was annihilation for the small group.

Exile

Nichiren spent three years in exile on Sado Island, first living in a small abandoned temple and later residing in another area. Though gradually apprentices such as Nitchō and Nikkō came to join him, the cold and hunger he suffered in the severe climate were indescribable. He shared a scant bowl of rice with his apprentices, and they huddled together at night to keep away the cold. While on the island, however, Nichiren was able to win a few followers. These simple, honest islanders secretly provided Nichiren with food and clothing without the shogunal steward's knowledge, enabling Nichiren and his small band to survive. Despite the extremes of suffering, Nichiren strove to deepen his teachings during this time of exile, and his chief works, *Eye Opening* and *The True Object of Devotion*, were written there.

In these writings, Nichiren stressed that in the period of the Decay of the Dharma, the *Lotus Sutra* was the one true teaching and that at such a time those who held to the sutra were bound to be persecuted. He spoke of his conviction that he himself was a great exponent of the *Lotus Sutra*, who moreover had the virtues of the master, the teacher, and the parent, and that he embodied Eminent Conduct Bodhisattva, the protector of the *Lotus Sutra*. This he expressed in the famous vows "I will be the pillar of Japan; I will be the eyes of Japan; I will be the ship of Japan."

The period on Sado Island, the nadir of misfortune and disappointment for Nichiren, was the turning point in his spiritual life, for it was then that a dramatic change appeared in his thought. He flung off his Tendai allegiance and stood alone, independent of any of the established sects, as his signature on *The True Object of Devotion*, "Nichiren, a priest of Japan," clearly indicates.

Amid public fears of an imminent Mongol invasion, Nichiren was pardoned in 1274. He returned to Kamakura, where the mood was somber. The apparent accuracy of his prediction in the *Treatise* may have been a factor in the pardon. Upon his return, Nichiren met a man with enormous influence in the shogunate, who asked whether he could predict the exact date of the invasion and inquired what countermeasures the government should take. But as before, when Nichiren submitted the *Treatise on the Establishment of the True Dharma and the Peace of the Nation,* the government failed to act on his advice. The faint hope that Nichiren had had in the shogunate disappeared, and in the summer of 1274 he retired to the seclusion of Mount Minobu, in Kai Province. There he determined to lead a life of splendid isolation.

Nichiren was not allowed to dwell alone for long. The followers who had scattered at the time of his exile regrouped around their master, coming in person to Mount Minobu for his teaching or bringing messages from other followers. Throughout the land, dharma successors relayed his words. Soon Nichiren became actively involved in the reconstruction of his organization, almost destroyed in the persecution.

To the small hermitage on Mount Minobu came heartfelt gifts from clerical and lay followers, gifts that sustained those on the lonely mountain who at first lacked even the essentials of food and clothing. Some followers made their way to Minobu so they could listen to Nichiren in person; one such cleric even came from Sado Island. Gradually the small hermitage expanded into a center for both clerics and lay followers.

It was when he was at Minobu that Nichiren finally changed from a policy of bringing the government around to his way of thinking, then using its power to spread faith in the *Lotus Sutra,* to a policy of bringing individuals to an awareness of themselves as holders of the sutra, emphasizing firm faith in the chanting of the sutra's name. The letters that he wrote at this time in reply to questions from followers in different parts of the country demonstrate how he taught the common people the principles of release in the next world and the meaning of, and joy in, the present existence.

Path to Release

Nichiren absolutely rejected the significance of the precepts taught by other Buddhist sects in support of ruling class ethics. Doing good works was not a requisite for fortunate rebirth, nor were evil deeds decisive in obstructing it. Nichiren even called himself "a priest without precepts." Even evil people could be saved through the merits of the *Lotus Sutra* in the present as well as in the future. The only precepts in a period of the Decay of the Dharma were keeping faith in the *Lotus Sutra* alone and devoted chanting of its title. These two practices surpassed all observance of the precepts in established Buddhism. These two practices alone, he taught, answered the needs of all people. Even the most stupid and the most ignorant were capable of chanting the sutra's title, for it was an "easy practice" in contrast to the difficult requirements for the ordained.

Thus Nichiren was able to promise hope in this world and the next even for the laity, including even evildoers and women, who were traditionally considered as beyond hope. To those who followed him, this self-styled son of outcasts was indeed the reincarnation of Eminent Conduct Bodhisattva and, through the merit of the *Lotus Sutra,* was the great leader in the time of the Decay of the Dharma.

Those of Nichiren's followers who held exclusively to the *Lotus Sutra* and chanted its title, whether warriors, farmers, outcasts, or women, were united within his group that "neither deferred to the noble nor hated the lowly, holding neither the high in regard nor the low in contempt" (*Attainment of Buddhahood Through Initial Aspiration for the Lotus*). The world that Nichiren spoke of was limited, both ideologically and religiously, but within it all class differences were abolished so that all could participate equally in the spiritual life. Nichiren, burning with a sense of mission and the realization of being a reincarnation of Eminent Conduct Bodhisattva, a practitioner of the essential teachings of the *Lotus Sutra,* and the parent of all Japanese, was the intermediary between the common believer and Shakyamuni, the universal absolute.

Within his band, the common person was freed of all arbitrary discrimination from those in power. The band acquired, accordingly, a strong sense of solidarity based on the philosophy of equality, and this was heightened by faith in the *Lotus Sutra* and chanting of its title.

In a letter to his followers, Nichiren wrote: "By intoning *'Namu Myōhō Renge-kyō'* ['Taking refuge in the *Lotus Sutra'*] you are assured of buddhahood; what is most important is your depth of faith. The root of the Buddha-Dharma is faith" (quoted from *Letter to Nichinyo Gozen*). Again, writing to the lord of Ueno, he stated, "Mixing other practices with [the chanting of] this *'Namu Myōhō Renge-kyō'* has grave results." Nichiren demanded that all previous religious practices be abandoned, for taking a stand on faith had to be single-minded. Such was the one practice that he demanded of his followers.

Nichiren did not seek to impose a heavy economic load on his followers by having them build temples or erect Buddha-images. Neither did he ask those who could not do so to abandon activities that society considered evil, nor those of little learning to undertake activities like sutra copying and chanting, which presupposed some learning. All that he required was that his followers recognize Shakyamuni alone as the one true, eternal Buddha, that they put their faith in the One Vehicle of the *Lotus Sutra* as the Buddha's ultimate purpose of his appearance in this world, and that they chant the title, the essence of the sutra. Nichiren faced the fact that evil in the Buddhist sense was a necessary and unavoidable part of the lives of common people of his time, but taught that this evil could be removed through the merit of chanting the title. The doctrine he taught was above all realistic, clear-cut, concise, and easy to practice.

As time went by, Nichiren's small band slowly recovered and expanded. The rigors of persecution and of the life on Mount Minobu took their toll on him, however. While Nichiren was still in his fifties, the severe climate increasingly affected his health, and starting around 1278 he took to his sick bed a number of times. Nine years after coming to Mount Minobu, in 1282, having regained a little strength, he determined to return to the birthplace he had never forgotten. His condition worsened in the course of the journey. He died in Musashi Province, at the residence of Ikegami Munenaka, a lay follower, surrounded by dharma successors and believers from all over the eastern provinces, on October 30, 1282, when he was just sixty years old.

Ippen
(1239–1289)

by Manabu Fujii

Warrior's Son

Ippen, the founder of the Ji sect, was the last of the great religious innovators of the Kamakura period (1185–1336). Seventeen years younger than *Lotus Sutra* exponent Nichiren, Ippen was also active during the turbulent period when Japan was threatened with a Mongol invasion.

The decisive factor in Ippen's religious life was his constant determination not to settle anywhere, neither at a temple nor at a simple hermitage, but instead to spend his life wandering throughout the country, preaching the benefits of the nembutsu (invoking the name of Amida) and urging people to establish a karmic affiliation with Amida Buddha. His interpretation of the nembutsu went further than did either Hōnen's or Shinran's (see biographies in part 1). He taught the merits and meaning of that practice to the people he met on his travels in a simple, easy-to-comprehend manner. Because the Buddhist practice of wandering was both the means and the end to him, he was called the Itinerant Holy Man.

The Ji sect is comparatively small today. In all of Japan it has only some four hundred temples and 350,000 members. Should this numerical inferiority be attributed to weaknesses inherent in Ippen's method of dissemination?

Between the end of the Kamakura period and the civil turmoil of the Northern and Southern Courts period (1336–1392), congregations of Ji followers grew explosively in all regions of the country. Other Pure Land sects, such as Hōnen's Jōdo and Shinran's Jōdo Shin sects, could not match the Ji sect's vigor in this period. Modern scholarship considers that the bands of Pure Land followers called Ikkō groups, which began to emerge at this time, tended to be affiliated not with Jōdo Shin's Hongan-ji, as was common later, but either with Ippen's Ji sect or with Ikkō Shunjō, a contemporary of Ippen.

Ji sect popularity plummeted during the latter part of the fifteenth century, when the base of the sect's support was penetrated by the renascent Hongan-ji organization under Rennyo (see biography in part 1). The weakness of the Ji sect's doctrinal position made it vulnerable to the incursions of a newly energetic Jōdo Shin, so Ji followers rapidly changed their affiliation to Hongan-ji.

Ippen was born into a prominent warrior family in Iyo Province, Shikoku, in 1239. His grandfather had received control of the province in 1205 as a reward for his support of the Minamotos. Ippen, therefore, was of a family that had dominated the region and that included an admiral who had controlled the Inland Sea. By the time of his birth, though, the family's fortunes had failed, as a result of its support for the imperial forces during the retired emperor Go-Toba's failed coup against the Kamakura shogunate in 1221. Ippen's grandfather was exiled to Mutsu Province in the far north of Honshu. An uncle of Ippen was murdered. Another of Ippen's relatives was deprived of the control of Iyo, and the family suffered the distress of separation and dispersal. Ippen's father became a Buddhist priest with the name of Nyobutsu and immured himself in an old Tendai temple, Hōgon-ji, in his native place, as if afraid of the public gaze. In such an atmosphere Ippen was born, and his early years were spent under the cloud of the family's disgrace.

Gaining Enlightenment

When he was ten, Ippen lost his mother. Like Hōnen, Dōgen, and Shinran, feeling the bitterness of impermanence as a youth, he threw himself into the Buddhist life. It was no doubt out of his grief that he later took a solemn vow to free all beings. The year his mother died, 1249, Ippen entered the priesthood at his father's wish, receiving the name Zuien. Three years later he was sent to Dazaifu on Kyushu to study the Pure Land teachings for twelve years. He studied first under Shōtatsu, one of the chief dharma successors of Shōkū (see biography in part 2), who was in turn one of Hōnen's successors and founder of the Seizan subsect of Jōdo. Ippen then studied under Kedai, also in the Seizan subsect, who gave him the name Chishin.

In 1263, when Ippen was twenty-four, his father died, and he returned home to Shikoku. He stayed there for seven years, but little is known about his life during this period. In 1271 he made a pilgrimage to Zenkō-ji in Shinano Province. While in retreat there, he copied a painting that impressed him deeply, depicting the parable of the two rivers and the white path; Chinese Pure Land master Shan-tao referred to this parable in his *Commentary on the Meditation Sutra*. On his return home Ippen made himself a hermitage and hung in it his copy of the Zenkō-ji painting. There he undertook ascetic practices. Next he went to a traditional site for religious practice, also on Shikoku, and for three years secluded himself in a cave. From here he returned home before setting out in 1274 on a journey to teach nembutsu. He visited Tennō-ji, made a pilgrimage to Mount Kōya, and from there went on to the Shinto shrine complex of Kumano, where he experienced a dramatic revelation that changed his way of thinking. (It should be noted that Shinto and Buddhism were not separate religions at the time.)

What had confronted him in his teaching among the people was the presence or absence of faith in nembutsu. According to *Wandering Sage Ippen*, an illustrated scroll depicting Ippen's life, on his way to Kumano he met a priest. Ippen said to him, "Accept this slip of paper bearing Amida's name, experience one instant [*ichinen*] of faith, and invoke Amida.'' The priest unexpectedly replied, ''I am not capable just at this moment of such single-minded faith. It would be wrong of me to take this slip.''

How could someone without faith in Amida's Original Vow be saved? Ippen's understanding of nembutsu, as a result of his religious practice on Shikoku, grew out of his own ideas; when he came to undertake actual teaching of nembutsu he had to ponder more deeply the meaning of a universal nembutsu that transcended the limits of personal comprehension.

Arriving at Kumano, Ippen sought an answer from the deity in the Hall of Witness. *Wandering Sage Ippen* relates that the deity appeared in the form of a mountain ascetic, and told Ippen, ''Living beings do not attain Pure Land rebirth through your teaching, for that was settled once and for all in the very instant that Amida Buddha gained perfect enlightenment ten eons ago. You should distribute your slips whether people have faith or not and whether they are pure or not.''

This revelation showed Ippen the depths of ''other-power,'' that is, total reliance on the saving power of Amida, and he gained a clear idea of the source and essence of nembutsu. For Ippen, human rebirth was not decided through faith in nembutsu or by invoking Amida. Faith and recitation, in fact, were themselves the residue of an interposing ''self-power,'' or reliance on one's own efforts. The rebirth of living beings was already decided by Amida's vow. If rebirth depended on humans themselves, faith and purity would be necessary. Because it depended instead on invoking Amida, constructs of human intellect and power such as faith or non-faith, purity or non-purity, were irrelevant. This then is how Ippen interpreted Amida's Original Vow of ''other-power.''

Ippen's predecessors in Pure Land teaching, Hōnen and Shinran, both promised that all, whether good or evil, noble or humble, male or female, would equally gain Pure Land rebirth through the merit of the nembutsu. The release that they spoke of pivoted on faith in the absolute being, Amida.

Ippen said, ''How silly it is that everyone laments their lack of faith when in fact their rebirth has been decisively settled. There is no decisive settlement in the hearts of foolish, ignorant beings; decisive settlement is through invoking Amida. Therefore, even if you have no faith that your rebirth has been decisively settled, if you leave it to your lips to invoke Amida, you will be reborn. Rebirth does not depend upon your attitude of mind; it is by invoking Amida that you will be reborn" (*Collected Dharma Talks in Harima Province*). Ippen considered that even faith was a working of the mind of the one being freed, and so he denied it. What lay at the root of his rejection of faith was the thought of all those without faith to whom Pure Land rebirth had been denied by earlier teachers.

Ippen expressed his new understanding in verse:

The name of Amida is the one universal [*ippen*] dharma;
The ten realms of existence are the one universal body;
The myriad practices, freed from thought, are the one
    universal realization.
One who invokes Amida is greatest among beings, a
    wondrously excellent lotus.

After that Ippen changed his name from Chishin to Ippenbō and began traveling throughout the country as a religious practice. The realization he had come to through the vision at Kumano signaled his enlightenment and the founding of the Ji sect.

The Single Name

The core of Ippen's teaching was not, however, toleration of lack of faith, but the certainty that rebirth in the Pure Land came about through invocation of Amida. All of Ippen's thought derived from this one belief. He wrote that the workings of the mind should not be discussed. In good and evil both, because the mind is deluded, it cannot be the key to emancipation. Invoking Amida itself brings rebirth. Ippen believed that Pure Land rebirth did not come through individual effort but through the name of Amida. He said that beyond the name of Amida, everything is phantasmal. Nothing else is to be depended upon. Conversely, he said, "Among the myriad living things, in the mountains and rivers, in the trees and grasses, in the blowing wind and the sound of the rising waves—there is nothing that does not invoke Amida" (*Sayings of Holy Man Ippen*). He believed the name of Amida represented the totality of truth, the whole of existence, and that it held the key to the inviolability of the eternal and the undying.

Ippen analyzed the six Chinese characters for "Take refuge in Amida Buddha" (*Namu Amida Butsu*) as follows: "*Namu* means all living beings; *Amida* is the dharma; *Butsu* is someone who has gained enlightenment. The six characters may be provisionally revealed as three—the living being, the dharma, and enlightenment—but ultimately they become one. Without the name of Amida, there is no living being taking refuge, no dharma to take refuge in, and no person of enlightenment" (*Collected Dharma Talks in Harima Province*). Ippen believed that the six characters for invocation of Amida represented the rebirth of living beings as well as Amida's own enlightenment. The name of Amida was the only refuge, and Amida did not exist apart from the six characters for his name. Ippen understood, in the six characters, Amida and living beings to be one; this was the realm of nonduality.

The actuality of rebirth did not reside in a person who invoked Amida's name, but in the name of Amida itself. When the essence of the name of Amida became identical with the oneness of living beings and the dharma, freedom was attained by embracing and receiving the name of Amida. This was reciting the nembutsu, establishing a relationship with the name of Amida.

As Ippen sought to convert people to nembutsu after his enlightenment at Kumano, he continually distributed small slips of paper on which was written "Take refuge in Amida Buddha; decisive settlement of rebirth: six hundred thousand people." This was intended to link the recipient with nembutsu. In distributing the slips and calling for people to recite the nembutsu, Ippen paid no attention to whether the recipient had faith or was of good moral character.

About invoking Amida, Ippen said that if a person thinks that one will attain rebirth through individual understanding or through invoking Amida, that person has not lost attachment to self and to self-power. Such a person will probably fail to achieve rebirth. To aspire for rebirth through invoking Amida meant that there remained an attachment to self in the form of aspiration; as a result, achieving rebirth was impossible. What Ippen meant by invoking Amida was abandonment of self-attachment and of faith, and invoking Amida with no interspersion of self. Of this he said that though you put your mind into the name of Amida, you should not take the name of Amida into your own mind. Ippen's "single utterance of the name of Amida," his "nembutsu meditation," was this: that Amida's name was to be invoked not as a function of the mind but as an expression of the realm where the workings of the mind no longer applied, the very nembutsu chanting the nembutsu.

Mission of a Sage Who Discarded Everything

It was from Ippen's thorough understanding of nembutsu meditation and his devotion to the name of Amida that his teaching of "discard all" originated. All concern for clothing, food, or shelter and all troubling thoughts of secular affection were to him expressions of attachment to self. Devoting himself completely to invocation of Amida, he abandoned his clerical rank, family ties, reliance on the intellect, and even a settled dwelling. For the rest of his life, he traveled the country as a wandering sage who had discarded everything to convert people to nembutsu.

Ippen's travels started after his vision at Kumano in 1274, when he was thirty-five. From Kumano he went to Kyoto, then to Kyushu, returning home to Iyo in the autumn of 1275 to spread his teachings there. In 1277 he went again to Dazaifu, Kyushu, visiting his Pure Land master Shōtatsu to report on the nature of his understanding and his hopes for dissemination by distributing amulets throughout the country. Next he went south along the west coast of Kyushu to Ōsumi Shōhachiman Shrine. On his return he traveled up the east coast of Kyushu. At that time work on fortifications against the second Mongol invasion was in full swing along the coast, interfering with Ippen's journey. In places he was taunted as a madman, and he often suffered from cold and hunger. Nevertheless, wearing a tattered robe, he never rested from his wanderings and his mission of distributing amulets. In Bungo, Kyushu, he gained the respect and patronage of a powerful warrior and met his first student, Shinkyō, who stayed with him to the end of Ippen's life.

In 1278 Ippen returned to Iyo, then crossed the Inland Sea to make a pilgrimage to Itsukushima Shrine in Aki Province and traveled along the Honshu coast teaching and converting. A well-known incident took place at this time when he was staying in Bizen. Living there was a famous warrior, called the Brave of Bizen, son of the chief priest of Kibitsu Shrine. Being away from home just then, the warrior had left his wife in charge of the household. His wife, though, believing in Ippen's teachings on liberation from birth and death, shaved her head and joined Ippen's band. On returning home, the husband exploded with rage when he heard what had happened. Without a moment's delay, he set off in pursuit of Ippen and caught up with the band several miles farther along in a busy marketplace. He rushed up to Ippen with drawn sword. Ippen, the son of warriors, did not blink an eye, but shouted, "Are you the son of Kibitsu Shrine?" It is said his reproving tone made the warrior's hair stand on end. The Brave of Bizen's anger immediately evaporated as he sat down to hear Ippen's teachings. Like his wife, he shaved his head and became a member of the wandering band. Such episodes occurred often during Ippen's travels, for dangers constantly surrounded him. Supporting him in his roaming practice were his warrior's passion and his fervent belief in his mission. By the end of the year, more than 280 men and women were ordained under him, and there were many of those who, like Shinkyō, accompanied him on his travels.

In the spring of 1279 Ippen and his band arrived in Kyoto, where they stayed at a temple and distributed amulets. In the summer Ippen left Kyoto for Zenkō-ji in Shinano Province, traveling the central mountain route. On the way, he conducted a special year-end nembutsu session at a market town. At this time, it is said, purple clouds appeared in the sky and miracles occurred. After this, good omens constantly accompanied Ippen's amulet distribution, or at least so the people of the time believed. It was said that sometimes flowers rained from the heavens or purple clouds hung in the sky. The *Book of Tengu,* a pictorial record that treats Ippen's travels very coolly, describes the omens as devices to attract the common people. "When people put their faith in Ippenbō, flowers fell." The same scroll also relates how the common people used Ippen's urine as a universal remedy. "Many drank urine, the master's urine, believing it to be a medicine for all sicknesses." This is not the place, though, to examine the truth or falsehood of the omens or the extent of people's ignorance. Ippen replied, when questioned about the significance of the omens, "Concerning the flowers, ask the flowers; concerning the purple clouds, ask the purple clouds; I do not know" (*Sayings of Holy Man Ippen*). The deep emotions of those who received his teachings led them to expect the appearance of good omens when Ippen spoke.

Dancing Nembutsu

Why did Ippen's teachings become so popular? On the way to Zenkō-ji, Ippen and his band stopped at the mansion of a warrior and distributed amulets to the people of the vicinity. Those who received the amulets invoked Amida and began to dance. This was probably the origin of the "dancing nembutsu" that was later to become a feature of the Ji sect. It had nothing to do with Hōnen's or Shinran's teaching of nembutsu; it did not evolve until Ippen's time.

Perhaps the most obvious reason is that Ippen's nembutsu practice was adopted in ordinary life. Already Ippen had stated that rebirth depended not upon humans but upon the name of Amida. He had also taught that within the name of Amida, Amida and living beings were indistinguishable, nondual. Immersed in the nembutsu meditation, human and Amida became one. "Meditation means seeing the Buddha," Ippen said (*Collected Dharma Talks in Harima Province*). One who dwelled in nembutsu meditation, putting all thought into the name of Amida, was already in the true enlightenment of Amida. Living, such a one was Amida. "Outside the nembutsu of the present, there is no nembutsu of the moment of death. The moment of death is ordinary life."

In contrast to Hōnen, for whom rebirth was experienced at the very moment of death, and to Shinran, for whom rebirth was decisively settled in one moment of faith in the course of daily life, Ippen discarded all self-attachment and sought in ordinary life for rebirth within the six characters for the nembutsu, stating that it was nembutsu chanting the nembutsu.

It is that moment, when "we are no longer ourselves: since our hearts are the heart of Namu Amida Butsu, our bodies' actions are the actions of Namu Amida Butsu, our words are the words of Namu Amida Butsu, there our living lives are the life of Amida Buddha, our dying lives are the life of Amida Buddha" (*Sayings of Holy Man Ippen*), that Ippen amplified. In that moment, no distinction remained between life and death, human and Amida. When a person gave the self completely to the name of Amida, through nembutsu of each thought, that person was no longer a person, but was, as far as words could express it, no different from Amida. Living, such a person was Amida.

Ippen did not believe, as did Hōnen and Shinran, that Amida was some kind of absolute being far superior to living beings. He made human being and buddha one, leading people to refuge in a universal life where there was as yet no separation between human and Amida. The core of rebirth was the name of Amida; through that name, "nembutsu chanting the nembutsu" in a state of no-self, human and buddha embraced and received each other within the name of Amida, becoming united and undifferentiated. Thus a human being was Amida.

This is why Ji followers made the suffix -*ami*, for Amida, part of their names. The significance of Ippen's freeing of the populace boils down to this. For those of the lower orders, to whom even Pure Land rebirth had been denied, Ippen's teachings indeed meant selfless rapture. Wherever Ippen went, therefore, frenzied followers began to perform a rapturous nembutsu dance.

Religious Wandering

Ippen's wanderings continued. In 1280 he set out from Shinano Province for Mutsu Province to visit the grave of his exiled grandfather. After that he went southward along the east coast of Honshu to Hitachi and Musashi provinces. In the spring of 1282, Ippen attempted to enter Kamakura, which was still reeling from the attempted Mongol invasion of the previous year. Prevented by military order from staying in Kamakura, he went to a village on the outskirts, where he lived for several months, then began his teaching activities along the Tokaidō, the highway between Edo and Kyoto. He made a pilgrimage to Mishima Shrine in Izu Province, then traveled to Owari Province, where he rested briefly at Jimmoku-ji. Next he went through Mino Province to Ōmi Province, where he stayed at Seki-dera and distributed nembutsu slips. In the summer of 1284 he returned to Kyoto and took up residence at the Shakyamuni Hall.

Ippen had been away from Kyoto for six years. During that time he had taught the dharma to large numbers of warriors and farmers and had gathered a considerable band of people who accompanied him on his travels. Many died of illness in the course of painful journeys. Ippen made two death registers, the famous *Death Registers for Clergy in Days Gone By,* one for male and one for female clergy, in which Shinkyō recorded the priests' names and the dates of their deaths. These are still preserved at the head temple of the Ji sect, Shōjōkō-ji in Kanagawa Prefecture.

From the Shakyamuni Hall, Ippen moved to other Kyoto temples, everywhere distributing nembutsu slips to people. At a place associated with Kūya, Ippen erected a special practice hall for dancing nembutsu. He had from his earliest days of retreat from the world revered Kūya as his teacher and predecessor.

Having spent forty-eight days in the capital, Ippen moved west of the city, and then set out for Inaba and Hōki provinces, continuing to distribute his nembutsu slips wherever he went. He made a pilgrimage to Nakayama Shrine in Mimasaka Province, traveling through the mountains of the central region; then, passing through Harima Province, he arrived at Settsu Province's Tennō-ji in 1286.

From Tennō-ji he made a pilgrimage to Sumiyoshi Shrine, then went into retreat near Prince Shōtoku's tomb. From there he went to Taima-dera, near Nara, to visit the Mandala Hall. Toward the end of the year he paid a visit to Iwashimizu Hachiman Shrine, then returned to Tennō-ji for a special nembutsu session. Without pausing to rest, he then set off again westward, traveling along the Inland Sea coast and visiting the grave of Kyōshin, a nembutsu practitioner who had died in 866. By the spring of 1287 he was at Mount Shosha, where he dedicated the *Hymn of Amida's Vow* in Kyōshin's memory.

Ippen next traveled farther west through Bizen and Bitchū provinces and made a pilgrimage to Kibitsu and Itsukushima shrines. At Itsukushima, he organized a special festival at the request of the shrine officials. In 1288 Ippen crossed the sea to Iyo, where he dedicated the three Pure Land sutras at Hata-dera in memory of his father, Nyobutsu. At the end of the year he made a pilgrimage to Ōmishima Shrine, to honor the tutelary deity of his family. It had been a relatively relaxed year, perhaps intended as a rest for an increasingly fatigued Ippen.

The following year, Ippen moved across Shikoku via Sanuki Province to Zentsū-ji and Mandara-dera. He crossed to Awaji Island, where his health steadily worsened. Realizing his death was near, Ippen went on to the Kannon Hall in Harima Province. He deposited some of the writings in his possession at Mount Shosha and burned the rest, saying, "All Shakyamuni's sacred teachings have completely become *Namu Amida Butsu*." He died in the summer of 1289, aged fifty. His grave can still be found in the grounds of Shinkō-ji in Hyōgo Prefecture.

Ikkyū
(1394–1481)

by Daisetsu Fujioka

Pure and Unconventional

"About forty years ago," wrote Ikkyū in his *Crazy Cloud Collection*, "I heard a priest in the dharma hall bragging about his family background and revealing who was of merchant or craftsman origin. What was this, I thought, and ran from the hall with my hands covering my ears. . . . Today there is gossip in the temples. There should be no toleration of gossip among the clergy about who is of high or low birth."

The episode reveals how difficult it was for the sixteen-year-old Ikkyū to put up with the abuses existing within officially sponsored Zen temples of his time. The eager, artless youth suddenly fled from the dharma hall, his hands over his ears, during a lecture by a senior cleric to the trainees. His inability to compromise and his incorruptibility were not just youthful idealism but remained an integral part of his character to his death at eighty-seven.

Ikkyū Sōjun was reputedly the son of Emperor Go-Komatsu and a noblewoman from the Southern Court. Though there is no conclusive evidence, it is now generally accepted that Ikkyū was of royal birth. As a result of slander, his mother was ousted from the palace while pregnant, and she gave birth to him in the house of a commoner. This misfortune may have lodged like an obstinate seed in his personality and been responsible for his later cynicism. As an unwanted child, he had been placed in a Zen temple as a trainee by the age of five.

It was a matter of great good fortune for Ikkyū that, at the age of sixteen, he went for instruction to Kennō Sōi of Kanzan Egen's lineage. Under Kennō, Ikkyū's concern for the purity of Zen and his righteous indignation found nourishment.

Within the Rinzai sect at that time there were two authoritative lineages. The first was that of Musō Soseki (see biography in part 2), responsible for the institutional development of the Five Mountains system covering some three hundred officially sponsored Rinzai temples. Sustained in the fourteenth and early fifteenth centuries by the patronage of the Ashikaga shoguns, the lineage was materially prosperous. Ashikaga support of the Five Mountains clerics led in time, however, to spiritual enervation as priests came to engage in literary pursuits instead of seeking enlightenment. Some even meddled in shogunate affairs and were active in the business of government.

The second lineage was that of Sōhō Myōchō (see biography in part 2), centering on Daitoku-ji, a temple founded with imperial support in 1324. Regarded with suspicion by the Ashikaga shoguns, this lineage devoted itself to developing a strict, orthodox Zen practice as a rationale for its existence. As a result, a considerable number of priests of Sōhō's lineage followed traditional Zen discipline, being proud of having no ties with the authorities, content in their honorable poverty, and unsparing in their practice. Kanzan Egen, one of Sōhō's chief dharma successors, was installed as first head of Myōshin-ji when it was dedicated in 1335. Under Kennō, Ikkyū was imbued with the spirit of Sōhō's lineage. He received from his master the name of Sōjun, literally ''essence of purity,'' reflecting his impressive purity of purpose. The death of Kennō in 1414 was a great shock to the twenty-year-old Ikkyū, who tried to drown himself in Lake Biwa. The following year he went to join Kasō Sōdon at his small retreat at Katada on the western shore of Lake Biwa. In joining Kasō, also of Sōhō's lineage, perhaps Ikkyū was trying to bring Kennō back to life through a new master.

Kasō was known for his harsh, unrelenting Zen. At first he refused Ikkyū admittance, but the young man remained undaunted. He slept at night in a small boat by the lakeside, then at dawn went to sit at the gate of Kasō's retreat. One day Kasō ordered his attendant to throw water on Ikkyū to drive him away, but on returning from a service in the village, found a wet, bedraggled Ikkyū still sitting at the gate, unmoving. Kasō, feeling Ikkyū's commitment, at last admitted him. Ikkyū's spirit was formidable. His life of practice under Kasō was that of a model student, a Zen trainee of Sōhō's lineage. One evening in 1420, when Ikkyū was twenty-six and in his sixth year of training under Kasō, he heard the caw of a crow and was startled into a great enlightenment. He went immediately to report the event to his master. Kasō responded coolly. "You have done no more than reach the understanding of an *arhat.* You have not reached the stage of a true Zen master." But Ikkyū was not the Ikkyū of before, for he was convinced of his enlightenment. "If you say that I have reached the stage of *arhat,* then that is enough," he replied. "I don't need to be a true Zen master." "If that is so, then you are a true Zen master after all," said Kasō, smiling. Ikkyū's six years of relentless practice had borne fruit, and he had come to an understanding of the great matter of birth and death.

Under Kasō, Ikkyū's purity of character gradually hardened into obstinate, uncompromising, righteous indignation. The words of Tettō Gikō, Sōhō's successor at Daitoku-ji, which Kasō had taught him, burned into his mind. Ikkyū quoted them in his *Crazy Cloud Collection:*

Those who practice Zen and follow the Way must strive to be pure in their everyday actions. Impurity in everyday actions is not allowed. They who can be called pure in everyday actions will, by penetrating the direct and indirect causes of one situation, arrive at the realm of understanding beyond reason. They strive tirelessly day and night. On occasion, they cut off the roots of ignorance and decide with clear understanding those things that even buddhas and demons have trouble perceiving. Repeatedly they bury their names and hide their traces. Under trees in a mountain forest they raise the direct and indirect causes of one situation. At these times they are without fault and of the utmost purity. Those, however, who say of themselves, "I am a good friend," who raise their staffs and fly whisks, gather a congregation and preach the dharma, and bewitch the sons and daughters of people; who covet fame and profit; who invite students into their rooms, promising to enlighten them concerning what is most profound, and thereby causing those gathered together to copy the speakers' words idly among themselves, while the speakers become biased: such clerics are not human, they are truly impure in their daily actions. Taking the Buddha's teachings, they use them to advance in the world; such clerics want only glory in this world.

When Ikkyū looked around him, he wondered if indeed there was anyone leading the Zen life of everyday purity that Tettō had spoken of. Of course there were the Five Mountains clerics, supported by the power of the government, more interested in literature than religion, but even the proud Daitoku-ji lineage had its own increasingly obvious troubles. Ikkyū burned angrily with righteous indignation. From the flames of his indignation emerged his reckless, unconventional side.

When he was twenty-eight, the thirty-third memorial service was held for Kasō's master, Gongai Sōchū, at Daitoku-ji's Nyoian. Ikkyū accompanied Kasō to the formal meal. The other priests were decorously wearing elaborate robes. Ikkyū alone was shabbily dressed in an ordinary cotton robe with straw sandals. Kasō asked him, "Why have you not come properly dressed?" Ikkyū answered composedly, "I alone enhance this meeting." Later, Kasō was asked by his dharma brother Nisshō who would succeed him upon his death. "Although he is somewhat crazy, Ikkyū Sōjun will," replied Kasō. We can therefore put the start of Ikkyū's unconventional bent to this time. This trait increased with the confrontation and rift with Yōsō Sōi, a dharma brother, after Kasō's death. It was particularly marked between the years 1445, when Yōsō was appointed to head Daitoku-ji, and 1458, when he died. This corresponded to the period between Ikkyū's fiftieth and sixty-fourth years. His crazy behavior is attested to in contemporary writings; the Tendai cleric and linked-verse master Shinkei wrote, "One who is mentioned frequently, for both his behavior and his mental state, is the priest Ikkyū. People say that everything he does is somewhat strange." Such irregular behavior was the other side of his unrelenting purity of purpose.

> Kasō's descendant does not know Zen.
> Who would speak of Zen before Crazy Cloud [Ikkyū]?
> For thirty years now
>   the burden has been heavy on my shoulders,
> This burden I have borne alone, the Zen of Sung-yüan.

In this sad verse in which Ikkyū speaks of a splendid isolation, like that of a pure lotus blooming in a muddy pond, one can feel his extreme irritation. Although he could ignore the Five Mountains priests, he deplored the appearance of inferior priests from his own lineage who reflected discredit on the name of their founder. When confronted by them, his anger would burst into flame. He could not forgive indolent, pleasure-seeking priests who brought shame on Sōhō's lineage and the purest of the Japanese Zen training centers. Herein lies the reason for Ikkyū's frenetic attack on Yōsō and his students. The glory-seekers of impure daily actions in Tettō's lecture were, Ikkyū thought, the clerics of Yōsō's lineage.

Confrontation with Yōsō

Yōsō Sōi was eighteen years older than Ikkyū and his senior among Kasō's disciples. Gentle in temperament and inclined to want to please everyone, he spared no efforts in building up the material prosperity of Daitoku-ji. His way of spreading the teachings, however, was to flatter the ruling classes while "selling" Zen to the masses. Here he was fundamentally at odds with Ikkyū, but over and above this difference of attitude was a sense of rivalry between the two that could not be overcome.

In the autumn of 1455, Yōsō rebuilt Yōshun-an in Sakai, and there he conducted teaching activities among the people of Sakai, instructing them in the five practices and giving his lectures in the vernacular so they would be easy for the merchant class to understand: "There are those among the merchants and others who say that they were able to attain the dharma in ten days. Others say that they were able to attain it in twenty."

The depth of the Zen understanding that Ikkyū had experienced when awakened by the caw of a crow, at the end of more than ten years of painstaking effort, became trivialized when the dharma was distributed to the people like a cheap commodity and by the willingness to devote ten or twenty days to an easy religious discipline. What was Yōsō but a heretic who would pour slopwater over the Buddha's head?

"Since the very beginning of Daitoku-ji, such an evil priest amid a band of great evildoers has been neither seen nor heard of!" complained Ikkyū harshly. The poem about Kasō's descendant quoted above is said to have been composed thirty years after Kasō's death and speaks plainly of the burden that was growing heavier as the confrontation with Yōsō increased in acrimony and Ikkyū's sense of isolation and eccentricity grew more intense.

The hundred or so poems that make up Ikkyū's *Self-Admonishments* are a vitriolic condemnation of Yōsō and his dharma successor, Shumpo Shōki. They employ the coarsest language that Ikkyū could devise. How he knew such obscene phrases is a mystery; but even more puzzling is why he, now an old man, a Zen priest who had attained an enlightenment that penetrated all things, should have expressed his anger in such a way, however foolish he thought Yōsō. Even though he was filled with anger and resentment, such behavior was not what was expected in one of the most famous clerics of his day. All in all he was an exception among those enlightened priests who had become as withered trees, withdrawn in their enlightenment.

Ikkyū's righteous indignation was not focused on the world of temples alone, for he demonstrated it toward secular society as well. Famine had broken out in 1460, causing widespread suffering. In the diary of the Five Mountains prelate Unsen Taikyoku, there is the poignant description of a group of boisterous, drunken young nobles returning home from flower viewing, who pass unseeing by a prostrate, homeless old woman, who weeps as she clutches to her the body of her dead child. Ikkyū also wrote, as an introduction to a poem, "Strong winds and floods, and the people are all anxious. Hearing that at night there are those who go out to banquets and sing and play the flute, I grieve." Similarly, in the poems "Beauty of Women" and "Courtesy of Women," he roundly criticized the behavior of the shogun's wife.

As the Ōnin War approached, social unrest increased, and the state of affairs grew more and more disquieting. It was natural that people should have become agitated in such a climate. During the turmoil, Ikkyū himself changed abode several times. In 1469 he fled to Takigi, midway between Kyoto and Nara, where he had first come in 1456, then to Sakai, and finally to Sumiyoshi. Inside and outside the capital, people flung themselves into their pleasures to overcome their disquiet, and as lewdness flooded the capital, Ikkyū lamented, "In every row of ten houses, four or five are now brothels. Lewd manners are proliferating everywhere. The fall of the nation approaches. How can I recall the poem of marriage joy?"

Love of the Attendant Mori

It is surprising that a man like Ikkyū should have become involved in a passionate love affair. An autumn 1494 entry in a nobleman's diary states:

> This year, the priest [meaning Giō Shōtei] is sixty-seven and is residing in Sakurazuka in Settsu. There is a secret about him. The priest Ikkyū was the son of Emperor Go-Komatsu, and therefore a prince, though nobody knows of this. Priest Shōtei is the true child of Ikkyū Sōjun and the true receiver of his dharma. They were truly father and son. How strange! How wonderful!

This would mean that Ikkyū had been thirty-two when Shōtei was born. Leaving aside the question of whether the report was true, it cannot be denied that Ikkyū loved many women. This is obvious from a single glance at the poems in his *Crazy Cloud Collection*. However much he deplored the lewdness and corruption of the city and denounced Yōsō for deceiving the women of the merchant class, the irony remains that Ikkyū himself was forced to suffer from his impulsiveness. Despite long years of Zen practice, he was unable to quench the fire of his passion. At times he would seek out the reason for his suffering and justify himself; at others, he would cloak himself in an extreme of self-loathing.

> If even the emperor could be lost in pleasure
>   with the deity of Wu-shan in a dream,
> How much more so should lesser beings
>   such as ourselves lose our way?
> The refined sage-king wept
>   [when he lost Yang Kuei-fei] at Ma Wei.
> These are clear examples;
>   they have not lost their force even today.

Even Emperor Hsüan-tsung was captivated by the beauty of Yang Kuei-fei. It could not be helped, therefore, if an insignificant person such as Ikkyū was ruined by lust. Such a rationale came of a self-righteousness born of desperation; should his involvement with women not somehow be understood as justified? Ikkyū certainly realized this. It was when he comprehended that his justification was hollow that he fell into the extremes of self-admonishment and self-ridicule:

> Who are the true masters of Daitō's [Sōhō's] lineage?
> There is no distinction between true and false,
>   and each has his own version of wisdom.
> Crazy Cloud himself—his actions too are fishy:
> All he has done is write love letters and erotic poems.

When he was suffering from the conflict between the realization that he himself was heir to the orthodox Zen of Kasō's line and the immorality in his dealings with women, he could only revile himself as human, susceptible to all the weaknesses of the flesh. He took the sobriquet "Crazy Cloud" and the pen name "Wind-Crazy," and he delighted in eccentric conduct. His threatened conversion to the Lotus and Pure Land sects was not merely a result of his hostility to Yōsō and his group but also an expression of the anguish and self-contradiction between his self-realization as a Zen priest and his sexual indulgence.

Finally, though, Ikkyū was able to acknowledge his innate, strong love in a natural way, released from such spiritual conditions:

> If I am thirsty, I dream of water.
> If I am cold, I dream of leather clothing.
> To dream of the bedchamber is my nature.

He acknowledged his desires to be as natural as the need to drink water and keep warm. It was a magnificent step in his spiritual growth. Zen teaches that one perceives what is green to be green, what is red to be red. Ikkyū developed this to embrace the realm of desire. Later, he was without feelings of guilt when he approached the opposite sex, and he expressed his love openly and honestly. Such a state of mind only came about when he was past seventy, tranquil now, his long-held animosity toward Yōsō and his followers gradually dying away following Yōsō's death.

The last, great love of the old man was a blind woman, Jihaku Shin, usually called Mori in English texts. Their love is recorded in a number of poems in the *Crazy Cloud Collection*.

Ikkyū wrote, "For some years I lived in a small dwelling in Takigi. The attendant Mori, having heard of me, already held me in affection; I knew of it, but remained undecided until now. In the spring of 1471 I met her by chance at Suminoe and asked her about her feelings. She replied that she was unchanged."

When Ikkyū and Mori met by chance in 1471, he was seventy-seven. From then on Mori seems always to have been at his side, looking after his needs. Ikkyū's feelings for her were extremely deep: "The blind attendant Mori has strong feelings of love. She refuses food and may lose her life. In sorrow and pain, I have composed some poems.'' It is not clear why she refused to eat, but Ikkyū's anguish is vividly described.

Once as Ikkyū gazed at Mori taking a nap, he discovered in her a beauty like that of the celebrated Yang Kuei-fei.

> The most elegant beauty of her generation!
> Her songs at banquets are the newest.
> A voice that pierces my heart,
>   that dimple in a flower-like face—
> She is spring in the begonia forest
>   of the T'ien-pao era.

Another time, Mori was riding in a cart; seeing her, Ikkyū wrote: ''I love to see Mori, so beautiful and good.'' One day when he saw her wearing a paper garment, he described her as ''so fresh and lovable.'' To him, everything about her was attractive.

There is only a single portrait of Mori, now in the Masaki Museum, Osaka. She is seated on a strip of tatami wearing a red kimono and a white overrobe, a drum and a stick beside her. The painting seems to date from a period close to Ikkyū's lifetime, so it provides a clue to what she was like. Though Ikkyū called her an ''attendant,'' which can mean the trainee who attends a senior priest, her charming clothes and long black hair serve to remind us that rather than a Buddhist cleric she was a woman entertainer from the secular world.

Ikkyū was overflowing with his love for Mori.

> The trees wither, the leaves fall,
>   but spring comes round again.
> Greenery grows, flowers bloom,
>   and old promises are renewed.
> Mori, should I forget my deep gratitude to you,
> Let me be reborn a beast for all eternity.

Mori wrote the following poem, which closely resembles a love song, that she may have sung to Ikkyū to a drum accompaniment:

> Floating, sinking, in my bed,
>> sleep of love, sleep of sadness,
> No solace but of tears.

Mori did not remain with Ikkyū until his death. The sadness of their parting is reflected in the next poem, prefaced by the words, "I had a lover, who was with me for many years. One day she left me, suddenly. I did not restrain her."

> The sadness of parting knows no bounds;
> The whiteness of my hair increases anew.
> Leaning on my length of bamboo,
> I think sadly upon a beautiful woman.
> I am sunk in thought the night through,
> My pillow is wet with tears.
> Alone in my bed I grow feeble with age.

Tears at their parting stream down the old man's cheeks. Now very frail, he has lost the fierceness he displayed toward Yōsō. From the evidence of Mori's name in a document, in the keeping of Daitoku-ji's Shinju-an, recording large donations by Mori for incense on the occasions of Ikkyū's thirteenth and thirty-third memorial services, it seems possible that their separation was brought about by something other than a quarrel.

Portrait of Ikkyū

There are two portraits from the Muromachi period (1336–1573) that draw our attention by their contrast. One is of Shinzei (see biography in part 2), in the collection of Saikyō-ji in Shiga Prefecture. Shinzei began an independent Pure Land movement in the Tendai sect; his portrait tells clearly of the austerity and purity of his daily life. His cleanly shaven head, his firm mouth, speak of a man with a clear vision of the ugliness of reality. Impressive also are his hands, palms together at the breast in reverence, and his Buddhist beads.

The other is Bokusai's portrait of Ikkyū, now in the Tokyo National Museum. His unkempt hair brings to mind the eccentric Chinese clerics Han-shan and Shih-te. A long scraggly beard covers his upper lip and chin. His lower jaw juts out, his nostrils angle upward, and his large lips are pursed. At first it seems perhaps strange to find Ikkyū portrayed as a boor; one cannot, however, overlook the deep wrinkles etched into his face from his eyes down his cheeks. These wrinkles come from a long history of pain. They are the wrinkles of the anxiety of a man who, in his essential purity, continuously suffers from the corruption he sees around him, one who, moreover, is a Zen priest and yet cannot escape the self-contradiction of being sunk in the mire of the senses. Ikkyū did not let his suffering go to waste. At the end he experienced splendid spiritual growth. He personifies the Renaissance man in Japan.

Ikkyū's poetry is by no means merely licentious. It is lofty and serious, but above all humane. With this in mind, another glance at his portrait shows him, unlike Shinzei, to be a human being, with warm blood coursing through his veins.

Rennyo
(1415–1499)

by Hitoshi Ōkuwa

Hongan-ji Poverty

It was around 1413, several years after the death of the third Ashikaga shogun, and the foundations of the Ashikaga shogunate were weakening. Three men from Katada in Ōmi Province, on the western shore of Lake Biwa, had crossed the mountains east of Kyoto and were about to descend into the capital. Resting in a wayside booth at the mountain pass, they mentioned to the old man in charge there that they were making a pilgrimage to Hongan-ji, in Ōtani, eastern Kyoto. "No one goes there," the old man told them, "everything there is lonely and desolate." Half in doubt, unable to believe that Shinran's mausoleum could have come to such a state, the three hurried along the road, only to find when at last they reached Hongan-ji, where Chion-in now stands, that the old man's words had been all too true.

The grandfather of Jirōsaburō, the leader of the three, had been converted by Kakunyo (see biography in part 2), Shinran's grandson and the one who transformed the Ōtani mausoleum into Hongan-ji. Kakunyo had subsequently opened a training hall for followers of the Jōdo Shin sect, at Katada, home of the three would-be pilgrims. Finding the reality of Hongan-ji so different from what he had heard from his grandfather and mother, Jirōsaburō was shocked. Then he heard a rumor that there was another temple, Bukkō-ji, that was disseminating the glad teachings of Shinran, so the three men hastened there. They found a flourishing temple where, one of them wrote, "people gathered in droves." Deciding that Bukkō-ji must certainly be the Jōdo Shin sect's most important temple, they paid their respects there and returned home rejoicing. Two years later, in 1415, Rennyo was born at the poor and desolate Hongan-ji.

Hongan-ji had been created out of Shinran's mausoleum. Originally, Shinran's eastern Japan followers had built a small memorial hall at the site of the grave in Ōtani and had given it into the care of Shinran's youngest daughter, a priest named Kakushinni. Kakunyo, Kakushinni's grandson, transformed the memorial hall into a formal temple, Hongan-ji, and attempted to unify the Jōdo Shin sect adherents all over the country under the leadership of Hongan-ji. There was, however, much opposition to his endeavors. Perhaps the most violent came from Senjū-ji, a temple in eastern Japan, founded by a direct disciple of Shinran, which had until this time flourished as the chief center of Shinran's adherents. Critical of Kakunyo and his attempts to enlarge the memorial hall, which the Senjū-ji adherents had in fact sponsored, Senjū-ji finally severed all connections with Hongan-ji and became an independent branch of the Jōdo Shin sect. Also in the vanguard of the opposition was Bukkō-ji of Kyoto. Other congregations that made moves toward independence were Kinshoku-ji in Ōmi Province and the Sammonto branch, consisting of five temples in Echizen Province. As a result, a century after Kakunyo's death Hongan-ji remained merely one small branch among many.

It was during Rennyo's lifetime that Hongan-ji became the chief temple of the Jōdo Shin sect, unifying virtually all of Shinran's adherents under its leadership and in the process forming the largest congregation in the history of Japanese Buddhism. Most scholars have credited this to Rennyo's charisma, but this is doubtful. The Jōdo Shin sect grants him reverence second only to Shinran, for Rennyo's role as the restorer of Hongan-ji; scholars, however, have considered him a man of shallow religious belief, a politician rather than a religious figure, praising him for his spread of the teachings at a popular level. Though it is difficult to see him as he really was, this very difficulty adds to the interest of his story.

"That Is Too Close"

As is common with many great men, much of Rennyo's life was a fight against adversity. He was born when his father, Zonnyo, who later was the chief priest of Hongan-ji, was not yet twenty. To make matters worse, his mother was not his father's legal wife, but apparently was a servant. Rennyo's life continued under a cloud. When he was six his mother disappeared, for Zonnyo was about to be betrothed to someone of his own standing. Rennyo's grief at losing his mother was such that until the end of his life he tried desperately to have her traced, but knowing neither her identity nor where she had gone, he met with no success, and in time she came to be regarded as a manifestation of Kannon of Ishiyama. His stepmother, a priest named Nyoenni, had no love for him, and soon Rennyo was surrounded by half-brothers and -sisters. Hongan-ji remained poor.

Growing up in such an environment, Rennyo gained a subtle understanding of the intricacies of human relationships, which was to stand him in good stead when he began his teaching campaign. Unlike the prosperous Bukkō-ji and the temples of other branches of the Jōdo Shin sect, Hongan-ji languished in the extreme of decline. Rennyo felt strongly that his mission was to restore Hongan-ji's fortunes. Such a sense of mission in adversity became a compelling whip. The young Rennyo drove himself relentlessly in his studies; many of the copies of the texts he used survive and enable us to trace the course of his studies.

Eventually he married and had children, but his hardships increased rather than diminished. Toward the end of his life he spoke of the poverty of those times. Unable to afford even a temporary servant, he was forced to wash his children's napkins himself. All of his children except the eldest son, Junnyo, were sent to live in large temples in the capital. Even so, sometimes Rennyo had no means to provide the three daily meals, and there were times when the family had to share a single serving of soup. They wore the handmade paper clothing of the very poor, with a strip of silk sewn into the end of the sleeve. We must, of course, discount some of this as a moralistic tale for comfortably reared grandchildren; by Zonnyo's later years, adherents were reaffiliating themselves with Hongan-ji, and the economic situation could not have been as bad as these stories suggest. They should be seen from Rennyo's point of view.

Zonnyo died in 1457. Rennyo was then in the prime of life at forty-two. Peasant leagues had risen in the provinces near Kyoto, and farmers, demanding the cancellation of debts, were destroying storehouses, the premises of wine merchants, and temples. The authority of the Ashikaga shogunate had plummeted, and the conflict in the deputy-shogun's family over rights of succession that was a prelude to the Ōnin War (1467–1477) had already erupted. Society was in the midst of change.

At Hongan-ji arrangements for Zonnyo's funeral proceeded amid many vicissitudes. Zonnyo's widow, Nyoenni, proposed that her son Ōgen succeed as head of Hongan-ji, and the matter seemed decided. Though younger than Rennyo, Ōgen was Zonnyo's eldest son by his legal wife, whereas Rennyo was illegitimate. No one objected. Zonnyo's younger brother, Nyojō, chief priest of the powerful Honsen-ji, however, arrived just then from northwest Honshu.

He vehemently opposed Ōgen's succession and set about changing people's minds. He emphasized that Zonnyo had already designated Rennyo as his heir, that Rennyo had made the requisite teaching tour of the eastern plains area, and that Rennyo, acting in place of Zonnyo, had made and distributed to adherents copies of scriptures; therefore his right to the temple was clear. Perhaps because many people secretly had high expectations of Rennyo, Nyojō's remonstrations succeeded, and support shifted from Ōgen to Rennyo. Nyoenni and Ōgen moved to Kaga Province, and Rennyo became the eighth head of Hongan-ji.

Rennyo immediately set out on a tour to spread the teachings. The leader of the three pilgrims, Jirōsaburō of Katada, who had been so disappointed in 1413, had long since reaffiliated himself with Hongan-ji and received the dharma name Hōjū. Now he headed a large number of adherents on the western shore of Lake Biwa. It was here that Rennyo went first, before extending his preaching to the south and east. Before him loomed the imposing presence of Mount Hiei and behind him, the powerful force of Senjū-ji, recently moved to Ise Province from eastern Japan.

Senjū-ji had as its head an impressive rival for Rennyo in Shin'e, who early had joined hands with the Tendai clergy on Mount Hiei to inhibit Hongan-ji's expansion. In early 1465, Mount Hiei priests accused Hongan-ji of heresies and made a surprise attack on Ōtani. Those adherents who happened to be there put up a fight, allowing Rennyo to make a narrow escape, but a number of buildings were destroyed. Jirōsaburō, from the town of Katada on Lake Biwa, hurried in indignation to Ōtani with eighty mounted warriors, and the powerful priest Nyokō, head of Jōgū-ji in Mikawa Province, who was in Kyoto at the time, also hastened to the aid of Hongan-ji. After much discussion of whether they should use force, Hongan-ji's adherents decided to follow Nyokō's suggestion and settle the matter with money. Nyokō therefore collected a large sum of money and used it to soothe Mount Hiei clerics' susceptibilities. Though Senjū-ji may have been behind the action, in the end Mount Hiei clerics were inspired more by the wish for ransom.

For Jirōsaburō and the other Katada adherents living at the foot of Mount Hiei, though, things were not resolved so easily. They made a stand in a town on the eastern shore of Lake Biwa and repelled the Mount Hiei forces. It was Japan's first rebellion by adherents of the Jōdo Shin sect, presaging an event that was to recur ever more often in the next century. Rennyo ordered the sect's adherents, who had flocked to the fight, to disperse. He probably realized that to take a stand against such a strong enemy as Mount Hiei would not help Hongan-ji's revival, which was then just beginning.

Following the destruction of Hongan-ji, Rennyo remained in hiding for a time in Kyoto before going to Ōmi Province. Eventually he arrived in 1467 at Jirōsaburō's training hall in Katada, but he was not allowed to remain long there. The people of Katada, with a reputation for piracy, were accused of stealing goods belonging to the shogun. Under this pretext, Sakamoto, at the foot of Mount Hiei, threatened battle. Finally open conflict broke out, with Katada losing. Rennyo managed to escape in time and took a boat to the southern shore of Lake Biwa, where he sought refuge at Mii-dera. The conflict between Katada and Mount Hiei was resolved by a monetary settlement, but the incident made Rennyo resolve to leave Ōmi Province. When the Katada adherents offered land on which to rebuild Hongan-ji, Rennyo refused, pointing to nearby Mount Hiei and commenting, "That is too close."

Success at Last

Around the middle of 1471, Rennyo moved "on impulse" to Yoshizaki, on the border between Echizen and Kaga provinces. Within two years, large crowds of adherents had gathered around him; the road was lined with some two hundred travelers' lodges run by temples, and a large temple town had come into being, with big gates to the north and south. Still, the Yoshizaki complex did not come into being quite so accidentally as Rennyo indicated. Knowing that after he had built up a sphere of influence in Ōmi Province it would be dangerous to remain there, he had long planned to go to the northwest area, and gradually his preparations took shape. Senjū-ji, already strong in the eastern region, had also moved into the northwest, intent on building a powerful base.

There was already, though, a long-established network of temples in the area affiliated with Hongan-ji, through the bridgehead of Zuisen-ji in Etchū Province, and its related temples. One such was Honsen-ji, belonging to Rennyo's uncle Nyojō, who had been instrumental in obtaining for Rennyo the highest position at Hongan-ji. Honsen-ji was now in the custody of Nyojō's widow, a priest named Shōnyoni. Rennyo's second son, Renjō, had been sent there for adoption, and two other sons, Rengō and Rensei, were also in charge of important temples in the district. Conditions were such that it took only Rennyo's arrival for things to begin to happen.

Though Rennyo later wrote that his selection of Yoshizaki as his base had been accidental, the site was on an estate belonging to Daijō-in, a subtemple of Kōfuku-ji in Nara. Two priests who headed this temple, Jinson and Kyōkaku, appear to have been related by marriage to Rennyo, and he had visited Nara before departing for the northwest, perhaps to ascertain Daijō-in's support for his undertaking. In addition, it appears that an important local temple in the Hongan-ji lineage, Hongaku-ji, was acting as co-supervisor of the Daijō-in estate, and prevailed on the provincial governor to make land available to Rennyo. Rennyo in fact arrived in Yoshizaki after all the pieces were in place.

Adherents of the Jōdo Shin sect soon flocked to Yoshizaki. This was not only because they understood Rennyo's teachings and were burning with devotion. Farmers intent on raising themselves by their own efforts, and the peasant leaders at their head, had in many places clashed with the civil and religious authorities by refusing to pay taxes and by raiding estates. Rennyo's teaching that Pure Land rebirth was ensured by relying on Amida was often their authority for denying and slighting the provincial governors, estate stewards, and temples and shrines. They endeavored to resolve their clashes with the authorities through the power of Amida, which meant in effect the strength of the band of adherents gathered at Yoshizaki. After the outbreak of the Ōnin War, confrontations between warrior bands became more and more violent, and again the participants tried to use the power of Yoshizaki.

Togashi Masachika, for example, competing with his brother Kōchiyo for the position of provincial governor, developed close ties with Yoshizaki, as a result of which Rennyo found himself drawn into the dispute whether he liked it or not. His painful experience in Ōmi Province prompted him to maintain neutrality as far as possible, to preserve his young band.

In 1473 he issued for the first time a list of prohibitions ("rules of conduct") for his followers at Yoshizaki. These included a ban on denigrating provincial governors and estate stewards and on belittling the various deities, and they urged his followers to respect society's code of conduct.

At times Rennyo even thought of leaving Yoshizaki in the hope of calming his ebullient followers. After all, they ignored his prohibitions, and in 1474 they sided with Masachika and overthrew Kōchiyo. It was the beginning of the armed uprisings by the Jōdo Shin sect leagues in that area. Masachika, confronted by the power of the sect's victorious adherents, realized that he himself could easily share his brother's fate and began to put pressure on the leagues, even attempting to attack Yoshizaki. For Rennyo only one action was possible. In 1475, faced with imminent danger, he sailed from Yoshizaki to a coastal town in Wakasa Province, then on to a site in Kawachi Province.

Rennyo remained there for a little over two years. From there he established new dissemination bases in Settsu and Izumi provinces, broadening his influence throughout the region surrounding the capital. Having now built up his power, Rennyo was ready to undertake the rebuilding of Hongan-ji, which had been destroyed in 1465. At the beginning of 1478, a new site was chosen at Yamashina, immediately east of Kyoto. By the summer of the following year, the memorial hall to Shinran was completed. Rennyo commented that he could not sleep for happiness. Shinran's image was transferred to the new hall from its sanctuary at Miidera late in 1479, and a great memorial service of appreciation for Shinran's teachings was held. In 1481 the Amida hall was finished, and by 1483 construction of the complex was completed, including moats, walls, and six blocks of buildings.

The temple prospered away from the tribulations of Kyoto and seemed an earthly paradise. A member of the nobility from Kyoto commented in his diary that its magnificence was unsurpassed. The proud Bukkō-ji led other congregations from Ōmi and Echizen provinces in giving allegiance to Hongan-ji, which soon controlled all of the Jōdo Shin sect adherents except those affiliated with Senjū-ji. In 1489, the seventy-four-year-old Rennyo handed over the temple to his fifth son, Jitsunyo, and retired from affairs, reflecting on the words of Laotzu: "When the task is accomplished and fame is achieved, to retire is the way of heaven." There are very few people about whom such words are as apt as for Rennyo.

He remained active until his death ten years later at the age of eighty-four.

Priest, Elder, and Village Head

What was the secret of Rennyo's success in expanding the influence of Hongan-ji to the extent he did? One answer lies in the very nature of his times. Able to develop appropriate tools for his ministry and to underpin them with an unambiguous teaching, he could exploit the opportunities offered by social change. An important key to understanding the large growth of Jōdo Shin sect congregations among peasants is the means by which the sect's tenets pervaded the farming villages.

Throughout the fourteenth century, thanks to the rift between the Northern and Southern courts, the power of the peasants grew remarkably. With the region surrounding Kyoto taking the lead, peasants began forming autonomous villages, destroying the authority of the proprietors of the old estates and ready to rebel in defense of their lives and freedom.

This raising of consciousness among the peasants eventually led them to a concern for their own release from the transient world. Bukkō-ji was the first to notice this phenomenon and set forth a doctrine that appealed to the peasants. This was that faith in the priest would ensure the believer of Pure Land rebirth. Those whose release was confirmed were listed in registers. Such a teaching and means of dissemination were plainly heretical from Shinran's stance, but they were above all simple to understand. Revere the religious leader, make offerings and donations as required, have your name recorded in the rebirth register, and go to paradise—the simplicity of the message brought peasants crowding to knock on Bukkō-ji's doors.

Hongan-ji's prosperity meant that this heresy had to be destroyed. Rennyo spent the latter half of his life grappling with it. The first half of his life had been spent firming his own religious understanding in preparation for combat. Shinran's personal struggle had been with his own suffering; Rennyo did not have this concern, for he had before him Shinran's clarification of the solution to the pain that all human beings share. He did not study to ensure his own release, but worked to secure the resurgence of Hongan-ji.

Thus Rennyo's faith and thought were true to Shinran, but they did not have the same urgency. Shinran's solution to the desperate fight, trust in Amida's power alone, was Rennyo's starting point. The foundation of Rennyo's religious ideas was that trust was the very crux of experience. Though it lacked Shinran's vehemence and force, in another sense it had great power in its very simplicity.

During his life, Rennyo produced some 220 letters that selected and condensed Shinran's doctrines for easy understanding. Even today they are still read aloud in Jōdo Shin sect temples and in the homes of the sect's adherents.

One of the most popular reads: "Those of this last age, ignorant men and women leading lay lives, should single-mindedly place deep trust in Amida Buddha. Do not waver from side to side, but with a single and undivided mind turn toward him to rescue you. However many your evil deeds, Amida Tathagata will free you." It is indeed condensed: Trust wholeheartedly in Amida, and he will rescue you. That was all. This idea of the primacy of faith fills large numbers of Rennyo's pastoral letters. With their simple slogans and their strength of description, the letters were able to give peace to the minds of those who heard them.

How did Rennyo advance on people, his letters as his weapon? Clearsighted, he was in no doubt: "Above all there are three people whom we must convert. They are the priest, the elder, and the village head," he wrote. It is obvious enough that if a priest changed allegiance, the congregation would all follow. Attention to elders and village heads, on the other hand, was an example of Rennyo's shrewdness. These were the leaders of the emerging autonomous villages; their conversion would bring the whole community of peasants with them. For example, the pilgrim of the opening paragraphs of this chapter, Jirōsaburō of Katada, was both the priest of a congregation, and, as the elder of Katada, the representative of increasingly independent peasants. A large factor in Rennyo's success was his attention to village leaders, who had been ignored by the other sects, and the way he reached them was through simple but direct letters of condensed doctrine.

"Make the Civil Law Your Foundation"

The expansion of Hongan-ji and Rennyo's success were in great part due to the strength of the peasants. Rennyo himself said, "I lean upon our adherents." He had to adopt a popular, reformist stance. For example, he rejected the custom, prevalent throughout Hongan-ji's Ōtani period, of leaders sitting on a higher level. Instead, Rennyo made a point of sitting among the congregation and speaking convivially with them, serving them warm sake in cold weather and chilled sake when it was hot. In the country he would sip humble millet porridge with the adherents as he spoke of Buddhism late into the night. His ability to be one with the common people was developed perhaps less out of respect for Shinran's avowal of the equality of all before Amida than from the influence of the peasant congregations. Even Rennyo's reformism could be taken as a reflection of the activities of the peasants, who fought for their independence and formed leagues.

If such a spirit had been integral to his thought, had welled up of its own accord from within him, would he have been so circumspect about the uprisings of the Jōdo Shin sect leagues? The sect's adherents disregarded him, far away at the time, when in 1488 they defeated Togashi Masachika and took over the virtual administration of the province. Rennyo sent a number of reprimands to the participants, but these were little more than a general warning against excess. The firm and unmoving Hongan-ji was not endangered by the actions of the leagues. Though leagues rose virtually wherever Rennyo went, that is still not evidence of his reformist leanings.

There is a story that has been handed down about Rennyo. "Holy man Rennyo noticed that a crow had flown into the garden, and it remained there for a considerable time. 'There is a heron in the garden,' he exclaimed. After a while priest Hōkei said, 'It really is a heron.' Holy man Rennyo was very pleased."

Where in this picture of the strong-willed leader of Hongan-ji is the man with the common touch?

Besides stressing the centrality of faith, Rennyo urged the Jōdo Shin sect's adherents to respect civil law. "Make the civil law your foundation; put the rules of ordinary conduct before you, act according to the rules of the world, and keep the faith of our tradition deep in your hearts."

When peasants, their power growing to the bursting point, became sure that their rescue was assured in Amida and therefore feared nothing, Rennyo, being afraid for the Hongan-ji congregation's future, preached compromise with the laws of society. Just as populism and authoritarianism coexisted in Rennyo, so did the seemingly contradictory tenets of the primacy of faith and the primacy of civil law. What merged them was Rennyo's overriding concern for the progress and prosperity of Hongan-ji. If populism and the primacy of faith were the secrets of Hongan-ji's successful development, then authoritarianism and the primacy of civil law ensured that development.

Rennyo studied the *Notes Lamenting Deviations,* the most popular of all of the works of the Jōdo Shin sect. A postscript to his copy of it says: "These sacred teachings are of the utmost importance to our tradition. They should not be shown to those who are not disposed to seek enlightenment." Having copied the work in his youth, he feared that its bold doctrine and radical expression could be misinterpreted, so he decided that its circulation should be discouraged. No influence of the *Notes Lamenting Deviations* can be detected in Rennyo's doctrine, and until the Meiji era when the work was reevaluated, hardly any members of the Hongan-ji congregation are known to have read it.

Rennyo used his incredibly numerous children skillfully to consolidate Hongan-ji's position. He married five times and fathered twenty-seven children—thirteen boys and fourteen girls. These he placed strategically around the country to make a bulwark for Hongan-ji. His sons headed Honsen-ji, Shōkō-ji, Kōkyō-ji, and Gantoku-ji in Kaga Province, and Kenshō-ji, Kyōgyō-ji, Kōzen-ji, and others in the provinces surrounding Kyoto. His daughters married clergy of other powerful temples. By these means Hongan-ji exerted great authority around the country. In his role as a mighty paterfamilias, Rennyo united the Jōdo Shin sect congregations.

Rennyo was, above all others, the one who brought the feudal religious organization to completion. It is perhaps inevitable that he has been assessed as an organizer and a politician rather than a religious figure. His flexibility in coping with the world is worthy of attention, however. More than any other religion in Japan, the faith of the Jōdo Shin sect is a reliable ethical guide for living in the present. In the fifteenth century it was Rennyo who brought this out. There is every chance that a new Rennyo could arise in modern times.

Takuan
(1573–1645)

by Daisetsu Fujioka

Surpassing the Parent

Takuan was born the son of a samurai, Akiba Tsunanori, in Tajima Province. His birth year, 1573, was the year that signaled the demise of the Ashikaga shogunate in name as well as fact, for it was then that Oda Nobunaga ousted the last shogun from Kyoto. Nobunaga's appearance on the stage of history brought a step closer to conclusion the civil war that had lasted almost a hundred years. The year of Takuan's birth was thus, in a sense, the final curtain on the medieval period in Japan, and he was a man of the new era.

From the middle of the fourteenth century, Tajima had been under the control of the Yamana family of provincial military lords. In 1580, however, the Yamanas were defeated. As a Yamana retainer, Takuan's father fell into adversity, and it was perhaps for that reason that two years later Takuan, barely nine years old, was placed in nearby Shōnen-ji, a Jōdo temple, and given the ordination name of Shun'ō.

At thirteen the young Takuan left Shōnen-ji—why, we do not know—and became a student of Kisen Saidō at a Zen temple, Sukyō-ji, in the same locality. Sukyō-ji was a venerable establishment, founded by the Yamana family as their family temple and entrusted to a high-ranking priest of Tōfuku-ji. There Takuan undertook strict Zen training under Kisen until the death of the latter when Takuan was nineteen. Fortunately for the grief-stricken Takuan, the lord of Izushi Castle invited Tōho Sōchū of Daitoku-ji to succeed Kisen. Tōho was an apprentice of Shun'oku Sōen, the 112th head of Daitoku-ji, and later himself became the head of that temple. Takuan's exposure as a youth to the Zen of Daitoku-ji through Tōho was a decisive factor in his life.

When the Ashikaga shogunate fell, the great Five Mountains temples found themselves bereft of patronage and suffered a decline in fortunes. Rinzai leadership gradually fell under the control of Daitoku-ji and Myōshin-ji, plus others of the same lineage. Throughout the Muromachi period (1336–1573), that lineage had maintained the spirit of Daitoku-ji's founder Sōhō Myōchō (see biography in part 2), its priests refusing to fawn on those in power and maintaining a strict form of Zen practice. This had given them strong pride; such was the spirit of Daitoku-ji Zen that became lodged firmly in the breast of the idealistic young Takuan.

In 1594 Tōho returned to Kyoto. He took Takuan with him, entrusting the youth to his own master, Shun'oku, who was then in a Daitoku-ji subtemple, Sangen-an. There, in the temple on which all his thoughts had been centered, Takuan received the dharma name Sōhō. Though Takuan came under the tutelage of other clerics in Daitoku-ji subtemples, the man he considered master was Shun'oku, the foremost priest of Daitoku-ji, and so it was unfortunate that the two were not of like mind. The master, not one to be content to practice Zen in the quiet of the temple, was a politician who was close to powerful provincial lords. Moreover, like his Five Mountains predecessors, he lived luxuriously.

After Tōho died in 1601, Takuan left Shun'oku's tutelage without hesitation and went to Sakai, in Izumi Province. A dharma brother of Shun'oku, Ittō Shōteki, whose Zen was the exact opposite of Shun'oku's, was in residence at Yōshun-an there. Ittō Shōteki loathed fame and sought seclusion, training his apprentices with the utmost severity. It was ironical that such Zen was being taught in a temple founded by the priest that Ikkyū had derided as the most false of all the masters since the founding of Daitoku-ji. Takuan had heard of Ittō Shōteki's style of Zen practice during the time he was under instruction at Sangen-an and had resolved to train to his very limits under Ittō Shōteki. Nevertheless, when Takuan arrived he did not go immediately to Yōshun-an; rather he entered the school of a cleric-poet residing at Daian-ji. This he did perhaps out of regard for his previous master's feelings. In his three years at Daian-ji, Takuan made a deep study of both poetry and the Confucian classics, the seed, no doubt, of the poetry and Confucian-based treatises he composed in later years.

After the death of this teacher in 1603, Takuan, then thirty, joined Ittō Shōteki and spent a year in formal meditation practice under his guidance. In 1604 he achieved enlightenment, receiving the seal of transmission from his master and the name of Takuan. He was Ittō Shōteki's only dharma successor.

In 1606 Takuan again met his old master Shun'oku. Perhaps wanting to test the strength of his former pupil, that master threw out a koan. Takuan, though, was not the man of six years earlier. Under Ittō Shōteki he had achieved great enlightenment. Even points that had left him baffled at Daitoku-ji he explained resourcefully, using clear logic. "A clever tongue!" Shun'oku commented venomously, but he was taken aback at Takuan's progress. Ittō Shōteki, on his sickbed back at Yōshun-an, murmured happily, "He has truly surpassed his parent." Ittō Shōteki died there the same year, no doubt relieved at having found such a worthy successor. It was shortly afterward that Akiba Tsunanori also died. Almost simultaneously Takuan lost both religious and natural fathers.

In 1609, at the age of thirty-six, Takuan was proposed as next head of Daitoku-ji, and was invested by order of the emperor as the 154th head. At that time, appointment as chief priest of Daitoku-ji and Myōshin-ji alone, among Zen temples, was the prerogative of the imperial house. For a Zen cleric, the height of ambition surely had to be heading a sect's head temple. Three days later, though, Takuan resigned his office and returned to Nan-

shū-ji, where he had lived since 1606. On this occasion he wrote a
poem:

> I have always been a roving seeker,
> Traveling clouds and flowing water:
> Spring in the capital,
> Dwelling at the venerable Daitoku-ji.
> It is too much.
> Tomorrow I embark on the Southern Sea [to Nanshū-ji].
> As the white seagull does not fly
> Toward the red dust of the world's troubles,
> I will not remain in the capital.

In 1611, after Shun'oku's death at the age of eighty-two, Takuan returned to Daitoku-ji to take up residence in a subtemple,
Daisen-in. Though there is no doubt that his return was due to
the need to rebuild Daisen-in, there is at the same time every
reason to believe that Takuan judged the time ripe, now that
Shun'oku's influence was no longer there, to restore to Daitoku-ji
some of the Zen spirit it had lost.

From that time, Takuan came into closer contact with those in
power. With his former master gone, Takuan's voice evidently
began to be heard. Perhaps his most devoted lay followers were the
lord of Izushi Castle, Koide Yoshimasa, and his son Yoshihide. A
great many of Takuan's surviving letters are addressed to Yoshihide; they reveal a much closer friendship than merely the relationship between a Zen cleric and a patron.

That same year, Takuan undertook to compile a chronological
biography of Daitoku-ji's founder, Sōhō Myōchō. Ikkyū had
written:

> Raise up the great lamp [the founder],
> Let it brighten the heavens.
> The phoenix carriages compete with each other
> Before the dharma hall.
> Eating the wind, dwelling in water—

No one records
Twenty years near the Gojō Bridge.

Sōhō Myōchō had spent twenty years living as a beggar under the Gojō Bridge in Kyoto, neither ingratiating himself with the authorities nor parading himself before society; rather, he secluded himself in order to undertake harsh practice. During his labors, Takuan must have found that the traditional spirit of Daitoku-ji had become engraved anew on his mind.

Daitoku-ji Regulations

As part of its policy to organize the state into a single political system, the Tokugawa shogunate formulated a plan that regulated religion in a variety of ways, creating a feudal hierarchy within the Buddhist sects and bringing overall control of the sectarian organizations into its own hands. During the fifteen years between 1601, when the first of the ordinances was issued to temples of the Shingon sect on Mount Kōya, and 1616, when the regulations for the Nichiren headquarters on Mount Minobu, Kuon-ji, were handed down, the Buddhist sects found themselves increasingly under government control even down to the smallest details. The majority of the hundred or so ordinances for temples were drafted by Sūden (see biography in part 2), the priest of Konchi-in at Nanzen-ji, who in 1608 had succeeded Seishō Jōtai as diplomatic advisor to the shogun, Tokugawa Ieyasu. Together with Tenkai (see biography in part 2), Sūden was a power in the inner circles of the shogunate and was involved in everything from religious policy to diplomatic correspondence.

In 1615 Sūden drafted legislation aimed at the Five Mountains temples and at Myōshin-ji and Daitoku-ji. It is a matter of interest that different regulations should have been promulgated for temples of the same Rinzai Zen. The Five Mountains Regulations comprised seven clauses. Of note were the elevation of Nanzen-ji, in clause 4, and the abolition, in clause 7, of the office of registrar of clerics that had been traditionally held by a Shōkoku-ji sub-temple. Sūden argued that because Nanzen-ji had been founded at the wish of an emperor, it was worthy of greater respect than any other Zen temple. Its clerics, therefore, could not be chosen from non-Nanzen-ji lineages. Further, the office of registrar of clerics, nominally held by the Shōkoku-ji subtemple Rokuon-in and administered in fact from a Rokuon-in hermitage called Inryōken, was of no more use and was to be abolished. Control of the Five Mountains temples was thereafter to be conferred, with the title of registrar, on whichever high-ranking priest from the Five Mountains temples was the shogun's trusted advisor. Sūden had accomplished, through the regulations, the preeminence of his own Nanzen-ji and the slick transfer of the privileges pertaining to the registrar's office from the Inryōken to his Konchi-in.

The Daitoku-ji Regulations comprised five clauses. Clause 2 reads: "The chief priest must be someone who has completed thirty years of Zen training under an eminent master, who has mastered the 1,700 koans, who has traveled to all the high-ranking priests for instruction, who is capable of conducting both clerical and secular affairs, and whose name has been forwarded to the shogunate for approval." The enforcement of strict conditions for appointment of the chief priest, something that was not broached in the Five Mountains Regulations, was clearly the work of Sūden, intent on wresting from the emperor the privilege of appointing chief priests of Myōshin-ji and Daitoku-ji and placing those appointments under shogunate control. If the clause were to be faithfully observed, it would be virtually impossible to find anyone capable of meeting the requirements. The thirty-six-year-old Takuan would have been automatically excluded, as would anyone of his comparative youth. It was a great problem for the affected temples.

Takuan must have been highly critical of the stipulations, but at the time he was not at Daitoku-ji, but in Izumi Province supervising the rebuilding of Nanshū-ji, destroyed by fire during the fall of Osaka Castle in 1615. In 1620 he returned to his birthplace and built a small retreat nearby, called Tōenken, in an apparent attempt to flee the anguish Daitoku-ji was suffering as a result of Sūden's policy and the shogunate's encroaching authority. He identified with an exiled Chinese statesman and poet who in despair threw himself into a river. Takuan spent seven years at Tōenken, his forty-seventh to fifty-fourth years. During that time he devoted himself to reading and deepened his friendship with the lord of Izushi Castle, Koide Yoshihide. It was at this time also that he composed the *Distinction Between Faith and Reason*.

Nevertheless, Takuan had not entirely abandoned the world. He paid careful attention to what was happening at Daitoku-ji and so was astounded when he heard in 1626 that the shogunate had censured Daitoku-ji and Myōshin-ji for their neglect of the 1615 Regulations. Early the following year, he left for Daitoku-ji and there proposed to the emperor that the dharma heir of the current chief priest Gyokushitsu be installed as the new head of Daitoku-ji. Having achieved a lightning coup, Takuan proceeded nonchalantly to Nanshū-ji. A little while later a stern censure was issued by the Kyoto shogunal deputy: "The award of purple and yellow robes, and the bestowal of the title of *seidō* [all indicative of the ranking of prelates] within the Five Mountains temples by sources other than the shogun are valid only if they preceded the Genna era [before the Regulations of 1615]." This came as a bitter blow to both Daitoku-ji and Myōshin-ji, which had continued to have their heads confirmed in office by imperial rescript even after the 1615 Regulations. As a result, purple-robe-level appointments after that time were not valid.

The Daitoku-ji subtemples were divided into two groups: the southern, centering on the subtemple Ryōgen-in, and the northern, centering on Daisen-in, to which Takuan had automatically succeeded as chief priest when he became the head of Daitoku-ji. Each group took a different stance toward the shogunate's action; the southern looked toward compromise, but the northern favored opposition. Takuan reconciled the divergent views and submitted a protest letter to the shogunate.

The letter was written in 1628 by Takuan himself, cosigned by Gyokushitsu and another, and forwarded to the shogunate in Edo through the Kyoto shogunal deputy. It was a long, point-by-point rebuttal of the Daitoku-ji Regulations of 1615, written in the informal mixed style using both Chinese characters and Japanese phonetic symbols rather than in pure, official Chinese. It naturally centered on the second clause.

The expressions "thirty years of Zen training" and "mastered the 1,700 koans," were, Takuan said, phrases used by Tokugawa Ieyasu to indicate practice in general and to intimate his desire that candidates should have undergone a strict Zen regimen. If that were not the case, then the instigator of the Regulations (i.e., Sūden) was ignorant of Zen.

A hatred of Sūden lies hidden beneath the moderation of the language. Takuan went on systematically pointing out the irrationality of the Regulations.

The expression "1,700 koans" refers, he explained, not to a specific number of koans but to the number of biographies of Zen masters given in the *Ching-te Record of the Transmission of the Lamp,* a Chinese work of 1004. It is therefore strange to assign thirty years to mastering them. For example, the founder of Daitoku-ji mastered 180, and the second head, Tettō Gikō, mastered 88. Both achieved great enlightenment.

Similarly, thirty years' training was unrealistic. A cleric who began Zen practice at fifteen or sixteen, and trained under a master for thirty years, would need at least a further five before being appointed chief priest. Further, if it was accepted that thirty years was the term necessary to train a student cleric, the master's life would end before it was possible to transmit the dharma, and where would Buddhism be then? There was no precedent of a master practicing for thirty years. Eisai (see biography in part 1) practiced for five years, Enni Bennen for seven, Guchū Shūkyū for six, Nampo Jōmyō for seven, Muhon Kakushin for six, and Musō Soseki (see biography in part 2) achieved great enlightenment at the age of thirty-one. Thus there was no need to spend thirty years, for there were a good many instances of young enlightened masters.

Takuan's letter drew the ire of the shogunate. Sūden noted in his diary, "It is absolutely against the will" of the shogunate. Early in 1629, the shogunate ordered the three signatories to Edo to answer for their action. The very priests who created the Regulations were among the shogunate officers who had to judge the case. Sūden demanded severe punishment, whereas his fellow advisor, Tenkai, pleaded for a lighter sentence. In the end, Takuan was sentenced to exile in Dewa Province, placed in the charge of one official, and Gyokushitsu was sentenced to exile in Mutsu Province, under the supervision of another official. All who had received appointments after 1615 without shogunate approval were deprived of their rank. Only one of the letter's signers was allowed to return to Kyoto; his crime was not thought serious enough to deserve punishment. At the same time, two Myōshin-ji clerics were also exiled. The charge against Takuan read: "In previous times, when Lord Ieyasu was considering Daitoku-ji Regulations, he invited three senior clerics . . . to visit him and give their opinions. For some months careful inquiry was made, and only then was the final decision taken. Considering that Takuan was not even at Daitoku-ji at that time, his coming forth now to violate and refute the Regulations amounts to neglect of the government, and in his arbitrarily putting forward his own views, there is something truly disgraceful." Emperor Go-Mizunoo abdicated as a result of the incident.

Exile

Takuan and his companions were sentenced to exile in the autumn of 1629. Takuan traveled with Gyokushitsu at first, but their ways parted on the fourth morning, in Shimotsuke Province. The two promised to meet again, should the transience of life allow, exchanged parting cups, and composed poems. Takuan arrived at his designated location and reported on his state of mind in a letter:

> Recently I spoke my mind on clerical matters, and because I have differed with the shogunate on them, I have been exiled to Dewa Province. This is a matter that will be discussed for two or three generations. I will be content if the fame [of the affair] lasts until the next life. As long as the mind is not clouded by illu-

sion, the sufferings of the body are of no import. To seek
physical ease through polluted actions is not what I should wish.

He may have felt that the authorities had punished him un-
fairly, and we can sense that he tried to rid himself of an insidious
feeling of unease by trying to convince himself of his own rec-
titude.

His life in exile was quite different from what he had contemplated, and he spent his days pleasurably rather than in the
misery he had expected. This was because of the extreme cordiality of the official responsible for him. Takuan describes life in exile
vividly in a New Year's letter sent to his brother in 1630:

> I have been given a house with a six-mat living room, a connect-
> ing room, a storeroom of three mats, and a servant's room.
> There is a double wall around the outside corridor to protect me
> from the cold. The bath and toilet are also built so as to be pro-
> tected from the wind. A large deerskin is spread under my sleep-
> ing place, so that I do not get chilled from below. All of this is
> through the consideration of the lord. I receive all the food I
> need. I was sent a quilted silk garment from Edo. The lord's
> wife also sent me a warm sleeveless jacket. When the lord is
> away on official business in Edo, he charges his retainers strictly
> to attend to my needs. All of them, from the senior counselors
> down, show as much concern for me as if I were the lord's grand-
> father.

The reality of his three years of exile, during which he was by no
means restricted in his activity, did not bear out the bitterness of
the verse he wrote on his arrival.

> Though, innocent, I have been sent into exile,
> I still see the moon
> From among the pines of Akoya.

In 1632 Takuan received a pardon and traveled to Edo. He
wrote a satirical verse at that time:

If it is the official will, Takuan will go;
Yet Musashi is squalid, Edo despicable.

The pardon had come as part of the general amnesty that followed the death of the shogun. Tenkai's efforts on Takuan's behalf no doubt also contributed to his release. It was not until 1634, though, that Takuan and his companion were allowed to return to Kyoto, six years after they had left. He had been back there only a brief time, enjoying again the life of a Zen cleric, when he had to return to Edo, obeying an urgent summons from the new shogun, Tokugawa Iemitsu.

Performing Priest

Iemitsu's invitation to Takuan stemmed from his need to find a new advisor on religious matters; Sūden had died and Tenkai was an old man. "It was the shogun's will to have someone to discuss temple administration and to act as an advisor," Takuan wrote, leaving no doubt that Iemitsu wanted a counselor regarding the shogunate's handling of temples. It was Yagyū Munenori who had been instrumental in securing Takuan's invitation to Edo. Yagyū, Iemitsu's swordsmanship master, declared that he had been brought to an understanding of the deepest secrets of swordsmanship through Takuan's Zen teaching. It is thought that their friendship began in the three years that Takuan spent in Edo after his release from exile in the north. Takuan wrote for Yagyū the famous *Miraculous Record of Immovable Wisdom*.

Iemitsu's attitude toward and treatment of Takuan were extraordinary by the standards of the day. Takuan vividly relates details of his life in letters to friends. A good description is in a letter written in 1637:

Once I was invited to a Noh play in the second ward of the castle, to which not even senior counselors had been invited. When the play ended I was invited to see some dancing. Then the senior counselor, Matsudaira Nobutsuna, came up at Iemitsu's request to invite me to pay respects at Tōshōgū Shrine, between the main and second wards, in the interval between Kyōgen performances. I was guided there by Nobutsuna. In the evening I was invited into the inner quarters and stayed there until ten in the evening talking alone with the shogun about all sorts of things. I sat talking, to one side of the charcoal brazier on the raised dais, not two feet from the shogun's knee! In such close proximity I sat for more than two hours; there was no one besides ourselves. When I returned to the Yagyū residence at around ten o'clock, my escort was Nakane Heijūrō. I could not have been better treated if I had been the lord of a province.

Iemitsu's favor increased as the years went by. In 1638 he announced that he would have a temple, called Tōkai-ji, built for Takuan. Iemitsu wanted to build something on the scale of Sūden's Edo residence. Takuan, fearing that he would find himself bound to Edo, firmly and repeatedly declined, but in the end was persuaded that it would be better to stay for the sake of Daitoku-ji and the dharma. For Takuan, though, the more support he received from the shogun and other high-ranking lords, the more pain he felt. His situation seemed all too far removed from the ideal of a Daitoku-ji cleric—the founder and his life as a beggar under the Gojō Bridge in Kyoto, or Tettō Gikō as he is revealed in his lecture to fame-seeking students. It seemed the ultimate irony that Takuan, a man who disliked fame and deplored the idea of flattering those in power, should be following the same road as the crafty Sūden, his opponent and predecessor. Even if he considered all he was doing was for Daitoku-ji in trying to restore its imperial privileges, it did little to help ease his affliction. "I am like a performing monkey pulled around at the end of a string," he lamented in a letter. How full of joy Takuan must thus have been when, in 1641, his claims were granted in their entirety. It is said that Iemitsu commented, "Takuan should be satisfied, for the order has been as he would wish." Takuan would have felt no dissatisfaction at all. The Daitoku-ji Regulations were a burden he had carried around with him for twenty-six years.

Takuan's life of seventy-two years closed at Tōkai-ji in Edo near the end of 1645. When he was on his deathbed, his apprentices pressed him for some last words. He took up his writing-brush and wrote the character for ''dream.'' He then threw down the brush and died. He had assimilated the fame-rejecting Zen of Daitoku-ji under Ittō Shōteki, and therefore the last part of his life, necessarily spent in close attendance on the shogun, would have seemed no more than a dream.

Takuan was not involved in politics to anywhere near the same extent as Sūden. The time for active involvement in setting up the new government was already past. Takuan's role was rather one of advisor to Iemitsu about the refinements of life.

Ryōkan
(1758–1831)

by Aishin Imaeda

Although at first glance these two poems by Ryōkan may seem rather ordinary, on closer acquaintance they reveal an infinite resonance:

> Hand in hand with the children,
> Picking young herbs in the spring fields:
> Could I be any happier?

> In my grass hut it is pleasant
> To stretch out my legs
> And hear the summer frogs
> Croaking in the hillside fields.

Put simply, Ryōkan was a man of love. He loved everyone equally. He gave the clothes off his back to a beggar who came to his hut. So that a thief could take his bedding from him, he rolled over, pretending to be asleep. If he had rice he joyfully gave some to birds or wild animals. He placed lice inside his robes, and left a leg outside his mosquito net so that the mosquitoes could drink his blood. He had boundless love for all living beings and all of nature.

Headman's Son

There are numerous anecdotes about Ryōkan and his eccentricities. But what has drawn people to him, now as in the past, has had nothing to do with behavior that might appear strange. However eccentric he was, he would not have been loved and respected so widely, now as in the past, but would have been forgotten as just another wandering priest.

Surprisingly few people realize that Ryōkan was a venerable Sōtō sect Zen priest. During the Edo period (1603–1868), there had already been a number of priests of that sect who spent their lives roaming the countryside as mendicants, never rising to a higher status, certainly never becoming heads of temples. Nevertheless they were widely praised by the common people for their learning and character; they left behind a heritage that continues to extend its influence today. Such people (like Tōsui, biography in part 2) were termed "wandering sages," the most typical of whom is without doubt Ryōkan. Because most of them tried to rid themselves completely of any egocentricity, spent their lives wandering, and tried not to talk of themselves, very little is known of them.

Ryōkan was born, possibly in December 1758, at Izumozaki in Echigo Province, long famous as a port of departure for the island of Sado and visited by many literary figures and artists. He was the eldest son of the town headman, Yamamoto Iori. Both of his parents had been adopted into the Yamamoto family. Iori was a skillful poet, known by his pen name Tachibana Inan, in the tradition of the great haiku poet Matsuo Bashō. His accomplishments apparently did not stretch to administration, however, and the family sank further and further into decline.

Ryōkan was called Eizō as a boy. From around the age of twelve he studied the Chinese classics under a Confucian scholar. After coming of age at fifteen, he began training to succeed his father as headman. Of an inherently religious predisposition, however, he could not warm to a job that required a certain worldly skill. At eighteen he entered the Sōtō sect temple of Kōshō-ji in a neighboring town and, on being ordained by its chief priest, was given the name Daigu Ryōkan. The need he had felt from childhood to seek enlightenment had directed him to the task of saving the world and benefiting others.

Apprentice to Kokusen

When he was twenty-one Ryōkan met Tainin Kokusen, a famous Sōtō priest then on a lecture tour of the area. Ryōkan accompanied him back to his temple, Entsū-ji, in Bitchū Province, some 650 kilometers from Izumozaki. There he became Kokusen's apprentice and practiced Zen under him. He must have been strongly attracted by the reformist zeal then sweeping Sōtō sect Zen and by the venerable personality of his master.

Ryōkan's motive for becoming a priest is puzzling, inasmuch as he grew up the privileged heir of a town headman. We can only conjecture. For a start, many of his brothers and sisters were interested in religion. Enchō, a younger brother, became a Shingon priest; a sister, Murako, became a cleric in a Lotus sect temple in her later years; another sister, Mikako, married the chief priest of a Jōdo Shin sect temple and later became a cleric with the name Myōgenni; and even his brother Yoshiyuki, who succeeded as headman in Ryōkan's place, later shaved his head and lived a secluded life. With such strong links to Buddhism, Ryōkan would seem to have been reared in a Buddhist atmosphere. The family fortunes were in decline, and disease and famine were rampant in the land; administering a poor, remote fishing community may have been too much for this vulnerable, sensitive youth.

Despairing of the transiency of the secular world, Ryōkan might have acutely felt that the only way open to him was the aspiration for enlightenment. For his own freedom and to free all sentient beings, he therefore chose the path of the homeless seeker of enlightenment.

Chinese clerics, including Ingen (see biography in part 2), introduced Ming-period Zen to Sōtō sect clerics around the middle of the seventeenth century. Their stimulus encouraged Gesshū Shūko, a Sōtō priest in Kaga Province, to take up the cry for reform in the sect. Enthusiasm for reform spread, and many Sōtō priests began seriously advocating a revival of Dōgen's Zen. It was at this time that intensive studies of the *Eye Treasury of the Right Dharma* began. In one generation, Gesshū's lineage became well known for the severity of its Zen training. Ryōkan's master, Kokusen, was the main apprentice of Kōgai Zenkoku, called "Demon Zenkoku," a master of that lineage. Ryōkan learned from Kokusen a pure, uncompromising style of Zen and spent more than ten years in strict training under him.

There were besides Ryōkan a large number of outstanding apprentices from all over the country studying with the famous master. One, called Senkei, silently went about his sole task of growing vegetables, involved neither in zazen nor in sutra chanting. Ryōkan was deeply impressed by Senkei's demeanor and looked on him as a model of living Zen. A poem he wrote in later years is a sample of his praise of Senkei, who must have substantially influenced him:

Ah, now I regret that I could not follow his example:
The priest Senkei is a seeker after the truth.

At Entsū-ji under the tutelage of Kokusen, Ryōkan thoroughly absorbed the essence of Dōgen's Zen in a religious atmosphere that reflected the sect's reformist zeal of later years. He revered Dōgen especially, regularly reading the *Record of Dōgen's Public Sayings* and having as his constant guide the section of the *Eye Treasury of the Right Dharma* called "Affectionate Words." It was also through his training under Kokusen that he discovered original, authentic Buddhist training, the practice of the wandering mendicants of the Buddha's time. Dōgen had advocated a return to the Buddhism of Shakyamuni, saying a cleric should go out during the day to beg alms and sit quietly in a grassy hut under a cliff at night doing zazen.

It was also at Entsū-ji that Ryōkan realized that to save others he must further his own religious training. He was severely critical of the growing number of Buddhist clerics who feigned enlightenment, boasted of their intelligence and learning, and greedily

snatched the donations of the simple country folk they deluded, all
the time making no attempt whatever to reflect on themselves.
Though Ryōkan did not like to criticize others, he was unable to
stomach the corruption and hypocrisy of temple Buddhism. In this
he was akin to Ikkyū when the latter left Daitoku-ji and refused to
cooperate with the authorities.

Ryōkan's independence of mind made him chafe at the bonds of
temple life, with all the restrictions of organization and hierarchy.
Thus he was strongly drawn to the kind of religious training taught
by Shakyamuni, which he had learned of through the Zen of
Dōgen explained to him by Kokusen and others. Ryōkan therefore
shifted his attention to the religious life that Dōgen had spoken of,
wanting to emulate Shakyamuni and return to the spirit of his
teachings. In this sense he inherited the basic concepts that Dōgen
himself formulated late in life. Perhaps this is why the Meiji era
Buddhist scholar Hara Tanzan (see biography in part 2) called
Ryōkan the greatest master after Dōgen.

Wandering Mendicant

Eventually Ryōkan set out on a journey to refine his practice,
visiting famous masters at Zen establishments around the country.
Because he never posed as a learned priest, these establishments apparently did not record his visits. He seems to have made his way
around either the Inland Sea region of Honshu or the island of
Shikoku.

While Ryōkan was undergoing the hardships of ritual wandering, in 1792 his father had gone to Kyoto where he had contacts
with imperial loyalists. He deplored the decline of the imperial
court, and in 1795, soon after writing *A Record of Heavenly Truth,* in
a fury of indignation he committed suicide by throwing himself
into the Katsura River, in the western part of Kyoto. Hearing
what had happened, Ryōkan set out for the city. After holding a
memorial service there for his father, he went to Mount Kōya to
further memorialize him.

That same year, the thirty-seven-year-old Ryōkan unexpectedly
returned to Echigo Province after an absence of seventeen years.

He may have felt nostalgia for his native landscape. For several years after his return, he lived near his birthplace, Izumozaki, moving from place to place in his continuing life of homeless wandering. He lived for a time on Mount Kugami and later at Hongaku-in and Mitsuzō-in temples. It is believed that he also traveled to Edo and Dewa Province during this period.

In 1804 he finally settled permanently at Gogō-an, a hermitage halfway up Mount Kugami. Then forty-six, Ryōkan was to remain there for twelve years. As the sun began to set he would return to his cottage and sit alone by the hearth. On rainy days he remained inside all day. He wrote Japanese and Chinese poetry, quietly discovering a way of life that suited him. The time at Gogō-an seems to have been the most satisfying of his life. He wrote:

> Mossy water,
> Telling of rocks and crevices
> In the mountain's shadow;
> Quietly, I too
> Grow transparent.

Enlightenment and Love

Ryōkan lived by begging and was untempted by worldly things. He loved nature and playing with the village children.

> Playing ball with the children
> Here in the village
> All through the spring day:
> How I wish
> It would never end!

He was completely indifferent to public criticism. He was great friends with a girl called Oyoshi, a maid in someone's house, and played marbles with a prostitute in Izumozaki. To him there was neither beauty nor ugliness, good nor evil, truth nor falsehood, delusion nor enlightenment, for he looked on everything without discrimination. Ryōkan had the serenity of nature itself, in his boundless love and thoroughgoing compassion. The nobility and richness of his character were the outcome of long, strict Zen practice that had cleared away the vines and creepers encircling his mind. This is the secret of the lasting affection in which Ryōkan has been held by all.

Ryōkan had only the bare necessities, for he had gone beyond all temptations of fame and fortune. He had no pretensions, treating all he met as equals. Even when he was drinking with visitors, his purity and lucidity were apparent to all present. Those who met him felt absolved and purified through his selflessness.

Though Ryōkan was a priest, he never preached or explained sutras. When he talked with friends or played with children, his pleasant smile impressed them with his goodness. This in itself was the true power of his Zen, something that cannot be found in Zen today, when many seek after appearance or fame.

A man who as a child met Ryōkan has described him for us:

The master [Ryōkan] stayed two nights at our house. He filled the house with harmony. Several days after his departure, people still felt the atmosphere of harmony. When we talked about the master, we felt that our hearts were purified. The master never spoke of the scriptures, nor did he ever urge others to do good. At our house he sometimes gathered firewood for the kitchen and sometimes did zazen in the tatami room. When he talked, he never quoted poetry or other literature, nor did he propound moral principles. He lived quietly, beyond description. One might be made virtuous just by meeting him.

Again, writing of his appearance:

The master was in exuberant spirits. He looked like a Taoist recluse. He was tall and very thin, with a high-bridged nose and long-slitted eyes. He was gentle but strict, and there was no odor of incense about him. . . . The master was even-tempered, showing neither joy nor anger. He was not hurried or confused in his talk, and his needs for sustenance were so limited as to seem ridiculous.

Around 1816, after more than a decade spent in seasoned simplicity, Ryōkan left Gogō-an and went to live in a cottage at Otogo Shrine at the foot of Mount Kugami. Some difficulty must have brought on the move. In 1827, in the winter of his sixty-ninth year, he could no longer support himself and was invited by a follower named Kimura Motoemon, a rich farmer of Shimazaki, to move into a dwelling on his estate.

It was about that time that the cleric Teishinni started visiting Ryōkan. The young woman was an apprentice in a Sōtō sect temple. She was attracted by Ryōkan's noble character, and after their first meeting they continued to meet occasionally and exchange poems, of which she later made an anthology entitled *Dewdrops on a Lotus Leaf*. One reads:

> You who I have long been waiting for
> Have come.
> Now that we are together
> What else could I want?

The old Ryōkan was delighted and cheered by her visits. She and Kimura Motoemon were with him when he died at the beginning of 1831, at the age of seventy-three. He was buried at Ryūsen-ji in the Kimura family plot.

Poetry and Calligraphy

Ryōkan fully expressed the purity and nobility of his character in poetry and calligraphy, which survive. He was a fine poet in both Japanese (*waka* poems) and Chinese, and a great calligrapher. At villagers' requests he wrote poetry that was unconventional and full of love.

As a poet and calligrapher, Ryōkan was not entirely self-taught. As with philosophy and Zen practice, he mastered the fundamentals of the classics, adopting only what suited him. He never ceased to study the classics and derive inspiration from them.

For example, he studied the work of famous Chinese calligraphers and representative Japanese calligraphy of the mid-Heian period. He had absolutely no connection with any school of calligraphy, however, and developed his style by himself. It has none of the usual pretensions of Zen clerics, but is completely original in its trimness, freshness, calm, and naturalness. The occasional mistakes reflect his nonchalance.

His poems are quite different from the kinds that were then in vogue. Instead he looked to earlier styles, of *The Anthology of Ten Thousand Leaves* and other early Japanese literature, the *waka* of Saigyō, and Dōgen's *Songs of the Way*. In Chinese poetry, he particularly admired the simple, natural styles of T'ao Yüan-ming and Han-shan, from which he learned much. He had no affiliation with any poetic school of his time. His is not the poetry of a professional but that of an amateur and outsider. This in itself is typical of Ryōkan: his joy and sadness, his pain and sorrow are conveyed without artifice, and indeed, so fresh is his writing that it draws us in a mysterious way. For example, when he quotes from *The Anthology of Ten Thousand Leaves* or from Dōgen, there is no sense of borrowing. Here appears Ryōkan's natural greatness as a poet; he broke new ground in Chinese and Japanese poetry. His art is founded on the perspective he attained through strict practice as a Zen priest and on his own incomparable humanity.

In conclusion, let us look at a poem that records one aspect of Ryōkan's feelings about life:

> All day long, from village to village,
> I have gone about, begging for food.
> The sun has set and the mountain path is long.
> The strong wind tears at my beard.
> My robes are like wisps of smoke.
> My wooden bowl is old and deformed.
> I do not grudge my lot, though cold and hungry,
> For many have gone this way before me.

Gesshō

(1813–1858)

by Yūsen Kashiwahara

Closing Years of the Shogunate

Gesshō was one of the Buddhist clerics who involved themselves actively in national affairs as imperial loyalists during the final years of the Tokugawa shogunate. To understand Gesshō, it is first necessary to understand the historical background of his times.

With the failure of the Tempō reform program (from 1841 to 1843), the shogunate entered its final decline. In 1853 American warships under Commodore Matthew Calbraith Perry and a Russian squadron under Vice Admiral Evfimii Vasil'evich Putyatin brought ultimatums to the Japanese government to open relations with the outside world. All the efforts of the shogunate immediately focused on how to deal with the problem. In 1854 treaties were concluded with the United States, Great Britain, and Russia, and in 1858, with the appointment of Ii Naosuke to the position of senior shogunal advisor, comprehensive commercial treaties were signed with those countries and with France and the Netherlands, bringing to an end the long period of national isolation.

Around the same time the shogunate found itself faced with another, internal issue, the selection of a successor to the ailing shogun. Two camps confronted each other: the majority of the

194

hereditary Tokugawa vassals backed the lord of the Kii domain, Tokugawa Iemochi, in opposition to the powerful lords of large domains in Echizen, Tosa, and Satsuma provinces, who supported the claims of Hitotsubashi Yoshinobu of the Mito domain in Hitachi Province. With his appointment as shogunal advisor, Ii Naosuke worked to have Iemochi raised to the position of shogun and, in so doing, attempted to strengthen autocratic government centered on the shogunate.

The Mito domain and the great lords who were supporters of Yoshinobu opposed Ii's policies on both the treaties with foreign powers and the succession issue. They accused him of signing the Harris Treaty (1858) without imperial approval and urged him to conduct government affairs in cooperation with the court, thereby advocating a process that became known as "the union of court and shogunate." Imperial loyalists from various domains aligned with court nobles to oppose the shogunate, under the slogan "Honor the emperor and expel the barbarians." Ii, determined to put an end to the opposition, punished the lords of Mito, Tosa, and Echizen and various members of the Kyoto court, including the minister of the left Konoe Tadahiro, the former imperial regent Takatsukasa Masamichi, and the imperial prince Shōren-in-no-miya Son'yū, and ordered the execution of samurai activists (known as "men of determination"). These executions were part of the Ansei Purge, in which more than a hundred people were put to death or imprisoned.

Ii Naosuke, the instigator, was assassinated outside the Sakurada gate of Edo Castle in 1860 by samurai from Mito. Following his death, the shogunate sought reconciliation with the court by proposing a marriage between Princess Kazu, sister of Emperor Kōmei, and the shogun. This proposal was favored even by the domains that had previously opposed the shogunate. Activists, however, continued to criticize the shogunate and, joining with disaffected courtiers, made "Honor the emperor and expel the barbarians" their rallying cry for the restoration of imperial rule. The "expulsion of barbarians" took a serious turn in 1862 when an Englishman was murdered by Satsuma extremists in a village near Edo, and in 1863 the Chōshū troops fired on French ships off their coast. Foreign retaliation was swift. British warships bombarded Kagoshima, the capital of the Satsuma domain, and a combined Western flotilla attacked Shimonoseki, the port that fired on the French. The offending domains had to desist in the face of superior power.

Having seen the futility of their campaign of "expulsion of the barbarians," opponents to opening the nation had to pull back, and thereafter the main strength lay with people who proposed opening the country while maintaining loyalty to the emperor. In 1866, one such leader, Kido Takayoshi, negotiated a secret military pact between the Satsuma and Chōshū domains. The following year anti-shogunate nobles and a number of domains set into motion events that would oust the shogunate. Backed by the powerful domains, they declared an imperial restoration; the governing apparatus of the shogunate was dismembered, bringing to an end nearly three hundred years of feudal rule.

To understand the character of the imperialist movement in which Gesshō was involved, one should be familiar with the substance of the argument for revering the emperor. As already stated, imperial loyalism shifted from national exclusion to opening the country, but there were two elements that remained constant. First, as one can surmise from the movement to unite the court and the shogunate, imperial loyalty did not automatically mean a negation of feudal rule. Consequently the imperialist movement, though it developed into an anti-shogunate movement, saw the emperor as sovereign in place of the shogun but otherwise looked to absolutist rule through feudal authority over a united country. Second, despite the change from an exclusionist to an open stance regarding foreign relations, deep down there remained the consciousness that foreigners were ultimately to be rejected. An essay of that period, *Speaking Quietly to a Friend,* says, "Expelling the barbarians requires that for now we have close ties with them." In league with foreigners, Japan could become strong; in other words, through friendship with the barbarians, Japan could advance economically and militarily, so that it would eventually be in a position to defend itself. Different in form, but the same in content, the idea of expelling the barbarians was basic.

Gesshō sympathized with the imperial loyalist movement from a Buddhist stance. Of course there were many other Buddhists at this time who similarly supported the imperialist movement. Gesshō, however, is probably the most widely known of the loyalist clerics, through the breadth of his involvement and his tragic end.

Gesshō the Man

Gesshō was born in 1813 in Osaka, the son of a physician. In 1827 he entered Jōju-in, the main Kiyomizu-dera subtemple in the Higashiyama district of Kyoto, where his uncle was the chief priest. Upon ordination he was given the name of Ningai. In 1835 his uncle and master died, and at the age of twenty-two Gesshō became chief priest of Kiyomizu-dera.

He had never been physically strong. Nevertheless he strove hard with his Buddhist training and worked to cultivate himself. Kiyomizu-dera had six subtemples, however, and disputes among them were far from uncommon. The reconstruction of the temple as a whole also fell on his shoulders. He sometimes went into Kyoto or visited the court nobles, seeking donations for the reconstruction work. In 1840 he allowed the temple's main image to be put on public display and averted bankruptcy with the offerings he thus received. For Buddhist training, he undertook special sessions of twenty-one and fifty days and made regular pilgrimages to Tō-ji and Kitano Temmangū Shrine. In this he was motivated by Kiyomizu-dera's origin as a place of rituals and petitions for the nobility and provincial lords. As a cleric he felt he should practice to acquire special powers. He was not, though, a practitioner who sought material benefits from his practice but one who kept the precepts very strictly indeed and governed himself with rigid discipline.

Fundamental to Gesshō's ideas about the importance of the precepts were the Ten Good Precepts, which prohibit the taking of life, stealing, adultery, lying, equivocation, slander, flattery, greed, anger, and wrong views. These are the most basic of the Buddhist precepts and were popularized during the Edo period (1603–1868) by Jiun (see biography in part 2) through his collection of essays called *The Way to Become a [Real] Person*. The Ten Good Precepts formed in Jiun's terms the "Vinaya of the True Dharma," the fundamental precepts that anyone, priest or lay person, could keep and that represented the basic attitude of one who had accepted the teachings of Shakyamuni. Gesshō devoted himself to keeping the Ten Good Precepts and regarded a moral life as meritorious. He composed a poem on each of the Ten Good Precepts. The fourth is on honesty:

> Better than living by falsehood,
> That I disappear cleanly
> Like the morning dew.

It clearly reflects the attitude of a man who was strict with himself.

Gesshō had a broad range of interests. As we have seen already, one was writing poetry in the form of thirty-one syllable *waka*. He left behind two verse-diaries. He was also skilled at painting, and many of his pictures survive, mainly careful studies on Buddhist themes. He made ceramics, and was proficient in seal carving. All in all, he was a sensitive man of culture.

For a serious Buddhist seeker like Gesshō, the responsibilities of being head of Kiyomizu-dera were all too troublesome. He often left the temple and secluded himself. In August 1853 he left without telling anyone and traveled until April 1854, from northwest Honshu to Shinano Province, and thence via the trunk route to Mount Kōya. It was then that he took the name Gesshō (Moon Illumination). One of the fifteen poems he wrote at the time of a full moon in the summer of 1854 reads:

> Though invited,
> Not going out into the world:
> The clear flowing mountain stream,
> The bright moon.

The high, lonely moon was his ideal. While away from Kiyomizu-dera, he continued to move among temples in the suburbs of Kyoto, living as a recluse. Finally he passed the position of Kiyomizu-dera chief priest to his younger brother, Shinkai, in March 1854, retiring at the age of forty-one. Shinkai, ordained at Kiyomizu-dera two years after Gesshō, was also a disciple of his uncle and is also known as an imperial loyalist cleric. Soon, though, Gesshō found himself drawn into the turmoil of national affairs despite his wish for a secluded life.

Political Involvement

From the autumn of 1854, Gesshō, as a writer of *waka*, frequently attended poetry readings at the house of Konoe Tadahiro. The Konoes were powerful patrons of Kiyomizu-dera, their family temple. Because Konoe Tadahiro was involved in the imperialist movement, advocating the expulsion of foreigners and the union of court and shogunate, Gesshō, through the poetry meetings, found himself becoming more and more deeply involved, and he willingly joined Konoe's movement. He very soon had connections with the leading court and samurai figures among the imperialists. First and foremost was the imperial prince Shōren-in-no-miya Son'yū. The prince had formerly lived at Ichijō-in in Nara, which supervised Jōju-in; the two therefore already knew of each other through their temples. After Son'yū moved to Shōren-in and became one of the central figures of the loyalist movement, their relationship deepened. Gesshō also associated with Takatsukasa Masamichi, who had been open-minded about the presence of foreigners but came to advocate their expulsion, thus becoming a sympathizer of Konoe Tadahiro and others. It is said that this change of mind was due to the persuasion of a family retainer who, incidentally, was also a powerful supporter of Jōju-in, being concerned with its financial affairs.

Eventually Gesshō's involvement in the pro-imperialist movement led him to meet famous samurai supporters as well. Of all the samurai supporters of the movement, Gesshō was closest to those from Satsuma. This had its origins in the fact that the lord of the Satsuma domain, too, was a strong supporter of Jōju-in. When that lord passed through Kyoto before or after a period of required residence in Edo, the head of Jōju-in always paid a formal visit to the lord's mansion in Kyoto. Gesshō was therefore eminently suitable as an intermediary between the Satsuma and Mito domain lords and the Kyoto nobility in matters such as the proposal of Yoshinobu as shogun, expulsion of foreigners, and moves to unite the court and shogunate. The lord of Mito also supported Jōju-in. Gesshō came into close contact with a number of high-ranking Satsuma retainers, and his closest political associate was Saigō Takamori, perhaps the most prominent of the Satsuma activists.

Despite his responsibilities to his temple, Gesshō could not stand idly by in the face of a foreign threat. He had performed rituals and petitions three times seeking for disaster to befall the foreign ships. The first American ship had appeared in 1846; British ships had followed in 1849. At that time the court had ordered rituals and petitions to stop their advance, and Kiyomizu-dera had been one of the temples that carried out the order. Russian ships appeared in 1852, and in the following year, as we have seen, came the American and Russian demands that Japan open itself to foreign intercourse. In February 1854, Kiyomizu-dera again participated in rituals and petitions to protect the nation from the foreign ships. Foreign intercourse grew all the greater following the signing of the commercial treaties in 1854, culminating on December 7, 1857, with the shogun's reception at Edo Castle of Townsend Harris, the first American consul. The court again ordered expulsion rituals and petitions to be conducted in early 1858 at seven temples and seven Shinto shrines. Kiyomizu-dera conducted a seven-day ritual for the purpose of expelling the "evil foreign influence." Gesshō, then, both officially and privately, was unavoidably drawn into the movement to expel the foreigners.

Gesshō came into frequent contact with Saigō during 1858, when key issues were the shogunal accession question and problems related to opening the country. Early that year, Gesshō and Saigō were closely involved in the attempt to have Hitotsubashi Yoshinobu declared the next shogun. Saigō had passed a letter

from Tokugawa Nariaki, the lord of the Mito domain and Yoshinobu's father, addressed to Takatsukasa Masamichi, into the
hands of the ailing shogun's wife. This letter sought the backing of
the Kyoto nobility for Yoshinobu's appointment. Further, Saigō
had gone to Kyoto carrying a letter from the shogun's wife addressed to Konoe Tadahiro and had used Gesshō's offices in
delivering it. The letter sought a private imperial edict to have
Yoshinobu designated her husband's successor. The direct result
was the issue of such an edict to the shogunate in May. Those in
favor of Iemochi's succession, however, managed to get Ii Naosuke appointed senior shogunal advisor in June. Naosuke concluded treaties with five countries during July and, upon the
shogun's death on August 15, had Iemochi appointed shogun, generally conducting affairs in an autocratic way.

In September, Saigō, seeking an imperial rescript, accepted
through Gesshō the commission to transmit it to Mito. He left
Kyoto on September 9 and went in great haste to Edo, arriving in
just five days, and delivered the imperial order to the Mito lord's
residence. He found, though, that both the lord of Satsuma and
his son, the current lord of Mito, had been placed under house arrest by the shogunate and forbidden audience at Edo Castle. Their
supporters were powerless to do anything, so Saigō then called
upon a fellow loyalist from Satsuma to go to Kyoto with the domain's reply. Once there, again through Gesshō, the imperial
order was returned via the Konoe family. When a further rescript
was issued to the Mito domain and to the shogunate, it was a Mito
retainer that delivered it to the lord. The document ordered, in the
name of a "union of court and shogunate," that aid be given the
Tokugawas so that the foreigners could be ousted from the country. The Mito lord sought the shogunate's advice on the rescript
on September 26. Immediately the shogunate sent its senior counselor to Kyoto to put a stop to the activities of the imperial court
and nobility and to condemn them for anti-shogunate activities.
As a result of this sudden about-face by the shogunate, loyalists
found themselves threatened with punishment. With an arrest on
October 14, the Ansei Purge began.

Thus by 1858 Gesshō had thrown himself completely into the

whirlpool of the loyalist movement. His devotion to the imperial cause is reflected in a poem he wrote at the time:

> For my country
> For the dharma
> Giving my life,
> Like dew,
> Here, now.
>
> Taking a bow and arrow,
> Though no warrior,
> My heart remains unchanging
> Till the end.

Road to Kinkō Bay

With the start of the Ansei Purge, Gesshō too found himself in danger. Konoe Tadahiro, now the minister of the left, asked Saigō, now returned from Edo, to give Gesshō his protection and urged Gesshō to flee from Kyoto. The very next day, Gesshō and his servant left for Osaka, guarded by Saigō and another supporter. Saigō returned alone to Kyoto to urge the minister of the right, Takatsukasa Yasuhiro, to give his support to the loyalist movement. A few days later, however, a Mito retainer and his son were arrested, and then a retainer of Takatsukasa Masamichi was also thrown into prison. Saigō found himself in very real danger. He immediately traveled to Osaka and the next day set out with Gesshō in a rented boat heading west on the Inland Sea. They arrived at Shimonoseki on November 7. Saigō intended to hide Gesshō in Satsuma and so proceeded there alone from Shimonoseki. Gesshō and his servant remained in hiding, passed from one loyalist home to another along the way.

Gesshō and his companion arrived in Satsuma on December 12, reaching the castle town of Kagoshima three days later. Gesshō and Saigō met the following day. Policy was in a turmoil. The lord of Satsuma had died suddenly on August 25. He had been succeeded by his nephew, a youth of nineteen, whose father held real power. The inner circles of the domain, dominated by this new lord's father, feared the shogunate's measures against the imperial activists and sought to suppress political activity in the domain. Consequently Satsuma was no place for Gesshō to hide. Into the bargain, the man on whom Saigō thought they could rely became seriously ill. Gesshō and his servant were therefore taken to a temple. The temple, however, immediately notified the domain authorities, who decided, on the pretext of exiling Gesshō to the neighboring province, to have him killed at the domain border.

At midnight on December 20, Saigō, Gesshō's escort to the temple, and some others, with Gesshō and his servant, escaped by boat across Kinkō Bay. Saigō and Gesshō decided to end their lives together then and there, throwing themselves in the sea. They were hauled back on board, but only Saigō could be resuscitated; Gesshō had died for his country. He was then forty-five years old. His last poem reads:

> What is it that I can do for the emperor?
> Soon my body will sink into the bay of Satsuma;
> The cloudless moon of my heart will finally
> Go into the waves of the offing
> Of the Satsuma inlet.

In February 1859, Saigō was exiled to the island of Ōshima. There he stayed until he was permitted to return to Satsuma in March 1862. Upon his return he resumed his anti-shogunate activities.

Gesshō's younger brother, Shinkai, also became an accomplished poet under Konoe Tadahiro and, again like his brother, involved himself deeply in imperial affairs. He was arrested by a shogunate official on February 8, 1859, and imprisoned in the western magistrate's office in Kyoto. Sent to Edo at the end of March, he died in prison there on April 21. He was thirty-eight. His final poem recalled his elder brother, drowned in Kinkō Bay, and his commitment to the same cause:

> Though the western sea
> And the eastern sky

Are different,
I feel as he did
About the emperor.

Gesshō's Imperial Loyalty

What motivated Gesshō's devotion to the imperial cause? A letter
quotes Gesshō as saying:

Though it would appear that it were not within the scope of the
work of clerics to involve themselves in national affairs, for the
sake of the country to eradicate that which is harmful, and for
the sake of the country to face difficulties—that is truly to be in
accord with the Buddha's will. To be born in the country and remain but a spectator to the causes that bring harm to the country is to live idly, certainly not according to the Buddha's will.

One must consider what it was that allowed Gesshō thus to com-
bine his Buddhism with devotion to the imperial cause.

First, as already mentioned, there had been a school of thought
that advocated the coexistence of the emperor and the Tokugawa
shoguns. Gesshō himself approved of this. In early 1858, during a
ritual at Kongōbu-ji on Mount Kōya conducted through the good
offices of Gesshō and his younger brother, Konoe Tadahiro
petitioned, "May the emperor reign ten thousand years! . . . May
the harmful influence of the barbarians from abroad be expunged!
. . . May the Great Tree [the shogun] be free from all care, and
long may the fortunes of war be his! May the nation be at peace,
and may the people be blessed with security and tranquility."

Gesshō shared in this spirit. The petition that the shogun "be
free from all care" shows that these men considered reverence for
the emperor, expulsion of the barbarians, and support for the
Tokugawas to be one and the same. Reverence for the emperor by
no means implied the denial of samurai rule and the feudal
system. From such thinking emerged the idea of uniting court and
shogunate, as well as the combined slogan of "Honor the emperor
and expel the barbarians." That Gesshō himself favored feudal

government is apparent in a poem he sent to a Shingon cleric who was being sent to Edo. In it Gesshō expresses the hope that the protection of the shogun might be the basis for the prosperity of Buddhism:

> For the sake of the dharma,
> Standing in the shadow of the Great Tree [the shogun]:
> I wish you to lay the foundation
> [for the flourishing of the dharma].

The attitude of the loyalist clerics toward the expulsion of foreigners was somewhat different from that of the samurai, which was centered on contempt of things foreign. The clerics' concern was Christianity and hindering its entry into Japan. A letter from Konoe Tadahiro, dated the same day as the petition above and addressed to Gesshō and his brother, mentions the demands of the American envoy, saying that these were dangerous, for they had the particular intent of propagating a false religion that would undermine the dharma, which guided the nation, and would undermine Japanese law as well. If the shogunate opened the country to foreign intercourse, Christian evangelism would be extensive and would have to be dealt with. Buddhist clerics, who had administered the religious inquiry system for the shogunate during the long years of the anti-Christian policy, were conscious of a crisis arising from a possible reintroduction of Christianity. To prevent Christianity from reentering the country, Buddhists expounded slogans about protecting the country and expelling the barbarians, and activist clerics like Gesshō emerged, involving themselves deeply in the imperial cause.

The political movement espoused by such men as Gesshō did not merely seek the continuance of the old order under the shogunate. There was also a fresh ambition to seek a new order, as loyalists looked to the restoration of a strongly political imperial system to create a new system from within the feudal organization. This was why the shogunate had to fight so strongly against the activists. The ideas and aspirations of the activists at first took the form of slogans like "Unity of court and shogunate" and "Honor the emperor and expel the barbarians." There was a later swing away from these to "Honor the emperor and open the country," and it was this slogan that heralded the Meiji Restoration of 1868. Gesshō's activity was confined to the earlier type; his life closed before his ideas ripened. As we have seen, the expulsion of foreigners remained a strong element even in the demands for the opening of the country. Gesshō was strongly motivated by this idea, as it related to a rejection of Christianity, and it was to remain alive in Buddhist circles well into the early years of the Meiji era.

Shimaji Mokurai
(1838–1911)

by Shiki Kodama

Jōdo Shin Temples in Chōshū

Shimaji Mokurai was the fourth son of the priest of a Jōdo Shin sect branch temple of Hongan-ji, called Senshō-ji, in a village in Suō Province. The year of Shimaji's birth saw the beginnings of the movement in the Chōshū domain for the Meiji Restoration of 1868. Feudal authority had declined there following severe unrest earlier in the decade.

Already in the Chōshū domain the long-awaited opportunity had arrived for samurai of ability to rise, whatever their family backgrounds, and doubtless the winds of change were also felt by the clever young Mokurai. During his youth he lived as a trainee at a number of temples around the domain, working hard at his studies.

There is an anecdote about Mokurai concerning the appearance of a ghost in the inner sanctuary of the main hall of Zensō-ji, a village temple. On closer investigation the "ghost" turned out to be Mokurai, then a trainee there. Each evening when he was sure everyone was asleep, he would steal into the sanctuary and read by the light of the votive lamps. Because he was dressed in white robes and remained standing, he was taken for a ghost. The story illustrates his diligence. To understand what he dreamed of achieving through study, it is necessary to examine the distinctive features of Jōdo Shin temples in the area at the end of the shogunate.

Ever since the domain had been established by the Mōri clan at the beginning of the seventeenth century, the lords had kept the Jōdo Shin temples under special supervision. For example, all Jōdo Shin temples in the domain were forced to affiliate with the Nishi Hongan-ji subsect and were strictly forbidden to change affiliation to the rival Higashi Hongan-ji (Ōtani) subsect. Further, all Jōdo Shin temples were placed under the supervision of Seikō-ji, newly established by the Mōri clan. These acts were no more than precautions against large-scale uprisings by Jōdo Shin sect followers, like those that occurred in the sixteenth century in the northwest region. The Mōris declared their support for Nishi Hongan-ji, but the cost was restraint of the large, medieval temples in the domain and the inclusion of all Jōdo Shin temples in the domain organization.

Large medieval Jōdo Shin temples based on a system of heredity had a number of smaller temples under their jurisdiction, again on a hereditary basis, with traditional rights of supervision over them. To contain the power of these large temples, it was necessary to give the smaller temples autonomy, weakening their connections with the large temples. This was the basis of the Mōris' policy toward the smaller temples. As a result, the large temples weakened, the smaller ones came to the fore, and all gradually came to be of equal rank. The table on the next page compares the numbers of supporters for temples in Kaga and Chōshū. It shows that in Kaga at the beginning of the Meiji era, most temples were either very large, with 800 or more supporting families, or very small, with fewer than 30. By contrast, Chōshū at the same time had a great number of medium-sized temples, with between 100 and 200 supporting families. This equality of temples was a feature of the Chōshū domain. Such temples were comparatively well-off and independent, so they had few of the strong feudal ties that bound large and small temples in the northwest region.

Distribution of Supporting Families Among Temples in Kaga and Chōshū

Number of supporting families	Number of temples	
	Kaga	Chōshū
0–30	98	42
31–60	26	64
61–120	52	111
121–240	52	166
241–360	24	57
361–480	7	15
481–600	6	12
601–800	14	7
801–1000	5	4
1001–1500	6	1
over 1500	11	0

For Domain and for Sect

In general, during the Tokugawa shogunate (1603–1868) temples were knit tightly together under the main-and-branch-temple system, and extremely strong feudal ties existed between higher- and lower-ranking temples. In areas like Chōshū, where temples had been equalized, however, though the hierarchical relationships continued to exist on paper, hierarchical control was comparatively weak, and lower-ranking temples were relieved of their traditional burden.

Furthermore, during this time it had been Hongan-ji's policy to pressure the older, traditional temples and to give smaller ones autonomy as a means of stabilizing its own central authority. For example, from the beginning of the period it had deliberately labored to associate temples with itself by conferring temple names, thereby weakening the ties between large and small temples. From the middle of the period it also adopted the system of conferring rank according to the amount of donations it received from a temple, irrespective of that temple's traditional status. As a result, even a small temple with no tradition could, through the size of its donations, obtain a higher rank than one ostensibly its senior. This tendency was particularly strong in Chōshū, where there was little economic difference between senior and junior temples. The competition for rank intensified, and the priests and supporters of branch temples went to pathetic lengths to raise their temples' status. Temples of the time were attracted by a system that allowed temples without tradition to advance in the world. By the end of the Edo period, not only temple status, but superior learning also, had become the passport to success. Sectarian disputes among priests grew animated, and the newer, medium-sized temples produced a large number of scholars.

Thus at the end of the Edo period, the Hongan-ji religious organization developed an environment that was unusual for feudal times, one that did not favor tradition and that encouraged the aspirations of the common people. Rivalry among branch temples was intense, though, and there was a constant feeling of tension that was not evident in other sects. The reason that Jōdo Shin priests strove so hard at their studies and at secular work, compared with priests of other sects, is related in part to this rivalry. Still, their aspirations were confined to raising their temple's rank and to success in their sectarian studies. Participation by branch temples in the administration of the sect was still impossible, with high administrative posts the monopoly of entrenched priest-officials and retainers of the headquarters temples, plus a small minority of extremely powerful temples. This caused discontent among priests at branch temples, particularly in Chōshū where so many temples were the same size.

Domain reforms then in progress had been initiated to draw forward the samurai of greatest ability, irrespective of family standing. Able priests in the domain, unable to participate in sect administration at Hongan-ji, could strengthen their influence in the domain by taking part in domain government, and in this way many talented Jōdo Shin priests became politically conscious. If at first they spoke for the domain, they wanted at the same time to speak for the Hongan-ji sect.

Chōshū, however, was only one small area; Hongan-ji's authority was nationwide. Trying to act for both sect and domain inevitably led to inconsistencies, but the domain, anticipating national unity and in the vanguard as the movement to "expel the barbarians" changed to advocating the overthrow of the shogunate, was in a position to proclaim that what was good for the domain was good for the country. Thoroughgoing reform by Hongan-ji on a national scale was impossible without national unity. Participation in domain government and work for national unity, therefore, did not basically contradict involvement in sectarian reform. When Nishi Hongan-ji led the Buddhist sects in joining the anti-shogunate and pro-imperial movement, there was less and less contradiction in saying, as Chōshū's Jōdo Shin priests did, that what they did for the domain they did also for the sect. In this way they moved enthusiastically into politics. Throughout his life, Mokurai was able to hold the view, without inconsistency, that what was good for Buddhism was good for the country, and this reflected his inability ever to deviate from the ideology of a Jōdo Shin priest from Chōshū at the end of the shogunate.

With the Loyalists

It was from such a background that Mokurai entered politics. Already active loyalists among the Jōdo Shin clergy had exerted considerable influence in the Chōshū domain. Their activities were backed by quite a large number of sympathizers among rich farmers and merchants. Lay people who were noted for giving financial help to the imperial activists often were also devoted Jōdo Shin followers, who had been involved in fund-raising for Hongan-ji since the 1830s. Such families were close to imperial loyalists among Jōdo Shin priests, as well, and were unsparing in their support. It should not be forgotten, either, that the rich farmers and merchants were increasingly effective liaison agents between lower-level samurai from Chōshū and the Jōdo Shin loyalist priests. In addition, Mokurai's activity after the Restoration was constantly supported by powerful figures like Kido

Takayoshi and Itō Hirobumi from Chōshū in the new government, people with whom he had formed ties before the Restoration.

Mokurai must have been in a lather of impatience as he watched the activities of Jōdo Shin loyalists in concert with low-level samurai and rich merchants and farmers. Returning home after studying in Higo and Aki provinces, Mokurai made his first political pronouncement in 1864, when the domain issued a ban against cremations as part of its anti-Buddhist policy. He strongly opposed this in a pamphlet entitled *On Funerals*. Then, in 1866, he and a colleague made a report to the domain authorities on the establishment at Seikō-ji of an ''Office of Reform,'' the education of Jōdo Shin priests, and improvements in morals, as well as the study of French military science. The report already shows the effect of Mokurai's idea that what was good for Buddhism was good for the country: ''We cannot just stand idly by as danger threatens the dharma. Nor can we ignore an emergency that threatens the nation's existence.''

He was then twenty-eight. That year he was adopted into the family of the priest of Myōsei-ji in a neighboring village and succeeded as the temple's sixteenth head. Soon afterward, he and his wife had their first child, a son called Toshio.

By this time even peasants and townspeople were joining the domain-instigated anti-shogunate movement. Jōdo Shin priests had formed the Diamond Corps and were involved in hard fighting. Mokurai remained for some while at Myōsei-ji, uncertain whether to bury himself in the country, protecting the integrity of the village temple and looking after his wife and child, or to involve himself in the anti-shogunate movement for ''the nation and the dharma.'' He finally made his decision in the autumn of 1868, leaving his family and traveling to Kyoto with a number of loyalist Jōdo Shin priests, determined to embark on a reform program at the head temple.

Advocating Separation of State and Religion

In Kyoto, Mokurai and other Chōshū priests demanded that Nishi

Hongan-ji immediately reform itself. Their main demands were that autocratic administration by hereditary families of priests and retainers be abolished and that priests from the branch temples be included in the sect's decisions. Despite the revolutionary nature of the demands, Nishi Hongan-ji accepted them with little resistance. This was probably owing both to the power of the Chōshū priests, backed by those at the center of the new government, and to the progressive outlook of Nishi Hongan-ji's head, Ōtani Kōson. Soon after his arrival in Kyoto, then, Mokurai found himself wielding power in sect administration, together with other Chōshū priests.

By this time Buddhism throughout Japan was facing unprecedented danger in the form of the widespread despoliation of everything Buddhist, under the slogan "Abandon the Buddha, Destroy Buddhism," that accompanied the order of the new government to separate Buddhism and Shinto at temples and shrines. The government attached great importance to Shinto, which underlay much of the thinking of imperial restoration, the ideal being unification of rites and government. In early 1868 the Department of Shinto Ritual was reestablished; it encouraged the independence of shrines and shrine priests from Buddhism so that they could promote government policies. Shortly afterward, the government issued the Separation Edict. With the promotion of a policy giving precedence to Shinto, certain scholars of "National Learning," took advantage of the climate of the times to promote an extreme anti-Buddhist stance, and the "Abandon the Buddha, Destroy Buddhism" movement sprang up nationwide.

The various Buddhist sects knew no way of combating the danger other than by relying on the Nishi Hongan-ji priests from Chōshū, who had connections with the central figures of the Meiji government. In particular, great expectations were placed on the skill of Mokurai, their leader, who thus found himself the representative of Japanese Buddhism resisting the oppressive policies of the new government.

In 1870 Mokurai and an associate managed to establish an office of Buddhist affairs at the Ministry of Popular Affairs to resist the order to close or amalgamate temples. This measure did not succeed, however, and in the following year the office was closed when the ministry was disbanded. Mokurai had been petitioning for the establishment of a ministry to administer Shinto and Buddhism jointly. He succeeded in this when in April 1872 the Ministry of Shinto Ritual, successor to the Department of Shinto Ritual (abolished in the previous year), was dissolved to make way for the Ministry of Religion. Buddhist circles were reassured for the time being, as government pressure on Buddhism lessened and Buddhism was again administered together with Shinto.

The new ministry, however, continued to promote Shinto over Buddhism, regarding Buddhism as no more than an instrument for enhancing the absolutist system and Shinto. Further, the Ministry of Religion attacked Buddhism's independence when it established the Great Teaching Institute to promote a new national ethic. Nevertheless, most Buddhist sects, just recovered from the excesses of anti-Buddhist pressures, submitted to the new order and made no attempt to extricate themselves from a humiliating situation in which the state and religion, and Shinto and Buddhism, were mixed together. Mokurai, though, deplored the state of affairs. Just as he was mulling what to do about it, he had a stroke of good fortune.

In January 1873 Mokurai and a group of scholars left on a study-tour of Europe at Nishi Hongan-ji's behest. This first travel to Europe by a group of religious figures had been promoted originally by Kido Takayoshi, a government leader from Chōshū. After surveying religious conditions in England, France, Germany, Switzerland, and Italy, Mokurai parted from his companions and traveled to Jerusalem by way of Greece and Turkey. From there he made a pilgrimage to Buddhist sites in India and returned to Japan in July the following year. The experience gave him the confidence necessary to take on the government over separation between the state and religion.

First of all, he had learned in Europe that Western rationalism had exposed the contradictions in Christianity, a religion feared by the Japanese, and that it was in decline. Buddhism, based on the law of cause and effect, had something which could not be denied even by modern science. Of all the Christian churches, it seemed only the Protestant ones had the power to hold their own in modern times. Mokurai felt that in Japanese Buddhism the Jōdo Shin sects, also having elements of monotheism, had the same kind of strength. His faith in Jōdo Shin grew ever stronger.

Second, in post-Commune Paris he had come to believe that separation of the state and religion was indispensable for any advanced nation, however strong. This belief led to his absolute conviction that Western rationalism was not inconsistent with his own long-cherished ideas. Already, in a document sent from Paris entitled *A Critique of the Three Articles of Instruction*, he had advocated separation of the state and religion, and after his return he bitterly attacked the government's religious policy, unfolding a campaign to extract Buddhism from the Great Teaching Institute. As a result of his efforts, the government permitted the four Jōdo Shin subsects to withdraw in January 1875, and by May the Great Teaching Institute itself was dissolved. That the various Buddhist sects and schools were gradually able to regain their autonomy was owing entirely to Mokurai's efforts.

Why did he espouse separation of the state and religion? Because he believed in democracy and rationalism? His foreign travels had convinced him of the supremacy of Buddhism, Jōdo Shin in particular, and he firmly believed that Buddhism would save Japan. The government favored Shinto nationalism, and Buddhism's position had weakened, so Buddhism had to be restored to its former status. He therefore opposed the Ministry of Religion's policy of giving precedence to Shinto and urged that Buddhism be freed from the Great Teaching Institute's control. To this end he espoused separation of the state and religion. Mokurai always acted to safeguard Buddhism's independence. That he did not advocate religious freedom for the individual is clear from his attitude to Christianity. From start to finish he attacked Christianity, always insisting that successful dissemination of the one true religion, Buddhism, especially as practiced by the Jōdo Shin sect, was the way to keep Christianity at bay. By advocating separation between the state and religion to resist absolutist rule, he was relatively advanced for his time, but for all his advanced ideas he did not oppose absolutism per se, wanting only that the new system should become stable so that Buddhism could be promoted and Christianity stamped out. For Mokurai, the promotion of Buddhism, especially Jōdo Shin Buddhism, was patriotic in itself. Specific measures to this end were first and foremost the strengthening of the head temple, Hongan-ji, and to this he gave his attention. He believed that what was good for the country was good for the dharma.

While people still believed in the new government, Mokurai's activities had wide support. With the growth of the People's Rights Movement from the mid-1870s, however, voices were increasingly raised against the Satsuma-Chōshū oligarchy that dominated the government. Mokurai's pronouncements on the role of religion were seen as toadying to the authorities. Not only did he lose popular sympathy, he was gradually exposed to heightening criticism.

From Sect Administrator
to Religious Disseminator

Mokurai was not attacked by Christians and Shintoists but, to his dismay, by a faction at Hongan-ji led by its chief priest, Ōtani Kōson, to whom he owed allegiance. Mokurai had once said, "I pray that I might give my all in serving the chief priest, and that I might long be his trusted helper in the castle of the dharma." The incident that brought the discord to a head is known as the Kitabatake Affair. On June 14, 1879, Ōtani unexpectedly announced that Hongan-ji would remove to Tokyo and at the same time Mokurai and other Chōshū officials would be dismissed. The appointment of a priest named Kitabatake Dōryū (see biography in part 2), originally from the Kishū domain, as head of the reform secretariat rocked society. Without a doubt it was a declaration of war by Ōtani's faction against the Chōshū group at Hongan-ji. The Chōshū group resisted that move by bringing in a man of their own, the governor of Kyoto. Eventually two members of the court nobility, who were central figures in the new government, persuaded Ōtani to reverse his decision, and all plans for a coup d'état were dropped. The administration of Hongan-ji and sectarian affairs continued as before, in the hands of Chōshū priests. Nevertheless, the fact that voices demanding Mokurai's ouster had been raised at Hongan-ji to such an extent made it clear that he was no longer indispensable.

Mokurai remained in office and, in close touch with Chōshū bureaucrats, continued to secure absolute rights for Hongan-ji in terms of religion. His political pronouncements, however, aroused little interest. From the late eighties, Christianity had become closely involved in practical social problems on a humanitarian basis; this won the approval of many socialists. In the face of Christian opposition to war and Christian involvement in other anti-government movements, Mokurai's criticisms began to seem merely strident, and he became more and more alienated from the people. His outright refutation of the liberals seemed only to reflect his servility toward the oligarchs.

Though Mokurai's political career had ended to all intents and purposes by the end of the 1870s, his religious teaching work continued to the last years of his life. His political pronouncements were conservative, but his religious talks, as one of the greatest and most eloquent of Hongan-ji's intellectuals, continued to draw people to him, and he won many converts, the fruit of a zealous spirit that sent him at times to Korea and Manchuria at an advanced age.

In 1905 Mokurai was sent to Gangyō-ji, in Iwate Prefecture, as director of religious education for northern Japan. The usual explanation for this is that the sect wanted to use his skill in developing a stronger base in an area that traditionally had only a small Jōdo Shin presence. Perhaps the real reason, though, was to weaken the power of the Chōshū clique at Hongan-ji by sending him far from the center. Undaunted, he threw himself into his work in Iwate with the help of his adopted son, obtaining much success. Through their efforts, several noted intellectuals became Jōdo Shin believers.

Mokurai is also remembered for his contributions to the development of journalism and women's education. With Kido Takayoshi he was involved in the publication in 1871 of Japan's first newspaper, a weekly, and also joined in the publication of a Buddhist magazine. In 1888 he established a girls' school affiliated with the White Lotus Society; this was the predecessor of the present Chiyoda Joshi Gakuen.

Mokurai died on February 2, 1911, when Chōshū influence in the central government had already weakened. He was seventy-three. With his death, the long implanted Chōshū faction at Hon-gan-ji disappeared completely. That his fervor and his power of action also came to an end was a misfortune for the Hongan-ji organization.

Shaku Sōen
(1859–1919)

by Kōnen Tsunemitsu

Young Priest

Shaku Sōen was one of the most remarkable figures in Japanese Buddhist circles in the late nineteenth and early twentieth centuries. By the time Buddhism had recovered from its decline in the early part of the Meiji era (1868–1912) and was riding once more upon a tide of reinvigoration, Sōen had become a figure representative of modern Japanese Buddhism.

Besides being a man of great wisdom, Sōen had spent many years in training as a Zen priest. Having early discerned the tendencies of his times, he turned his gaze abroad, always in search of new knowledge. Of all his contemporaries, he was the one who involved himself the most appropriately in promotion of Buddhism among national leaders. Perhaps his greatest accomplishment was his role in planting the seed of Buddhism in America, as a Japanese representative at the World's Parliament of Religions in Chicago in 1893. It was through the contacts he made then that Suzuki Daisetz (see biography in part 1) was sent to America in 1897 to work with Paul Carus, the editor at Open Court Publishing Company in Illinois. Later a number of Sōen's apprentices and their apprentices went to America and were instrumental in establishing a Buddhist, particularly Zen, movement there. Sōen's overseas activities are therefore discussed in some detail after a review of his life as a whole.

Sōen was born in 1859, in a town in Echizen Province, the second son in a family of two boys and four girls. His given name was Tsunejirō. As a child he was outgoing and a leader among the children. Though small for his age and not robust in health, he was persevering. He learned reading and writing at the local temple school.

Sōen's father was a severe man and deeply religious; his mother was warmly compassionate. Sōen was ordained at the age of eleven at the request of his elder brother, Ichinose Chūtarō. As the elder son and heir, Chūtarō could not follow his inclination to become a priest and therefore asked Tsunejirō to do so in his place. The direct incentive was the visit of Ekkei, later head of Myōshin-ji. Ekkei was related to the Ichinose family and had returned to take part in a celebration marking his mother's longevity. The immediate family and their relations had all gathered, and there the young Tsunejirō was urged by all to become as fine a priest as Ekkei. Tsunejirō, moved by his family's encouragement, announced he would become Ekkei's apprentice. Eventually he accompanied Ekkei to Kyoto and in 1871 entered a Myōshin-ji subtemple called Tenju-in, where Ekkei lived.

Sōen studied under a number of masters, undertaking various kinds of training. At seventeen he was entrusted to the care of Shungai at Kennin-ji, under whom he spent several years learning how to act as a Zen priest. Following this master's death, he went to a temple on Shikoku; temple duties there relating to the needs of the numerous supporters prevented him from studying, though, so he left. Next he traveled to Mii-dera, where he studied the *Abhidharma Storehouse Treatise,* and on to Okayama Prefecture where he threw himself into training under Ekkei's master. Returning to Kyoto, he received Ekkei's permission to go to Kamakura to train under the head of Engaku-ji, Imakita Kōsen, one of Ekkei's dharma brothers. Sōen was then twenty-one.

Completion of Training

Sōen devoted himself to his training. Kōsen soon realized that he was no ordinary student and made every effort to further his practice. Sōen, too, put his heart and soul into his training and at the age of twenty-five received certification of enlightenment from Kōsen. Afterward Kōsen made a special journey to visit Ekkei to request that he be given Sōen as an apprentice. Ekkei agreed.

In 1884 Sōen, contemplating the course of social change in Japan, concluded that Buddhism was too conservative. Realizing that Buddhism had to be in tune with its age, he enrolled at Keiō University. Its founder, Fukuzawa Yukichi, commented that Sōen would surely become the head of one of the great temples someday. He gave the young man every encouragement and invited him to recite sutras on the family's annual memorial days. Sōen studied English with high hopes and determined to accomplish great things overseas.

In the spring of 1887 Sōen graduated from Keiō. Fukuzawa and others collected money to enable him to travel to Ceylon for study. In his three years there he mastered Sanskrit and strictly observed the Theravada precepts. From Ceylon he went to India, visiting the Buddhist holy places, and returned to Japan via Siam and China. On his return he edited a book about southwestern Buddhism. Kōsen was delighted to see him again and in appreciation of his achievements, on December 8, 1889, had him promoted. Sōen became the priest of Hōrin-ji, on the outskirts of Tokyo. Large numbers of people came there from all over Japan to receive his instruction.

It was around this time that at the request of the Organization of Buddhist Sects he joined Shimaji Mokurai (see preceding biography) and others in compiling the *Essence of the Buddhist Sects,* a task they completed in the summer of 1891. Kōsen died suddenly in January 1892, and Sōen succeeded Kōsen as head of the Engaku-ji subsect of Rinzai Zen while he was still only thirty-two years old. It was rare in the Buddhist world for one so young to reach such a high position.

World's Parliament of Religions

The World's Parliament of Religions opened in Chicago in September 1893. It had been planned as part of the World's Columbian Exposition commemorating the four hundredth anniversary of the European discovery of America. Sōen was one of several Japanese delegates. There was considerable opposition to Sōen's decision to go to America. Critics said that heads of large temples should not go away on a whim but should rather remain at their temples and receive visitors. Nevertheless Sōen went despite opposition.

The text of Sōen's speech, entitled "The Law of Cause and Effect, as Taught by the Buddha," was read for him at the meeting on September 18 by the chairman, Dr. J. H. Barrows, and was influential in planting the seed of Buddhism in the United States. Another important result of the Parliament was the meeting between Sōen and Carus, which would result in Suzuki Daisetz being sent to America in 1897.

Sōen wrote in the introduction to the Japanese translation of Carus's *The Gospel of Buddha:*

> When I traveled to the United States last year and stayed in Chicago, a scholar came to me one day urging that if we wished to teach Buddhism there, we should first convince Carus of the Tathagata's excellence. As both an eminent philosopher and a scholar of comparative religion, Carus is a beachhead here for us. If he could be brought to understand the true meaning of Buddhism, it would be better than converting a hundred thousand ordinary people. Eventually we were able to shake his hand cordially, and after we had had many discussions about religion, I realized that scholar had indeed been right. What resounded like a thunderclap from the doctor's tongue has taken the form of a treatise and flown to us from a corner of heaven as *The Gospel of Buddha.* What great pleasure it gives me!

The substance of their conversations is recorded in Sōen's travelogue *Notes on Crossing to America.* He also describes Carus's appearance:

September 3. Fine. Dr. Carus came. The doctor, as I had heard, has an outstanding reputation in literary circles. He held a black straw hat in his hand, and wore a suit. His hair and beard were unkempt and seemed for a long time to have been strangers to the barber's scissors. . . . He seems very unusual, like a Taoist sage. Though he wore no diamond on his finger, his eyes were piercingly bright. He had a large build. After our first momentous greetings, he courteously congratulated me on having undertaken such a long journey and on my bravery at having crossed the high seas of the great ocean despite the opposition of some people.

The description is accurate. Immediately afterward they began discussing the soul. The cordiality of their association deepened with time, and the opportunity to introduce Buddhism to America would come soon. Sōen returned to Japan. In 1895, when a joint training institute was set up for the priests of Kenchō-ji and Engaku-ji, Sōen was recommended as its head. He also continued to work hard for his sect in creating a corpus of religious texts and determining sectarian regulations.

Latter Half of Sōen's Life

In 1903, the leadership of Rinzai's Kenchō-ji and Engaku-ji subsects was united in Sōen. The following year, after the outbreak of the Russo-Japanese War, he visited the war zone as a member of a group of eminent figures. Sōen had lost a treasured and beloved apprentice named Uemura Sōkō, who had begun religious training under him before graduating from university. Sōen had put much meticulous effort into training this apprentice, and when Sōkō was eventually called up and sent off to the front, Sōen had given Sōkō his small curved staff, held by Zen masters when teaching, as a mark of encouragement. Tragically, Sōkō was killed just before the end of the war, and Sōen lost heart. In April 1905 he resigned as head of Engaku-ji and Kenchō-ji and retired to the nearby Tōkei-ji.

A year or two earlier, when he had still been head of the subsects, Sōen had welcomed an American couple, Mr. and Mrs. Alexander Russell, to Engaku-ji and instructed them in Zen. They practiced intensely and achieved much. Delighted with their experience, they invited Sōen to America to teach. In June 1905, he thus departed again for the United States. Arriving in San Francisco, he stayed with the Russells and taught Zen widely. Suzuki Daisetz, already working at Open Court Publishing Company in Illinois, accompanied Sōen as interpreter and attendant. This was the first formal teaching of Zen in America. Sōen spent eight months in San Francisco then went on to Chicago, where he visited his old friend Carus and spoke about Zen. Next he went to New York and Washington, where he met President Theodore Roosevelt and visited a number of universities. Deciding that as he had come so far already he might as well go on to Europe, he crossed the Atlantic and, meeting a Japanese leader of progressive education who happened to be there as well, toured together with him before going on to India, where he visited the sacred site of Bodhgaya and made a vow to the Buddha. He then went to Ceylon to visit old friends and spoke to many people. It was September 1906 before he returned to Japan, having been away a year and a half.

On his return, he formed a group called the Blue Cliff Society, which included a number of politicians and financiers. It met three times a month, with Sōen lecturing on the *Blue Cliff Records*. Every session attracted an audience of several hundred students and people from various walks of life.

Sōen was known throughout the country as the greatest Zen figure of his time. In October 1912 he was invited by the president of the Manchurian Railway Company to visit southern Manchuria and to teach Zen there. The following year he traveled to Taiwan. In September 1915 he was appointed president of Hanazono Gakuin, the Rinzai university, and in June the following year, once again became the head of the Engaku-ji subsect. In September 1917 he attempted a long journey through northern and southern China, Manchuria, and Korea, but his health began to fail and steadily worsened from that time onward. He died peacefully on November 1, 1919, aged sixty, leaving the following death verse:

> Lightly approaching, illness is now my constant attendant.
> From my mind I exclude Mara and the Buddha as well.
> Where is it—returning to the source?
> In the vastness of the universe I build my hut.

Dharma Successors
Who Went to the United States

Sōen planted the seed of Buddhism, and Zen in particular, during his second visit to the United States. His dharma successors, over the first and second generations, maintained that transmission.

In 1894, a year after Sōen had returned from the World's Parliament of Religions in Chicago, Carus sent him a proof copy of *The Gospel of Buddha*. Sōen had Suzuki Daisetz translate it into Japanese, and it was published in Japan in 1895. When in 1897 Carus requested Sōen to find someone proficient in English and classical Chinese to work as a translator at Open Court Publishing Company, Sōen immediately thought of Suzuki and sent him to assist Carus. Suzuki stayed at Open Court Publishing Company for eleven years, during which time he translated Laotzu's *The Way and Its Power* and Ashvaghosha's *Discourse on the Awakening of Faith in the Mahayana* into English and published his own *Outlines of Mahayana Buddhism* in English. He took the opportunity to travel to England and France. During Sōen's second visit to the United States, Suzuki acted as his assistant, interpreting his speeches, lectures, and instructions on zazen.

Shaku Sōkatsu had been an apprentice of Shaku Sōen's master, Kōsen. In January 1893, after Kōsen's death, he became Sōen's apprentice. He followed Sōen's guidance fervently, but at the end of his training he refused to become the master of a temple. Sōen therefore charged him with reviving the lay group that Kōsen had founded in Tokyo, the Forgetting Both Society (the name refers to the famous Zen series of ox-herding pictures). In 1906 Sōkatsu decided to travel to the United States and live there for an extended time in order to teach Zen, taking with him a number of lay followers, both men and women, from the Forgetting Both Society. He delayed his departure until August so that his oldest apprentice could graduate from university. They disembarked at Seattle and traveled by train to Oakland. At Hayward, a two-hour trolley ride from Oakland, he bought a small farm to make the group self-reliant. There Sōkatsu set up the American branch of the Society and began to teach Zen. Though he had, through his master, Sōen, the support of the Russells in San Francisco, the farm failed because of his own and his followers' inexperience. Financial difficulties forced them to abandon it and settle in San Francisco. About that time his supporters in Japan were urging him to return at least for a short period. Returning in the spring of 1908, he spent six months in Japan, during which time his health began to deteriorate. Nevertheless he returned to the United States as planned. Sōen sent him the following poem at the time of his departure:

> Throughout the many roads, north, south, east, and west,
> All people seek the wind of truth;
> Though America is far from this place,
> It is my earnest desire
>   that compassion be sent to ease the suffering there.

A year and a half later, in the summer of 1909, Sōkatsu returned to Japan for good with most of his followers. He had been unable to fulfill his original aim. One apprentice who had accompanied him to America in 1906, Sasaki Shigetsu, decided to remain in America and continue Sōkatsu's work.

Shigetsu was born the son of a Shinto priest in Kagawa Prefecture, Shikoku, in 1882. His mother was his father's concubine, but because his father's wife had not given birth to any children, he was entered in the family register as legitimate. After completing elementary school, he went to Tokyo to be apprenticed to a sculptor. He later studied sculpture at Tokyo Bijutsu Gakkō (now Tokyo University of Fine Arts and Music), graduating in April

1905. While a student, he had studied Zen enthusiastically at Sōkatsu's Forgetting Both Society. When he heard that Sōkatsu was planning to go to the United States, he immediately asked to join the group. In America he worked as a houseboy and studied painting at the California Institute of Art. After Sōkatsu returned to Japan, Shigetsu worked as a sculptor and gave Zen talks; gradually he devoted more and more time to Zen activities. He returned to Japan to be ordained as a Zen priest. After training intensively at the Society's temple and receiving authority to teach, he was ordained as a Rinzai priest. In 1922 he returned to America, settling in New York and concentrating on teaching Zen to Americans. He founded a temple called Sōkei-an at his apartment in February 1930 and established the Buddhist Society of America. He lectured on Zen and gave instruction in zazen exclusively to Americans not of Japanese ancestry. Gradually his followers increased in number. "Welcome those who come," he would say, "don't run after those who leave, do not answer if you have not been asked, and do not seek followers."

After the outbreak of the Second World War, Shigetsu, like other Japanese nationals in the United States, was placed in an internment camp. Inclined to obesity, he suffered from high blood pressure, and as his health worsened, his American followers did all they could to gain his release. Unsuccessful, they tried one last method, marriage to an American citizen. In 1944, Ruth Fuller Everett, the widow of a Chicago attorney, married the chronically ill Shigetsu. His release came too late, though, and he died on May 17, 1945, aged sixty-four. In 1949 Ruth Fuller Sasaki went to Japan; at Ryūzen-an, within the Daitoku-ji complex in Kyoto, she worked to establish a base in Japan where foreigners could study Zen, thus extending Sōen's lineage.

While Sasaki Shigetsu worked mainly on America's East Coast, another of Sōen's students, Senzaki Nyogen, spent most of his life promulgating Zen on the West Coast. There is an element of mystery about Senzaki. He was born in Siberia; abandoned as a baby, he knew neither the date of his birth nor who his parents were, but thought his father was Chinese. Rescued by a Jōdo priest from Japan, he was adopted by a member of the priest's temple, a shipwright named Senzaki. The name Nyogen was given him by the Jōdo priest. He studied classical Chinese from the age of eighteen and was ordained at a Sōtō sect temple in Tokyo called Sōsen-ji. Despite the difference in sect, he was a faithful apprentice of Shaku Sōen.

Shaku Sōen's biography notes: "The Mentorgarten, a training facility for orphans, was founded by Senzaki Nyogen. A student [of Sōen's], he entered the Shikayama Sōdō in 1896, spending five years under Sōen's instruction. He returned home voluntarily and taught Buddhism there. When the master [Sōen] went to America in 1905, he soon followed and remained there."

It is unclear whether Nyogen's decision to go to the United States was as simple as related above; his real purpose might have been to raise funds for the Mentorgarten. When Sōen's English follower, Thomas Kirby (dharma name, Sōkaku) came to the United States, Nyogen worked with him teaching Zen. He established the Mentorgarten Meditation Hall in San Francisco in 1928 and continued to teach Zen despite constant financial difficulties. The Mentorgarten Meditation Hall moved to Los Angeles in 1931, and Nyogen gave Zen guidance to Americans who were mostly not of Japanese ancestry. His training methods were strict. There is the story of the American apprentice who, on returning to the United States after Zen training in Japan, greeted Nyogen familiarly with "Hello, Senzaki." That apprentice was expelled. Nyogen's ministry in the United States lasted more than fifty years, ending only with his death in 1958, at the age of about eighty-one, in his East Second Street Zendo in Los Angeles.

Furukawa Gyōdō, another direct apprentice of Shaku Sōen, also taught Rinzai Zen in California. He was born on December 8, 1872, in Shimane Prefecture. As a boy, he always had a weak constitution and in fact had almost died soon after birth. He miraculously recovered during the funeral preparations. Placed in a temple while still a child, he later became an apprentice of Daikō, the priest of Manju-ji in Shimane Prefecture. Following a strict regimen under Daikō, and then under Bitchū Kuhō, he traveled to Engaku-ji in Kamakura and entered the tutelage of

Shaku Sōen. Gyōdō succeeded Sōen and became head of the Engaku-ji subsect in 1920. Invited by Senzaki Nyogen to teach Zen in the United States, Gyōdō left Yokohama in the summer of 1931. Nyogen at that time was in San Francisco, and Gyōdō, finding the customs very different and doubtless feeling the strain of working with the penniless Nyogen, fell ill and was forced to return to Japan at the beginning of the following year. Though he spent only a short time in America, Gyōdō helped nurture the seed of Buddhism that Sōen had planted.

Kiyozawa Manshi

(1863-1903)

by Yūsen Kashiwahara

Japanese Buddhism in the Meiji era (1868-1912), liberated after a long period of feudal control, was filled with a sense of mission to elucidate the original faith of the Buddha. At the beginning of the period, priests of the Jōdo and Shingon sects, such as Fukuda Gyōkai and Shaku Unshō (see biographies in part 2), stimulated Buddhist circles with their efforts to restore the precepts. In the 1870s and 1880s, Shimaji Mokurai (see earlier biography) and the lay Buddhist Ōuchi Seiran attempted to revive Buddhism by allying it to the enlightened thought of the times. Inoue Enryō (see biography in part 2) strove to reinterpret Buddhism in the light of Western philosophy. Following the Sino-Japanese War of 1894 to 1895, Japan entered a period of hardship and privation, and people looked for ways to develop inner spiritual resources. Religions responded by seeking a faith that could sustain a life lived in truth. Christians were prominent; in Buddhism too there was vigorous activity, with a new liberal movement called the Buddhist Pure Believers' Association, a new Nichirenism, and the "Way-Seeking" movement of Chikazumi Jōkan (see biography in part 2). The greatest impact on thinking Buddhists and intellectuals, however, was made by the spirituality movement of Kiyozawa Manshi.

230

Manshi was the son of a low-ranking samurai. After elementary schooling he studied English and medicine in Nagoya and in 1878, at the age of fifteen, enrolled in Higashi Hongan-ji's school in Kyoto for young Jōdo Shin sect priests. At that time Higashi Hongan-ji paid students fifty yen per year to study at the school, which provided education for the most gifted of the sect's priests. The brilliant Manshi selected that school because it could provide the education his family could not afford. Because only priests could enroll there, he was ordained and received the name Kenryō. There was perhaps more than that to his selection of the school, though. His parents, particularly his mother, were fervent Jōdo Shin sect adherents, and he had been raised in a pious atmosphere. This no doubt naturally turned his attention to the school, where he took the first steps along the road he was to walk as one of the great luminaries of the Jōdo Shin sect.

In 1882, when Manshi was nineteen, Higashi Hongan-ji ordered him to go to Tokyo for further study. He enrolled in a preparatory school for Tokyo Imperial University (which became the University of Tokyo). He consistently led his class, which included many future leaders of Japan's government and industry. Enrolling at the Tokyo Imperial University, Manshi studied philosophy and in 1887 began work toward a graduate degree in philosophy of religion.

The most influential of Manshi's teachers was Ernest Fenollosa, best known for his promotion of the study of fine arts in Japan. From Fenollosa, Manshi learned Hegelian philosophy. During his student years, Manshi was also connected with the Philosophy Association of Inoue Enryō, the Buddhist scholar who founded the forerunner of Tōyō University in 1887, and Katō Hiroyuki, educator and president of the Tokyo Imperial University. Manshi founded that organization's *Magazine of the Philosophy Association* and shared responsibility for editing it. As he continued his study of Western philosophy, he continued his investigations into religion and Buddhism as well, endeavoring to reformulate basic Buddhist concepts in philosophical terms. His understanding was that Buddhist philosophy had an organic structure determined by the dualism of the finite and the infinite, inasmuch as Buddhism taught the relationship between relative, finite human beings and the absolute, infinite Buddha. This was an epoch-making interpretation, for it gave the complexity of Buddhist teachings a place in modern philosophy for the first time. What Manshi was attempting was a restructuring of Buddhist philosophy, not of the religious belief itself. The question of the finite and infinite remained a lifelong concern and was, in a religious sense, at the root of his sense of personal release.

Religious Life

In March 1888 the Kyoto municipal government, in financial straits, passed control of its middle schools to Higashi Hongan-ji, and in July Manshi was recalled from Tokyo to serve as a principal. He decided to abandon the path to Tokyo power and influence out of obligation to the sect authorities for their support of his scholarly efforts. The same year he married into the family of the priest of a Higashi Hongan-ji sect temple, Saihō-ji, in Aichi Prefecture, and took his wife's family name, Kiyozawa. He was then twenty-five.

In July 1890 he resigned as principal but went on teaching. He lectured at Higashi Hongan-ji's highest educational institution, the Takakura Daigakuryō, chiefly on the philosophy of religion. His course there focused on the problem that had been with him since his university days, the relationship between the finite and the infinite. He also taught the concept of self-power and other-power in Buddhism, the problem of the spirit, religious good and evil, and the nature of religious tranquillity. His lectures were noted for their progress from philosophical to religious topics. They were published in 1892 as *A Skeletal Outline of the Philosophy of Religion;* an English translation was introduced by Noguchi Zenshirō the following year at the World's Parliament of Religions in Chicago.

After resigning as principal in 1890, Manshi made unrelenting efforts to discover the basis of his own religious understanding. He assumed the appearance and garb of a priest, gave up smoking and eating meat, separated himself from his family, and entered a life of severe religious austerity. Interested in their way of life, he visited religious ascetics around Kyoto and in 1892 made a special trip on foot to Ise to address the summer session of the Buddhist Youth Association. The way of life that he was later to sum up in the phrase "the Minimum Possible" grew out of this experience of religious austerity.

From this time on, Manshi moved toward the ideas of Shinran as presented in the *Notes Lamenting Deviations* and became increasingly attracted to the Jōdo Shin teaching of other-power. The purpose of his religious training, therefore, was not ascetic self-discipline or the enlightenment and perfection of self, as practiced by the non-Pure Land traditions. Rather, by discovering his own limitations, he hoped to understand through direct experience the meaning of a finite being, which had concerned him since his student days. Having realized his limited self, he strove to give himself up to the Buddha, the infinite and absolute being.

As a result of the rigorous life he was leading, Manshi contracted tuberculosis in 1894. He wanted to continue teaching university and high school classes but was dissuaded by the concern of those around him. Taking a leave of absence, he rented a room for himself and his family in a Zen temple called Dōyō-ji, in Hyōgo Prefecture. He spent almost a year there recuperating, and the period unexpectedly turned out to by a very useful one of spiritual growth. Beginning his convalescence, Manshi wrote, "The old Tokunaga [Manshi] is dead; his body is yours to do with as you like." He took his friends' advice to heart and faithfully followed the regimen set out by the doctors. He was forced to change his way of life; instead of trying to test his limits, he had to accept himself as he was. Because in those days tuberculosis was virtually incurable, death could never have been far from his mind. A constant foreboding, together with the passive life he was leading, allowed him to develop his religious views on the relationship between the finite and the infinite. Personal experience had verified his complete faith in the absolute and infinite Buddha. In his diary of the time, *Jottings of Convalescence,* he wrote, "Religion is that which brings peace of mind and quietness of spirit concerning the questions of life and death." During this period Manshi certainly confronted the questions of life and death, and he arrived at an understanding and appreciation of Shinran's teachings of absolute other-power, taking refuge in Amida with just a single thought of faith. He later wrote in his diary: "When I reflect, it was during my period of convalescence in 1894 and 1895 that my ideas concerning human life underwent a change. Though I had been able to refute the fallacy of self-reliance, I was still moved to action by human affairs. My concern for sectarian matters in 1895 therefore caused my involvement in the reform movement of 1896–97." Manshi could not help deeply involving himself in the movement to reform sect administration at Higashi Hongan-ji.

Sect Reform Movement

In the Meiji era, Higashi Hongan-ji (an Ōtani subsect) faced financial ruin, partly because of its heavy financial contributions to the new government following the Meiji Restoration, but mainly because of the huge expense of rebuilding the head temple in Kyoto. The complex had burned down four times since 1788, most recently during the civil war in 1864. Reconstruction of the main and founder's halls began in 1879, and work was finally completed in April 1895. These halls are still standing. Their reconstruction was an enormous task for the sect, and its debts rose to 3.3 million yen by 1894. Consequently, fund-raising and debt repayment had become the administrators' main concern, to the neglect of religious matters. The situation spurred Manshi and other like-minded people to urge, once the building program had been completed, that the sect return as quickly as possible to giving religious matters priority.

In July 1895 Manshi broke off his treatment and returned to Kyoto. There he presented to the Hongan-ji secretariat a petition with twelve signatures, including his own, demanding reform. Because of the meager response, in October Manshi and his friends confined themselves in Shirakawa in Kyoto and founded a group commonly known as the Shirakawa Party, as a base for the reform movement. Still continuing his life of voluntary privation, in October the following year Manshi began publishing a magazine called *Timely Opinions on the Ecclesiastical World*, in which the group appealed to those within and without the Jōdo Shin sect for reform of the religious establishment to be achieved through spiritual reform. The reaction was extensive; the sect's young priests, in particular, rallied to the cause. In November 1896 Shinshū University (later Ōtani University) students, including three of Manshi's followers, published in the ordinary newspapers a manifesto addressed to "our respected fathers, brothers, fellow clerics, and lay followers." In it they attacked the sect's financial disorder and advocated the encouragement of religious teaching. Hongan-ji immediately expelled all the signers. The students continued their campaign, however, sending speakers around the country, contributing articles to the newspapers, and helping edit their magazine. Students from Jōdo Shin sect middle schools joined the movement, and well-known Jōdo Shin scholars, including Murakami Senshō, Inoue Enryō, and Nanjio Bunyiu (see biographies in part 2), added their voices to the demands, supporting the reform movement. In January 1897 an office for Ōtani subsect administrative reform was established in Kyoto, and all the reform groups federated, bringing supporters to Kyoto from all over Japan. The Shirakawa Party made ten demands for reform, centering on the democratization of Hongan-ji administration, including revision of the law on the sect's temples, establishment of a council of branch temples, and a change in the constitution of the senior offices; reforms in financial management; and reform in religious promotion, including a scheme for religious education activities, a plan to encourage study, and provisions for the appointment and promotion of personnel.

As the reform movement grew in intensity, those responsible for administration at Hongan-ji were replaced, and the expelled students were reinstated. The sect accepted some of the Reform Federation's demands and, to stimulate religious study, set up an Association to Inquire into Doctrine. This turned out to be no more than a forum for religious discussion, however. In a number of other ways also, the demands for reform were not being met. An anti-reform movement was begun by hardliners with traditional views on sectarian studies. Regional opposition groups also ap-

peared. They condemned the Shirakawa Party for falsifying doctrine and causing a collapse of religious principles.

Ahead of its time, the reform movement was doomed. The
Reform Federation disbanded in November 1897, and its voice,
the *Timely Opinions on the Ecclesiastical World*, ceased publication the
following year after seventeen issues. Though the movement itself
had collapsed, its spirit lived on. In fact, it might be said that the
collapse was fortunate for the future of Manshi's religious activity.
He was now able to concentrate all his efforts on spiritual questions, specifically those concerning Buddhist spirituality and other-
power faith. He wrote in explanation of the decision to disband
the Federation: "The disbanding is only a matter of form, not
spirit. The form of what we finish today without regret will, I
hope, eventually be transfigured as spirit." This was what Manshi
called spirituality.

Spirituality Movement

After returning home to Aichi in 1897, Manshi went to Tokyo in
September of the next year at the request of the new head of
Higashi Hongan-ji. He stayed with an old friend and while there
happened to read the Greek Stoic philosopher Epictetus, whose
writings were suggestive for the direction his own spirituality was
to take. His stay in Tokyo was connected with the proposed move
of Shinshū University to the capital. In 1899 Higashi Hongan-ji
offered to appoint him its acting dean. He accepted on the conditions that it move to Tokyo and that he would be responsible for
the curriculum. Having already experienced the obstinate power
of sect authorities, Manshi planned removal of the university from
the sect's control and establishment of a broad-based religious
educational facility. Hongan-ji accepted Manshi's recommenda-
tions and put him in charge of construction. Work began in 1900,
and the ceremony to mark the move was held in October of the
following year. Manshi was appointed the first dean. At the ceremony, he affirmed that Shinshū University's main purpose was
to instill strong faith in Jōdo Shin sect teachings among people
capable of disseminating them to others in turn. The university

offered a variety of courses, including indoctrination in the Jōdo Shin sect faith in other-power. This was to be expected at a sectarian university, but it was also an attitude based on the spirituality that Manshi advocated.

In June 1899 Manshi had moved to Tokyo's Bunkyō Ward. By September of the following year, a number of former Shinshū University students that had taken part in the reform movement and others were living in his house. The young Buddhists who gathered around Manshi called his residence the Lively Wide Cavern. In June 1902 the young people moved to another house in the same ward, which became the new Lively Wide Cavern, but they went to Manshi's house every day to discuss religion. In addition, every Sunday there was a lecture for visitors at the Lively Wide Cavern on spirituality. Later, one member recalled, "This house was for us the Pure Land in this world." Another also said, "When I think about those things now I could weep for joy." The Lively Wide Cavern produced a number of prominent scholars.

The Lively Wide Cavern began publishing a magazine called *Spiritual World* in January 1901. Its introductory editorial stated, "Those who seek to pass through the valley of suffering and sorrow and to play in the fields of peace and joy, come to us!" It was clearly addressed to all who had experienced the bitterness of the confusion in the late 1890s. For the inaugural issue Manshi wrote an essay titled "Spirituality," presenting his ideas to the world at large for the first time. *Spiritual World* became the voice of spirituality, and three thousand copies of every issue were printed. Until his death, Manshi always wrote on spirituality, and residents of the Lively Wide Cavern as well as people both inside and outside the Jōdo Shin sect contributed articles. Eventually the ideas of spirituality became widely known among young priests and among intellectuals with an interest in religion. *Spiritual World* continued to be published by like-minded people even after Manshi's death, and though the Lively Wide Cavern later moved several times, both continued until 1918.

The year 1902 was difficult for Manshi. First, he had to leave Shinshū University, the center of his hopes. Trouble among the Hongan-ji authorities extended to the university, and there was a movement to expel the man that Manshi had placed in charge of administration. Further, the students themselves wanted the university to be accredited so that it could give teaching qualifications, of use in real life. There was little comprehension of the education based on religious ideals that Manshi contemplated. Manshi accepted his administrator's resignation on October 21 and submitted his own the following day. That same year, Manshi lost a son (June 6) and his wife (October 7), and his own health deteriorated. After resigning, he returned to his wife's hometown in Aichi Prefecture. He said, "This has been a devastating year. My child has died. My wife has died. The university has collapsed. If I break down also, everything will be gone."

The following year Manshi himself died. His tuberculosis had never shown any sign of improvement after 1895. He continually coughed up blood and suffered hemorrhaging of the lungs, but despite that did not cut back on his activities. Another son died of illness on April 9. His own faith remained firm in adversity, and he continued to lecture on spirituality. But his final hour was soon to come. On June 3 he hemorrhaged heavily. The next day he had another severe hemorrhage. He finally died before dawn on June 6, aged forty. A week before his death he wrote an article called "My Beliefs." It is famous not only as his last writing but also as a crystallization of the ideal of spirituality.

Manshi's Thought

Manshi said that the philosophical works that had most influenced him were the *Notes Lamenting Deviations,* the works of Epictetus, and the *Agama sutras.* The first reveals the essence of Shinran's Jōdo Shin sect other-power faith. He admired Epictetus's idea that one who clearly comprehends what the self is will suffer no external harm or pain, for the perception of suffering is caused when the self is lost, when the mind is captured by something other than the self. The *Agama sutras,* scriptures of early Buddhism, had until then attracted little attention in Mahayana Japan. Manshi, however, discovered in those early works a record of the living Shakyamuni and was greatly influenced by the practical teachings of transience, suffering, and non-self that are basic to Buddhism. It was the essence of Manshi's spirituality that allowed him to unite organically, without contradiction, Shinran's teachings, standing at the apex of Mahayana other-power Buddhism, with the self-understanding of Epictetus and early Buddhism's ideal of religious practice, the *Agama sutras*. Spirituality, though based on reliance in the power of the other, was above all a means of personal release. It was not just a philosophy but necessarily had to be applied in daily life.

Manshi's spirituality means regarding all things without desire and seeking spiritual self-sufficiency. To this end, one must attain perfect peace of mind, which is none other than the boundless compassion of the absolute, infinite Buddha. Manshi taught that one must entrust oneself, body and spirit, to that compassion. Spirituality means perfect freedom. Because all is entrusted to the Buddha's boundless compassion, one should live completely according to his teachings and no one else's. If one is forced temporarily to submit to another authority, it is the Buddha's will, not one's own, and is therefore not a cause of suffering. Rather it is a state of perfect religious autonomy. Spirituality also means taking a subjective stance. Faith in the Buddha's compassion means faith in the Buddha's power. Through such faith, all is fulfilled. Spirituality is thus a realm completely different from those of scholarship or ethics, which infinitely pursue objective discussions of judgments of right or wrong, good or bad.

Spirituality is clearly based upon the Jōdo Shin teachings of absolute other-power. It was expounded in a way, though, that tended to diverge from traditional sectarian commentaries on the teachings. As a result, traditionalists often looked askance at it. It is also a very intellectual concept, so it was not understood by the masses of believers, who since the Edo period (1603–1868) had been taught a simple ethic, although it did catch the imagination of the intelligentsia and the younger priests. It therefore never spread widely through the Jōdo Shin sect. It did, however, have the effect of bringing a breath of the fresh air of modernity into the doctrinal complexity and rigidity of traditional sectarian understanding, and furthermore, through its elucidation of the independent and subjective nature of religion, free and unbounded by any constraints, it brought an awareness of true autonomy to a religion within which there had long been confusion among politics, learning, ethics, and faith itself. In this sense, spirituality can even today be appreciated for its ability to show religion's role in the modern world, rather than merely in terms of its place within Jōdo Shin Buddhism.

Suzuki Daisetz
(1870–1966)

by Daisetsu Fujioka

Three Epochs

The introduction to the Japanese edition of the collected works of Suzuki Daisetz says:

> Over half a century, spanning the Meiji, Taishō, and Shōwa eras [1868–1989], breasting the upheavals of history and the changing currents of intellectual life, Suzuki Daisetz was a thinker who was able to influence the minds of his contemporaries deeply and fundamentally, while constantly remaining aloof from the crowd.
>
> Suzuki was not only a first-rate Buddhist scholar, with works such as *Studies in the History of Zen Thought* and *Fundamental Thought of Rinzai* credited to his name, but also a religious practitioner of uncommon dedication, who spent his long life striving virtually without cease to root Zen truth in people's lives and thinking. His writings and promotion efforts took him abroad many times, and the present upsurge in interest in Zen in Europe and America can be largely attributed to his moral influence. It was Suzuki's accomplishment that he understood

modern currents of thought and fathomed the contradictions in modern civilization; he propounded a Zen that offers relief from the anxiety of his contemporaries.

Although the introduction does not mention his study of Zen influence on Japanese culture, it shows the high esteem in which he was held in Japan. Few Japanese have received such extravagant praise.

His writings fill over a hundred volumes. In a way it is ironic that such a vast production, along with an equally broad exposure through lectures and talks, should have served to promote a Zen that cautions against depending on the written word or considering the sutras the only source of truth. On the other hand, perhaps Zen requires a special kind of transmission, inasmuch as it can only be explained indirectly and repetitiously.

Born in Kanazawa in 1870, the young Suzuki Teitarō traveled to Tokyo at the age of twenty-one and entered Tokyo Semmon Gakkō, predecessor of Waseda University. Meiji absolutism had been established with the promulgation of the Imperial Constitution two years previously and with the convening of the first Imperial Parliament in 1890. Suzuki soon left the university and concentrated on Zen training under Imakita Kōsen at Engaku-ji in Kamakura. This was not his first exposure to Zen, but as his first real Zen training, it must have decided his life's course. Little is known about the doubts and worries he brought with him to his training, but it is likely he was less troubled by the oppressive atmosphere of his times than by feelings of isolation after the death of his father, a doctor, and during the long years of poverty in which he was raised by his beloved mother, who died the year before he went to Tokyo.

Imakita Kōsen died in 1892, and Suzuki continued studying under his successor, the thirty-four-year-old Shaku Sōen (see biography in part 1). In the meantime he enrolled in the non-regular course at Tokyo Imperial University (later University of Tokyo) on the recommendation of his friend, the philosopher Nishida Kitarō, but his zealous practice of Zen continued. In December 1895, in his fifth year of training, he is said to have attained enlightenment. This experience became a major premise in his thought.

One writer noted that a momentous meeting marked each of the three important stages in the development of Suzuki's thought. The first was with Shaku Sōen and the second, with Paul Carus. In 1897, at Sōen's recommendation, Suzuki went to the United States to act as editorial assistant to Carus, a philosopher and publisher, who managed the Open Court Publishing Company in the suburbs of Chicago. Suzuki lived at Carus's house for eleven years. During this time he improved his English and made English translations of Laotzu's *The Way and Its Power* and Ashvaghosha's *Discourse on the Awakening of Faith in the Mahayana.* In 1907 he published his own *Outlines of Mahayana Buddhism.* He also studied European intellectual methodology and gained a wide knowledge of Buddhism.

The third important meeting was with Beatrice Lane, whom he married in 1911, when he was forty-one. Marriage to someone of her deep understanding of Buddhism must have been important for him, but there is no direct evidence of her influence on his thought.

Of greater importance was the year 1919, when Sōen died. In that year Suzuki retired as English professor at Tokyo's Gakushūin and went to Ōtani University in Kyoto as professor of Buddhist philosophy. There he began the publication of an English-language magazine, *The Eastern Buddhist,* and became interested in the nembutsu tradition of Buddhism. His first book on Zen, *Essays in Zen Buddhism, First Series,* was published in 1927, when he was fifty-seven. In the following decade, before writing *Zen Buddhism and Its Influence on Japanese Culture* in 1938, he produced a flood of works on Zen. His nembutsu studies had worked as a catalyst to release in literary form his accumulated ideas and experience concerning Zen.

Two Wheels of a Cart

Putting Suzuki's vast literary output into order is a task yet to be completed, but broadly speaking his writings fall into two categories, those explaining the nature of Zen enlightenment in philosophical terms and those dealing with the centrality of Zén to Japanese culture.

In 1883, when Suzuki was in middle school, he met Fujioka Sakutarō, later a scholar of Japanese literature, and Nishida Kitarō, who was to become a philosopher and a lifelong friend and was to greatly influence Suzuki's thinking. In cast of mind, Suzuki and Nishida were quite different. Whereas Nishida was intellectual, with a scientific bent, Suzuki was intuitive and poetic; Nishida's logicality contrasted with Suzuki's emotionalism. Their temperaments were also reflected in their scholarship, and their interaction gave birth to two great intellectuals. They were like two wheels of the same cart.

Suzuki describes Nishida as follows: "Nishida has a strong, scientific mind. His honesty forces him to pursue something he does not understand to the very end, and he does not give up until he has studied it to its limits. This combination of personal honesty and intellectual acuteness has built his philosophy."

Nishida wrote of Suzuki: "You are a man rich in scholastic ability and insight. Although you say you are troubled by unbearable incidents that often arise in your relationships with people, you always behave like moving clouds and a running stream. I have many friends and associates, but none is as singular as you. You do not look like the most powerful, but you would seem to be. Intellectually I owe you a great deal." Suzuki's Zen helped form Nishida's philosophy.

In the introduction to Nishida's *A Study of Good,* Suzuki wrote: "Nishida's philosophy of absolute nothingness or his logic of the self-identity of absolute contradictions is difficult to understand, I believe, unless one is passably acquainted with Zen experience. Nishida himself was a good student of Zen and always deplored the fact that the Zen advocates, especially those who are regarded as its authorized exponents, are utterly ignorant of, or indifferent to, Western philosophy or the Western way of thinking." Of course it was at Suzuki's suggestion that Nishida practiced Zen.

Suzuki also tried to learn from Nishida's philosophy. In a letter written during his last years to one of his favorite students, Akizuki

Ryōmin, Suzuki says, " 'Sorrow' is lacking in modern Zen. Thus it is not motivated to contribute to society. Neither has it any 'theory,' as Nishida always said. To satisfy Westerners, you need theory. . . . I feel it would have been good for me to have read more of Nishida's books." Nishida is supposed to have advised Suzuki, as the latter continued writing about Zen, "Be more theoretical, be more theoretical!"

Perhaps Suzuki's philosophical concept of the "logic of absolute affirmation and absolute negation," which he used to explain the inexplicable enlightenment, the ultimate purpose of his Zen, was owing to Nishida's advice. It is certain that his contact with Westerners made him acutely aware that even Zen had to be considered in philosophical terms. Explaining the concept, he showed typical breadth of intellect. "To say that 'Mind is Mind because it is No-mind' is to say that the negative is in itself positive, that both the negative and the positive are mutually neither one nor the other, in regard to the absolute. 'Neither one nor the other' is 'itself.' This I call Zen logic. 'Absolute affirmation and absolute negation' is also 'nonconceptual conceptualization' and 'unconscious consciousness.' All else I leave to the philosophers."

This was his own concept, but he left it to other philosophers to clarify and develop it. His lack of rigor is also apparent in a comment in his biography of Imakita Kōsen: "Zen priests are not what they were. In ethics, in learning, in integrity, in dignity, they are not the men of old. All that can be said of their way of life is that they live in temples. Otherwise they are no different from other men in the world at large. I am not asking whether this is good or bad; but it is something that Zen priests should consider." As a lay practitioner, Suzuki always saw the Zen establishment from the outside. It must have struck him that the reality was considerably different from the essence of Zen that he constantly sought. He must have had harsh criticism for individual priests as well as for the establishment as a whole. Yet, in his massive output of writings, there is little expression of it.

This reluctance derives from his personality. It was as unlike him to harden his heart and criticize harshly as it was to think something through scientifically. Rather, he absorbed himself in free, wide-ranging speculation in a field that was liberated from all shackles.

Zen Must Be Learned from Experience

Commentaries on Suzuki are full of praise and awe at his thought and achievement, which is to be expected. He focused modern thought on a Zen that was moldy and dust-covered, and he gave it a philosophical backing. He saw the place of Zen in the history of philosophy and strove to elucidate it with modern speculative methodology. His introduction of Zen to the West and explanation of its profound influence on Japanese culture was a major achievement.

Most Japanese commentators on Suzuki have been eminent philosophers (who learned of him through Nishida's philosophy), friends and students, or people who knew him during his time as a professor at Ōtani University.

Of those who were neither acquaintances nor pupils, that is, who knew of him only through his writings, none seem to have been willing to comment on his ideas. Why is it that his writings on Zen philosophy, though admired, have not been analyzed and followed up?

Possibly it is because few people have experienced Zen, or enlightenment. Because his thought is based on Zen, it cannot be analyzed with logic or dialectics. His student Akizuki once said to him, "I want to understand Zen and have read your books as diligently as I can. But however much I read, I still can't gain a clear understanding. All I have learned is that only by attaining enlightenment myself will I understand Zen." Suzuki replied, "That is enough. That is what I have written."

This koan-like exchange makes us ask why Suzuki wrote so voluminously. Why should he have formulated the "logic of absolute affirmation and absolute negation" and the "logic of suchness"? Perhaps we have to consider that all of his writings are skillful means to lead us to Zen enlightenment through direct experience, like a finger pointing to the moon. In the preface to his book *Zen,* Suzuki wrote, "Reading this book through should give you an idea of what modern Zen is. However, Zen is not only knowledge; above all it is direct experience. Therefore I believe that it goes without saying that it is impossible to be satisfied with just the intellectual basis." Consequently, if we try to discuss Suzuki's philosophical weaknesses in terms of that intellectual basis, we probably bring upon ourselves the rejoinder, "Give up your verbal conceptions and first sit. After you have sat and attained enlightenment, then try using words again."

Umehara's Criticism

In an essay in the August 1966 issue of the journal *Vision,* the young philosopher Umehara Takeshi attacked Suzuki's theories of Japanese culture. Umehara appears to have been the first to criticize Suzuki seriously. The essay strongly impressed all who esteemed Suzuki and was, in its way, refreshing, especially for those who had not been able to articulate their dissatisfaction with the vagueness of the nonsystematic and elusive nature of his thought. Just after the essay was published, Suzuki died on July 12 at the age of ninety-five. This lent an element of drama to the proceedings.

Umehara presumably had had no Zen training or experience of enlightenment, so he did not focus his criticism on what Suzuki wrote about the realm of the absolute, which is enlightenment, but focused it rather on Suzuki's other major interest, Japanese culture. The question of Zen influence on Japanese culture is historical and would not require Zen training to answer.

Suzuki published *Zen Buddhism and Its Influence on Japanese Culture* in 1938, and it created a sensation in the West. In 1940 it was translated into Japanese by Kitagawa Momoo and was widely read in Japan. Explaining the extent of Zen's influence on Japanese culture, Suzuki wrote, "While the Japanese have always felt close to nature, Zen greatly increased that feeling of closeness and undoubtedly gave it a philosophical and religious basis." He is emphasizing that the Japanese had always loved nature and lived in harmony with it, and that this attitude had been intensified through Zen. He mentioned areas such as the fine arts, the warrior ideal, Japanese swordsmanship, Confucianism, the tea ceremony, *haiku* poetry, and the Noh drama as being particularly influenced by Zen, and went on to explain in what ways.

Umehara's criticism of Suzuki's arguments is variegated, but its main thrust is that Suzuki's idea that Zen alone was the creative power in Japanese culture reveals a partiality to Zen. After all, Umehara says, other Buddhist sects, such as Shingon, where his own interest lay, also have had an important influence on Japanese culture. Because Suzuki was writing for Westerners, he was responsible for having given them "the misconception that Zen, and Zen alone, fostered the Japanese love of nature, for Western readers have been fascinated by the fluent style and wealth of quotations in a book that actually is full of inaccuracies concerning that love of nature."

Umehara then turned to Suzuki's *Japanese Spirituality*. "Japanese spirituality" is a term Suzuki coined to distinguish what he considered true Japanese spirituality from the nationalist spirit of that time. According to Suzuki's book, "Japanese spirituality" was not fully awakened in the Heian period (794–1185); it was in the Kamakura period (1185–1336) that it was deeply cultivated through Zen and Pure Land teachings.

Umehara's criticism is severe.

Suzuki writes that Japanese spirituality was awakened in the Kamakura period. Why did this occur through Zen and Pure Land teachings, and not through the Nichiren branch, for example? To elucidate this, Suzuki would need to have criticized Nichirenism in a substantial way, but in fact he makes no mention of it and just says Japanese spirituality was awakened by Zen and Pure Land teachings. Reading *Japanese Spirituality*, I felt tempted to give this somnambulant Japanese spirituality a hefty blow to wake it from its long sleep. But then I realized that the one fast asleep was Suzuki; Japanese spirituality had been brilliantly realized in Prince Shōtoku [see biography in part 2], in Gyōgi, in Kūkai, in Saichō [see biographies in part 1], and the sleeping Suzuki mistook something awake and vibrant for something still to be awakened.

The old scholars who had nothing but admiration for Suzuki must have been appalled.

What Umehara addresses is the ambiguity of a brilliant concept whose ideas are not borne out by fact. I do not know whether Suzuki ever saw the essay, but if he had, I am sure he would have said, "I leave all this and more up to students of Buddhist history."

War Responsibility

Umehara criticized Suzuki on another count, as well.

> Suzuki says that Zen advocates a spirit of "passive, peaceful" force. Isn't "passive" or "peaceful" force a contradiction in terms? . . . This work, published in 1940, advocating peaceful or passive force, may have been intended as a tacit criticism of the "active force" of the government's policy of aggression of the time, but it played a historical role in promoting respect for "passive, peaceful" military force in Japan.
>
> Suzuki thought these kinds of force were of considerable importance, placing the chapters "Zen and the Warrior" and "Zen and *Kendō* [Japanese swordsmanship]" immediately after "Zen and the Fine Arts." This speaks to us of a certain tendency toward militarism in his thought, the same militarism that Japan has embraced since the early Meiji era.

Immediately after the Second World War, Suzuki published *The Building of a Spiritual Japan,* in which he criticized Shinto nationalism and addressed the restructuring of Japan on the guiding principle of Japanese spirituality. Umehara had very little patience with a Suzuki who could say casually in the book, "I can now declare explicitly and publicly that I believed from the beginning that Japan would lose the war, and that I even thought that to lose would be good for Japan"; "If I had referred directly to [Japanese spirituality], I would have incurred the displeasure of the authorities and not been allowed to publish."

The young men of Umehara's generation, who had been swept

up in a reckless war and constantly faced death, had discovered a way of escape in the idea of the identity of life and death, and had carried Suzuki's book with them to the battlefield. The story that Suzuki liked to recount, from the record of the Chinese Ch'an priest Fa-yen, about the burglar who taught his skill to his son, gave these young men a way of living with death. After the war, Umehara and others felt betrayed by Suzuki's disavowals, hence the bitterness of Umehara's criticism.

If Suzuki had thought that the war would be lost, why did he not have the courage to say so? While expounding the virtues of great compassion, he stood silently by and watched large numbers of Japanese being killed day by day. Is it not strange that one who had attained enlightenment at the age of twenty-five should have been afraid of the authorities and of speaking his mind? Of all Umehara's criticisms, this cuts closest to the bone.

At this point we should turn again to the nature of Zen enlightenment. Suzuki is not alone in bearing responsibility for the war. He was a man of conscience and did criticize it in a small way. He was a free spirit, however, who had experienced Zen and was supposed to be different from timid academics afraid to swim against the tide. If enlightenment really exists, and if Suzuki really attained it, he bears a far heavier responsibility for the war than ordinary contemporaries.

Later Umehara wrote of Suzuki in *Vision* (June 1968), "Just after my criticism of him appeared in *Vision,* he died. I was filled with remorse and felt we had lost a great man. Suzuki was a great thinker who made us aware of the true spirit of our country at a time when that spirit seemed forgotten."

The Suzuki that I believe will remain in our hearts for years to come is not the Suzuki of the philosophers and students who are supposed to have understood him best and who have showered him with praise, but the Suzuki fiercely criticized by Umehara out of love.

PART TWO
Brief Biographies

by Hitoshi Ōkuwa

PRINCE SHŌTOKU (574–622). The first Japanese imperial family member to understand and accept Buddhism, Prince Shōtoku is revered as the father of Japanese Buddhism. Born as Prince Umayado, the second son of Emperor Yōmei, in 593 he was appointed crown prince and regent for his aunt, the reigning empress Suiko. He instituted a new style of government, making the national government firmer, adopting a system of court ranks, sending missions to China, promulgating the Seventeen-Article Constitution, and ordering compilation of two official histories, the *Records of the Emperors* and *Record of the Nation*. Because of Prince Shōtoku's deep faith in Buddhism, in 594 he issued a proclamation urging the promotion of Buddhism based on the Three Treasures (the Buddha; Buddhist law, or dharma; and community of Buddhists, or sangha). The following year he became a student of Eji, a priest from the kingdom of Koguryo on the Korean peninsula. The learning center that he erected for the purpose later became Hōryū-ji. Two historically documented statements attest to the prince's faith: "Avoid evil, undertake good," and "This world is illusion; only the Buddha is truth." These statements have been highly esteemed as testaments to the prince's deep understanding. Other writings attributed to him, such as the phrase "sincerely reverence the Three Treasures—the Buddha, dharma, and sangha" in the Seventeen-Article Constitution, and three commentaries, on the *Queen of Shrimala Sutra, Vimalakirti Sutra,* and *Lotus Sutra,* are considered by some to have come from another hand.

DŌSHŌ (629–700). The first transmitter to Japan of the Hossō teachings, Dōshō was active in the mid- to late seventh century. Dōshō was born of the Funa family in Kawachi Province. After ordination he lived at Gangō-ji, where he became renowned for his virtue and adherence to the precepts. In 653, he and several others went to T'ang China as student priests. In China, Dōshō studied the Consciousness Only doctrine under Hsüan-tsang and maintained a close friendship with K'uei-chi, one of Hsüan-tsang's dharma successors. He also received Ch'an instruction under another priest. In 660, he returned to Japan with a large number of sacred texts, which he deposited in a Zen hall he built within Gangō-ji. He worked for the dissemination of the Hossō teachings and also traveled the country teaching the elements of engineering and transportation, digging wells by roadsides, building boats at fords, and constructing bridges. The famous Uji Bridge in Kyoto is said to have been built by Dōshō. In 698 he led a dedication ceremony at Yakushi-ji, "opening the eyes" of an embroidery representing Amida Buddha; the emperor, in gratitude, appointed him senior assistant high priest. Dōshō died in 700 at the age of seventy-one. In accordance with his own request, he became the first person in Japan whose body was cremated.

SHINJŌ (d. 742). A scholar-priest from the kingdom of Silla on the Korean peninsula, Shinjō brought the Kegon teachings, based on the *Flower Garland Sutra,* to Japan. Seeking the dharma, he went first to China, where he studied the Flower Garland doctrine under Fa-tsang, the third patriarch in China's Hua-yen (Kegon) lineage. He arrived in Japan somewhat before the middle of the eighth century, taking up residence at Daian-ji. Rōben (see biography in part 2), hearing of his arrival, requested that he lecture on the *Flower Garland Sutra,* but Shinjō did not agree. In 740, however, he accepted the emperor's invitation to lecture on the sutra; this took place at what was to become the Lotus Hall of Tōdai-ji. Shinjō lectured on the sixty-volume version of the sutra, assisted by three priests, taking three years to complete the series. The emperor and nobility attended the first lecture, and an offering of one thousand bales of dyed cloth was made. Kegon studies thereafter took root at Tōdai-ji and prospered as the *Flower Garland Sutra* became the principal sutra revered within Nara Buddhism. Shinjō had many dharma successors, including Rōben.

DŌJI (d. 744). A scholar-priest of Daian-ji during the early part of the eighth century, and the third transmitter of Sanron (Three Treatises) doctrines to Japan, Dōji was born of the Nukata family in Yamato Province and entered the priesthood as a child. He studied Sanron doctrine at Hōryū-ji and Hossō doctrine at Ryūmon-ji. In 701 he traveled to China in an official embassy; there he visited famous masters and sought out sutras. While making a deep study of Sanron in particular, Dōji also studied esoteric Buddhism under Shubhakarasimha. He returned to Japan in 718 and worked hard to spread knowledge of Sanron. In 729, the emperor appointed him to supervise the rebuilding of Daian-ji; he renovated the temple based on the plan of Hsi-ming temple in T'ang China. Later in the same year he was appointed preceptor, and in 737 he lectured on the *Golden Light Sutra* at the imperial palace. After his return from China he wrote *A Fool's Idea*, criticizing the degeneration of male and female clerics and discussing how clerics should conduct themselves. He died in 744, at the age of about seventy. Two of his poems appearing in a collection of poetry in Chinese, *Yearnings for the Ancient Chinese Style,* assembled around 751, are admirable expressions of his attitudes.

RŌBEN (689–773). Rōben was a scholar-priest of the Kegon sect and the founder of Tōdai-ji. A descendent of immigrants from the kingdom of Paekche on the Korean peninsula, he was born in either Ōmi or Sagami Province. He studied Hossō doctrine early in life, under Gien. Through his efforts, the Korean priest Shinjō (see earlier biography) gave lectures on the *Flower Garland Sutra* at Konshō-ji (the predecessor of Tōdai-ji) in 740, paving the way for the eventual erection of the statue of the Great Buddha (Vairo-cana). In the New Year of 742 he gave a lecture on the *Golden Light Sutra* to bring about a revival of the fortunes of Buddhism. Gradually he became more and more politically involved. To-gether with court official Tachibana no Moroe and Gyōgi (see biography in part 1), he aided Emperor Shōmu with the construc-tion of the Great Buddha at Tōdai-ji. At the completion of the statue he was appointed the first chief priest. In 756, as a leading Buddhist figure, he was made senior assistant high priest. In 760, fearing the degeneration of the Buddhist religion, he joined with another leading priest, Jikun, to prevent the decay. In 763 he was appointed high priest. He is remembered more as the prototype of a cleric with close political connections than for his scholarly work in Hossō and Kegon studies.

JITCHŪ (726?–815?). A Kegon priest of the late eighth century, who brought Tōdai-ji to completion, Jitchū studied under Rōben (see preceding biography) and succeeded him as the superinten-dent of repairs to Tōdai-ji. He established the structure of that temple in terms of both buildings and administration. In 764, when the eastern pagoda was being erected and the base of the fin-ial proved hard for the carpenters to put in place because of its weight, Jitchū himself climbed the pagoda and attached the base to the rooftop. Again in 771, when the construction of auxiliary columns in the Great Buddha Hall ran into problems, Jitchū had the work completed in a scant eight months. He also assisted with repairs on the halo behind the Great Buddha in 799. These attest to his carpentry and building skills. Jitchū was also skilled in other areas, particularly temple administration, and made every effort to establish proper temple ceremonial. He originated an annual service in Fukū Kenjaku-in; this continued without intermission between 752 and 809. He also began the ceremony marking the day of the Buddha's death, and this continued for fifty-three years, between 761 and 814. He is said to have died during the early ninth century; some records mention that he died in 815, aged eighty-five, others say he was over ninety.

ENNIN (794–864). Ennin, a Tendai priest, became the third head of Enryaku-ji. Posthumous title: Jikaku Daishi. Born of the Mibu family in Shimotsuke Province, he entered Mount Hiei and became an apprentice of Saichō (see biography in part 1) when he was fifteen. In 838 he went to study in China, where he learned Sanskrit and esoteric Buddhism. Intending to return to Japan the following year, he found himself remaining in China when his ship was driven back by adverse winds. He visited famous old temples, beginning with those on Mount Wu-t'ai, and later in Ch'ang-an he studied the Diamond Realm and Womb-Store Realm teachings, as well as T'ien-t'ai Concentration and Insight practices. He returned to Japan in 847. The travel record he kept during the stay in China is well known; it was translated into English by Edwin O. Reischauer as *Ennin's Diary*. Ennin was appointed an official court priest in 848 and head of the Tendai sect in 854. He built Tō-in to house the sutras, ritual implements, and manuals he had brought back with him and built the Monju-dō as a hall for the four meditation practices. He also erected the Chū-do and Hokke Sōji-in at Yokawa, thus strengthening the temple fabric and working to fulfill Saichō's aspirations. He promoted the practice of meditation through ninety days of walking and chanting Amida's name, also known as nembutsu meditation; this eventually resulted in the development of Pure Land teachings. He was the author of many works, including commentaries on the *Diamond Peak Sutra* and the *Sutra of Good Accomplishment*.

DŌSHŌ (798–875). Dōshō, a Shingon priest, was one of Kūkai's (see biography in part 1) ten chief dharma successors. He founded Hōrin-ji in Yamashiro Province. Born of the Hata family in Sanuki Province, he entered Buddhism as a child, studied Sanron doctrine at Gangō-ji, and was ordained as an annual quota priest in 816. He received the *Vinaya of Four Categories* precepts at Tōdai-ji two years later, then roamed the country practicing various Buddhist traditions. Meeting Kūkai at Takaosan-ji, Dōshō received esoteric initiation under him and studied Shingon doctrine. In 830 he was invited to be officiating priest for a ceremony of repentance by recitation of the Buddha names, which was held at the imperial palace. In 836 he became chief priest of Kōryū-ji and reconstructed it after a fire destroyed it. In 842, he was the officiating priest for a ceremony held at Danrin-ji in Saga, and between 863 and 864 he was appointed lecturer at three Buddhist ceremonies. He was appointed provisional preceptor in 864 and junior assistant high priest in 874. He was a skilled engineer and repaired the collapsed embankment on the Ōi River during the 830s and 840s. Some considered him the reincarnation of Gyōgi.

ENCHIN (814–891). As the fifth head of Enryaku-ji, Enchin founded the Jimon subsect of Tendai. Posthumous name: Chishō Daishi. Born of the Wake family in Sanuki Province, he was a nephew of Kūkai (see biography in part 1). At fifteen he entered Mount Hiei and studied under Gishin, not leaving the mountain for twelve years. In 857 he went to China. First he studied the Siddham script of Sanskrit at a temple in Fukien; then at Mount T'ien-t'ai he made a deep study of T'ien-t'ai doctrine. In Ch'ang-an he studied esoteric Buddhism and received initiation. During his six years in China he collected many Buddhist works, and on his return to Japan, took up residence at Sannō-in on Mount Hiei. He frequently lectured and conducted Buddhist services at court. In 859 Enchin moved to Mii-dera; he became its chief priest in 866. He was appointed head of the Tendai sect two years later and received imperial permission to make Mii-dera an official site for esoteric transmission. This led to the schism within Tendai between the Sammon (Mount Hiei) and Jimon (Mii-dera) subsects. Enchin favored esoteric teachings over the traditional Tendai teachings based on the *Lotus Sutra,* and under him Tendai esotericism reached its greatest influence. His writings are collected in the *Anthology of Enchin's Writings.*

YAKUSHIN (827–906). The priest who received the patronage of the former emperor Uda, Yakushin, founded the Hirosawa lineage of the Shingon sect. Posthumous name: Hongaku Daishi.

He was born of the Ki family (one record says Shinaji) in Bingo Province and was the younger brother of Gyōkyō, founder of Iwashimizu Hachiman Shrine. Yakushin became a student of Buddhism at a young age, residing at Daian-ji in Nara, where he received ordination and studied esoteric Buddhism. He studied Hossō doctrine at Gangō-ji and later received esoteric initiation at Tō-ji. In 894, Yakushin was appointed head of Tō-ji. Owing to the success of his rites on behalf of a court lady, he was given a mountain villa in the Higashiyama district of Kyoto, which he made into a temple called Enjō-ji. This success also led to the former emperor Uda seeking ordination under him. In 899 Uda became a priest at Ninna-ji, and in 901 he received dharma initiation at Tō-ji. Yakushin died at Enjō-ji in 906. His writings include the *Procedures for the Ritual for the Diamond Realm.*

SHŌBŌ (832–909). Shōbō is known as the restorer of Shingon esotericism. He was a renowned scholar of Sanron doctrine, advocating the unity of exoteric and esoteric teachings, and he was also the founder of Daigo-ji, founder of the Ono lineage of the Shingon sect, and regenerator of the Shugendō movement. Posthumous name: Rigen Daishi. A descendant of Emperor Kōnin, Shōbō was born on Shiaku Island, Sanuki Province. In 847, at the age of fifteen, he received ordination under Shinga, the younger brother of Kūkai and one of his chief dharma successors, at Jōkan-ji. He studied Sanron doctrine at Gangō-ji, as well as Hossō and Kegon doctrines at Tōdai-ji. In 874 Shobō established Shōgyō-in (Daigo-ji's predecessor) on Mount Kasatori as a result of a dream; this temple later received imperial patronage. In 875 he built Tōnan-in as a center for the Sanron sect, within Tōdai-ji, and made that the center for esoteric studies within the Nara sects. His honors included heading Jōkan-ji, superintending the seven official temples, and heading both Tōdai-ji and Tō-ji. He popularized Shingon esoteric Buddhism and regenerated Shugendō, through his restoration of Kimpusen and Ōmine. His works include *Notes on the Commentary on the Great Sun Sutra* and *Procedures for the Ritual for the Womb-Store Realm.*

RYŌGEN (912–985). The Tendai priest Ryōgen rejuvenated Mount Hiei. Posthumous name: Jie Daishi. Also called Ganzan Daishi. A native of Ōmi Province, he entered Mount Hiei at the age of twelve. In 928 he received the precepts from Son'i, then head of the Tendai sect. He studied both esoteric and exoteric traditions under a number of masters and was renowned for his scholarship. In 937, Ryōgen debated with the Hossō priest Gishō of Gangō-ji during the *Vimalakirti Sutra* ceremony at Kōfuku-ji, and in 963 he defeated Hōzō of Tōdai-ji in a debate at the imperial palace. Ryōgen worked strenuously to restore academic standards within Tendai, reviving doctrinal study. He was appointed head of Tendai in 966. During his nearly twenty-year term in office, he rebuilt the Mount Hiei temple buildings that had been destroyed in the disastrous fire of 966. In particular he restored the Yokawa area and built Eshin-in there. He was raised to senior high priest in 981. In 984 he built Hōdō-in in the western precinct. Ryōgen died on the third day of the following New Year; the popular title by which he is known, Ganzan Daishi, derives from the date of his death *(gan,* "new year," and *zan,* "third," with *daishi,* "great teacher"). He wrote many works, including *On the Nine Types of Rebirth in the Pure Land of Utmost Bliss.*

GENSHIN (942–1017). Tendai priest Genshin, through his adoption of the Chinese Shan-tao school's oral nembutsu, laid the foundations for development of Japan's Pure Land (Jōdo) movement. He was born of the Urabe family in Yamato Province. His father died when he was seven; soon after, he entered Mount Hiei with Ryōgen (see preceding biography) as his teacher. At thirteen he shaved his head and received formal ordination with the dharma name Genshin. Because he lived in Eshin-in at Yokawa, and there underwent religious training and wrote his many works, he is also known as Assistant High Priest Eshin. In 978 he gained recognition as a skilled scholar and debater, and in 985 he produced his famous *Essentials of Deliverance,* systematizing Pure Land doctrine for the first time. This was an epoch-making work in the history of development of the Pure Land teachings, for as a result those teachings began to be widely disseminated. A copy was sent to Chou Wen-te in China, who sent it to Mount T'ien-t'ai, praising Genshin as the "Japanese Small Shakyamuni Tathagata." In 986 Genshin compiled the *Nembutsu Assembly of Twenty-five Like-minded People and Ritual for Nembutsu* and gathered people around him to practice nembutsu meditation. In 1004 his apprentice declined an appointment as provisional junior assistant high priest, so the appointment went to Genshin, but Genshin retired the following year. Genshin died in 1017, his hands in the Amida position. His works other than those mentioned above include *Essentials of the One-Vehicle Teaching* and *Essentials of Contemplating the Mind.*

JŌJIN (1011–1081). Tendai priest Jōjin, who received imperial patronage in China, was the son of a renowned calligrapher. He entered Daiun-ji in Yamashiro Province when he was six. Jōjin was fond of calligraphy and studied both exoteric and esoteric doctrines. In 1053 he received imperial appointment as a holy teacher at Sōji-in on Mount Hiei, where he recited the *Lotus Sutra.* In 1072, at the age of sixty-one, he went to China with another priest and traveled to the sacred sites on Mounts T'ien-t'ai and Wu-t'ai, then settled in a temple. In 1074, during a severe drought, Jōjin performed a rain ritual at China's imperial palace. Because of the efficacy of his ritual, the emperor bestowed upon him the title of Great Master Shan-hui. Later Jōjin lived at another temple; he died in China at the age of seventy. His activities in China are recorded in detail in his *Record of a Pilgrimage to Mounts T'ien-t'ai and Wu-t'ai.* On his companion priest's return to Japan, Jōjin sent with him more than five hundred religious documents to Japan and donated to Daiun-ji the sixteen statues of the Buddha's disciples that the Chinese empress had given him. Jōjin's other works include *Notes on the Lotus Sutra* and *Description of the Meditation Sutra.*

RYŌNIN (1072–1132). Ryōnin was a Tendai priest who taught *yūzū nembutsu* (mutually inclusive nembutsu) and founded the sect of that name. Also called Kōjōbō. A native of Owari Province, he studied Tendai doctrine on Mount Hiei, including esoteric doctrines and the Tendai tradition of musical chanting of sutras. In 1109 he built two temples in the Ōhara district just north of Kyoto, which specialized in musical chanting. Later ages called him the restorer of musical chanting. The Ōhara district had long been known as a place where wandering nembutsu ascetics gathered, and musical chanting had strong ties with nembutsu. Ryōnin himself practiced perpetual chanting of the nembutsu on particular days. In 1117 he had a vision of Amida Buddha, the content of which he expressed in the verse "One person is all people, all people are one person; one practice is all practices, all practices are one practice." This is the mutually inclusive nembutsu, called a direct revelation of Amida. After returning to Kyoto in 1124, Ryōnin expounded his teachings to the retired emperor Toba and the court nobility. He later traveled around the country and established Shūraku-ji in Settsu Province as his main temple. This is now Dainembutsu-ji.

KAKUBAN (1095–1143). Kakuban founded the Shingi (New Meaning) subsect of Shingon. He is the founder of the Dembō-in subsidiary of the Hirosawa lineage. Posthumous title: Kōgyō Daishi. A native of Hizen Province, Kakuban entered Buddhism at the age of thirteen, at Nanna-ji in Kyoto. He went on to study various esoteric traditions at Mount Kōya, Mii-dera, and Daigo-ji. Given patronage by the retired emperor Toba, in 1126 he founded Dembō-in in Kii and in 1132, Daidembō-in on Mount Kōya. Kakuban became chief priest of Daidembō-in in 1134 and took charge of Kongōbu-ji on Mount Kōya. Because of the violent opposition of the Mount Kōya priests to his doctrines, however, Kakuban retired the following year to Mitsugon-in, removing himself from affairs and immersing himself in esoteric meditation. When Mitsugon-in was destroyed by angry Mount Kōya priests in 1140, Kakuban and his followers escaped to Mount Negoro, where he established a temple called Emmyō-ji. The conflict with Mount Kōya continued, and Kakuban never returned. He died at Emmyō-ji near the end of 1143. His numerous works include the *Esoteric Explanation of Amida.*

MONGAKU (d. 1203). A Shingon priest and ascetic, Mongaku is known as the restorer of Takaosan-ji. His lay name was Endō Moritō. Skilled in martial arts, he was assigned to guard Jōsai-mon'in, a daughter of Emperor Toba. After accidentally killing a noblewoman when he was eighteen, he entered religion in remorse and made an ascetic pilgrimage around Kumano and other mountains of spiritual potency, achieving great powers. Around 1177 Mongaku went to Mount Takao near Kyoto and, lamenting the desolate state of Takaosan-ji, vowed to restore the temple and went among the people raising funds to this end. Having forcibly extracted a donation from the retired emperor, Go-Shirakawa, however, he was exiled to Izu Province. While there it is said he became acquainted with Minamoto no Yoritomo, urged Yoritomo to take up arms against the Tairas, and traveled to Kyoto to obtain a decree to Yoritomo from the retired emperor urging this course of action. Following the subsequent establishment by Yoritomo of the Kamakura shogunate, Mongaku appealed to Yoritomo as a patron to help him restore Takaosan-ji. He also vowed to do repair work on Tō-ji. After Yoritomo's death in 1199, Mongaku served the Taira descendants planning a rebellion and was again exiled, this time to the island of Sado. He died in grief there. He was violent in temperament and was said to be a "rough holy man, one who threw himself into his practice, but had no learning." In later times Mongaku became a topic for literature and plays. His story has been popularized through legend.

CHŌGEN (1121–1206). Chōgen, a Jōdo priest, was active in the reconstruction of Tōdai-ji. He entered Daigo-ji at the age of twelve and studied Shingon doctrine; later he made pilgrimages to sacred mountains throughout the country, practicing perpetual nembu-tsu chanting. He traveled to China three times between 1167 and 1177, studying engineering and architecture as well as Buddhism there. After Tōdai-ji was destroyed in 1180 during the Taira-Minamoto War, Hōnen proposed in 1181 that the sixty-year-old Chōgen should head a campaign to raise money for its reconstruction. Chōgen traveled the country, unifying popular support and encouraging donations; at the same time he put his efforts into teaching and leading the people. He promoted public works and the religious merit of building temples, erecting statues, and holding services. In 1195 the reconstruction of Tōdai-ji was finished, with the completion of the Indian-style Great Buddha Hall designed by Chōgen. The work had demonstrated his political and technical gifts; he contributed greatly to the development of Kamakura art and the renaissance of Nara Buddhism, to say nothing of the economic foundation of Tōdai-ji itself in the form of manorial rights. Chōgen wrote a *Collection [Telling How] the Nembutsu Invocation Created Good,* probably in 1203.

JŌKEI (1155–1213). Hossō priest Jōkei, stimulated by the new movements in Kamakura Buddhism, worked for the renaissance of the Nara sects. Also called Gedatsu Shōnin of Kasagi-dera. He is known as the regenerator of the Hossō sect. His father was Fujiwara no Sadanori, a poet, and his grandfather was a prominent political figure of the time. The family suffered death and exile through involvement in the Heiji Disturbance of 1159, and two years later Jōkei entered Kōfuku-ji, headed at the time by his uncle. In 1192, disappointed with the greed for fame in Buddhist circles, Jōkei adopted the life of a recluse at Kasagi-dera in Yamashiro Province, outside Nara. It is said that the direct cause of his withdrawal was that people sneered at the simple priest's robe he wore at the annual ceremony expounding the *Golden Light Sutra* at the imperial palace. He moved to Kaijūsen-ji in 1208 and died there five years later, at the age of fifty-eight. Kujō Kanezane, when he was imperial regent, called Jōkei "the virtuous sage of the Last Age." Jōkei restored the ordination platform at Tōdai-ji, practiced the chanting of Shakyamuni Buddha's name, promoted the cult of Prince Shōtoku (see biography in part 2), and revived the doctrine of Consciousness Only. He was also the author of the *Kōfuku-ji Petition,* which was instrumental in having the Pure Land nembutsu movement banned. His works include *Litany on Maitreya* and *Aspiring to the Way in Foolishness and Delusion.*

SHUNJŌ (1166–1227). In the early Kamakura period, Shunjō studied the Vinaya teachings in China and restored the Ritsu (Vinaya) sect in Japan. Also known as Gazen and Fukaki. Posthumous titles: Daikō Shōhō Kokushi, Getsurin Daishi. Born in Higo Province, Shunjō received ordination in 1184 at Kanzeon-ji in Dazaifu, on Kyushu, and first trained in the esoteric tradition of the Tendai sect. Becoming convinced of the need for the precepts, he went to China in 1199. There he studied the Nanshan school of Vinaya and T'ien-t'ai doctrine. He returned to Japan after a twelve-year stay, bringing back with him more than two thousand Buddhist texts. At the invitation of Eisai (see biography in part 1) he went to live at Kennin-ji. Later he became very popular with the imperial family, nobility, and top-ranking military families; among his patrons were Emperors Go-Toba, Juntoku, and Chūkyō, and the Kamakura regent Hōjō Yasutoki. In 1218 he was given the Kyoto temple Sen'yū-ji by a senior vassal of the Hōjō family; this temple was later renamed Sennyū-ji and became the center for the restoration of Japan's Tendai and Ritsu sects. Among his several dharma successors was Jōshun, who succeeded him as the head of Sennyū-ji. Shunjō wrote the *Method of Nembutsu Meditation* and *Principles and Manners for Zazen*.

MYŌE (1173–1232). A pioneer in the movement to reinvigorate the established Buddhist sects in the face of the new movements of the early Kamakura period, Myōe is called the restorer of the Kegon sect. Also known as Kōben. He was born in Kii Province, the son of a Taira father and a Fujiwara mother. He entered religion when he was eight, following the deaths of both parents. At sixteen he went to study under Mongaku (see earlier biography), the priest who had urged Minamoto no Yoritomo to revolt. Myōe read Fa-tsang's *Discussion of the Five Teachings and the Ten Sects* and the verse portion of the *Abhidharma Storehouse Treatise*. He later studied Kegon doctrine, esoteric Buddhism, Siddham script, and Zen (under Eisai; see biography in part 1). Much as he loved learning, he knew the importance of religious practice and was particularly strict in the observance of the precepts. He had many supporters, drawn by his purity, among whom were the retired

emperor Go-Toba, Kenreimon'in (consort of Emperor Takakura), and Hōjō Yasutoki. At the urging of his master Mongaku,
Myōe lived at Toganoo near Kyoto, and there made Kōzan-ji
the center for the revival of the Kegon sect. As the representative of the declining exoteric and esoteric sects, he came into confrontation with the proponents of the new sects of Kamakura
Buddhism; he is particularly famous for his *Smashing the Wheel of
Heresy*, a criticism of Hōnen's *Collection of Passages on the Original
Vow and the Nembutsu*. Among his other writings are *On Venerating
the Three Treasures Thrice Daily* and *Record of the Workings of Faith
[Regarding] the Mantra of Light and the Sprinkling of Sand.*

BENCHŌ (1162–1238). A dharma successor of Hōnen and second
patriarch of the Jōdo sect, Benchō founded the Chinzei subsect of
Jōdo. Also known by the names Ben'a and Shōkōbō. Was popularly called Chinzei Shōnin and Niso Shōnin. Posthumous title:
Daishō Shōshū Kokushi. Born in Chikuzen Province, Kyushu,
Benchō belonged to a branch of the Fujiwara family. He entered
religion in his infancy and in 1183 went to Mount Hiei to study
Tendai doctrine. In 1190 he returned to Kyushu. Deeply disturbed by the death of his younger brother, he visited Hōnen in Kyoto
in 1197 and became his apprentice. After a profound study of the
Pure Land doctrines, Benchō returned in 1204 to his native province, where he spread the nembutsu teachings, built halls for nembutsu practice, and, most importantly, established Zendō-ji as the
main Jōdo temple on Kyushu. At Ōjō-in in Higo Province he composed the *Personal Seal [Attesting] to the Transmission of the Nembutsu in
the Latter Days* and formalized Jōdo tradition in the Chinzei
subsect. He was succeeded by his apprentice Ryōchū. When,
more than a century after Hōnen's death, the Chinzei subsect
established itself in Kyoto at Hōnen's mausoleum as the orthodox
sect of Jōdo (modern Jōdo is the Chinzei subsect), Benchō was
given the title of Niso Shōnin (Second Patriarch, Holy One).
While emphasizing oral nembutsu, Benchō also affirmed the
possibility of attaining Pure Land rebirth through a variety of
other practices. His works include *Collection of the Essentials of the
Jōdo Sect* and *Discussion on the Teachings of the Jōdo Sect.*

SHŌKŪ (1177–1247). Shōkū, another dharma successor of Hōnen, founded the Seizan subsect of the Jōdo sect. Also called Gedatsubō and later Zen'e. The eldest son of the lord of Kaga and adopted son of a givernment minister, Koga Michichika, he joined Hōnen at the age of fourteen. Shōkū made a profound study of Pure Land writings, beginning with Shan-tao's *Commentary on the Meditation Sutra*. He also received the Mahayana precepts and studied the essentials of other sects under venerable masters. Shōkū helped Hōnen with the compilation of the *Collection of Passages on the Original Vow and the Nembutsu* in 1198, and the following year he lectured on it in Hōnen's place at the residence of Kujō Kanezane. Sentenced to exile at the time of the 1207 persecution, Shōkū was entrusted to the noted Tendai priest Jien instead. Later he studied Tendai doctrine, Shingon, and, under Jien, Tendai esotericism. In 1213 Jien gave him the temple Ōjō-in at Nishiyama, and Shōkū took up residence there. That is how his subsect came to be called Seizan, which is another pronunciation for the characters for Nishiyama (its present head temple, however, is Kōmyō-ji at Ao). Shōkū began a variety of practices at Ōjō-in, including perpetual nembutsu chanting, ceremonies dedicated to Amida six times a day, and formal discussion; he also put great effort into spreading the Pure Land teachings. Shōkū's doctrines were strongly Tendai-oriented and aristocratic. His writings include *Admonition [Concerning] Protecting and Striving* and *Nembutsu Dharma Words in Japanese*.

KAKUJŌ (1194–1249). Another restorer of the Ritsu sect, Kakujō was called by many a reincarnation of Ganjin (see biography in part 1). He is also known as the restoring founder of Tōshōdai-ji in Nara. Also known as Gakuritsu and Kūjō. Posthumous name: Daihi Bosatsu. Born in Yamato Province, Kakujō entered Kōfuku-ji as a young child. In 1212 he took up residence at Jōki-in, built at Kōfuku-ji by Jōkei (see biography in part 2) as a center of Vinaya studies, and there studied the Vinaya. Later he studied Kegon doctrine under Myōe (see biography in part 2) at Kōzan-ji and centered his efforts on studying and practicing the precepts under Kainyo of Saidai-ji following Jōkei's death. In 1236, together with Eizon (see following biography) and other priests, he accepted the precepts for himself, without the presence of a precepts transmitter, at the Lotus Hall of Tōdai-ji. These priests sought the restructuring of their age's Buddhism, which tended toward frivolity and ostentation. In 1238 he was invited by Eizon of Saidai-ji to introduce the community ceremony of the *Vinaya of Four Categories*; he acted as one of the three precepts transmitters for the ceremony. Emperor Shijō and his empress, together with the court nobility, received the bodhisattva precepts in the ceremony. By imperial order Kakujō took up residence in Tōshōdai-ji in 1243 and there worked hard to restore the Ritsu teachings and rebuild the halls. His writings include *Collection of Writings on the Chapter of Manifest and Unmanifest* and *Doubts Concerning the Bodhisattva Precepts*.

EIZON (1201–1290). Ritsu priest Eizon was the restoring founder of Saidai-ji in Nara. Also known as Shien Shōnin. Posthumous name: Kōshō Bosatsu. Born in Yamato Province, he became a priest at Tōdai-ji in 1217. Later he made a thorough study of esoteric teachings on Mount Kōya and at Daigo-ji. Concluding that the decline of the precepts was deplorable, he took up residence at Saidai-ji and studied the Vinaya under Kainyo of Saidai-ji in 1235. In 1236, he took part in a self-imparted precepts ceremony with Kakujō (see preceding biography) and others, determined to spread the precepts of the Nara sects and striving to increase Vinaya study. Later he won many followers among the nobility and was precepts transmitter for the retired emperor Go-Saga and other members of the imperial family. He was invited to court many times to give lectures and to administer the precepts. Eizon went to Kamakura at the invitation of the Hōjō family and was received there with reverence by the ranking retainers and military leaders, many of whom received the precepts from him. He also worked among members of the outcast class, giving them the bodhisattva precepts, and established sanctuary areas where no hunting or fishing was allowed. He is said to have given the precepts to more than ninety thousand people during his long life and to have established more than one thousand sanctuaries. His writings include *Collected Writings Concerning the Commentary on the*

Sutra of the Perfect Net and an autobiographical record called the *Record of Eizon.*

NINSHŌ (1217–1303). Ninshō was also a Ritsu priest who, like Chōgen and Eizon (see biographies in part 2), was well known for his social concern and efforts toward public welfare. Also known as Ryōkan Shōnin. Posthumous name: Ninshō Bosatsu. Born in Yamato Province, he was taught by his mother from infancy to have faith in Monju Bodhisattva. After his mother's death, he was ordained at Tōdai-ji. He studied under Eizon of Saidai-ji and learned the Vinaya from Kakujō (see biography in part 2). Stimulated by the revival of Vinaya studies within the Nara sects, Ninshō went to the eastern plains region in 1252 and took up residence at Sanzon-ji in Hitachi Province. In 1261 he went to Kamakura, where he lived at Shaka-dō and strived to teach and administer the precepts. The support and faith Ninshō received from the Hōjō family and many members of the shogunate enabled him to establish a number of temples, including Kōsen-ji in 1261 and Gokuraku-ji in 1267. Skilled at temple management, he also served as chief priest of Tahō-ji, Godai-dō, and the Kamakura Great Buddha temple. In addition he served in senior positions at Tada-in in Settsu, Tōdai-ji in Nara, and Shitennō-ji in Osaka. Giving care and effort to the plight of the poor and homeless, Ninshō built two centers, Hiden-in and Keiden-in, to care for the ill and needy. He had 189 bridges built and 71 roads constructed and repaired; people called him a living tathagata and an enlightened master of healing.

ISSAN ICHINEI (1247–1317). A Chinese Lin-chi priest, Issan Ichinei advanced the development of Southern Sung–style Ch'an among Kyoto Zen temples. A native of T'ai-tsu in China, he first practiced Ch'an, then studied the Vinaya and T'ien-t'ai, traveling from master to master and residing on Mount Pu-t'o. In 1299 the Chinese emperor sent him to Japan as an envoy; Japanese authorities, thinking him a spy, imprisoned him at Shuzen-ji on the Izu peninsula. When he was pardoned, Ichinei went to live at Kenchō-ji in Kamakura. He won the support of the Kamakura regent Hōjō Sadatoki and other leading clerical and lay figures in the eastern plains region. In 1300 the retired emperor Go-Uda invited him to become the third head of Nanzen-ji in Kyoto. His influence made Southern Sung Ch'an popular among the Zen temples of Kyoto. Because he also had considerable knowledge of Confucianism and secular literature, he attracted many followers. Ichinei left a lasting legacy in his apprentices, many of whom, like Musō Soseki (see biography in part 2), became leading figures in Rinzai Zen. His teachings are preserved in the *Record of National Teacher Issan.*

SōHō MyōCHō (1282–1337). The founder of Daitoku-ji, Sōhō Myōchō, commonly known as National Teacher Daitō, opposed the Japanization of Rinzai Zen. Posthumous titles: Kōzen Daitō Kokushi, Kōshō Shōtō Kokushi. Also known by the names Kōshō Daiji, Unkyō Shinkō, Kanjō Myōen, Emman Jōkō, and Daichi Shōkai. Born in Harima Province, he first studied Tendai doctrine on Mount Shosha; later he turned to Zen and studied under Kōhō Kennichi, a propounder of a syncretistic Zen style. Dissatisfied with this Japanized type of Zen, he entered the tutelage of Nampo Jōmyō, who taught a Southern Sung–style Ch'an, and received the seal of enlightenment at the age of twenty-five. In 1308 Myōchō secluded himself at a hermitage in the Higashiyama district of Kyoto, and in 1326 he went to a hermitage at Murasakino in Kyoto. There many people visited to seek his instruction, and it was there that he established Daitoku-ji with the support of the retired emperor Hanazono and others. In 1325 he debated with Tendai and Shingon priests at the imperial palace and so greatly impressed Emperor Go-Daigo that the emperor raised Daitoku-ji to the same high status as Nanzen-ji. Myōchō followed a severe style of Zen practice and was unable to get along with Musō Soseki (see following biography), one of the central figures of Five Mountains Zen. His many dharma successors included Tettō Gikō and Kanzan Egen. He wrote the *Record of Daitō, Evening Dialogue at Shōun-an, Dharma Words of National Teacher Daitō,* and capping phrase commentaries on koan collections.

Musō Soseki (1275–1351). Musō Soseki was a preeminent figure within Rinzai's Five Mountains temples, receiving many titles as national teacher—Musō, Shōgaku, Fusai, Gen'yū, Buttō, and Daien. Born in Ise Province, he entered religion as a child. After studying Tendai and Shingon doctrines, he turned to Zen and finally became a dharma successor of Kōhō Kennichi of Kenchō-ji in Kamakura. Soseki retreated from places near political power and secluded himself in the mountains in various districts. In 1325, however, he went to reside at Nanzen-ji at the order of Emperor Go-Daigo. Later he went to Kamakura at the invitation of the Kamakura regent Hōjō Takatoki, and there resided at Jōchi-ji and Engaku-ji. He founded Erin-ji in Kai Province, through the invitation of Hōjō Sadatoki. Around 1334 Soseki returned to Nanzen-ji at the request of Emperor Go-Daigo. Later he retreated to Rinsen-ji at Saga and concentrated on teaching his apprentices. Continuing to receive the patronage of the nobility and military leaders, he established Tenryū-ji and Saihō-ji in Kyoto. He took a leading role in Zen affairs as the most influential figure of his time in the Five Mountains temples. His dharma successors included Gidō Shūshin (see biography in part 2). Among his many works are the *Collection of the Discussions in Dreams, Rinsen-ji Regulations,* and *Record of National Teacher Musō.*

Kakunyo (1270–1351). The third head of Hongan-ji, Kakunyo, endeavored to give a social meaning to the Jōdo Shin sect, based on the thought of his great-grandfather Shinran (see biography in part 1), and was successful in establishing the framework of the Hongan-ji organization. His posthumous name was Shūshō; his childhood name Kōsen; and he was also known as Gōsetsu. The son of Shinran's grandson Kakue, Kakunyo was born in Kyoto and at the age of four was sent to study under a Jōdo priest. He went on to study Tendai and the doctrines of the Nara sects. In 1286, at the age of sixteen, he was ordained, and the next year he received the sect's teachings from Shinran's grandson Nyoshin at Ōami. In 1290 Kakunyo went with his father to the eastern provinces to visit places associated with Shinran. In 1294 when

Shinran's thirty-third memorial service was held, Kakunyo composed the address, called *Litany of Gratitude*. The following year he wrote Shinran's biography. Kakunyo did not succeed to the position of caretaker of Shinran's mausoleum until 1310 because of litigation by his uncle, Kakue's younger half-brother. After the succession was resolved, Kakunyo gradually established the authority of Hongan-ji on the basis of its supervision of the mausoleum. He wrote *Notes on Holding Fast*, a collection of two sermons by Shinran, with commentary; *Notes of Oral Transmissions; Essay to Correct False Faith;* and other works to establish his own position among Jōdo Shin followers as part of Shinran's lineage. Other works include *Gist of [Shinran's] "Teaching, Practice, Faith, Attainment"; Essay on the Greatest Essence; Essay on the Original Vow;* and *Biography of the Venerable Priest [Hōnen] from Collected Materials*. Kakunyo is famous for disowning his eldest son, Zonkaku, and denying him the Hongan-ji leadership.

GIDŌ SHŪSHIN (1325–1388). Rinzai priest Gidō Shūshin was an outstanding figure in Five Mountains literary circles during the Northern and Southern Courts period (1336–1392). Also called Kūge. A native of Tosa Province, he entered religious life at thirteen; the following year he received the precepts, then studied esoteric Buddhism on Mount Hiei. Turning to Zen, Gidō entered Tenryū-ji, where he studied under Musō Soseki (see biography in part 2). After Musō's death, he followed Ryūzan Tokken of Kennin-ji. In 1360 he was invited by Ashikaga Motouji, the shogunal deputy for the eastern provinces, to go to Kamakura, where he resided first at Engaku-ji, then, from 1366 on, at Zempuku-ji. In 1371 Gidō founded Hōon-ji with the support of the powerful Uesugi family. In 1380 he went to head Kennin-ji at the order of the shogun, Ashikaga Yoshimitsu. Then, after going to Nanzen-ji in 1386, he retired to one of its subtemples. Noble-minded and with high ideals, he had no liking for clerical participation in government. Nevertheless, he taught Zen and Southern Sung scholarship to Motouji's son Ujimitsu and the shogun and tried to bring harmony to the tense relationship between the Kamakura and Kyoto branches of the Ashikaga family. He contributed to the shogun's establishment of Shōkoku-ji and to the determination of ranking within the Five Mountains system. Though he made repeated strictures against Zen priests involving themselves in literary activities and Confucian studies, accusing them of forgetting their true allegiance, he himself was a poet. Gidō and Zekkai Chūshin, a brother dharma successor of Musō Soseki, have been called the bright jewels of Five Mountains literature. His works include *Recorded Sayings of Gidō Shūshin* and *Kūge's Instructions on Daily Life*.

NISSHIN (1407–1488). Nisshin was a purist who came into conflict with the authorities over his attempts to make the Nichiren sect the national religion. Also called Kuonjō-in. He was born in Kazusa Province and began religious training as a child at Myōsen-ji in the same province. He later practiced religious austerities at Nakayama Hommyō-ji. At eighteen he was sent to take charge of Gokoku Kōshō-ji in Hizen Province, Kyushu, setting him on his course of spreading the Nichiren sect. At that time the sect was concerned that the shogun accept it as a national religion, and to this end it was conducting a popular campaign to gain support among the common people. Nisshin established a number of temples, including Ichijō-ji in Settsu Province, and preached throughout Kyushu and southwestern Honshu. In 1439 he went to Kyoto and the following year wrote *Establishing Righteousness to Protect the Nation* to present to the shogunate. Incurring the anger of the shogun, he was imprisoned and cruelly tortured. Nisshin was pardoned a little over a year later, after the shogun had been murdered. Despite the fact that his speech was impaired as a result of the cutting of his tongue during the torture, he continued preaching. He died at Hommyō-ji in Kyoto aged eighty-one. His many works include *Notes on the Correct Principle of Subduing Evil*, *Notes on the Transmission of the Lamp*, and *Notes from Haniya*.

SHINZEI (1443–1495). The founder of the Shinzei subsect of Tendai, Shinzei was born in Ise Province. Posthumous titles: Enkai Kokushi, Jishō Daishi. Shinzei first studied at Kōmyō-ji in Ōmi Province and was ordained at thirteen. After study at Mitsuzō-in in Owari Province, at eighteen he went to Mount Hiei where he remained for twenty years. In 1477 he was promoted to provisional senior assistant high priest. Six years later he retired to Seiryū-ji at Kurodani and began the practice of reciting 60,000 nembutsu daily. He was impressed with *Essentials of Deliverance* by Genshin (see biography in part 2) and lectured on it widely. In 1486 he restored Saikyō-ji in Ōmi Province, a temple closely associated with Genshin, and made it his headquarters. Shinzei proposed unifying the practice of oral nembutsu and the observance of the Mahayana precepts. Many nembutsu practitioners among his followers had such fervent faith that they drowned themselves to attain rebirth in the Pure Land. He won the support of many of the nobles and high-ranking military families. Emperor Go-Tsuchimikado received the Mahayana precepts from him, and emperor-to-be Go-Kashiwabara, the ten nembutsu recitations. He established temples in many places—Saikō-ji in Echizen Province, Sairai-ji in Ise Province, and Sairen-ji in Iga Province, among others. Shinzei built well over a hundred centers for nembutsu practice in various districts and gave his efforts to the conversion of the ordinary people. He is said to have written the name of Amida more than one hundred thousand times. He wrote *Advanced Words of Religious Instruction*.

KAISEN (d. 1582). Kaisen, a priest of the Myōshin-ji subsect of Rinzai Zen, died in the flames of Erin-ji. Also known as Shōki and Daitsū Chishō Kokushi. A native of Mino Province, he was born of the Toki family. He received dharma transmission from Ninshū Sōju of Myōshin-ji and later lived at Sōfuku-ji in Mino. After Kaisen moved to Erin-ji in Kai Province to become head of that temple, he received the patronage of the great warlord of the district, Takeda Shingen. In 1582, Oda Nobunaga burned the temple down in anger because an opposing lord was sheltered there. Kaisen and more than a hundred other people took refuge in the upper portion of the main gate, but they were unable to escape the fierce flames, and all perished. At his death Kaisen quoted the verse of a Chinese poet: ''Doing zazen, I need not the cool of mountain or stream; when body and mind are controlled, even the flame's heat is cool." His age at death is not recorded.

EKEI (d. 1600). Rinzai priest Ekei became a clever political tactician. Also known as Yōho. Born in Aki Province of the family of lords of Ginzan Castle, he was ordained at ten at Tōfuku-ji in Kyoto and called Junzōshu. He entered Nanzen-ji as a record keeper; then, after going to live at Taikō-an in the Tōfuku-ji complex, he inherited from his master the position of chief priest of Ankoku-ji in Aki. Ekei was trusted by a powerful lord of the region and became involved in political affairs. In 1583, when Toyotomi Hideyoshi besieged the castle of Takamatsu, belonging to that lord's vassal, Ekei acted as an intermediary to arrange peace terms. He gained the trust of Hideyoshi also and was granted an annual income of about 11,000 kiloliters of rice from land in Iyo Province. Through Hideyoshi's patronage, Ekei was able to rebuild and restore the temples of Ankoku-ji, Tōfuku-ji, and Jōten-ji in Hakata. He became the 224th head of Tōfuku-ji in 1598. Ekei fought against Tokugawa Ieyasu in the Battle of Sekigahara in 1600; being on the losing side, he was arrested at Kennin-ji in Kyoto and executed. He was later represented as the archetypical figure of the evil priest, but he appears to have been an astute man, who predicted the downfall of Oda Nobunaga and the rise of Hideyoshi well before the event.

MOKUJIKI ŌGO (1537–1608). A Shingon priest and favorite of Toyotomi Hideyoshi, Mokujiki Ōgo was also famous as a master of linked verse. Also known as Mokujiki Shōnin and Kōsan Shōnin. Was first called Nissai, later Ōgo. His lay name was Junryō. Born in Ōmi Province, he first served the local lord, but in 1573, at the age of thirty-six, went to Mount Kōya and was ordained there. Ōgo then secluded himself at Kokuoku-ji on Mount Kōya and practiced Buddhism intensely. He worked on the construction and repair of many temples, such as Hase-dera and Murou-ji, and founded Kōsan-ji on Mount Kōya. In 1585, when Toyotomi Hideyoshi was about to attack Mount Kōya, Ōgo persuaded him to leave without destroying the complex. He was trusted by Hideyoshi, and under Hideyoshi's orders embarked on the construction of a Great Buddha hall at Hōkō-ji in Kyoto the following year. Having received the title "Mokujiki Kōsan Shōnin" from Hideyoshi, it was Ōgo who performed the funeral rites when Hideyoshi died. The following year he was placed in charge of Hideyoshi's shrine, Toyokuni Jinja. After Hideyoshi's son was defeated in the Battle of Sekigahara in 1600, Ōgo retired to a small temple in Ōmi Province, studied linked verse, and in 1603 published a collection of rules for linked verse composition.

KYŌNYO (1558–1614). The founder of Higashi Hongan-ji, head temple of the Ōtani subsect of Jōdo Shin, Kyōnyo was born at Ishiyama Hongan-ji in Osaka, the eldest son of the eleventh head of Hongan-ji, Kennyo. Also called Kōju, and Shinjō-in posthumously. He was ordained at the age of twelve in 1570, the year that Oda Nobunaga's conflict with Ishiyama Hongan-ji began, and Kyōnyo took part in the campaign, aiding his father. In 1580 the court ordered Kennyo to enter into peace negotiations with Nobunaga. Under the peace terms, Kennyo had to vacate Ishiyama Hongan-ji, so he went to Saginomori in Kii Province. Kyōnyo, however, refused to withdraw; with his supporters, he held Ishiyama Hongan-ji more than three months. Kennyo repudiated Kyōnyo for this action, but pardoned him two years later, and Kyōnyo became the twelfth head of Hongan-ji when his father died in 1592. The following year he yielded his position to his younger brother Junnyo and retired at Toyotomi Hideyoshi's order. Nevertheless he continued to act as the sect's head, endorsing grants to trainee priests and setting up a branch temple in Osaka. To all intents and purposes Hongan-ji had split into two. In 1602 Tokugawa Ieyasu granted Kyōnyo some land in Kyoto, and the following year Kyōnyo established Higashi Hongan-ji, installing the founder's statue he received from the eastern provinces.

SŪDEN (1569–1633). Rinzai priest Sūden, an advisor to the Tokugawa shoguns in the early seventeenth century, was known as the "black-robed counselor." Also known as Ishin. Posthumous title:

Enshō Honkō Kokushi. The son of an Ashikaga family vassal, he entered Nanzen-ji as a young child, also studying at Daigo Sambō-in and Shōkoku-ji. He was singled out by Seishō Jōtai, a Rinzai priest and diplomatic advisor to Toyotomi Hideyoshi and Tokugawa Ieyasu, and in 1605 became the 270th head of Nanzen-ji at the age of thirty-six. Through Jōtai he became acquainted with Ieyasu and in 1608 was called to Sumpu, where Ieyasu was living in retirement, to write diplomatic correspondence. Sūden drafted the proclamation sent to Mexico that banned Christianity and expelled Christian priests. From around 1611 Sūden, together with the Kyoto shogunal deputy, was charged with the supervision of religious affairs. Between 1612 and 1615 he drafted legislation for Ieyasu, including laws controlling the imperial court and the regulation that the court could grant purple robes to priests only with shogunate approval. He was also responsible for the series of regulations governing Buddhist institutions. It was Sūden as well, acting on Ieyasu's orders, who formulated the pretext whereby Ieyasu was able to resume the attack on Toyotomi Hideyori after the Winter Siege of 1614–1615. After the death of Ieyasu, Sūden advocated giving him the Yoshida Shinto posthumous title of Daimyōjin. In this he was opposed by, and finally lost to, Tenkai (see biography in part 2) who wanted Ieyasu to receive the title of Gongen, based on Sannō Ichijitsu Shinto, which was closely connected with the Tendai Buddhist sect. Sūden argued for the severe punishment and exile of Takuan (see biography in part 1) and other priests of Daitoku-ji and Myōshin-ji in 1627, at the time of the "purple robe incident." Besides sermons, he wrote an important diary called the *Diary of National Teacher Honkō*.

NICHIŌ (1565–1630). The Nichiren sect priest Nichiō founded the *fuju fuse* ("neither give nor accept") movement that later developed into a Nichiren subsect. Also known as Ankokubō Nissen, he later changed his name to Ankoku-in and Busshō-in. Born the son of a wealthy merchant in Kyoto, Nichiō entered Myōkaku-ji in Kyoto at the age of nine and became an apprentice of Nichiden. He made a thorough study of Nichiren doctrine and strongly emphasized the importance of faith. In 1592 he became the twenty-first head of Myōkaku-ji at the age of twenty-seven. In 1595 he opposed the sect's participation in a service that Toyotomi Hideyoshi had planned, commemorating the completion of the Great Buddha image at Hōkō-ji. A dispute arose among the priests of all the sects, with controversy particularly fierce in the Nichiren sect. Nichiō based his objection on the Nichiren doctrine that followers should neither receive donations from nonbelievers, such as Hideyoshi, nor give donations to them. He was opposed by the majority of Nichiren priests, who believed that offerings from the country's ruler were allowable. Defeated, Nichiō submitted a memorial to Hideyoshi and retired to Tamba Province. The conflict continued; in 1600 Tokugawa Ieyasu exiled Nichiō to the island of Tsushima, where he spent twelve years before being pardoned. The ban on the "neither give nor accept" doctrine was lifted for a time but imposed again later. It was not until 1874 that the Fuju Fuse subsect, based on that doctrine, could be formally established. Among Nichiō's works are the *Treatise on Protecting the Correct Principles* and *Treatise on Prohibiting the Slander of Giving*.

TENKAI (1536–1643). Tendai priest Tenkai was greatly trusted by Tokugawa Ieyasu. He was responsible for a publication of the Buddhist canon that is usually called the Tenkai edition. Posthumous name: Jigen Daishi. Born in Mutsu Province, he studied Confucianism at the Ashikaga Academy in Shimotsuke Province in 1560. Though he wished to return to Mount Hiei, where he had previously studied, Tenkai was unable to do so because Oda Nobunaga had destroyed all the temples on the mountain. In 1570 Tenkai debated with several clerics who had descended from Mount Hiei, winning the devotion of the local lord, Takeda Shingen. Later he returned to Mount Hiei. In 1600, knowing of plans to attack Tokugawa Ieyasu, Tenkai held a ritual at Yakushi-dō, in Kanda, to protect the nation; he thus gained Ieyasu's respect. He was successful in solving the discord on Mount Hiei and received the rank of high priest. In 1613 he was appointed head of Nikkōzan, and he taught Sannō Ichijitsu Shinto to Ieyasu. Tenkai also had a hand in the promulgation of the various regulations issued to temples, nobles, warriors, etc. After Ieyasu's death he advised the Tokugawa shoguns Hidetada and Iemitsu concerning shogunal government and thus contributed to the establishment of Tokugawa power. In 1625 Tenkai founded Tōeizan Kan'ei-ji in Edo and there held rituals for national tranquillity. In 1633 he completed the Tenkai edition of the Buddhist canon.

GENSEI (1623–1668). Gensei, a Nichiren priest, advocated the importance of the precepts and clerical regulations. Also called Nissei, Myōshi, Taidō, Kūshi, Genshi, and Fukashigi. Born in Kyoto, he used his mother's family name, Ishii. At twelve he went to serve the lord of the Hikone domain in Ōmi Province. Hearing a priest of Sennyū-ji speak on the *Lotus Sutra,* he developed an aspiration for the Buddhist Way and expressed his wish to be ordained then and there. This was not allowed, however, and it was not until he was twenty-five that he entered the priesthood under Nippō of Myōken-ji and trained according to Nichiren doctrine. In 1655 he founded Chikuba-an (later named Zuikō-ji) in Yamashiro Province. He placed great importance on practice, advocating the Lotus Vinaya. Gensei planned for a new growth in sect prosperity. He was a good poet and exchanged work with a number of noted poets. He also corresponded with the Ming refugee and poet Ch'en Yüan-yun, resulting in the book *Collection of Poetry Exchanged by Gen[sei] and Yüan[-yun].* He is also famous as an advocate of filial piety, and in this sense worked for a growth in secular ethics within Nichiren sect doctrine. His works include the *Grassy Mountain Collection,* a collection of letters, poetry, and essays; *Legends of Filial Devotion to Shakyamuni's Teachings;* and *Twenty-four Followers of Shakyamuni.*

INGEN (1592–1673). Chinese Ch'an priest Ingen founded Japan's Ōbaku sect. Posthumous names: Butsuji Kōkan Zenji, Keizan Shushutsu Zenji, Kakushō Emmyō Zenji, Daikō Fushō Kokushi, Shinkū Daishi. Born in Fukien Province, China, he was ordained at the age of twenty, attracted to the cult of Kannon at Mount Po-t'a. He studied at Mount Huang-po and received Lin-chi Ch'an dharma transmission. At forty-five he became the head of his temple. Ingen went to Japan in 1654 at the invitation of his apprentice, Itsunen, who had gone to Japan earlier and had become the head of Kōfuku-ji in Nagasaki. Many Zen priests, including Tetsugen (see following biography), came to study under Ingen in Nagasaki and his name became increasingly well known. The following year, the head of Kyoto's Myōshin-ji and others invited Ingen to move to Fumon-ji in Settsu Province, and in 1658 he went to Edo and was given an audience with the shogun, Toku-gawa Ietsuna. In 1660 he was granted land in Yamashiro Prov-ince and there established Ōbakusan Mampuku-ji (completed in 1662). Ingen's Zen incorporated nembutsu practice, and it also had a strong tantric element. Emperor Go-Mizunoo and many of the court nobility gave him their patronage. His works include the *Record of National Teacher Fushō* and *Extended Record of National Teacher Fushō.*

TETSUGEN (1630–1682). Ōbaku priest Tetsugen is remembered as the compiler of the Japanese printed edition of the complete Bud-dhist canon. Also known as Dōkō. Born in Higo Province, he was at first associated with the Jōdo Shin sect, but as a result of in-fluence by Saigin, a Jōdo Shin priest accused of leanings toward Zen, Tetsugen left that sect and went to Nagasaki in 1655, where he met Ingen and changed to the Ōbaku sect. Tetsugen accom-panied Ingen when he went to Fumon-ji in Settsu Province and was apprenticed to Ingen's chief apprentice, the Chinese priest Mokuan. In 1668 Tetsugen determined to print the entire canon and, basing himself at Gekkō-ji in Osaka, appealed for public financial support. Myōu Dōnin of Kannon-ji donated 1,000 plat-inum coins, and Ingen loaned his copy of the Ming edition of the canon. Building Hōzō-in within Mampuku-ji as a work cen-ter, Tetsugen set to work making the printing blocks. Though he later received the support of the lord of the Kumamoto domain, most of the work was financed by popular contribution. The names and amounts donated were recorded on the blocks. In 1681 the 6,771 volumes were finally completed, after Tetsugen had twice used all his funds for famine relief, necessitating further fund-raising. The more than 60,000 blocks are preserved at Hōzō-in. His *Zen Master Tetsugen's Dharma Words in Kana* was published in the Japanese syllabary, reflecting his concern for teaching women, who at that time were taught only the syllabary and not Chinese characters. Tetsugen died of illness while engaged in relief work during the great famine of 1682.

TŌSUI (d. 1683). Tōsui was a Sōtō sect priest who chose to practice a life supported by begging, outside the restrictions of temples. He is also known as Unkei. Born in the Kyushu province of Chikugo, he received ordination under Igan Shūtetsu, then resided at Tōkō-ji in Shimabara, also on Kyushu. When Tōsui left that temple he built a retreat on Honshu, where he lived in seclusion for eight years. He then accepted an invitation to head Hōgon-ji in Settsu Province, but disliking the pressure of priests and lay people, he one day disappeared from the temple. When his apprentice was amazed to meet him selling straw sandals along the road to Ise, Tōsui replied that he was practicing physical austerities. Later he begged along a riverbank in Kyoto and took care of the sick. He also sold straw sandals at Ōtsu, in Ōmi Province. In his old age Tōsui was offered the patronage of a rich Kyoto merchant, but refused all support, asking only that he be given the household's leftover rice to brew vinegar. Calling himself Dōzen the Vinegar Seller, Tōsui lived in a Kyoto district famous for its bands of retired performers. People there called him a beggar sage.

ENKŪ (d. 1695). Japan's best-known carver of Buddhist statues, Enkū, was an itinerant Rinzai sect priest, a native of Mino Province. Little is known about his life. His carvings show an innate talent and have the originality of a true artist. Enkū entered the priesthood at a young age. He made a pilgrimage to Mount Fuji at the age of twenty-two and also went to Mount Hakusan in Kaga Province. Later he rebuilt Miroku-ji in Mino. He was a wandering ascetic of Shugendō, a mixture of esoteric Buddhism with Japan's tradition of mountain practice, going into the precipitous fastnesses of sacred peaks. He also secluded himself in caves, and many caves are now associated with him—including Ōta Gongen Cave and Reimonge Cave, both on Ezo Island, and Iwaya Kannon Cave, in Mino Province. Enkū carved his distinctive Buddha figures using only a kind of hatchet, chipping away the wood at great speed in a wholly concentrated state of mind. He also exhibited religious power, giving prophecies and holding rituals. His activities extended to Ezo Island; although he stayed only two years, more than forty of his carvings have been found there. His farflung religious teaching activities are worthy of note.

DAITSŪ (1649–1716). Although Ryōnin (see biography in part 2) started the practice of "mutually inclusive nembutsu" and is recognized as the founder of the Yūzū Nembutsu sect, it was Daitsū who was responsible for raising it to an independent sect nearly six hundred years later. Also called Yūkan and Ninkō. Born of a prosperous farming family in Settsu Province, he early developed an affinity to nembutsu under his father's influence. Daitsū became a religious ascetic at the age of twenty-five, fervently practicing the Buddhist Way, and studied Hokke (Lotus), Tendai, and Zen doctrines at various temples. In 1681, when he was thirty-two, he was ordained by Ryōkan of Dainembutsu-ji. Deploring the slack atmosphere prevailing within the Jōdo sect, Daitsū appealed to the shogun and had conditions corrected. Later he worked for the independence of Yūzū Nembutsu from its parent Jōdo sect, and in 1688 the shogunate granted this. The following year he succeeded as head of Dainembutsu-ji. In 1695 he was able to establish a main-and-branch-temple system and to formulate regulations for a sect academy, establishing the sect's organization. While traveling the country teaching, Daitsū also wrote the *Description of the Teachings of Yūzū Nembutsu* in 1703, a systematic exposition of mutually inclusive nembutsu doctrine, outlining the origins of the name of the sect and clarifying the meaning of the all-permeating faith in Amida that the sect's founder Ryōnin experienced. Other works by Daitsū include *Faith and Discernment of Yūzū Nembutsu*.

EKŪ (1644–1721). The first head of the Higashi Hongan-ji academy, scholar-priest Ekū established the foundations of Jōdo Shin scholarship in the late seventeenth and early eighteenth centuries.

Also called Egan and Shūkōdō. Posthumous name: Kōonbō. Born at Zenryū-ji in Ōmi Province, Ekū even as a child expressed a wish to withdraw from the world. At seventeen, he went to Mount Hiei. After about three years, he left and went to study under Rinzai priests Ryūkei Shōsen and Enchi in Kyoto. Through the latter he was invited in 1670 to enter Myōshin-ji's training hall; he left in 1683. In the meantime, in 1680 he had accepted the temple members' invitation to enter Saifuku-ji in Kyoto. Besides lecturing at the academy that he had worked hard to establish, he explored the repositories at Kōzan-ji, a Kegon sect temple near Kyoto founded by Myōe (see biography in part 2), and Nison-in, a Jōdo sect temple in Saga. Ekū received the faith and support of a rich Osaka merchant and began lecturing, principally at Honsen-ji in Osaka, winning many followers. His extant writings and records are extremely numerous. He studied the three principal Pure Land sutras and other Jōdo Shin sect texts, produced works of secular ethics to simplify doctrine, and did detailed research into the origins of the Jōdo Shin sect. Among his many works is *Forest Collection,* a detailed survey of doctrines, history, and traditions of the Jōdo Shin sect.

HŌTAN (1659–1738). The restorer of the Kegon sect, Hōtan was famous as a debater with priests of other sects. Also called Sōshun and Kerei Dōnin. Born in Etchū Province, he was ordained at Mount Hiei and studied Tendai doctrine. Eventually Hōtan decided to restore the Kegon sect in Japan as a result of his study of Kegon texts. In 1707 he published *Notes on the Kegon Five Teachings,* expressing his standpoint. The Shingon priest Ekō wrote *Exposition on the Esoteric Manuals* to refute him, and Hōtan replied with *Quintessence of the Kegon and Tendai Sects.* He engaged in scholarly dispute with learned scholars of other sects as well. Against the Zen sect he wrote *Iron Wall and Piece of Cloud,* a critique of one hundred cases in the *Blue Cliff Records,* and against Shingon, another book. In reaction to the refutations composed by Shingon priests, he wrote a further book. Hōtan's attack on nembutsu, *Clarification of Pure Land Rebirth,* received the rebuttal of Jōdo Shin scholars such as Hōrin (see following biography). Hōtan replied with another

284   BRIEF BIOGRAPHIES

book. He was also attacked by Tendai and Nichiren priests and replied to them without weakening his own position. In 1723 he founded Daikegon-ji in Kyoto. He left many other works.

HŌRIN (1693–1741). Hōrin, the fourth head of studies of the Nishi Hongan-ji subsect of Jōdo Shin, was a great Jōdo Shin scholar. Also called Erin, Nikkei, or Shōkashi. Posthumous name: En'yōin. Born in Kii Province, the son of the priest of a subtemple at Saginomori, Hōrin showed promise from an early age and at eighteen lectured on Hōnen's *Collection of Passages on the Original Vow and the Nembutsu.* When a widespread doctrinal misunderstanding occurred, he made a name for himself by clearing it up. He entered the sect's academy at the age of twenty-six. Hōrin became an assistant lecturer and succeeded as head of Shōsū-ji in Ōmi Province. He composed *Discussion of the Pure Land* to answer Hōtan's (see preceding biography) attack on nembutsu and later wrote *A Laughable Discourse on the Mantis [Trying to Stop a Chariot] with Its Elbow,* which made him famous. Hōrin left a great number of works dealing with one of the central topics of Jōdo Shin doctrine, practice and faith. After his death he was criticized for his views about the symbol of faith and non–Pure Land teachings. This led to the Meiwa dispute and split Nishi Hongan-ji into two branches.

HAKUIN (1685–1768). Hakuin is remembered as the restorer of the Rinzai sect and as a teacher of Zen among the common people. Also called Ekaku and Kōrin. Posthumous titles: Shinki Dokumyō Zenji and Shōshū Kokushi. Born in Suruga Province, he was ordained at fourteen and thereafter practiced Zen in many places, seeking a master. In 1708 he gained his first experience of enlightenment under Shōtetsu of Eigan-ji in Echigo Province. He then practiced Zen under Tekiō Etan in Shinano Province, who forced him to reflect upon his conceit. The training Hakuin performed under Tekiō was very strict, and it was from Tekiō that he received his certification of enlightenment. In 1718 he was granted rank by Myōshin-ji in Kyoto, and from then on he traveled around the country teaching Zen. When he read the *Lotus Sutra* in 1726 he understood his master Tekiō's true intent for the first time. Hakuin restored Shōin-ji in Suruga Province and founded Kannon-ji, Shimmuryō-ji, and Ryūtaku-ji in Izu Province, where he spent his later years. He devised ways of bringing the common people to an understanding of Zen, emphasizing the oneness of daily life and Zen and placing much importance on the observance of secular ethics. Despite certain limitations, his influence on modern Rinzai has been great. He wrote *Poison Stamen of the Briar Thicket,* his recorded sayings, and is famous for his works on secular ethics, such as *The Embossed Tea Kettle* and *Leisurely Talks in a Boat in the Evening.*

GŌZEI (1721–1794). Scholar-priest Gōzei, of the Nishi Hongan-ji subsect of Jōdo Shin, is noted as the compiler of *Biographies of Wondrously Good People.* Also known as Kingan and Gomyōkaku. Posthumous name: Jitsujō-in. Born in Iga Province, he studied at the Hongan-ji academy and was known for the accuracy of what he recorded. In 1761 the sect sent him to Iwami and Aki provinces to stamp out widespread heresy. Gōzei was invited to live at Jōsen-ji in Iwami, but this was opposed by the members of Myōgaku-ji in Iga, where he had been born. Finally the members appealed to the head temple. He wrote a commentary entitled *Sources for the Essentials of Jōdo Shin Sect Teachings* for the edition of Jōdo Shin works that was compiled at that time. In response to the rise of anti-Buddhist polemics from scholars of "National Learning," Gōzei wrote *Argument Against Prejudice and Criticism,* advocating the unity of Shinto, Confucianism, and Buddhism. He also wrote a number of works dealing with secular ethics. His most famous work, *Biographies of Wondrously Good People,* is noteworthy as portraying the ideal type of religious person according to the standards of the mid-Edo period. It provided the stimulus for many later works of the same kind.

JIUN (1718–1804). Jiun founded the Shingon movement known as the Vinaya of the True Dharma, or Shōbōritsu, and compiled a thousand-section work on Sanskrit, *Guide to Sanskrit Studies.* Posthumous name Onkō, he called himself Katsuragi Sanjin and Hyakufuchi Dōshi, and sometimes Maitramegha (Sanskrit for

Jiun). He was the son of a samurai from Sanuki Province. At the age of eleven he started Neo-Confucian studies and entered the Buddhist priesthood at Hōraku-ji in Kawachi Province. At fourteen he began studies of esoteric Buddhism and Siddham (a Sanskrit script) and of Confucian texts and Chinese history, prose, and poetry. Gradually Jiun immersed himself further in the study of the Vinaya, and in 1744, five years after becoming the chief priest of Hōraku-ji, he moved to Chōei-ji and there proclaimed the Shingon Vinaya of the True Dharma doctrine. He later settled into a life of seclusion at a hermitage on Mount Ikoma in Settsu Province. There Jiun completed his life's work, the *Guide to Sanskrit Studies*. When he was fifty-three, he went to live at Amida-ji in Kyoto and there began teaching the Ten Good Precepts: abstention from killing, stealing, adultery, lying, frivolous language, slander, equivocation, greed, anger, and wrong views. He wrote *Sermons on the Ten Good [Precepts], The Way to Become a [Real] Person,* and *Priest Jiun's Dharma Words,* and worked hard to bring the common people into contact with Buddhist life. In 1776 Jiun went to live at Kōki-ji in Kawachi Province and restored that temple. In 1786, with permission from the shogunate, he set up the Shōbōritsu subsect within the Shingon sect, establishing Kōki-ji as its head temple. Finally, in 1792, Jiun set up an ordination platform at Kōki-ji.

Mokujiki Gyōdō (1718–1810). An itinerant priest of the Shingon sect, Mokujiki Gyōdō was a prolific carver of Buddhist statues. Also called Godō, Myōman, and Gogyō Bosatsu. Born in Kai Province, he entered the priesthood at the age of twenty-one, in 1739. At forty-four he took the vows of a *mokujiki* (literally "tree-eater"), an extreme form of asceticism whose followers eat only wild fruits and vegetables. From the time he was fifty-five until his death, he traveled throughout Japan, carving more than 1,000 Buddhist statues to fulfill a vow he had made. His subjects included the twelve heavenly generals, the Buddha of Healing, Prince Shōtoku (see biography in part 2), the Buddha's disciples, and the eleven-faced Kannon Bodhisattva. Gyōdō did not follow the accepted tenets of religious sculpture, but rather carved with freedom and individuality. Though he was formally affiliated with the Shingon sect, his severe practice, which formed the basis for his faith, included elements of nembutsu and Zen. In addition to countless statues, Gyōdō left many poems with a Buddhist flavor. Until his images were discovered by the folk craft movement in the early nineteenth century, he had been almost completely forgotten. His experiences are recorded in an autobiographical work, *Record of Dedication of Sutras.*

TOKUHON (1758–1818). Jōdo ascetic Tokuhon was a native of Kii Province. Also called Myōrenja Gōyo and Shō Amida Butsu. His family name was Tabuse. When he was three, a neighbor's child died, and Tokuhon recited the nembutsu out of a feeling of the world's transience. He asked to be ordained when he was eight, but was refused. At twenty-four he received ordination under Daien of Ōjō-ji. In 1782 he performed an ascetic practice at Gesshō-ji, eating only one bowl of boiled barley a day for thirty days. He later practiced austerities at other sites. In 1798 he received the bodhisattva precepts at Hōryū-ji and later settled at Kachiodera in Settsu Province, where he undertook religious teaching activities. In 1817 Tokuhon went to live at Ikkō-in in Edo, at the request of the head of the Jōdo sect. His *Record of Tokuhon* says, "Reverence is to be wholehearted." He taught that in secular life nembutsu dwells in a mind that is completely reverent. He tried to show the unified nature of nembutsu and life.

ENTSŪ (1754–1834). Entsū, a Jōdo priest, is remembered as a defender of the Buddhist interpretation of cosmology. Also called Kagetsu, Mugeshi, and Fumon. A native of Inaba Province, he entered the Nichiren sect priesthood at the age of six, but later was expelled from the sect for advocating internal reform. He changed to the Tendai sect, living at Mount Dai and Mount Hiei, then studied at Chishaku-in in Kyoto and resided at Shakuzen-in. Late in life Entsū changed to the Jōdo sect and entered Eshō-in within Jōdo's head temple, Zōjō-ji in Edo. Wishing to defend the dharma in the face of Copernican theory, he studied the Gregorian calendar and Western astronomy. He asserted that Buddhist cosmology, which places Mount Sumeru in the center of the universe, can be understood in terms of superhuman sight and insight, and said that Western calendrical theory agrees with the Mount Sumeru theory and Indian calendrical theory. Entsū drew up a model of Mount Sumeru and a spherical model to explain the movement of the sun and moon. His defense was much used by other Buddhist writers. His works include the *Experimental Theory of Mount Sumeru.*

TOKURYŪ (1772–1858). As tenth head of the academy of the Higashi Hongan-ji subsect of Jōdo Shin, the popular teacher Tokuryū sought to relate Buddhist teachings to secular ethics. Also known as Shōun, Fusōshitsu, Kōju-in. Born at Muishin-ji in Echigo Province, he was known from childhood for his wisdom; he composed poetry by the age of seven. After visiting Edo with his father when he was eleven, Tokuryū traveled among various teaching facilities and temples and studied the doctrines of many sects. He took a post at the Hongan-ji academy, lecturing on doctrine, and became head of the academy in 1847. Tokuryū took part in the defense of Buddhism against the attacks of non-Buddhist scholars, and he wrote several works about self-administered precepts. He also produced an attack against Christianity. He worked to popularize doctrine and to develop secular ethics. Tokuryū received the patronage of an Ōmi merchant, as a result of which he wrote a book about daily ethics in merchant families. Tokuryū was said to be the most virtuous of all the academy heads.

GESSHŌ (1817–1858). Gesshō, a priest of the Nishi Hongan-ji subsect of Jōdo Shin, was active in the imperialist movement in the late Tokugawa shogunate period. Also called Chien and Shōkyō. Born at Myōen-ji in Suō Province, he became chief priest of that temple. At fourteen he traveled to Kyushu and later to the Kyoto region and the eastern provinces, studying and mingling with Confucian scholars and poets. Gesshō made a name for himself with his poetry, and is famous for his verse: "If a man of ambition leaves his native place and does not succeed in becoming a scholar, he should never return.'' Having heard that the Portuguese conquered other countries in the name of Christianity, Gesshō resolved that the Jōdo Shin sect would protect Japan. He was widely known for his proposition that no foreigners should be allowed to enter Japan. He mixed with imperial activists, advocating an extreme anti-shogunate position. Gesshō went to Kyoto at the invitation of the head of Hongan-ji. Meeting an imperial loyalist with a school in Kyoto, he spoke on coastal defense in Kii Province, and his suggestions were acted upon. When the shogunate proposed to develop Ezo Island, Gesshō was named by the sect to establish the Jōdo Shin sect there. Before he could go, however, he contracted an illness and died. Hongan-ji published Gesshō's *Treatise on Buddhist Defense of the Nation* after his death.

SESSHIN (1808–1877). The twenty-seventh head of Kōshō-ji, founder of the independent Kōshō-ji subsect of Jōdo Shin, was also active in the imperial loyalist movement in the final years of the Tokugawa shogunate. Also called Honjaku. Posthumous name: Daikyōkishin-in. The second son of Takatsukasa Masamichi, a former regent, Sesshin entered Kōshō-ji at the age of two in 1810. He was ordained in 1818 and succeeded as temple head. At that time Kōshō-ji was affiliated with a Nishi Hongan-ji subsect, which leaned toward imperial loyalism as a result of the activities of its priests from the Chōshū domain. Sesshin was influenced by this, but from around 1864 he veered rather to the policy of uniting court and shogunate. He met with political leaders but took an independent stance. After the Meiji Restoration of 1868 he was active in the movement to protect Buddhism. In 1868 he appealed to the heads of the various Buddhist sects, and in 1869 he set up a Buddhist Ethics Association to emphasize the inseparability of Buddhist and secular laws and to expel false religions. He had also formed an alliance among the five Jōdo Shin subsects to combat false religions. With the formation of the government's Ministry of Religion in 1872, Sesshin supported the establishment of the Great Teaching Institute, the training institute for Buddhist and Shinto priests, and became its head. He was against the efforts of Shimaji Mokurai (see biography in part 1) and others from the Nishi

Hongan-ji subsect who opposed the Great Teaching Institute and sought to withdraw the Jōdo Shin sect. When they succeeded in doing so in 1875, Sesshin alone remained and the following year made the Kōshō-ji subsect independent.

SADA KAISEKI (1818–1882). Sada Kaiseki, a Nishi Hongan-ji subsect Jōdo Shin priest, provided scholarly support to Buddhism around the time of the Meiji Restoration. Also called Danshiki, Tōzōsai. Posthumous name: Shōgetsu-in. Born in Higo Province, he later entered Shōsen-ji in the same province. He studied first under a Confucian scholar and doctor. At eighteen he went to Kyoto, where he studied the *Abhidharma Storehouse Treatise* and the doctrine of Consciousness Only. Following a return to his home, Kaiseki went to meditate in the mountains, living in a hermitage. On a second visit to Kyoto, he studied Zen at Tōfuku-ji and Nanzen-ji. In the meantime he had read Mori Shōken's *In Defense of Buddhism* and was impressed with the sentence "The difficulties Buddhism is facing derive from astronomy and geography." Kaiseki set about studying calendrical theories, then organized groups of supporters and gave lectures in various places. In defense of the Mount Sumeru theory of Buddhist cosmology, he produced a spherical model, and he actively opposed Western culture and Japan's governmental policy of westernization. When Buddhism faced the "Abandon the Buddha, Destroy Buddhism" movement after 1868, he emphasized the contribution Buddhism could make to the national good and developed a unique economic theory. Because he was a conservative who adhered strictly to the self-sufficient feudal economic system, the government did not accept his ideas. In his later years Kaiseki changed to the Tendai sect and lived at a temple in Tokyo. His writings include *Detailed Accounts of the Spherical Model* and *Theory That Buddhism Develops the Nation.*

FUKUDA GYŌKAI (1806–1888). Jōdo priest Fukuda Gyōkai, an authority on Japanese Buddhism, was revered as a pillar of Buddhism for his support of the religion during a period of persecution. Also called Shin'a and Kenrenja Ryūyo. Born in Musashi Province, he received the precepts and entered Dentsū-in as a young child. He studied Jōdo doctrine, then Tendai doctrine. In 1866 Gyōkai became priest of Ekō-in in the Edo area; in 1876, head of Dentsū-in, where he had been ordained; in 1879, head of Zōjō-ji and leader of the Jōdo sect in the eastern plains area; and in 1885, head of the sect's head temple, Chion-in in Kyoto, and leader of the whole sect. At the time of the "Abandon the Buddha, Destroy Buddhism" movement after 1868, he defended Buddhism and advocated religious reform regardless of sectarian affiliation. In 1882 Gyōkai called upon sect heads and supporters to establish a Buddhist promotion agency, headed by him, to publish a small-type edition of the Buddhist canon. This was completed three years later. He was an excellent scholar and skillful poet, and became the most famous figure of his time in Buddhist circles. His writings include *Answering Questions [Viewing] Snow Through the Window*.

UGAI TETSUJŌ (1814–1891). Another Jōdo priest active in the defense of Buddhism was Ugai Tetsujō. Also called Zuirenja Jun'yo, Kiyū Dōnin, Shōō, Kokei, Kokyōdōshu. Born in Chikugo Province, he entered the priesthood at five. Going to Kyoto, he studied Confucianism and Buddhism. Next he went to Edo, where he entered Zōjō-ji and studied Jōdo doctrine. In 1861 Tetsujō entered Jōkoku-ji in Musashi Province. Having read an anti-Buddhist tract called *Correction of the Errors of Buddhist Doctrine*, published in Chinese in 1868 by a Christian missionary in China, Joseph Edkins from England, he entered into the lists of Buddhism's defense with two works, *First Defeat of*, and *Second Defeat of "Correction of the Errors of Buddhist Doctrine."* Later Tetsujō published a number of other works. In response to the "Abandon the Buddha, Destroy Buddhism" movement following the Meiji Restoration, in Tokyo he formed the Buddhist Ethics Association in 1869, with himself as head, and appealed to the government to build defenses against Christianity. He opened a Jōdo seminary in Yamaguchi in 1870. In 1872 he became head of the Jōdo sect and two years later, head of Chion-in. Working to establish Chion-in as the head temple of the Jōdo sect, he reformed sect regulations and opened a conference of branch temples throughout the country.

HARA TANZAN (1819–1892). Hara Tanzan, a Sōtō sect priest, introduced medical and physical science into Buddhist studies and contributed greatly to religious studies during the late nineteenth century. His childhood name was Ryōsaku and his posthumous names Kakusen and Kakusō. He was the eldest son of a retainer of the Mutsu domain. In 1833, at the age of fourteen, Tanzan went to Edo, where he studied Confucianism at the academy for Tokugawa shogunate retainers; he also studied medicine. Though ordained at Sōsen-ji in Edo, he studied Zen mainly in the Kyoto region. He went to Sōtō sect head temple Eihei-ji in 1855, for the ceremony marking qualification as a Sōtō priest, and entered Shinshō-ji in Kyoto the following year. Later he moved to Saijō-ji in Sagami Province. In such works as *A Record of Experiments Concerning Buddhist Dharma* and *The Theory That Delusion and Disease Have the Same Origin*, he attempted to elucidate Buddhism experimentally and scientifically. In 1872 he was licensed by the government to preach, but two years later he took his name off the priests' register. In 1879 he became the first lecturer in Indian philosophy at the Tokyo Imperial University (now University of Tokyo) and lectured on Fa-tsang's commentary on Ashvaghosha's *Discourse on the Awakening of Faith in the Mahayana*. He resumed his priest's position the following year. In 1885 he was elected to the Imperial Academy (now the Japan Academy), and he became assistant head of the Sōtō sect in 1887. His other works include the *Collection of Kakusō [Hara Tanzan]*.

OGINO DOKUON (1819–1895). Rinzai priest Ogino Dokuon was another Buddhist defender of the late nineteenth century. Also called Shōju. Born in Bizen Province, he first studied under a Confucianist. Later he went to Kyoto, was ordained, and trained at Shōkoku-ji. In 1868 he joined the Jōdo Shin priest Sesshin (see biography in part 2) and others in establishing the Buddhist Ethics Association to oppose Christianity and combat the "Abandon the

Buddha, Destroy Buddhism'' movement. In 1872, Dokuon and representatives from other sects proposed that the government establish the Great Teaching Institute to educate Buddhist and Shinto priests. Dokuon was appointed head of that institution when it was founded and also was made head of the Rinzai sect. When the Jōdo Shin sect was working to withdraw from the Great Teaching Institute, he advised the government to oppose the issue. In 1875, with Fukuda Gyōkai (see biography in part 2) and others, he argued that Buddhism was beneficial to the nation and presented the government with a white paper opposing the anti-Buddhist movement and proposing reform of the clergy. He was a conservative but defended Buddhism with great energy. Advocating a Zen that is available to everybody, he established a lay practice center at Shōkoku-ji and played a major role in the development of lay Buddhism. He wrote *Records of Taikō [Ogino]* and *Biographies of Zen People of Our Day.*

SHICHIRI GŌJUN (1835–1900). Shichiri Gōjun was noted for his great success in encouraging faith in the Nishi Hongan-ji subsect of Jōdo Shin. Also called Shōkashi. He was born at Myōkyō-ji, in Echigo Province, and entered the priesthood when he was ten. Gōjun studied at the Nishi Hongan-ji academy, starting when he was thirteen, under a number of noted Jōdo Shin sect priests. In 1864 he entered Mangyō-ji in the city of Fukuoka and took the surname Shichiri. When a question arose in 1879 about whether Nishi Hongan-ji should move to Tokyo, he went to Kyoto at the order of the head of the sect, Ōtani Kōson, and occupied an important executive position in the sect administration there until 1881. Gōjun returned to his own temple in January 1882 and concentrated on teaching religion in ways appropriate to people's understanding and on educating the younger generation. Great numbers of people flocked from all over the country to hear his talks on Buddhism. It is said that inns lined the road to his temple to accommodate his followers.

KITABATAKE DŌRYŪ (1820–1907). Nishi Hongan-ji priest Kitabatake Dōryū is remembered as a proponent of organizational reform in his sect. Born at Hōfuku-ji in Kii Province, he studied for more than twenty years and became a councilor at the Nishi Hongan-ji academy. Failing to win support for his proposal to reform Nishi Hongan-ji's administration, however, he returned to his home. When anti-shogunate forces caused a commotion in Yamato Province, he organized a force of Buddhist cleric-soldiers at the order of the local lord and was awarded samurai status for his success. After the Meiji Restoration of 1868, Dōryū studied German and opened a private academy in Tokyo. With the breakdown in the affairs of the Nishi Hongan-ji sect in 1878, he once again advocated administrative reform and was appointed to a responsible post. He traveled to Europe and the United States in 1881, searched for Buddhist remains in India, and returned to Japan only after seven years of travel. He urged the establishment of a Buddhist university, but incurred the wrath of Buddhist clerics for proposing moral reform among Buddhist clergy. Dōryū's uncompromising response was to take himself off the clerical register. He had many friends in political circles and mingled with government leaders. His writings include *Telling Politicians and Religious Leaders*.

UCHIYAMA GUDŌ (1874–1911). Sōtō sect priest Uchiyama Gudō was executed for involvement in the High Treason Incident of 1910, an anarchist plot to assassinate Emperor Meiji. Born in Niigata Prefecture, his childhood name was Keikichi; he was ordained at twenty-three and took over Rinsen-ji in Hakone in 1904, around the time he was studying socialism under the journalist and socialist leader Sakai Toshihiko. Sympathetic with the movement, he came into close contact with the anarchist leader Kōtoku Shūsui around 1905. Gudō ran a secret printing press at Rinsen-ji and gradually moved toward anarchist thought. A famous sentence in a secretly published work, "Emperors and princes, the wealthy, and great landlords, all are leeches sucking the blood of the people," was a principal cause for his sentence of execution. He supported freedom from taxation for small farmers, the abolition of conscription, and the end of the emperor system, but appears to have joined these with a Zen spirit of "no labor, no eating'' and of not taking life. In 1909 he was arrested for violations of the Publishing and Explosives Laws and was imprisoned the following year; it was while he was serving his sentence that his associates were arrested for treason. Implicated in the plot, he was sentenced to death in January 1911 and executed on January 24. His writings include *Mottoes of Imperial Soldiers* and *Awareness of Mediocrity*.

SHAKU UNSHŌ (1827–1909). Shaku Unshō, a Shingon priest, supported a movement to restore emphasis on the bodhisattva precepts. He was born in Izumo Province of the Watanabe family; he later assumed the surname of Shaku. Ordained at nine, in 1844 he went to Mount Kōya to study Shingon doctrine and practice. After receiving the Ten Good Precepts recommended by Jiun (see biography in part 2), he secluded himself at Seichō-ji in Settsu Province, then at Kōki-ji in Kawachi Province, devoting himself to religious training. He lamented the corruption of the clergy in the late nineteenth century and urged reform. Unshō worked against the "Abandon the Buddha, Destroy Buddhism" movement on the grounds that Confucianism and Buddhism support Shinto, which was being promoted by suppression of Buddhism. He established a school in Tokyo for study of the precepts in 1889, formed an Association of the Ten Good Precepts, published a magazine called *Jewel Cave of the Ten Good [Precepts]*, and worked for the revival of emphasis on those precepts. Unshō had many patrons from government and financial circles, including the son of the Mitsubishi financial empire's founder. From about 1897 on, he toured the country advocating the unity of the three teachings (Confucianism, Buddhism, and Shinto). He stressed that the teachings of Buddhism do not change with time and opposed the Buddhist reform movement of the "New Buddhists." His writings include *Great Principles of Buddhism*.

INOUE ENRYŌ (1858–1919). Buddhist intellectual and thinker Inoue Enryō worked to establish a philosophical basis for Buddhism. He was born in an Echigo Province temple affiliated with the Higashi Hongan-ji subsect of Jōdo Shin. As a child he was called Kishimaru, and later Shūjō. He studied English, first in 1873 at Takayama and the following year at Nagaoka, becoming an assistant teacher there at the age of sixteen. In 1877 he entered the training institute for Higashi Hongan-ji, then in 1878 was sent as a scholarship student to a preparatory school for Tokyo Imperial University (the present University of Tokyo). In 1885 he graduated in philosophy from that university. Three years later he set up a bookstore called Philosophic Publications. With Shimaji Mokurai (see biography in part 1) and others he took part in the formation of a cultural and political association called the Society for Political Education, and in its periodical *The Japanese* he advocated nationalism and attacked Christianity. In 1887 he also established an institute of philosophy, the Tetsugakukan, which was the forerunner of Tōyō University. Inoue strongly recommended protecting the nation, encouraging patriotism, and supporting the secular law. He also urged an intellectual awakening of the Buddhist clergy and the popularizing of East Asian studies, including Japan studies. In 1896 Inoue obtained a doctorate for his work *Systematization of Buddhist Philosophy*. From 1899 on, he poured his energy into social education, setting up a Morals Society and a kindergarten, and traveling around the country giving lectures. To combat popular superstitions he established a center for the study of spirit phenomena in Tokyo and published works on the subject, such as *Lectures on Ghosts;* he was even called Doctor Ghost. His other works include *New Theory on Destroying Evil* and *Enlivening Buddhism*. He died in Manchuria.

NANJIO BUNYIU (1849–1927). As a pioneer of Indological and Buddhist research based on original materials, Nanjio Bunyiu has an excellent reputation in the West as well as in Japan. As a child he was called Kakumaru and Kakujun. He was also called Matsuzaka and Sekika. A priest of the Higashi Hongan-ji subsect of Jōdo Shin, he was born in Mino Province. In 1876 Gennyo, the head of Higashi Hongan-ji, sent the twenty-seven-year-old Bunyiu and another young priest to study at Oxford University. There Bunyiu researched Sanskrit Buddhist texts under Max Müller. With Müller, he published Sanskrit editions of the *Sutra of*

Infinite Life and *Amitabha Sutra* (also called the *Larger* and *Smaller Sukhavati-vyuha*). His name was secured for posterity with the publication in 1883 of his *A Catalogue of the Chinese Translation of the Buddhist Tripitaka*, commonly known as the "Nanjio Catalogue." Upon his return to Japan in 1884 he took a teaching post at the Tokyo Imperial University (now University of Tokyo). In 1887 Bunyiu toured Buddhist sites in India and China. The following year he gained his doctorate, and in 1906 he became a member of the Imperial Academy (now the Japan Academy). In 1914 he was appointed president of Shinshū (now Ōtani) University. Other works include the Sanskrit edition of the *Sutra of the Appearance of the Good Doctrine in [Sri] Lanka*, an English translation called *A Short History of the Twelve Japanese Buddhist Sects*, and an autobiography, *Nostalgic Record*.

MAEDA EUN (1857–1930). Maeda Eun, a Buddhist scholar and priest of the Nishi Hongan-ji subsect of Jōdo Shin, was the eldest son of the priest of Saifuku-ji in a village in Ise Province. He later succeeded as head of the temple. He was also called Shisen and Ganjun. After studying classical Chinese and Buddhist texts, he went on to train in Buddhist doctrine under various Nishi Hongan-ji teachers. He also studied Tendai doctrine at Mii-dera. In 1889 Eun worked with the lay Buddhist Ōuchi Seiran and others to establish the Great Alliance to Revere the Emperor and Serve the Buddha, a patriotic and strongly nationalistic movement. In 1891 the head of Nishi Hongan-ji appointed him chief of educational affairs; in 1898 he was appointed assistant head of the Nishi Hongan-ji academy; in 1900 he became a lecturer in humanities at Tokyo Imperial University; and in 1903 he became president of the Takanawa Buddhist University (now Ryūkoku University). That same year he issued a personal interpretation of Hongan-ji doctrine, receiving a doctorate for his *On the History of Mahayana Buddhism*. Because this was seen as denying that Mahayana was preached by the Buddha himself, Eun was forced to give up his priesthood the following year. He was reinstated, however, in 1905. He was the chief editor of the *Great Japan Supplementary Tripitaka*, a compilation of works not included in the previously published *Great Japan Revised Tripitaka,* in which he also participated. In 1906 he was appointed president of Tōyō University, and in 1922, president of Ryūkoku University. His works include *An Outline of the Tendai Sect, An Outline of the Sanron Sect,* and *A History of the Pure Land Teachings in India.*

MURAKAMI SENSHŌ (1851–1929). Murakami Senshō, a scholar of Buddhism and Buddhist history, was born of a family connected with the Higashi Hongan-ji subsect of Jōdo Shin. He was also called Fujū Dōnin. He was born in Tamba Province, entered Nyūgaku-ji in Mikawa Province in 1875, and took the surname of Murakami. He studied Buddhism at Higashi Hongan-ji's academy, then became a lecturer at the Sōtō sect's academy (now Komazawa University) and Inoue Enryō's (see biography in part 2) Tetsugakukan. In 1890 he succeeded Hara Tanzan (see biography in part 2) at Tokyo Imperial University; in 1917 he became professor of Indian philosophy there, and the following year was elected to the Imperial Academy (now the Japan Academy). He had long urged the need for historical research into Buddhism. In 1894 he began a magazine called *Buddhist History Grove* on that subject. He published *Outline of Japanese Buddhist History* and *Chronology of Chinese and Japanese Buddhism* in 1898 and received his doctorate the following year. In 1899 he opened a Buddhist studies center in Kanda, Tokyo, actively involving himself in the Buddhist intellectual movement. He wrote *The Unification of Buddhism* in 1901; as a result of that, Higashi Hongan-ji stripped him of his priesthood for writing that Mahayana is not the direct teaching of the Buddha. In 1924, however, he became a lecturer for Higashi Hongan-ji and two years later became president of Ōtani University.

CHIKAZUMI JŌKAN (1869–1931). The brilliance of Chikazumi Jōkan, a Higashi Hongan-ji subsect priest, impressed religious and intellectual circles in the early twentieth century. Basing his activities on his organization called the Way-Seeking School, he saw the *Notes Lamenting Deviations* as his ideal. Born in Saigen-ji in Shiga Prefecture, he graduated from Tokyo Bunka University. Initially connected with the formation of the Greater Japan Buddhists' and People's Alliance, he began in January 1899 to publish the journal *Religion and State Review* to make Buddhism an officially recognized religion and to pursue political issues. After returning to Japan in 1902, following a study of the religious systems of Europe and the United States sponsored by Higashi Hongan-ji, however, he distanced himself from political questions and put his energy into promoting Shinran's thought and standing forth as an independent teacher. He established the Way-Seeking School in 1902, published a magazine called *Seeking the Way*, and built Gudō ("Way-Seeking") Hall in Tokyo. In advocating Buddhist spirituality he exerted a particularly deep influence on young people, such as university students. His works include *Life and Faith, Repentance Record, Lingering Taste of Faith,* and *Faith of the Holy Man Shinran.*

KAWAGUCHI EKAI (1866–1945). Tibetan explorer and linguist Kawaguchi Ekai was affiliated with the Ōbaku sect. Born in Sakai, he graduated in 1891 from Inoue Enryō's (see biography in part 2) Tetsugakukan in Tokyo. Kawaguchi began studying under Shaku Unshō (see biography in part 2) in 1894. He also studied Southern Buddhism and, becoming convinced of the necessity of bringing original Buddhist texts to Japan, resolved to go to Tibet even though that nation was closed to foreigners. In 1897 Kawaguchi went to Darjeeling, near India's border with Tibet, and there studied the Tibetan language. Two years later he entered Tibet alone via a hidden route in Nepal, becoming the first Japanese ever to visit Tibet. He studied Lamaism at Sera but was expelled when his nationality was discovered, and he returned to Japan in 1903. At the end of 1904 Kawaguchi returned to India, where he studied Sanskrit at the Central Hindu College in Benares. In 1913 he entered Tibet again and brought back with him the Tibetan canon and many other Buddhist manuscripts. Later he became a lecturer at Taishō University; published Chinese-Tibetan translations of several sutras, a Tibetan grammar, and other works; and made many contributions to the development of modern Buddhist studies. His works include *Three Years in Tibet* and *Lay Buddhism.*

ŌTANI KŌZUI (1876–1948). Explorer Ōtani Kōzui became the twenty-second head of Jōdo Shin's Nishi Hongan-ji subsect, succeeding his father, Ōtani Kōson. His religious name was Kyōnyo. After graduating from Gakushūin University, he studied in Europe. In 1899 he traveled to China and Tibet, then went on to make a study tour of India and Europe. On his way back, in 1902, he planned to enter the Central Asian region from Russia, but he returned to Japan upon the death of his father the following New Year and became head of Nishi Hongan-ji. Seven years later he went to India and Europe again, sending others into China's western regions where they excavated many Buddhist sites. He retired from his various clerical positions in 1914, taking responsibility for vast debts arising from financing of his expeditions, his contributions to the Russo-Japanese War (1904–1905), the building of a villa on Mount Rokkō, and the establishment of a Buddhist junior high school. Afterward he traveled in China, India, and Europe and managed enterprises in China and the Pacific region. During the Second World War he encouraged the development of a nationalistic thought movement and became a member of the House of Councilors, the upper house of Japan's bicameral legislature, and held a cabinet post.

ITŌ SHŌSHIN (1876–1963). An advocate of the Selfless Love movement, which exerted a great influence on early-twentieth-century Japanese thought, Itō Shōshin was expelled from the Jōdo Shin priesthood for advocating Selfless Love while he was a research student at Shinshū (now Ōtani) University. Itō then secluded himself in a hall called Dainichi-dō. In 1903 he began publishing the magazine *Selfless Love*. The base of the early Selfless Love movement was Itō's Dainichi-dō, where he was joined by two fellow students. There members led a communal life, though the individuality of each person was valued. There were rich and poor, holders of all kinds of belief. The economist Kawakami Hajime gave up his teaching position to join the Garden of Selflessness. There were about a hundred members around the country. Writings about the Garden of Selflessness were published and in its most prosperous period, *Selfless Love* had a readership of four thousand. The first

Garden of Selflessness closed in 1906 because members were needed to practice selfless love rather than just to disseminate its teachings. *Selfless Love* featured many essays preaching socialism and peace from the standpoint of universal and absolute love. Itō was in contact with leading socialists and anarchists; at the time of the High Treason Incident of 1910 he wrote an article called "Revelation of the High Treason Incident," and was imprisoned. During the Russo-Japanese War he wrote critical essays that reveal his pacifism.

East Asia

Sea of Japan

JAPAN

Mt. Wu-t'ai

KOREA

Yellow River

Yellow Sea

Pacific Ocean

Lo-yang

ang-an

East China Sea

Yang-chou

Yangtze River

CHINA

Ming-chou

Mt. Ching

Mt. A-yu-wang

Mt. T'ien-t'ung

CHEKIANG

Mt. T'ien-t'ai

Mt. Huang-po

FUKIEN

Yang-chou

Yangtze River

Kuang-chou

Mt. Ching

Ming-chou

Mt. A-yu-wang

Mt. T'ien-t'ung

Mt. T'ien-t'ai

South China Sea

Mt. Huang-po

CHEKIANG

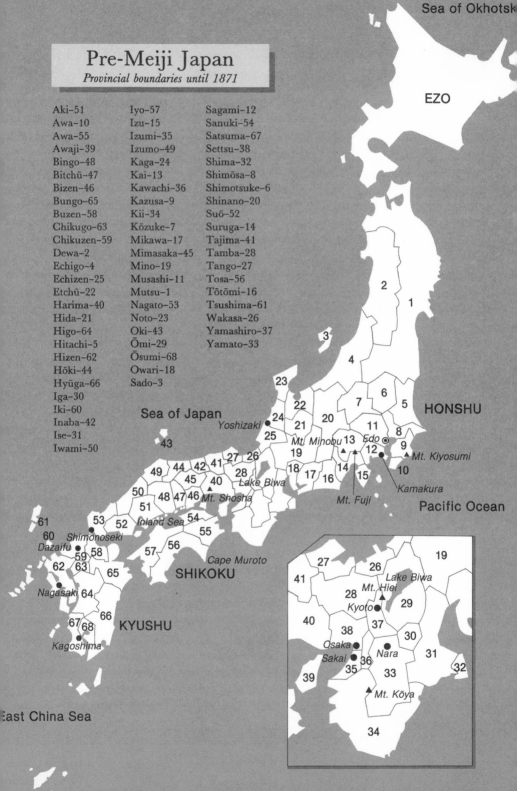

Chronological Guide

JAPANESE HISTORY	WORLD HISTORY
	ca. 460–528 Life of Bodhidharma, first patriarch of Chinese Ch'an (Zen) Buddhism, said to have gone to China from India.
	515–ca. 577 Life of Hui-ssu, transmitter of Buddhist teachings to Chih-i, organizer of the T'ien-t'ai sect in China.
538 (552?) Syong Myong, king of Paekche on the Korean Peninsula, presents an image of the Buddha to the Japanese court.	*538–597* Life of Chih-i, founder of T'ien-t'ai Buddhism in China.
	549–623 Life of Chi-tsang, a founder of the San-lun school of Buddhism in China.
552 Soga and Mononobe clans begin to fight over acceptance of Buddhism.	*557–610* Life of Yen Tsung, who restores Chinese Buddhism after its persecution by the emperor.
	561–632 Life of Kuang-ting, Chih-i's disciple and successor as patriarch of the T'ien-t'ai sect in China. He compiles his master's

JAPANESE HISTORY	WORLD HISTORY

WORLD HISTORY

lectures into *Textual Commentary on the Lotus Sutra, Profound Meaning of the Lotus Sutra,* and *Great Concentration and Insight.*

562 Japanese-held territory on the Korean Peninsula is lost to the peninsular Silla Kingdom.

562–645 Life of Tao-cho, a pioneer who follows T'an-luan's thought and promotes Pure Land teachings in China.

570–632 Life of Mohammed; founding of Islam.

577 Buddhist priests (three male, one female), two Buddhist artisans, and scriptures are sent to Japan by another king of Paekche.

584 Buddhist sanctuary is built within the Ishikawa residence of Soga no Umako, where Zenshinni and two other female priests (the first Japanese Buddhist priests) reside.

585 Mononobe no Moriya burns down a Buddhist stupa and hall and abandons a Buddhist statue.

588 Soga no Umako founds Asuka-dera (Hōkō-ji), the first Buddhist temple for male priests.

590–640 Pope Gregory founds the Papal States in Italy.

593 Prince Shōtoku is appointed regent and builds Shitennō-ji.

594 Prince Shōtoku proclaims the propagation of the Three Treasures.

594–657 Life of Niu-t'ou Fa-jung, Ch'an priest who writes commentaries on the *Diamond* and *Vimalakirti* sutras and founds the Ox Head sect.

596 Asuka-dera is completed.

596–667 Life of Tao-hsüan, founder of the Lü (Vinaya) school of Chinese Buddhism and compiler of the *Further Collection of Essays on Buddhism,* a collection of 296 documents on Buddhism from the

JAPANESE HISTORY	WORLD HISTORY
	time of its introduction to China until the mid-seventh century.
601 Prince Shōtoku founds Ikaruga Palace.	*600–664* Life of Hsüan-tsang, Chinese priest and translator who takes Buddhist texts from India for translation into Chinese.
603 Administration of Prince Shōtoku begins. Twelve grades of cap rank (the first system of courtly ranks) are established.	*602–668* Life of Chih-yen, second patriarch of the Hua-yen (Flower Garland) sect in China.
604 Prince Shōtoku promulgates the Seventeen-Article Constitution.	
607 Construction of Hōryū-ji is completed. First embassy to China.	*613–681* Life of Shan-tao, Chinese patriarch of the Ching-t'u (Pure Land) sect of Buddhism, said to have written *Commentary on the Meditation Sutra.*
615 Prince Shōtoku completes commentaries on the *Queen of Shrimala, Vimalakirti,* and *Lotus* sutras.	
622 Prince Shōtoku dies.	
625 Ekan of Koguryo officially transmits the Sanron sect to Japan.	*632–682* Life of K'uei-chi, disciple of Hsüan-tsang who helps his master organize the Fa-hsiang school of Chinese Buddhism.
	635–713 Life of I-ching, translator and priest who studies at Nalanda, India, for ten years and writes *A Record of the Buddhist Kingdoms in the Southern Archipelago* and *Biographies of Eminent Priests of the T'ang Who Sought the Dharma in the Western Regions.*
	637–735 Life of Shubhakarasimha, Buddhist who introduces Chen-

yen (True Word) esoteric Buddhism into China.

638–713 Life of Hui-neng, Chinese Buddhist priest of the Southern Ch'an school who becomes its sixth patriarch after a long and bitter controversy with his rival Shen-hsiu of Northern Ch'an. The *Platform Sutra of the Sixth Patriarch* is attributed to Hui-neng.

645 The government announces a policy of support for Buddhism.

643–712 Life of Fa-tsang, Chinese Buddhist who organizes the Hua-yen school of Buddhism on the basis of Tu-shun's teachings.

645–649 Taika Reforms (political and economic reforms) are carried out.

660 Dōshō officially transmits the Hossō sect to Japan.

652–710 Life of Shikshananda, who takes the Sanskrit text of the *Flower Garland Sutra* to China, where he helps translate it into Chinese.

670 Fire destroys Hōryū-ji.

671–741 Life of Vajrabodhi, first patriarch of esoteric Buddhism in China, who was born in India.

677–744 Life of Nan-yüan Huai-jang, talented disciple of Hui-neng who promotes his own style of Ch'an.

678 Dōkō introduces the Ritsu sect.

680 Construction of Yakushi-ji begins.

680–748 Life of Hui-jih, Pure Land priest who studies in India.

689 Asuka Kiyomihara Code (penal and administrative law) is promulgated.

700 Dōshō dies and becomes the first person in Japan to be cremated.

JAPANESE HISTORY	WORLD HISTORY

701   Court promulgates the Clerical Code, rules for male and female Buddhist clerics.

702   Taihō Code (fundamental legal code revising the Asuka Kiyomihara Code) is promulgated.

710   The capital is transferred to Heijōkyō (Nara).

705–774   Life of Amoghavajra, esoteric Buddhist teacher and translator who was born in India and becomes a disciple of Vajrabodhi in China. He brings esoteric Buddhist texts from Ceylon to China.

711–782   Life of Chan-jan, who promotes the works of Chih-i and is called the sixth patriarch. His writings include commentaries on Chih-i's three major works and *Summary of Concentration and Insight.*

712   Compilation of *Record of Ancient Matters,* Japan's oldest extant chronicle, is completed.

717   Gyōgi is forbidden to teach Buddhism to the general populace.

718   Dōji returns to Japan with the *Golden Light Sutra.*

717–741   Reign of Leo III as Byzantine emperor. He restores order to the empire, repels the Arabs, and reforms the army and legal and fiscal systems. His measures against image worship open the great iconoclastic controversy that continues until 843.

720   Compilation of *Chronicles of Japan,* the oldest official history, is completed.

723   Law of Three Generations is promulgated to encourage the cultivation of wasteland. A dispensary for medicinal herbs and a hospital/asylum is built at Kōfuku-ji.

728   Court distributes copies of the *Golden Light Sutra* to the provinces.

735   After returning from T'ang China, Gembō transmits the Hossō sect.

720–814   Life of Pai-chang Huai-hai, Chinese Ch'an priest who draws up a monastic constitution that is more detailed than and, in some respects, contrary to the Vinaya.

738–839   Life of Ch'eng-kuan, fourth patriarch of the Hua-yen sect in China.

740 Shinjō explicates Kegon sect teachings (*Flower Garland Sutra*) at Tōdai-ji.

741 Emperor Shōmu orders establishment of one temple for male clergy and one for female clergy in each province.

743 Law to encourage reclamation of land is promulgated. Emperor Shōmu issues an edict to cast an image of the Great Buddha.

745 Gyōgi is raised to the newly created rank of senior high priest.

747 Casting of the image of the Great Buddha begins.

749 Gyōgi dies.

752 Dedication ceremonies are held at Tōdai-ji for the Great Buddha.

754 Chinese priest Ganjin arrives in Japan and sets up an ordination platform at Tōdai-ji.

757 Yōrō Code (fundamental legal code revising the Taihō Code) is promulgated.

759 Ganjin establishes Tōshōdai-ji.

763 Ganjin dies.

766 Dōkyō is given the title of "dharma king."

746–805 Life of Hui-kuo, Chen-yen priest who receives esoteric teachings from Amoghavajra and is considered the seventh patriarch in transmission of esoteric Buddhism or the fifth patriarch of the Chen-yen sect. He transmits esoteric Buddhism to Japanese priest Kūkai in 805.

756 Donation of Pepin, French territorial donation to the pope that establishes a basis for the Papal States.

771–853 Life of Kuei-shan Ling-yu, Ch'an priest who receives the teaching of Pai-chang Huai-hai.

780–841 Life of Tsung-mi, disciple of Ch'eng-kuan and fifth patriarch of the Hua-yen sect in China.

JAPANESE HISTORY	WORLD HISTORY
785 Saichō builds a small hermitage on Mount Hiei.	
788 Saichō founds Enryaku-ji.	
794 Capital is transferred to Heiankyō (Kyoto), marking the beginning of the Heian period.	
797 Kūkai writes *Indications of the Goals of the Three Teachings*.	
804 Saichō and Kūkai go to China.	
806 Kūkai brings the Shingon sect to Japan, and Saichō establishes the Tendai sect.	*807–869* Life of Tung-shan, co-founder of the Ts'ao-tung (Sōtō) sect of Chinese Ch'an Buddhism.
	814–890 Life of Yang-shan Hui-chi, Ch'an priest who transmits the teaching of Kuei-shan Ling-yu and founds his own sect.
819 Kūkai founds Kongōbu-ji on Mount Kōya. Saichō asks for government permission to found an ordination platform on Mount Hiei.	
820 Saichō writes *Treatise on the Mahayana Precepts*.	
821 Kūkai repairs the Mannōike reservoir in Sanuki Province.	
822 Saichō dies. Mount Hiei is given permission to set up its own ordination platform.	
828 Kūkai opens a school, Shugei Shuchi-in, next to Tō-ji for Buddhist, Confucian, and Taoist studies.	
835 Kūkai dies.	
847 Ennin returns from three years of study in China.	

JAPANESE HISTORY	WORLD HISTORY

858   Enchin returns from five years of study in China. Fujiwara no Yoshifusa becomes imperial regent.

867   Death of Lin-chi I-hsüan, founder of the Lin-chi (Rinzai) sect of Ch'an Buddhism in China.

868   Enchin establishes Mii-dera as an esoteric transmission site, leading to a split between Tendai's Sammon and Jimon subsects.

874–875   Shōbō establishes Daigo-ji at Mount Kasatori and builds Tōnan-in within Tōdai-ji as a Sanron sect center.

881   Shinnyo, priest and imperial prince, dies on the way to India.

887   Fujiwara no Mototsune becomes imperial regent.

894   End of embassies to China because of political instability there.

899   Retired emperor Uda becomes a Buddhist priest under Yakushin and enters Ninna-ji.

ca. 900   Borobudur, one of the world's greatest Buddhist monuments, is built in central Java under the Sailendra dynasty.

905   Compilation of *Collection of Ancient and Modern Japanese Poems,* the first in a series of anthologies of native verse compiled by imperial command.

919–987   Life of I-chi, priest who lays the foundation for restoration of the T'ien-t'ai sect in China.

938   Kūya chants the nembutsu in Kyoto.

951   Kūya constructs Rokuhara-mitsu-ji.

963   Debate at the imperial palace between Ryōgen of Mount Hiei and Hōzō of Tōdai-ji.

JAPANESE HISTORY	WORLD HISTORY

966 Fire destroys most buildings on Mount Hiei. Ryōgen becomes head of the Tendai sect and starts rebuilding.

968 Conflict between Tōdai-ji and Kōfuku-ji over landownership.

972 Kūya dies.

985 Genshin sets forth the Pure Land doctrine in *Essentials of Deliverance.*

ca. 986–987 Yoshishige no Yasutane composes *Records of Pure Land Rebirth in Japan.*

993 Open hostility between followers of Ennin and Enchin; Enchin's followers are forced to leave Mount Hiei.

1000 Court forbids unauthorized behavior by priests of Kōfuku-ji.

1017 Fujiwara no Michinaga becomes grand minister of state.

1018 Ninkai holds ritual for rain at the Shinsen'en.

1022 Fujiwara no Michinaga completes the main hall at Hōjō-ji.

1035 Brawl between the priests of Enryaku-ji and Mii-dera.

1042 Enryaku-ji (of the Tendai Sammon subsect) priests burn down Mii-dera (of the Tendai Jimon subsect).

1051–1062 Earlier Nine Years' War (military campaign waged intermittently by the imperial court

1002–1069 Life of Huang-lung Hui-nan, Lin-chi Ch'an priest and first patriarch of the popular Huang-lung lineage.

against the magnate of Mutsu Province).

1052 First year of Decay of the Dharma period.

1053 Fujiwara no Yorimichi constructs the Phoenix Hall of Byōdō-in, Kyoto.

1054 Final schism between the western (Roman) and the eastern (Orthodox) churches occurs, because of controversy between Pope Leo IX and the Byzantine patriarch over southern Italy.

1063–1135 Life of Yüan-wu K'och'in, Ch'an Buddhist who compiles *Blue Cliff Records*.

1072 Jōjin goes to China on pilgrimage and collects many Buddhist works.

1075 Emperor orders construction of six imperial temples in Kyoto.

1081 Jōjin dies in China.

1083–1087 Later Three Years' War (military campaign in which Minamoto no Yoshiie subdues the fractious magnate of Dewa Province).

1086 Beginning of government by retired emperors.

1096–1099 First Crusade.

1100s Angkor Wat, a Buddhist temple complex at Angkor, Cambodia, is built by the Khmer king Suryavarman II.

1113 Priests from Enryaku-ji destroy the hall of Kiyomizu-dera belonging to Kōfuku-ji in a feud over the right to appoint Kiyomizu-dera's head priest.

1124 Ryōnin founds the Yūzū Nembutsu sect.

1126 Chūson-ji is constructed at Hiraizumi.

JAPANESE HISTORY	WORLD HISTORY

1134 Kakuban becomes head of Daidembō-in and Kongōbu-ji (resulting in foundation of the Shingi subsect of Shingon).

1140 Kakuban flees Mount Kōya and moves Daidembō-in to Mount Negoro.

1156 Hōgen Disturbance (military conflict arising from rivalries within imperial families).

1159 Heiji Disturbance (clash between Minamoto no Yoshitomo and Taira no Kiyomori).

1167 Taira no Kiyomori is appointed grand minister of state.

1168 Eisai goes to China and returns with Chōgen.

1175 Hōnen establishes exclusive-practice nembutsu and founds the Jōdo sect.

1180 War between the Minamoto and Taira clans begins, and Taira no Shigehira burns down Tōdai-ji and Kōfuku-ji because of their support of the Minamoto.

1181 Chōgen takes charge of fundraising for rebuilding Tōdai-ji.

1185 Mongaku restores Takaosan-ji at Mount Takao. Minamoto clan defeats the Taira clan. Dedication ceremony for the repaired Great Buddha Hall at Tōdai-ji.

1186 Debate at Shōrin-in at Ōhara between Hōnen and Kenshin.

1187 Eisai goes to China again.

1163–1228 Life of Ju-ching, Ts'ao-tung Ch'an priest whose teaching is transmitted by the Japanese priest Dōgen, founder of the Sōtō sect in Japan.

1178–1249 Life of Wu-chun, Lin-chi Ch'an priest who promotes Ch'an fused with Confucianism and Taoism and teaches Japanese priests, such as Enni Bennen, thus greatly influencing the development of the Rinzai sect in Japan.

1183–1260 Life of Hui-k'ai, Chinese Ch'an Buddhist later known as Wu-men, who composes *The Gateless Gate,* 48 dialogues well known in Ch'an Buddhism.

JAPANESE HISTORY	WORLD HISTORY

1191 Eisai returns from China and disseminates Zen teachings.

1192 Minamoto no Yoritomo receives the title of shogun and establishes a shogunate at Kamakura, marking the beginning of the Kamakura period.

1198 Hōnen composes *Collection of Passages on the Original Vow and the Nembutsu.* Eisai composes *Propagation of Zen as a Defense of the Nation.*

1199–1216 Reign of King John in England; granting of the Magna Carta.

ca. 1200 Angkor Thom, another temple complex at Angkor, is built by Khmer king Jayavarman VII.

1201 Shinran joins Hōnen's followers.

1202 Eisai establishes Kennin-ji.

1204 Hōnen signs the *Seven-Article Injunction.*

1205 Kōfuku-ji criticizes exclusive-practice nembutsu.

1206 Hōnen's apprentices, including Gyōkū and Junsai, are exiled. Myōe founds the Kegon sect at Kōzan-ji.

1206–1227 Genghis Khan leads the Mongols in conquest of northern China and Central Asia.

1207 Exclusive-practice nembutsu is banned; Hōnen is exiled to Shikoku, Shinran to Echigo.

1211 Hōnen returns to Kyoto.

1212 Myōe composes *Smashing the Wheel of Heresy,* opposing nembutsu. Hōnen dies.

1214 Eisai presents his *Drink Tea and Prolong Life* to the shogun, Minamoto no Sanetomo.

1215 Eisai dies.

JAPANESE HISTORY	WORLD HISTORY
1217 Dōgen goes to Kennin-ji and studies Rinzai sect Zen under Eisai's successor, Myōzen.	
1218 Shunjō becomes head of Sen'yū-ji and revives the Ritsu sect.	
1221 Jōkyū Disturbance (retired emperor Go-Toba's attempt to overthrow the shogunate).	
1223 Dōgen and Myōzen go to China.	
1224 Shinran establishes the Jōdo Shin sect.	
1227 Dōgen returns from China and establishes the Sōto sect.	
1232 Formulary of Adjudications (legal code) is established by the Kamakura shogunate for its vassals.	
1236 Kakujō takes the *Vinaya of Four Categories* precepts with three other priests and starts to revive the Ritsu sect.	
1244 Dōgen establishes Daibutsu-ji (Eihei-ji).	
1253 Nichiren expounds the Lotus belief and establishes his sect. Dōgen dies, leaving *The Eye Treasury of the Right Dharma* uncompleted.	
1260 Nichiren presents *Treatise on the Establishment of the True Dharma and the Peace of the Nation* to the Kamakura regent, Hōjō Tokiyori.	*1260–1294* Kublai Khan rules China and the Mongol Empire from the Pacific Ocean to the Mediterranean Sea, with his capital at Peking. He builds roads, canals, and hospitals and encourages art and science.
1261 Nichiren is exiled to Izu for two years.	

JAPANESE HISTORY	WORLD HISTORY

1262   Shinran dies.

1268   Nichiren warns the government of foreign invasions.

1271   Nichiren is exiled to Sado Island.

1274   Nichiren is pardoned and goes into seclusion on Mount Minobu. Ippen establishes the Ji sect. First Mongol invasion.

1281   Second Mongol invasion.

1282   Nichiren dies.

1289   Ippen dies.

1294   Ninshō constructs a hospital and an asylum.

1300   Issan Ichinei becomes head of Nanzen-ji and popularizes Chinese Southern Sung dynasty Zen.

1324   Sōhō Myōchō founds Daitoku-ji.

1333–1336   Kemmu Restoration (attempt of Emperor Go-Daigo to restore imperial rule).

1336   Fall of the Kamakura shogunate, marking the beginning of the Muromachi period, and separation of the Northern and Southern courts.

1338   Ashikaga Takauji is appointed shogun.

1339   Musō Soseki founds Tenryū-ji.

1270   Eighth Crusade, the last crusade of real importance.

1271–1295   Marco Polo travels throughout the Mongol Empire.

1272–1340   Life of Tung-ming Hui-jih, Ch'an Buddhist of the Ts'ao-tung lineage, who visits Japan and propagates Ch'an.

ca. 1300   European Renaissance begins in Florence.

1335–1418   Life of Tao-yen, Lin-chi Ch'an priest and the emperor's political and military adviser.

1337–1453   Hundred Years War; English and French kings fight for control of France.

JAPANESE HISTORY	WORLD HISTORY
1342 Ashikaga shogunate establishes the Gozan ranking system for Rinzai sect temples.	
1371 Gidō Shūshin founds Hōon-ji.	
1386 Ashikaga shogunate amends the Gozan ranking system and places Nanzen-ji at the apex.	*ca. 1376–1382* John Wycliffe and his followers translate the Bible into English.
1392 Reconciliation of the Northern and Southern courts.	
1397 Ashikaga Yoshimitsu begins construction of the Temple of the Golden Pavilion in Kyoto.	*1429* Joan of Arc saves France from English conquest.
1440 Ashikaga shogunate imprisons Nisshin over his efforts to make the Nichiren sect into the national religion.	*ca. 1454* Johann Gutenberg invents printing with movable metal type.
1457 Rennyo is appointed head of Hongan-ji.	*1455–1485* Wars of the Roses in England end with the founding of the Tudor dynasty.
1465 Enryaku-ji Tendai priests burn down the Jōdo Shin sect's Hongan-ji in Ōtani.	
1467–1477 Ōnin War (clash between the allies of the Hosokawa and the Yamana).	
1471 Rennyo makes Yoshizaki the teaching center of the Jōdo Shin sect.	
1474 Jōdo Shin sect followers participate in an uprising in Kaga Province.	
1479 Rennyo rebuilds Hongan-ji in Yamashina.	
1481 Ikkyū dies.	

JAPANESE HISTORY	WORLD HISTORY
1482 Ashikaga Yoshimasa begins construction of the Temple of the Silver Pavilion in Kyoto.	
1488 Jōdo Shin sect followers in Kaga defeat the provincial governor.	*1492* Columbus discovers America.
1496 Rennyo founds Ishiyama Hongan-ji in Osaka.	*1497–1499* Vasco da Gama sails around Africa to India and back, giving Portugal the opportunity to establish a monopoly on trade in spices from the Far East to Europe.
1499 Rennyo dies.	
1501 Hosokawa Masamoto brings Nichiren and Jōdo priests together in debate.	
1506 Jōdo Shin sect uprisings spread throughout the north-western region.	*1509* Erasmus writes *The Praise of Folly.*
	1517 The Protestant Reformation begins in Germany.
	1519–1522 Ferdinand Magellan circumnavigates the globe.
	1521 Martin Luther is excommunicated.
1524 Enryaku-ji Tendai priests burn down Nichiren sect temples in Kyoto.	
1531 Kaga uprising disintegrates.	
1532 Nichiren sect followers and Rokkaku Sadayori burn down the Jōdo Shin sect's Hongan-ji.	*1534* Reformation begins in England as Henry VIII makes himself head of the church after his excommunication for divorcing Catherine of Aragon.
	1534–1564 Presbyterianism, developed by John Calvin in Switzerland, gains English Puritans and French Huguenots as adherents.
1536 Enryaku-ji Tendai priests burn down Nichiren sect temples in Kyoto.	

JAPANESE HISTORY	WORLD HISTORY

<table>
<tr><td></td><td>1542–1551   St. Francis Xavier introduces Roman Catholicism to India and Japan.</td></tr>
<tr><td>1543   First musket is introduced to Japan.</td><td>1543   Copernicus publishes his theory that the earth revolves around the sun.</td></tr>
<tr><td></td><td>1546   Martin Luther dies.</td></tr>
<tr><td>1549   First Christian missionaries arrive.</td><td></td></tr>
<tr><td>1560   First major victory for Oda Nobunaga over Imagawa Yoshimoto's army.</td><td>1555   Peace of Augsburg grants to each prince of the Holy Roman Empire the right to choose Catholicism or Lutheranism, but not Calvinism, as the religion of his state. In general, Lutheranism prevails in northern Germany and Catholicism in southern Germany and the Rhineland.</td></tr>
<tr><td>1563   Jōdo Shin sect uprising occurs in Mikawa, accompanied by conflict with Tokugawa Ieyasu.</td><td></td></tr>
<tr><td>1570   Jōdo Shin sect followers in Echizen fight against Oda Nobunaga.</td><td>1566–1642   Life of Yüan-wu, Lin-chi Ch'an priest who has many talented disciples, including Ingen, founder of the Ōbaku sect in Japan.</td></tr>
<tr><td>1571   Oda Nobunaga destroys Mount Hiei.</td><td></td></tr>
<tr><td>1573   Fall of the Ashikaga shogunate.</td><td></td></tr>
<tr><td>1575   Jōdo Shin sect uprising in Echizen is subdued by Oda Nobunaga's army.</td><td></td></tr>
<tr><td>1579   Religious debate is held in the castle town of Azuchi between representatives of the Jōdo and Nichiren sects.</td><td></td></tr>
<tr><td>1580   Kennyo of Hongan-ji accepts peace negotiations with Oda Nobunaga and leaves Ishiyama Hongan-ji, placing pressure on the Jōdo Shin sect uprising in Kaga.</td><td>1580–1645   Life of Chi-kuang, founder of a subsect of the Lü sect in China, who instructs many disciples.</td></tr>
</table>

JAPANESE HISTORY	WORLD HISTORY

1582 Kaisen dies when Oda Nobunaga burns down Erin-ji. Assassination of Oda Nobunaga.

1582 Pope Gregory XIII issues the Gregorian calendar, correcting the errors of the Julian calendar of 46 B.C.

1588 English fleet defeats the Spanish Armada.

1589 Toyotomi Hideyoshi bans Christianity.

1595 Nichiō is briefly exiled for refusing to participate in the dedication of the Great Buddha at Hōkō-ji, advocating the Fuju Fuse ("neither give nor accept") doctrine.

1600 Nichiō is exiled for twelve years for refusal to debate the Fuju Fuse doctrine. Battle of Sekigahara, resulting in victory for Tokugawa Ieyasu.

1602 Kyōnyo founds Higashi Hongan-ji, dividing the Jōdo Shin sect into the Hongan-ji (Nishi) and Ōtani (Higashi) subsects.

1603 Tokugawa Ieyasu is given the title of shogun, marking the beginning of the Edo period.

1609 Takuan becomes head of Daitoku-ji.

1612 Tokugawa shogunate bans Christianity.

1613 Tokugawa shogunate issues regulations concerning the necessity of shogunal approval in imperial conferral of purple robes.

1615 Tokugawa shogunate issues regulations to head temples of the main sects. Fall of the Toyotomi

JAPANESE HISTORY	WORLD HISTORY

family. Regulations Governing the Imperial Court and Nobility are promulgated.

1619 Tokugawa shogunate appoints Sūden registrar of priests.

1625 Tenkai founds Kan'ei-ji, in Edo.

1627 Purple Robe Incident.

1629 Takuan is exiled for three years.

1630 Nichiō and his Fuju Fuse subsect followers are persecuted.

1631 Tokugawa shogunate bans construction of new temples.

1633 Tenkai completes publication of the Buddhist canon. Tokugawa shogunate issues the first National Seclusion Edict.

1634 Takuan becomes the shogun's advisor on religious affairs.

1635 Tokugawa shogunate appoints supervisors of shrines and temples in domains.

1637–1638 Shimabara Uprising (Christian peasant uprising in the Shimabara domain).

1639 Tokugawa shogunate issues the last National Seclusion Edict in the aftermath of the Shimabara Uprising; seclusion continues until 1854.

1640 Government institution for religious inquisition is established.

1618–1648 Thirty Years' War; Protestants in Holy Roman Empire rebel against oppression by Roman Catholics.

1632–1652 Shah Jahan builds the Taj Mahal in India.

1633 Inquisition forces Galileo to repudiate the Copernican system.

JAPANESE HISTORY	WORLD HISTORY

"Temple guarantee" system and system of registering family Buddhist temple affiliation begin.

1645   Takuan dies.

1654   Ingen arrives in Nagasaki.

1659   Ingen founds Ōbakusan Mampuku-ji and establishes the Ōbaku sect.

1665   Tokugawa shogunate issues regulations for all temples.

1681   Tetsugen completes wood blocks for printing the complete Buddhist canon in 6,771 volumes.

1688   Yūzū Nembutsu sect receives shogunal permission to be independent of the Jōdo sect.

1691   Hiden subsect of the Nichiren sect is banned.

1707   Hōtan revives the Kegon sect.

1716   Hakuin restores Shōin-ji.

1716–1745   Kyōhō Reforms (first of a series of three financial and agrarian reform programs carried out by the shogunate).

1723   Hōtan founds Daikegon-ji and engages in debate with other sects.

1746   Jiun founds the Vinaya of the True Dharma (Shōbōritsu) movement.

1642–1658   Oliver Cromwell leads supporters of parliament in defeating royalist armies; Charles I is beheaded in 1649. Cromwell rules as military dictator, suppressing the Church of England and decreeing Puritanical laws.

1648   Peace of Westphalia concludes the Thirty Years' War, redrawing French-German borders.

1689–1725   Peter the Great carries out westernizing reforms and establishes Russia as major military power.

1707   England, Scotland, and Wales form the United Kingdom of Great Britain.

1748   Montesquieu completes *The Spirit of Laws*.

JAPANESE HISTORY	WORLD HISTORY
1758 Hakuin founds Ryūtaku-ji.	
	1775–1783 American Revolutionary War.
	1776 Adam Smith writes *The Wealth of Nations*.
1782 Temmei Famine.	*1781* Immanuel Kant writes *Critique of Pure Reason*.
1787–1793 Kansei Reforms of Matsudaira Sadanobu (second of the shogunate's reform programs).	*1788–1860* Life of Arthur Schopenhauer, exponent of a metaphysical doctrine of the will that prepares the way for existential philosophy and Freudian psychology.
	1789 French Revolution begins.
1792 Russian ships arrive at Nemuro, Ezo Island.	
1797 Jiun establishes an ordination platform at Kōki-ji and sets up Shōbōritsu as a subsect of Shingon.	*1800–1894* Life of Brian Houghton Hodgson, British Resident in Nepal who gathers many Buddhist texts.
1804 Jiun dies. Ryōkan settles at Gogo-an on Mount Kugami.	*1804* Napoleon crowns himself emperor of France.
	1805 Battle of Trafalgar; Nelson defeats the French-Spanish fleet, enabling Britain to blockade Napoleonic France.
	1807 Hegel publishes his *Phenomenology of Mind*.
	1815 Napoleon escapes from Elba and is defeated by Wellington at Waterloo.
	1823 United States issues the Monroe Doctrine, warning Europe against interfering in the Western Hemisphere.

JAPANESE HISTORY	WORLD HISTORY

1825 Tokugawa shogunate orders foreign ships repelled.

1831 Ryōkan dies.

1833 Tempō Famine.

1835 Gesshō becomes head of Kiyomizu-dera.

1837 Uprising of Ōshio Heihachirō.

1838 Large-scale roundup of Nichiren Fuju Fuse subsect followers.

1841–1843 Tempō Reforms of Mizuno Tadakuni (third of the shogunate's reform programs).

1823–1900 Life of Max Müller, German philologist and pioneer in bringing Indian religious texts to the attention of Europeans.

1832 Goethe completes *Faust.*

1832–1907 Life of Henry Steel Olcott, co-founder with Madame Blavatsky of the Theosophical Society.

1839–1842 Opium War; China is forced to cede Hong Kong to Britain and to open other ports to trade.

1843–1922 Life of Thomas William Rhys Davids, founder of the Pali Text Society and perhaps the most forceful figure in editing and translating the texts of the Theravadins.

1844–1900 Life of German philosopher Friedrich Nietzsche.

1845–1849 Sikh Wars; British conquest and annexation of the Punjab, in northwestern India.

1848 Karl Marx and Friedrich Engels publish the *Communist Manifesto* in Germany.

1850–1864 T'ai P'ing Rebellion; rebel believers in a Chinese form of Puritan Protestantism win control of central provinces; the Manchus subdue them with the aid of foreign mercenaries.

JAPANESE HISTORY	WORLD HISTORY
	1852 Eugène Burnouf's French translation of the *Lotus Sutra* is published posthumously.
1853 Arrival of American ships under Commodore Matthew C. Perry and Russian ships under Vice Admiral E. V. Putyatin.	
1854 United States and Japan sign the Treaty of Peace and Amity (Kanagawa Treaty).	*1854–1856* Crimean War begins as a dispute over control of Christian holy places in Jerusalem.
	1854–1899 Life of Henry Clarke Warren, editor of Buddhaghosa's *Visuddhimagga*.
	1854–1920 Life of Hermann Oldenberg, German Indologist and Buddhologist, one of the two most prominent scholars, with Thomas William Rhys Davids, of Pali texts.
	1856–1870 Christians persecuted in Korea; missionaries are executed.
	1857–1859 Indian (Sepoy) Mutiny; a widespread but unsuccessful rebellion against British rule in India and a source of inspiration to later Indian nationalists. Transfer of government from the East India Company to the British crown.
1858 Gesshō dies fleeing the shogun's supporters.	
1858–1859 Ansei Purge (widespread purge of political leaders and court nobles who oppose the shogunate's policy of opening Japan to diplomatic and trade relations with the West).	
1860 Sakuradamon Incident (assassination of Ii Naosuke).	*1859* Charles Darwin publishes *On the Origin of Species by Means of Natural Selection.*
	1861–1865 American Civil War.
	1862–1943 Life of Sir Mark Aurel Stein, who follows the route of Alexander the Great and publishes *Serindia* (1921) and *Innermost Asia* (1928), and who is partly responsible for the rediscovery of Tunhuang.

JAPANESE HISTORY	WORLD HISTORY

1863 U.S. President Abraham Lincoln issues the Emancipation Proclamation.

1865 Satsuma domain promotes the "Abandon the Buddha, Destroy Buddhism" movement.

1865–1869 Leo Tolstoy writes *War and Peace.*

1866 Alliance between the Satsuma and Chōshū domains.

1866–1942 Life of Theodore Stcherbatsky, Russian scholar of Buddhism and translator of many texts, notably *Buddhist Logic.* His book *The Central Conception of Buddhism and the Meaning of the Word "Dharma"* is one of the classics in the field.

1867 Shogun returns political rule to the emperor. The Satsuma and Chōshū forces proclaim an "imperial restoration."

1868 Promulgation of the Imperial Oath of Five Articles, a statement of national policy. Separation Edict is promulgated, ordering the separation of Shinto and Buddhism. Edo is renamed Tokyo. Meiji Restoration, marking the beginning of the Meiji era (period). Buddhist Ethics Association is formed in Kyoto.

1869 Suez Canal opens.

1869–1937 Life of Louis de La Vallée Poussin, Buddhologist and translator of many critical Buddhist texts, including Vasubandhu's *Abhidharmakośabhāṣyam.*

1870 Government orders promotion of Shinto.

1871 Uprising by supporters of the Mikawa Dharma Preservation Society. Abolition of domains and establishment of prefectures. System of registering family Buddhist temple affiliation is abolished.

1872 Ministry of Religion is established and issues the Three Articles of Instruction. Great Teaching Institute is established; Sesshin becomes its first head. Government instruction officials are installed to enlighten people through religion. Permission is given to priests to eat meat, marry and

JAPANESE HISTORY	WORLD HISTORY

let their hair grow. Shimaji Mokurai compiles *A Critique of the Three
Articles of Instruction.*

1873–1881   Land Tax Reform.

1873–1945   Conscription Ordinance
(law making military service com-
pulsory for all males).

1875   Jōdo Shin subsects withdraw
from the Great Teaching Institute.

1877   Satsuma Rebellion (the last
major armed uprising against the
government and its reforms).

1879   Hara Tanzan is appointed
first lecturer in Indian philosophy
at Tokyo Imperial University.

1883   Nanjio Bunyiu publishes *A
Catalogue of the Chinese Translation of
the Buddhist Tripitaka.*

1889   Meiji Constitution is promulgated. Shaku Unshō forms the
Association of the Ten Good Precepts.

1892   Shaku Sōen becomes head of
Engaku-ji.

1893   Shaku Sōen attends the
World's Parliament of Religions in
Chicago.

1895   Kiyozawa Manshi and others
call for reform within the Ōtani
subsect of Jōdo Shin.

1897   Suzuki Daisetz goes to the
United States as editorial assistant
to Paul Carus.

1878–1945   Life of Paul Pelliot, col-
lector of manuscripts from Central
Asia and publisher of *La Mission
Pelliot en Asie Centrale* in 1924.

1882   Germany, Austria, and Italy
sign the Triple Alliance defense
pact.

1894–1895   Sino-Japanese War; Japan wins control of Korea, For-
mosa, and the Pescadores Islands.

1895   Wilhelm Conrad Rontgen,
Univesity of Würzburg physicist,
discovers X-rays.

1896   First modern Olympic Games
are held at Athens, Greece.

JAPANESE HISTORY	WORLD HISTORY

1899   Buddhist Pure Believers' Association is formed. Kawaguchi Ekai becomes the first Japanese to enter Tibet, and studies Tibetan Buddhism.

1900   German physicist Max Planck formulates the quantum theory.

1901   Kiyozawa Manshi starts *Spiritual World* magazine.

1900–1901   Boxer War; China attempts to end its exploitation by killing foreigners and destroying foreign installations. U.S., Russian, British, French, and German troops subdue the Chinese, capturing and looting Peking and forcing China to pay for damage to foreign property.

1903   Kiyozawa Manshi dies.

1903–1983   Life of Étienne Lamotte, Louvain Buddhologist; author of the classic *Histoire du Bouddhisme Indien des origines à l'ère Saka* and translator of many important Buddhist texts.

1904–1905   Russo-Japanese War; Japan astonishes the world by defeating the Russians with relative ease.

1905   Itō Shōshin founds the Selfless Love movement's first institute. Shaku Sōen visits the United States again.

1910   Uchiyama Gudō and others are implicated in the High Treason Incident of 1910. Annexation of Korea.

1911   Shimaji   Mokurai   dies. Uchiyama Gudō is executed for treason.

1912–1926   Reign of Emperor Taishō (beginning of the Taishō era).

1913   Kawaguchi Ekai re-enters Tibet and brings out the Tibetan canon and other manuscripts.

1914–1918   World War I.

1916   Albert   Einstein   publishes "The Foundation of the General Theory of Relativity."

JAPANESE HISTORY	WORLD HISTORY
	1917 Russian Revolution.
1919 Shaku Sōen dies.	*1919* Treaty of Versailles is signed.
	1920 League of Nations holds its first meeting at Geneva, Switzerland.

.

Glossary

Abbreviations used are "C" for Chinese, "J" for Japanese, and "S" for Sanskrit.

"Abandon the Buddha, Destroy Buddhism" 廃仏毀釈 [J: *haibutsu kishaku*] Nationwide anti-Buddhist movement that followed the government's 1868 decree to separate Shinto and Buddhism.

Akashagarbha Bodhisattva 虚空蔵菩薩 [J: Kokūzō Bosatsu; S: Ākāśagarbha Bodhisattva] Central bodhisattva in the Womb-Store Mandala of esoteric Buddhism, and the object of worship in the ritual to strengthen the memory (Mantra of Akashagarbha).

Amida Buddha 阿弥陀仏 [J: Amida Butsu; S: Amitābha (or Amitāyus) Buddha] Buddha of the Western Pure Land and the focus of nembutsu in Pure Land Buddhism. *Amitābha* means infinite light, and *amitāyus* means infinite life. Also called Amida Tathāgata.

Amida sage 阿弥陀聖 [J: *Amida hijiri*] Wandering ascetic; an epithet for Kūya.

arhat 阿羅漢 [J: *arakan*] Highest stage in Theravada Buddhism, one of the two main streams of Buddhism, attained by one who has completely eliminated the defilements and so is free from rebirth and all attachment to desire.

assistant high priest 僧都 [J: *sōzu*] Second highest rank in the Bureau of Clergy, with four subdivisions (*daisōzu, gon-daisōzu, shōsōzu,* and *gon-shōsōzu*).

bessho 別所 Specialized training center where ascetics who felt dissatisfied with the training and practices of established Buddhist temples secluded themselves.

biku 比丘 [S: *bhikṣu*] Male Buddhist cleric. See official priest.

bikuni 比丘尼 [S: *bhikṣuṇī*] Female Buddhist cleric. See official priest.

bodhisattva 菩薩 [J: *bosatsu*] The Sanskrit term *bodhi* means buddhahood; *sattva*, living being. One who devotes oneself to attaining enlightenment not only for oneself but also for all sentient beings.

bodhisattva precepts 菩薩戒 [J: *bosatsu-kai*] Precepts contained in the *Sutra of the Perfect Net;* also called the Brahmajala precepts.

buddha 仏陀 [J: *budda*] In Sanskrit, a title meaning "one who is enlightened."

Buddha of Healing 薬師仏 [J: Yakushi Butsu; S: Bhaiṣajya-guru Buddha] Buddha of the Land of Emerald in the east.

Buddhist Ethics Association 諸宗道徳会盟 [J: Shoshū Dōtoku Kaimei] Association founded in 1868 in Kyoto and the following year in Tokyo by Sesshin, Ugai Tetsujō, Fukuda Gyōkai, and others, in reaction to the "Abandon the Buddha, Destroy Buddhism" movement.

Bureau of Clergy 僧綱 [J: Sōgō] From 624 on, a board of priests appointed by the court to regulate Buddhism, consisting of three ranks, *sōjō, sōzu,* and *risshi,* each with a number of subdivisions. By the 13th century the ranks were honorary and had no supervisory function.

ceremony of repentance by means of the Buddha names 仏名懺悔 [J: *butsumyō sange*] Penitential service at the imperial court in which the names of the three thousand buddhas were recited to purify the court and the country; discontinued after the 15th century.

Ch'an 禅 [J: *zen;* S: *dhyāna*] Originally meaning meditation, it became the name of a Buddhist sect based primarily on the practice of meditation. According to tradition, the Indian priest Bodhidharma went to China and transmitted the teaching in the 7th century, and thus began the Ch'an sect in China.

chanting of Shakyamuni Buddha's name 釈迦念仏 [J: *Shaka nembutsu*] Form of Shakyamuni worship developed in reaction to the popular Amida faith after the 13th century.

Clerical Code 僧尼令 [J: *sōni-ryō*] Legal code promulgated in 718 to regulate male and female priests.

cleric-soldier 僧兵 [J: *sōhei*] Armed lower-ranking priests attached to great Buddhist institutions, such as Kōfuku-ji and Enryaku-ji, in the 11th and 12th centuries.

community ceremony 布薩 [J: *fusatsu;* S: *upavasatha*] Regular meeting of priests and other members of a temple community held twice monthly to expound the doctrine and the precepts.

Concentration and Insight 止観 [J: *shikan;* C: *chih-kuan;* S: *śamatha-vipaśyanā*] Method of meditation that helps one to cease deluded thought and attain enlightenment, established in the 6th century by Chih-i, founder of the T'ien-t'ai sect in China.

Consciousness Only 唯識 [J: *yuishiki;* S: *vijñapti-mātratā*] Doctrine that all phenomena are produced from the "store-consciousness" (*ālaya-vijñāna* in Sanskrit), the last of the eight levels of consciousness, based on the *Treatise on the Establishment of the Doctrine of Consciousness Only.*

Daiseishi Bodhisattva 大勢至菩薩 [J: Daiseishi Bosatsu; S: Mahā-sthāmaprāpta Bodhisattva] Bodhisattva representing wisdom.

Dazaifu 太宰府 Government headquarters in northern Kyushu from ca. the 7th through 12th century.

Decay of the Dharma 末法 [J: *mappō*] Period of the last and decadent dharma after Shakyamuni Buddha's death; in Japan it is believed to have begun in 1052. Other periods are those of the True Dharma and the Counterfeit Dharma.

Department of Shinto Ritual 神祇官 [J: Jingikan; also known as Department of Divinity] High government office established in 1868 following an ancient precedent, to control all Shinto priests and shrines. It was demoted in status in 1871, placed under the aegis of the Great Council of State (Dajōkan) and renamed the Ministry of Shinto Ritual (Jingishō). In 1872 it was reconstituted as the Ministry of Religion (Kyōbushō), and was abolished in 1877.

dharma [J: *hō*] Buddhist teaching, Truth.

dharma master 法師 [J: *hōshi*] Title given to an eminent priest.

Diamond Realm 金剛界 [J: Kongō-kai; S: Vajra-dhātu] Realm representing the wisdom aspect of Mahavairocana. The Diamond Realm mandala is a representation of this. The Diamond and Womb-Store realms are the two aspects of Mahavairocana and the two central tenets of esoteric Buddhism.

Eminent Conduct Bodhisattva 上行菩薩 [J: Jōgyō Bosatsu; S: Viśiṣṭacāritra Bodhisattva] Bodhisttva entrusted by Shakyamuni Buddha with spreading the teachings of the *Lotus Sutra.*

Emma 閻魔 [J: Emma; S: Yama] Lord of the underworld.

Five Mountains system 五山制度 [J: *gozan* or *gosan seido*] The ranking system of Rinzai temples in Kamakura and Kyoto by the Kamakura and Ashikaga shogunates during the 14th and 15th centuries.

fuju fuse 不受不施 ["neither give nor accept"] Sixteenth-century movement (later subsect) founded by Nichiō within the Nichiren sect that refused to give donations to, or accept them from, nonbelievers.

Garden of Selflessness 無我苑 [J: Muga'en] The base of Itō Shōshin's movement of Selfless Love, where adherents lived and practiced.

grand minister of state 太政大臣 [J: *dajō-daijin*] Policy-making rank in the *ritsuryō* system of government.

Great Council of State 太政官 [J: Dajōkan] Central administrative organ in the *ritsuryō* system of government established in the late 7th and early 8th centuries.

Great Teaching Institute 大教院 [J: Daikyōin] Institute founded within the Ministry of Religion in 1872 to propagate state ethics.

haiku 俳句 Japanese poetic form using seventeen syllables.

high priest 僧正 [J: *sōjō*] Highest rank in the Bureau of Clergy, with three subdivisions (*daisōjō, gon-daisōzu, shōsōzu,* and *gon-shōsōzu*).

hijiri 聖 Wandering religious figures and Buddhist priests who were credited with magical powers, often attained during seclusion in mountains. Civil-engineering works like the building of bridges and roads are often attributed to them, and they were in close contact with the common people through their knowledge of medical and magical means of curing illness.

holy teacher 阿闍梨 [J: *ajari* S: *ācārya*] Title given to officially appointed eminent priests of the Tendai or Shingon sect and to priests who received Tendai or Shingon esoteric initiation.

Huang-lung 黄竜 [J: Ōryō] Lineage of the Lin-chi sect of Ch'an Buddhism in China, founded in the 11th century by Hui-nan on Mount Huang-lung and brought to Japan by Eisai in 1191.

Hu-ch'iu 虎丘 [J: Kukyū] Chinese Ch'an Buddhist lineage taken to Japan by Enni Bennen in the 13th century. Also called Yang-ch'i (Yōgi in Japanese).

junior assistant high priest 少僧都 [J: *shōsōzu*] Rank in the Bureau of Clergy.

"just sitting" 只管打坐 [J: *shikan taza*] Dōgen's Zen emphasized this method of attaining enlightenment without depending on koans as codified meditation subjects.

Kamakura regent 執権 [J: *shikken*] Office of the Kamakura shogunate and de facto ruler, starting in 1203.

kambun 漢文 Classical Chinese texts, and texts written in Chinese by Japanese authors.

kami 神 Japan's indigenous Shinto deities, widely incorporated into Buddhism during the 11th and 12th centuries through their identification with Buddhist figures of worship.

Kannon Bodhisattva 観音菩薩 [J: Kannon (or Kanzeon) Bosatsu; S: Avalokiteśvara Bodhisattva] Compassionate bodhisattva.

Kegon 華厳 [C: Hua-yen] Buddhist sect emphasizing the teachings of the *Flower Garland Sutra*. Its doctrine was systematized by Fa-tsang in the 7th century in China. The Korean priest Shinjō, who lectured on the sutra in Nara, is considered the founder of the Japanese branch.

kendō 剣道 Japanese swordsmanship.

koan 公案 [J: *kōan;* C: *kung-an*] A conundrum used by the Rinzai sect to awaken spiritual insight, for example, "What is the sound of one hand clapping?"

labor tax 調 [J: *chō*] See rice tax.

Lin-chi 臨済 [J: Rinzai] Ch'an sect founded in the 9th century by Lin-chi I-hsüan and taken to Japan by Eisai.

linked verse 連歌 [J: *renga*] Form of poetry that flourished mainly from the 13th through 16th century.

Lively Wide Cavern 浩々洞 [J: Kōkōdō] Residence of Kiyozawa Manshi and his group, and the base of his spirituality movement.

Mahavairocana Tathagata 大日如来 [J: Dainichi Nyorai; S: Mahā-vairocana Tathāgata] Central tathagata in the Shingon sect. An expression of the truth of the universe, from which all things are born.

Mahayana 大乗 [J: Daijō; S: Mahāyāna] Literally, "Great Vehicle." One of the two main branches of Buddhism, practiced in such countries as Tibet, China, Korea, and Japan.

main-and-branch-temple system 本末制度 [J: *hommatsu seido*] Tokugawa shogunate's legal system of controlling Buddhist temples, established in the 17th century.

mandala 曼陀羅 [J: *mandara;* S: *maṇḍala*] Geometric design representing the universe. Used in esoteric Buddhism and the Nichiren sect to illustrate fundamental religious doctrine.

mantra 真言 [J: *shingon*] Literally, "truthful utterance." In Buddhism it refers to sacred verses and words, important in esoteric sects, such as Chen-yen and Shingon.

Ministry of Civil Administration 治部省 [J: Jibushō] Government ministry involved in imperial funerals, mausolea, and diplomacy; it was under the control of the Great Council of State in the *ritsuryō* system of government.

Ministry of Religion 教部省 [J: Kyōbushō] Government ministry established in 1872 in place of the Ministry of Shinto Ritual and abolished in 1877.

mokujiki 木食 Literally, "tree-eater." Extreme form of asceticism whose followers eat only wild fruits and vegetables.

Monju Bodhisattva 文殊菩薩 [J: Monju Bosatsu; S: Mañjuśrī Bodhisattva] Personification of the Buddha's wisdom.

mudra 印相 [J: *ingei* or *inzō;* S: *mudrā*] Hand position or gesture represent-

ing Buddhist enlightenment. Through mudras a practitioner is believed to be able to become one with the Buddha.

National Learning 国学 [J: Kokugaku] Textual and interpretive study of
Japanese classical literature and ancient writings that began in the
17th century; also termed the nativist movement.

national teacher 国師 [J: kokushi] Honorary title, often posthumous,
given to eminent priests by an emperor.

nembutsu 念仏 Repetition of the phrase Namu Amida Butsu—"I take
refuge in Amida Buddha"—as a way of attaining enlightenment.

Nichiren sect [J: Nichiren-shū] Japanese Buddhist sect founded by Nichiren, based on the Lotus Sutra.

official certification system for clergy 公験制度 [J: kugen seido] System set
up by the government in the 8th century of giving newly ordained
priests certificates of ordination and of receipt of the precepts.

official priest 官僧 [J: kansō] Officially ordained priests were given ordination certificates and were called shami and shamini. They were then
qualified to receive the precepts, at which point they were given
precepts certificates and called biku and bikuni.

ordination certificate 度牒 [J: dochō] Certificate issued by the government
to priests who were officially ordained. The practice began in the 8th
century.

ordination platform 戒壇 [J: kaidan] Dais used in a ceremony in which
one accepts the Buddhist precepts.

"other-power" 他力 [J: tariki] Total reliance on the saving power of
Amida Buddha.

preceptor 律師 [J: risshi] Rank in the Bureau of Clergy, with three subdivisions (dairisshi, chūrisshi, and gon-risshi).

precepts certificate 戒牒 [J: kaichō] Certificate issued by the government
to official priests who received the precepts. The practice began in the
8th century.

precepts transmitter 戒師 [J: kaishi] Priest qualified to give the precepts
to those entering the clergy.

privately ordained priest 私度僧 [J: shido-sō] Priest who was not officially
ordained.

produce tax 庸 [J: yō] See rice tax.

provisional high priest 権僧正 [J: gon-sōjō] Rank in the Bureau of Clergy.

provisional junior assistant high priest 権少僧都 [J: gon-shōsōzu] Rank in
the Bureau of Clergy.

provisional preceptor 権律師 [J: gon-risshi] Rank in the Bureau of Clergy.

provisional senior assistant high priest 権大僧都 [J: gon-daisōzu] Rank in
the Bureau of Clergy.

rice tax 租 [J: *so*] The rice tax (*so*), produce tax (*yō*), and labor tax (*chō*) were the basic taxes under the *ritsuryō* system established in the 7th century.

Rinzai. See Lin-chi.

ritsuryō system 律令制度 [J: *ritsuryō seido*] System of centralized autocracy between the 7th and late 10th centuries, modeled on the T'ang Chinese legal system and structured around comprehensive penal and administrative codes.

''self-power'' 自力 [J: *jiriki*] Reliance on one's own efforts, in contrast to ''other-power'' (reliance on Amida Buddha).

senior assistant high priest 大僧都 [J: *daisōzu*] Rank in the Bureau of Clergy.

senior high priest 大僧正 [J: *daisōjō*] Rank in the Bureau of Clergy.

Shakyamuni [J: Shaka or Shakamuni; S: Śākyamuni] Literally, ''Sage of the Shakya Tribe.'' The historical buddha and founder of Buddhism, who lived in India about 2,500 years ago.

shami 沙弥 [S: *śrāmaṇera*] Male Buddhist novice. See official priest.

shamini 沙弥尼 [S: *śrāmaṇerī*] Female Buddhist novice. See official priest.

Shingon 真言 [C: Chen-yen; S: Mantra] Buddhist sect emphasizing esoteric practice, taken to China from India in the early 8th century and to Japan by Kūkai in the early 9th century.

Shingon esotericism 東密 [J: Tōmitsu] Esoteric teachings systematized at Tō-ji by Kūkai, in contrast to Tendai esotericism.

Shinto 神道 [J: Shintō] Japan's indigenous religion, involving cults of deities of natural forces.

Shugei Shuchi-in 綜芸種智院 School of Buddhism and Confucianism founded next to the Kyoto temple Tō-ji by Kūkai in 828.

''silent illumination'' Zen 黙照禅 [J: *mokushō Zen*] Tranquil form of sitting meditation in the Ch'an sect.

Sōtō. See Ts'ao-tung.

spirituality movement 精神主義運動 [J: *seishin-shugi undō*] Early-20th-century movement initiated by Kiyozawa Manshi emphasizing self-knowledge and faith in the Buddha over scholarship or ethics.

Ta-hui 大恵 [J: Daie] Chinese Ch'an lineage of the Lin-chi sect that was founded in the 12th century by Ta-hui Sung-kae. It emphasizes sudden enlightenment through koan practice.

tathagata 如来 [J: *nyorai;* S: *tathāgata*] Literally, ''thus come.'' One who has come from the Truth; an epithet of a buddha.

Tendai 天台 [C: T'ien-t'ai] Buddhist sect emphasizing the *Lotus Sutra,* established in the 6th century in China by Chih-i and in Japan by Saichō in 806.

Tendai esotericism 台密 [J: Taimitsu] Esoteric teachings established within the Tendai sect by Ennin and Enchin in the 9th century, in contrast to Shingon esotericism.

three stages of conversion 三願転入 [J: *sangan tennyū*] Shinran's concept of conversion, involving good actions, exclusive-practice nembutsu, and, finally, realization of "other-power."

Ts'ao-tung 曹洞 [J: Sōtō] Chinese Ch'an sect, founded in the 9th century in China by Tung-shan Liang-chieh and taken to Japan by Dōgen in 1227. It stresses the attainment of self-enlightenment through seated meditation, in contrast to Lin-chi Ch'an, which emphasizes the koan method.

ubai 優婆夷 [S: *upāsikā*] Female lay Buddhist.

ubasoku 優婆塞 [S: *upāsaka*] Male lay Buddhist.

Vairocana Buddha 盧遮那仏 [J: Rushana Butsu] Principal buddha in the Kegon and Shingon sects.

Vinaya 律 [J: *ritsu;* C: *lü*] One of the Three Baskets (S: *Tripiṭaka*) of the Buddhist canon, comprising the writings concerning precepts and conduct for the Buddhist clergy (the other baskets are those comprising sutras and commentaries). Also the name of Chinese and Japanese Buddhist sects.

waka 和歌 Japanese poetic form using thirty-one syllables.

Way-Seeking 求道 [J: *gudō*] Early-20th-century movement emphasizing Shinran's teachings, initiated by Chikazumi Jōkan.

Womb-Store Realm 胎蔵界 [J: Taizō-kai; S: Garbha-dhātu] Realm representing Mahavairocana's aspect of dynamic enlightenment, which underlies and nurtures all phenomena. This and the Diamond Realm are the two aspects of Mahavairocana and the two central tenets of esoteric Buddhism.

Documents

Abbreviations used are "C" for Chinese, "J" for Japanese, "S" for Sanskrit, and *"T"* for *Taishō Shinshū Daizō-kyō* (popularly called *Taishō Tripiṭaka,* ed. Junjirō Takakusu et al., 55 vols. Tokyo: Daizō Shuppan, 1924–29), a compilation of sacred Buddhist works. The numbers following *"T"* indicate text numbers in that collection.

Abbreviated Chronicles of Japan 日本紀略 [J: Nihon Kiryaku]. (A history of Japan to 1036.)

Abhidharma Storehouse Treatise 阿毘達摩倶舎論 [J: Abidatsuma Kusha-ron (abbreviated as Kusha-ron 倶舎論); C: A-p'i-ta-mo chü-she-lun; S: Abhidharmakośa]. By Vasubandhu, ca. 400–480. *T* 1558, 1559.

Admonition [Concerning] Protecting and Striving 鎮勧用心 [J: Chinkan Yōjin]. By Shōkū.

Advanced Words of Religious Instruction 奏進法語 [J: Sōshin Hōgo]. By Shinzei, 1492.

Agama sutras 阿含経 [J: Agon-gyō; C: A-han-ching]. In the Chinese canon, these consist of the following:

    1. *Long Discourses* [J: Jō-agon-gyō; C: Ch'ang a-han-ching; S: Dīrghāgama]. *T* 1.

    2. *Middle-Length Discourses* [J: Chū-agon-gyō; C: Chung a-han-ching; S: Madhyamāgama]. *T* 26.

    3. *Grouped Discourses* [J: Zō-agon-gyō; C: Tsa a-han-ching; S: Saṃyuktāgama]. *T* 99.

4. *Discourses Treating Enumerations* [J: Zōitsu-agon-gyō; C: Tseng-i a-han-ching; S: Ekottarāgama]. *T* 125.

Amitabha Sutra (Smaller Sukhavati-vyuha) 阿弥陀経 [J: Amida-kyō; C: A-mi-t'o-ching; S: Sukhāvatī-vyūha]. *T* 366, 367.

Answering Questions [Viewing] Snow through the Window 雪窓答問 [J: Sessō Tōmon]. By Fukuda Gyōkai.

Anthology of Enchin's Writings 智証大師全集 [J: Chishō Daishi Zenshū]. By Enchin.

The Anthology of Ten Thousand Leaves 万葉集 [J: Man'yō-shū]. (Translated by Ian Hideo Levy as *The Ten Thousand Leaves: A Translation of Man'yōshū, Japan's Premier Anthology of Classical Poetry,* vol. 1. Princeton, N.J.: Princeton University Press, 1981.)

Argument Against Prejudice and Criticism 僻難対弁 [J: Byakunan Taiben]. By Gōzei, 1765.

Aspiring to the Way in Foolishness and Delusion 愚迷発心集 [J: Gumei Hos-shin-shū]. By Jōkei, 1192.

Attainment of Buddhahood Through Initial Aspiration for the Lotus 法華初心成仏鈔 [J: Hokke Shoshin Jōbutsu-shō]. By Nichiren, 1277.

Awareness of Mediocrity 平凡の自覚 [J: Heibon no Jikaku]. By Uchiyama Gudō.

Basics of Tendai 依憑天台集 [J: Ehyō Tendai-shū]. By Saichō, 813.

Biographical Chronology of Gyōgi 行基年譜 [J: Gyōgi Nempu]. Comp. 1175.

Biographies of Wondrously Good People 妙好人伝 [J: Myōkōnin-den]. By Gōzei, 1842.

Biographies of Zen People of Our Day 近世禅林僧宝伝 [J: Kinsei Zenrin Sōhō-den]. By Ogino Dokuon.

Biography of the Venerable Priest [Hōnen] from Collected Materials 拾遺古徳伝 [J: Shūi Kotoku-den]. By Kakunyo, 1301.

Blue Cliff Records 碧巌録 [J: Hekigan-roku; C: Pi-yen-lu]. Comp. by Yüan-wu K'o-ch'in, 1125. *T* 2003. (Translated by Katsuki Sekida in *Two Zen Classics: Mumonkan and Hekiganroku.* Tokyo: Weatherhill, 1977.)

Book of Tengu 天狗草紙 [J: Tengu Sōshi]. Comp. 1296.

Buddhist History Grove 仏教史林 [J: Bukkyō Shirin]. (Magazine published by Murakami Senshō, 1894–1897.)

The Building of a Spiritual Japan 霊性的日本の建設 [J: Reiseiteki Nihon no Kensetsu]. By Suzuki Daisetz.

A Catalogue of the Chinese Translation of the Buddhist Tripitaka: The Sacred Canon of the Buddhists in China and Japan 大明三蔵聖教目録 [C: *Ta-Ming san-tsang sheng-chiao mu-lu*]. (Translated by Nanjio Bunyiu. Oxford: Clarendon Press, 1883.)

Ching-te Record of the Transmission of the Lamp 景徳伝灯録 [J: Keitoku Dentō-roku; C: Ching-te ch'uan-teng-lu]. Comp. by Tao-yüan, ed. by Yang-i, 1004. (Partially translated by Chang Chung-yüan as *Original Teachings of Ch'an Buddhism: Selected from the Transmission of the Lamp.* New York: Vintage, 1971.)

Chronicles of Japan 日本書紀 [J: Nihon Shoki]. Comp. 720. (Translated by W. G. Aston as *Nihongi: Chronicles of Japan from the Earliest Times to A.D. 697.* Tokyo: Tuttle, 1972.)

Chronology of Chinese and Japanese Buddhism 和漢仏教年契 [J: Wakan Buk-kyō Nenkei]. By Murakami Senshō, 1898.

Clarification of Pure Land Rebirth 念仏往生明導箚 [J: Nembutsu Ōjō Meidōsatsu]. By Hōtan.

Collected Biographies of Kōbō Daishi 弘法大師全集 [J: Kōbō Daishi Zen-shū]. Comp. 1934.

Collected Dharma Talks in Harima Province 播州法語集 [J: Banshū Hōgo-shū]. By Ippen. Probably Kamakura period.

Collected Writings Concerning the Commentary on the Sutra of the Perfect Net 梵網 経古迹文集 [J: Bommō-kyō Koshaku Monjū (full title: Bommō-kyō Koshakki Bugyō Monjū 梵網経古迹記輔行文集)]. By Eizon.

Collection of Ancient and Modern [Japanese] Poems Continued 続古今[和歌]集 [J: Shoku Kokin [Waka]-shū]. Comp. by Fujiwara no Motoie et al., 1265.

Collection of Kakusō [Hara Tanzan] 鶴巣集 [J: Kakusō-shū]. By Hara Tan-zan.

Collection of National Polity 経国集 [J: Keikoku-shū]. Comp. by Minabuchi no Hirosada et al., 827. (An anthology of prose and verse in Chinese.)

Collection of Passages on the Original Vow and the Nembutsu 選択本願念仏集 [J: Senchaku Hongan Nembutsu-shū]. By Hōnen, 1198. (Partially trans-lated by Kōshō Yamamoto as *The Senchakushū by Genkū* in *Shinshū Seiten: The Holy Scripture of Shinshū,* pp. 161–167. Honolulu: Honpa Hon-gwanji Mission of Hawaii, 1955.)

Collection of Poetry Exchanged by Gen[sei] and Yüan[-yun] 元々唱和集 [J: Gen-gen Shōwa-shū]. Comp. by Gensei, 1662.

Collection of the Discussions in Dreams 夢中問答集 [J: Muchū Mondō-shū]. By Musō Soseki, 1342 or 1344.

Collection of the Essentials of the Jōdo Sect 浄土宗要集 [J: Jōdo-shū Yōshū]. Comp. by Benchō, 1237.

Collection of Writings on the Chapter of Manifest and Unmanifest 表無表章文集 [J: Hyōmuhyōshō Monjū]. By Kakujō.

Collection [Telling How] the Nembutsu Invocation Created Good 南無阿弥陀仏作 善集 [J: Namu Amidabutsu Sazen-shū]. By Chōgen, probably 1203.

Commentary on Fa Li's Annotations on the Vinaya of Four Categories 四分律 疏飾宗義記 [J: Shinbunritsu-sho Shokushū Giki (abbreviated as Shokushū Giki 飾宗義紀); C: Ssu-fen-lü-su shih-tsung i-chi]. By Ting-pin.

Commentary on the Meditation Sutra 観無量寿経疏 [J: Kammuryōju-kyō-sho; C: Kuan-wu-liang-shou-ching-su]. By Shan-tao. *T* 1753.

Commentary on the Sutra of the Principle of Wisdom 大楽金剛不空真実三昧耶経般若波羅蜜多理趣釈 [J: Dairaku Kongō Fukū Shinjitsu Sammaya-kyō Hannya Haramita Rishu-shaku (abbreviated as Hannya Rishu-shaku 般若理趣釈 and as Rishu-shaku 理趣釈); C: Ta-lo-chin-kang pu-k'ung chen-shih san-mei-yeh-ching pan-jo po-lo-mi-to li-ch'ü-shih]. By Amoghavajra. *T* 1003.

Continued Chronicles of Japan 続日本紀 [J: Shoku Nihon-gi]. Comp. by Fujiwara no Tsugutada et al., 797. (A history covering the years 697 to 791.)

Correction of the Errors of Buddhist Doctrine 釈教正謬 [J: Shakkyō Seibyū; C: Shih-chiao cheng-miu]. By Joseph Edkins, 1868.

Crazy Cloud Collection 狂雲集 [J: Kyōun-shū]. By Ikkyū. (Partially translated by Sonja Arntzen as *Ikkyū and the Crazy Cloud Anthology*. Tokyo: University of Tokyo Press, 1986.)

A Critique of the Three Articles of Instruction 三条教則批判建白書 [J: Sanjō Kyōsoku Hihan Kempaku-sho]. By Shimaji Mokurai.

Death Registers for Clergy in Days Gone By 往古之過去帳 [J: Ōgo no Kako-chō]. By Ippen and Shinkyō.

Description of the Meditation Sutra 観経抄 [J: Kangyō-shō]. By Jōjin.

Description of the Teachings of Yūzū Nembutsu 融通円門門章 [J: Yūzū Emmon-shō]. By Daitsū, 1703.

Detailed Accounts of the Spherical Model 視実等象儀詳説 [J: Shijitsu Tōshōgi Shōsetsu]. By Sada Kaiseki.

Dewdrops on a Lotus Leaf 蓮の露 [J: Hasu no Tsuyu]. By Ryōkan and Teishinni. (Translated by Nobuyuki Yuasa in *The Zen Poems of Ryokan*. Princeton, N.J.: Princeton University Press, 1981.)

Dharma Words of National Teacher Daitō 大燈国師法語 [J: Daitō Kokushi Hōgo]. By Sōhō Myōchō.

Diamond Peak Sutra 金剛頂経 [J: Kongōchō-kyō; C: Chin-kang-ting-ching; S: Vajraśekhara-sarvatathāgatatattvasaṃgraha-sūtra]. *T* 865.

Diary of National Teacher Honkō 本光国師日記 [J: Honkō Kokushi Nikki]. By Sūden. (Diary covering the years 1610 to 1633.)

Discourse on the Awakening of Faith in the Mahayana 大乗起信論 [J: Daijō Kishin-ron; C: Ta-ch'eng ch'i-hsing-lun]. Attributed to Ashvaghosha. *T* 1666, 1667. (Translations: D. T. Suzuki, *Açvaghosha's Discourse on the Awakening of Faith in the Mahāyāna*. Chicago: Open Court, 1900; Yoshito S. Hakeda, *The Awakening of Faith in Mahayana, Attributed to Aśvaghosha*. New York: Columbia University Press, 1967.)

Discussion of the Five Teachings and the Ten Sects 華厳一乗教義分斎章 [J: Kegon ichijō Kyōgibunzai-shō (abbreviated as Kegon Gokyō-shō 華厳五

教章); C: Hua-yen i-ch'eng chiao-i-fen-ch'i-chang)]. By Fa-tsang. *T* 1866.

Discussion of the Pure Land 浄土折衝篇 [J: Jōdo Sesshō-hen]. By Hōrin, 1731.

Discussion on the Teachings of the Jōdo Sect 浄土宗名目問答 [J: Jōdo-shū Myōmoku Mondō]. By Benchō.

Distinction Between Faith and Reason 理気差別論 [J: Riki Sabetsu-ron]. By Takuan.

Doubts Concerning the Bodhisattva Precepts 菩薩戒遣疑鈔 [J: Bosatsukai Kengi-shō]. By Kakujō, 1246.

Drink Tea and Prolong Life 喫茶養生記 [J: Kissa Yōjō-ki]. By Eisai, 1211. (Translated in De Bary, ed., *Sources of Japanese Tradition* I [see Suggested Reading], pp. 237–240.)

The Eastern Buddhist (English-language magazine published by Ōtani University, 1921–.)

Eliminating Errors Concerning the Lotus 法華去惑 [J: Hokke Kowaku]. By Saichō, 818.

The Embossed Tea Kettle 遠羅天釜 [J: Orategama]. By Hakuin, 1748. (Translated by R. D. M. Shaw. London: George Allen and Unwin, 1963.)

Enlivening Buddhism 仏教活論 [J: Bukkyō Katsu-ron]. By Inoue Enryō.

Ennin's Diary, the Record of a Pilgrimage to China in Search of the Law 入唐求法巡礼行記 [J: Nittō Guhō Junrei Kōki]. By Ennin, ca. 847. (Translated by Edwin O. Reischauer. New York: Ronald Press, 1955.)

Esoteric Explanation of Amida 阿弥陀秘釈 [J: Amida Hishaku]. By Kakuban.

Essay on the Greatest Essence 最要抄 [J: Saiyō-shō]. By Kakunyo, 1343. (Partially translated by Kōshō Yamamoto as ''The Saiyōshō by Kakunyo Shōnin'' in *Shinshū Seiten: The Holy Scripture of Shinshū*, pp. 285–286. Honolulu: Honpa Hongwanji Mission of Hawaii, 1955.)

Essay on the Original Vow 本願抄 [J: Hongan-shō]. By Kakunyo, 1337.

Essay to Correct False Faith 改邪抄 [J: Gaija-shō]. By Kakunyo, 1337.

Essays in Zen Buddhism, First Series 禅論文集第一 [J: Zen Ronbun-shū Daiichi]. Published by Suzuki Daisetz, 1927. Reprint. London: Rider, 1949, 1958.

Essays on Protecting the Nation 守護国界章 [J: Shugo Kokkai-shō]. By Saichō, 818.

Essence of the Buddhist Sects 各宗綱要 [J: Kakushū Kōyō]. Comp. by Organization of Buddhist Sects.

Essentials of Contemplating the Mind 観心略要集 [J: Kanjin Ryakuyō-shū]. By Genshin, probably 1017.

Essentials of Deliverance 往生要集 [J: Ōjō Yōshū]. By Genshin, 985. (Partial translations: A. K. Reischauer, ''Genshin's Ōjō Yōshū: Collected Essays on Birth into Paradise'' in *Transactions of the Asiatic Society of Japan,* 2d ser., 7, Dec. 1930, pp. 16–97; Kōshō Yamamoto, ''The Ōjōyōshū by Genshin'' in *Shinshū Seiten: The Holy Scripture of Shinshū,* pp. 157–160. Honolulu: Honpa Hongwanji Mission of Hawaii, 1955.)

Essentials of the Lotus 法華肝心 [J: Hokke Kanjin]. By Tokuitsu.

Essentials of the One-Vehicle Teaching 一乗要決 [J: Ichijō Yōketsu]. By Genshin.

Establishing Righteousness to Protect the Nation 立正治国論 [J: Risshō Chikoku-ron]. By Nisshin, 1440.

Eulogy for Kūya 誄 [J: Rui]. Comp. by Minamoto no Tamenori (d. 1011).

Evening Dialogue at Shōun-an 夜話記 [J: Yuwa-ki]. By Sōhō Myōchō.

Excellent Words About the Lotus 法華秀句 [J: Hokke Shūku]. By Saichō, 821.

Experimental Theory of Mount Sumeru 実験須弥山説 [J: Jikken Shumisensetsu]. By Entsū.

Exposition on the Esoteric Manuals 密軌問弁 [J: Mikki Momben]. By Ekō, possibly 1711.

Extended Record of National Teacher Fushō 普照国師広録 [J: Fushō Kokushi Kōroku]. By Ingen.

Eye Opening 開目抄 [J: Kaimoku-shō]. By Nichiren, 1272. (Translated by Kyotsu Hori as *St. Nichiren's Kaimoku-shō: Open your Eyes to the* Lotus Teaching. Tokyo: Nichiren Shu Overseas Tokyo Propagation Promotion Association, 1987.)

The Eye Treasury of the Right Dharma 正法眼蔵 [J: Shōbō Genzō]. By Dōgen, 1231–1253. (Translated by Kōsen Nishiyama as *Shōbōgenzō: The Eye and Treasury of the True Law.* Tokyo: Nakayama Shōbō, 1988.)

Faith and Discernment of Yūzū Nembutsu 融通念仏信解章 [J: Yūzū Nembutsu Shinge-shō]. By Daitsū.

Faith of the Holy Man Shinran 親鸞聖人の信仰 [J: Shinran Shōnin no Shinkō]. By Chikazumi Jōkan.

First Defeat of ''Correction of the Errors of Buddhist Doctrine'' 釈教正謬初破 [J: Shakkyō Seibyū Shoha]. By Ugai Tetsujō.

Five Classics 五経 (*Classic of Changes, Classic of History, Classic of Poetry, Collection of Rituals, Spring Autumn Annals*) [J: Gokyō; C: Wu-ching].

Flower Garland Sutra 華厳経 [J: Kegon-kyō (full title: Daihōkōbutsu Kegon-kyō 大方広仏華厳経); C: Hua-yen-ching; S: Buddha-avataṃsaka-nāma-mahā-vaipulya-sūtra]. *T* 278, 279, 293.

A Fool's Idea 愚志 [J: Gushi]. By Dōji.

Forest Collection 叢林集 [J: Sōrin-shū]. By Ekū, 1717.

Fundamental Thought of Rinzai 臨済の基本思想 [J: Rinzai no Kihon Shisō]. By Suzuki Daisetz.

General Advice on the Principles of Zazen 普勧坐禅儀 [J: Fukan Zazengi]. By

Dōgen, 1227. (Translated by Yūhō Yokoi and Daizen Victoria in *Zen Master Dogen: An Introduction with Selected Writings,* pp. 45–47. Tokyo: Weatherhill, 1976.)

The Genkō Era's History of Buddhism 元亨釈書 [J: Genkō Shaku-sho]. Comp. by Kokan Shiren, 1322.

Gist of [Shinran's] "Teaching, Practice, Faith, Attainment" 教行信証大意 [J: Kyōgyōshinshō Taii]. By Kakunyo, 1328.

Golden Light Sutra 金光明経 [J: Konkōmyō-kyō; C: Chin-kuang-ming-ching; S: Suvarṇaprabhāsa-sūtra]. *T* 663, 664, 665.

The Gospel of Buddha. By Paul Carus. Chicago: Open Court, 1915.

Grassy Mountain Collection 草山集 [J: Sōzan-shū]. By Gensei, 1674. (Translated by Burton Watson as *Grass Hill: Poems and Prose by the Japanese Monk Gensei.* New York: Columbia University Press, 1983.)

Great Concentration and Insight 摩訶止観 [J: Maka Shikan; C: Mo-ho chih-kuan]. Comp. by Kuan-ting from lectures by Chih-i, 594. *T* 1911. (Partially translated by Neal Donner and Daniel B. Stevenson as *The Great Calming and Contemplation.* Honolulu: University of Hawaii Press, 1993.)

Great Japan Revised Tripitaka 大日本校訂大蔵経 [J: Dai Nihon Kōtei Daizōkyō]. Comp. by Fukuda Gyōkai et al., 418 vols. Tokyo: Kōkyō Shoin, 1880–1885.

Great Japan Supplementary Tripitaka 大日本続蔵経 [J: Dai Nihon Zoku Zōkyō]. Comp. by Maeda Eun et al., 751 vols. Kyoto: Zōkyō Shoin, 1905–1912.

Great Perfection of Wisdom Sutra 大般若波羅蜜多経 [J: Daihannya Haramitta-kyō (abbreviated as Daihannya-kyō 大般若経); C: Ta-pan-jo po-lo-mi-to-ching; S: Mahāprajñāpāramitā-sūtra]. *T* 220.

Great Principles of Buddhism 仏教大原理 [J: Bukkyō Daigenri]. By Shaku Unshō.

Great Sun Sutra 大日経 [J: Dainichi-kyō (full title: Daibirushana Jōbutsu Jimbenkaji-kyō 大毗盧遮那成仏神変加持経); C: Ta-jih-ching; S: Mahā-vairocanābhisaṃbodhivikurvitādhiṣṭhāna-vaipulyasūtrendrarāja-nāma-dharma-paryāya]. *T* 848.

Guide to Sanskrit Studies 梵学律梁 [J: Bongaku Shinryō]. By Jiun.

Heart Sutra 般若心経 [J: Hannya Shin-gyō (full title: Hannya Haramitta Shin-gyō 般若波羅蜜多心経); C: Pan-jo hsing-ching (Pan-jo po-lo-mi-to hsing-ching); S: Prajñāpāramitāhṛdaya-sūtra]. *T* 251.

A History of the Pure Land Teachings in India 印度浄土教史 [J: Indo Jōdokyō-shi]. By Maeda Eun.

Hymn of Amida's Vow 別願和讃 [J: Betsugan Wasan]. By Ippen.

Illustrated Life of the Revered Master of Hongan-ji 本願寺聖人伝絵 [J: Hongan-ji Shōnin Den'e]. By Kakunyo, 1295.

In Defense of Buddhism 護法資治論 [J: Gohō Shiji-ron]. By Mori Shōken.
Indications of the Goals of the Three Teachings 三教指帰 [J: Sangō Shiiki]. By Kūkai, 797. (Translated by Yoshito S. Hakeda in *Kūkai: Major Works*. New York: Columbia University Press, 1972.)
Instructions for the Zen Cook 典座教訓 [J: Tenzo Kyōkun]. By Dōgen, 1237. (Translations: Yūhō Yokoi, *Regulations for Monastic Life*. Tokyo: Sankibō Busshorin, 1973; Thomas Wright, *Refining Your Life: From the Zen Kitchen to Enlightenment*. Tokyo: Weatherhill, 1983.)
Iron Wall and Piece of Cloud 鉄壁雲片 [J: Teppeki Umpen]. By Hōtan. (A critique of one hundred cases in the *Blue Cliff Records*.)

The Japanese 日本人 [J: Nihonjin]. (Magazine edited by Inoue Enryō, published in Tokyo by Seikyōsha, 1888–1891.)
Japanese Spirituality 日本的霊性 [J: Nihonteki Reisei]. By Suzuki Daisetz. (Translated by Norman Waddell, comp. by Japanese National Commission for UNESCO. New York: Greenwood Press, 1988.)
Jewel Cave of the Ten Good [Precepts] 十善宝窟 [J: Jūzen Hōkutsu]. (Magazine published in Tokyo by Shaku Unshō, 1893–1938.)
Jottings of Convalescence 保養雑記 [J: Hoyō Zakki]. By Kiyozawa Manshi.
The Journey of the T'ang Great Master to the East 唐大和上東征伝 [J: Tō Daiwajō Tōsei-den]. By Ōmi no Mifune.

Kōfuku-ji Petition 興福寺奏状 [J: Kōfuku-ji Sōjō]. By Jōkei, 1205.
Kūge's Instructions on Daily Life 空華日用工夫集 [J: Kūge Nichiyō Kufū-shū]. By Gidō Shūshin, late 14th century.

Later Chronicles of Japan 日本後紀 [J: Nihon Kōki]. Comp. by Fujiwara no Otsugu et al., 842.
A Laughable Discourse on the Mantis [Trying to Stop a Chariot] with Its Elbow 笑蟷臂 [J: Shōrōhi]. By Hōrin, 1732.
Lay Buddhism 在家仏教 [J: Zaike Bukkyō]. By Kawaguchi Ekai.
Lectures on Ghosts 妖怪学講義 [J: Yōkaigaku Kōgi]. By Inoue Enryō.
Legends of Filial Devotion to Shakyamuni's Teachings 釈門孝伝 [J: Shakumon Kōden]. By Gensei.
Leisurely Talks in a Boat in the Evening 夜船閑話 [J: Yasen Kanna]. By Hakuin, before 1741. (Translations: R. D. M. Shaw in *The Embossed Tea Kettle*, op. cit., pp. 25–47; Trevor Leggett in *The Tiger's Cave: Translations of Japanese Zen Texts*, pp. 142–156. London: Rider, 1964.)
Letter to Nichinyo Gozen 日女御前御返事 [J: Nichinyo Gozen Gohenji]. By Nichiren, 1277.
Life and Faith 人生と信仰 [J: Jinsei to Shinkō]. By Chikazumi Jōkan.
Life of the Great Priest 大唐伝戒師僧名記大和上鑑真伝 [J: Daitō Denkaishi Sōmeiki Daiwajō Ganjin-den (abbreviated as Daiwajō-den 大和上伝)]. By Ssu-t'o.

Lingering Taste of Faith 信仰の余瀝 [J: Shinkō no Yoreki]. By Chikazumi Jōkan.

Litany of Gratitude 報恩講私記 [J: Hōonkō Shiki]. By Kakunyo, 1292 or 1294.

Litany on Maitreya 弥勒講式 [J: Miroku Kōshiki]. By Jōkei.

Lotus Sutra 妙法蓮華経 [J: Myōhōrenge-kyō (abbreviated as Hoke-kyō 法華経); C: Miao-fa lien-hua-ching; S: Saddharmapuṇḍarīka-sūtra]. *T* 2190. (Translations: Johan H. C. Kern, *Saddharma Puṇḍarīka. The Sacred Books of the East*, vol. 21. New York: Dover, 1963; Bunnō Katō et al., *The Threefold Lotus Sutra*. Tokyo: Kōsei, 1975; Senchū Murano, *The Lotus Sutra*, 2d ed. Tokyo: Nichiren Shu Shimbun, 1991; Leon Hurvitz, *Scripture of the Lotus Blossom of the Fine Dharma*. New York: Columbia University Press, 1976; Burton Watson, *The Lotus Sutra*. New York: Columbia University Press, 1993.)

Magazine of the Philosophy Association 哲学会雑誌 [J: Tetsugakukai Zasshi]. (Published in Tokyo by Kiyozawa Manshi, 1887–1892.)

Mantra of Akashagarbha 虚空蔵求聞持法 [J: Kokūzō Gumonjihō (full title: Kokūzō Bosatsu Nōman Shogan Saishōshin Darani Gumonjihō 虚空蔵菩薩能満諸願最勝心陀羅尼求聞持法); C: Hsu-k'ung-tsang ch'iu-wen-ch'ih-fa]. *T* 1145.

Master Ganjin's Secret Method 鑑上人秘方 [J: Gan Shōnin Hihō; Ch: Chen-shang-jen pi-fang]. By Ganjin.

Memorial Presenting a Record of Newly Imported Sutras and Other Items 弘法大師御請来目録 [J: Kōbō Daishi Goshōrai Mokuroku]. By Kūkai, 806. (Translated by Yoshito S. Hakeda in *Kukai: Major Works*, pp. 140–150. New York: Columbia University Press, 1972.)

Method of Nembutsu Meditation 念仏三昧方法 [J: Nembutsu Zammai Hōhō]. By Shunjō.

Miraculous Record of Immovable Wisdom 不動智神妙録 [J: Fudōchi Shimmyō-roku]. By Takuan. (Translated by William Scott Wilson as *The Unfettered Mind: Writings of the Zen Master to the Sword Master*. Tokyo: Kodansha International, 1986.)

Miraculous Stories from the Japanese Buddhist Tradition 日本霊異記 [J: Nihon Ryōiki]. By Kyōkai, early 9th century. (Translated by Kyoko Nakamura as *Miraculous Stories from the Japanese Buddhist Tradition: The Nihon Ryōiki of the Monk Kyōkai*. Cambridge, Mass.: Harvard University Press, 1973.)

A Mirror Illuminating the Provisional and the Real 照権実鏡 [J: Shō Gonjitsu-kyō]. By Saichō.

Mirror of the East 吾妻鏡 [J: Azuma Kagami]. (A history of the Kamakura shogunate, 1180–1266.)

A Mirror of the Orthodox and the Heterodox 中辺義鏡 [J: Chūhengi-kyō]. By Tokuitsu.

Mottoes of Imperial Soldiers 帝国軍人座右之銘 [J: Teikoku Gunjin Zayū no Mei]. By Uchiyama Gudō.

"My Beliefs" 我信念 [J: "Waga Shinnen"]. By Kiyozawa Manshi. (Translated by Bandō Shōjun in *The Eastern Buddhist* [see Suggested Reading], pp. 141–152.)

Nembutsu Assembly of Twenty-five Like-minded People and Ritual for Nembutsu 二十五三昧式 [J: Nijūgo Zammai Shiki]. By Genshin, 986.

Nembutsu Dharma Words in Japanese 和字念仏法語 [J: Waji Nembutsu Hōgo]. By Shōkū.

New Theory on Destroying Evil 破邪新論 [J: Haja Shinron]. By Inoue Enryō.

Nirvana Sutra 涅槃経 [J: Nehan-gyō (full title: Daihatsu Nehan-gyō 大般涅槃経); C: Nieh-p'an-ching; S: Mahāparinirvāṇa-sūtra]. T 374–376.

Nostalgic Record 懐旧録 [J: Kaikyū-roku]. By Nanjio Bunyiu.

Notes from Haniya 埴谷抄 [J: Haniya-shō]. By Nisshin, 1470.

Notes Lamenting Deviations 歎異鈔 [J: Tanni-shō]. Attributed to Yuienbō, late 13th century. (Translations: Ryōsetsu Fujiwara, *The Tanni Shō: Notes Lamenting Differences*. Ryukoku Translation Series 2. Kyoto: Ryukoku University, 1962; Bandō Shōjun and Harold Stewart, "Tannishō: Passages Deploring Deviations of Faith." *The Eastern Buddhist*, n.s., 13, no. 1 [Spring 1980]: 57–78; Dennis Hirota, *Tannishō: A Primer*. Kyoto: Ryukoku University, 1982.)

Notes of Oral Transmission 口伝鈔 [J: Kuden-shō]. By Kakunyo, 1331.

Notes on Crossing to America 渡米紀程 [J: Tobei Kitei]. By Shaku Sōen.

Notes on Holding Fast 執持抄 [J: Shūji-shō]. By Kakunyo, 1326. (Translated by D. T. Suzuki as "Tract on Steadily Holding to [The Faith] by Kakunyo Shōnin." *The Eastern Buddhist*, 7, nos. 3–4 [July 1939]: 363–375.)

Notes on the Commentary on the Great Sun Sutra 大日疏鈔 [J: Dainichi Shoshō]. By Shōbō.

Notes on the Correct Principle of Subduing Evil 折伏正義抄 [J: Shakubuku Shōgi-shō]. By Nisshin, 1438.

Notes on the Kegon Five Teachings 華厳五教章匡真鈔 [J: Kegon Gokyōshō Kyōshin-shō]. By Hōtan, 1707.

Notes on the Lotus Sutra 法華経註 [J: Hoke-kyō-chū]. By Jōjin.

Notes on the Transmission of the Lamp 伝燈抄 [J: Dentō-shō]. By Nisshin, 1470.

One-Page Testament 一枚起請文 [J: Ichimai Kishōmon (also called Ichimai Shōsoku 一枚消息)]. By Hōnen, 1212. (Translated by The Buddhist Churches of America as "Ichimai Kishōmon by Hōnen Shōnin" in *Mahādharma, a Quarterly Review,* [March 1951]: 18.)

On Funerals 送葬論 [J: Sōsō-ron]. By Shimaji Mokurai.

On the Buddha-nature 仏性抄 [J: Busshō-shō]. By Tokuitsu.

On the History of Mahayana Buddhism 大乗仏教史論 [J: Daijō Bukkyōshi-ron]. By Maeda Eun.

On the Nine Types of Rebirth in the Pure Land of Utmost Bliss 極楽浄土九品往生義 [J: Gokuraku Jōdo Kuhon Ōjōgi (also known as Kuhon Ōjōgi 九品往生義)]. By Ryōgen.

On Venerating the Three Treasures Thrice Daily 三時三宝礼釈 [J: Sanji Sambōrai-shaku]. By Myōe, 1215.

Outline of Japanese Buddhist History 日本仏教史綱 [J: Nihon Bukkyōshi-kō]. By Murakami Senshō.

An Outline of the Sanron Sect 三論宗綱要 [J: Sanron-shū Kōyō]. By Maeda Eun.

An Outline of the Tendai Sect 天台宗綱要 [J: Tendai-shū Kōyō]. By Maeda Eun.

Outlines of Mahayana Buddhism 大乗仏教概論 [J: Daijō Bukkyō Gairon]. By Suzuki Daisetz. London: Luzac, 1907.

Personal Seal [Attesting] to the Transmission of the Nembutsu in the Latter Days 末代念仏授手印 [J: Matsudai Nembutsu Jushuin]. By Benchō, 1228.

Poison Stamen of the Briar Thicket 荊叢毒蕊 [J: Keisō Dokuzui]. By Hakuin, 1758.

Precepts for Perfect and Sudden Enlightenment 一心戒文 [J: Isshin Kaimon (full title: Denjutsu Isshin Kaimon 伝述一心戒文)]. By Kōjō.

Priest Jiun's Dharma Words 慈雲和上法語 [J: Jiun Wajō Hōgo]. By Jiun.

Principles and Manners for Zazen 坐禅事儀 [J: Zazen Jigi]. By Shunjō.

Procedures for the Ritual for the Diamond Realm 金剛界次第 [J: Kongōkai Shidai]. By Yakushin.

Procedures for the Ritual for the Womb-Store Realm 胎蔵界行法次第 [J: Taizōkai Gyōbō Shidai]. By Shōbō.

Procedures of the Engi Era 延喜式 [J: Engi-shiki]. Compiled 905–927. (Partially translated by Felicia G. Bock as *Engi-shiki: Procedures of the Engi Era*. Tokyo: Sophia University, 1970 [books 1–5], 1972 [books 6–10].)

Propagation of Zen as a Defense of the Nation 興禅護国論 [J: Kōzen Gokoku-ron]. By Eisai, 1198. (Partially translated in De Bary, ed., *Sources of Japanese Tradition* 1 [see Suggested Reading], pp. 236–237.)

Queen of Shrimala Sutra 勝鬘師子吼一乗大方便方広経 [J: Shōman Shishiku Ichijō Daihōben Hōkō-kyō (abbreviated as Shōman-gyō 勝鬘経); C: Sheng-man shi-tzu-hou i-ch'eng ta-fang-pien fang-kuang-ching; S: Śrīmālādevī-siṃhanāda-sūtra]. *T* 353. (Translated by Alex Wayman and Hideko Wayman as *The Lion's Roar of Queen Śrīmālā*. New York: Columbia University Press, 1974.)

Quintessence of the Kegon and Tendai Sects 円宗鳳髄 [J: Enshū Hōzui]. By Hōtan.

Recorded Sayings of Gidō Shūshin 義堂語録 [J: Gidō Goroku]. By Gidō Shū-shin.

Record of a Pilgrimage to Mounts T'ien-t'ai and Wu-t'ai 参天台五台山記 [J: San Tendai Godaisan-ki]. By Jōjin, 1073.

A Record of Clergy in the Enryaku Era 延暦僧録 [J: Enryaku Sōroku]. By Shitaku.

Record of Daitō 大燈語録 [J: Daitō Goroku]. By Sōhō Myōchō.

Record of Dedication of Sutras 納経帳 [J: Nōkyō-chō]. By Mokujiki Gyōdō.

Record of Dōgen's Public Sayings 永平広録 [J: Eihei Kōroku]. By Dōgen.

Record of Eizon 感身学正記 [J: Kanjin Gakushō-ki]. By Eizon.

A Record of Experiments Concerning Buddhist Dharma 仏法実験録 [J: Buppō Jikken-roku (later called Shinshō Jikken-roku 心性実験録)]. By Hara Tanzan.

A Record of Heavenly Truth 天真録 [J: Tenshin-roku]. By Tachibana Inan (Yamamoto Iori).

Record of National Teacher Fushō 普照国師語録 [J: Fushō Kokushi Goroku]. By Ingen.

Record of National Teacher Issan 一山国師語録 [J: Issan Kokushi Goroku]. By Issan Ichinei, 1317.

Record of National Teacher Musō 夢窓国師語録 [J: Musō Kokushi Goroku]. By Musō Soseki.

Record of Shinran's Dreams 親鸞夢記 [J: Shinran Muki]. By Shinran.

Record of the Workings of Faith [Regarding] the Mantra of Light and the Sprinkling of Sand 光明真言土砂勧信記 [J: Kōmyō Shingon Dosha Kanjin-ki]. By Myōe, 1228.

Record of Tokuhon 徳本行者語 [J: Tokuhon Gyōja-go]. By Tokuhon.

Records of Pure Land Rebirth in Japan 日本往生極楽記 [J: Nihon Ōjō Gokuraku-ki]. By Yoshishige no Yasutane, ca. 986–987.

Records of Taikō [Ogino] 退耕録 [J: Taikō-roku]. By Ogino Dokuon.

Records of Tōdai-ji 東大寺要録 [J: Tōdai-ji Yōroku].

Regulations for Ch'an Temples 禅苑清規 [J: Zennen Shingi; C: Ch'en-yüan ch'ing-kuei]. Completed by Chang-lu Tsung-tse, 1103.

Regulations for Life at Eihei-ji 永平清規 [J: Eihei Shingi]. By Dōgen, 1237–1249. (Translated by Yūhō Yokoi in *Regulations for Monastic Life*. Tokyo: Sankibō Busshorin, 1973.)

Regulations for the Annual Quota Students of the Tendai Lotus Sect 天台法華宗年分学生式 [J: Tendai Hokke-shū Nembun Gakushō-shiki]. By Saichō, 818. (Partially translated in De Bary, ed., *Sources of Japanese Tradition* 1 [see Suggested Reading], pp. 127–132.)

Regulations of Pai-chang 百丈清規 [J: Hyakujō Shingi; C: Pai-chang ch'ing-kuei]. Comp. by Pai-chang Huai-hai, 785–805.

Religion and State Review (later *Seeking the Way*) 政教時報 [J: Seikyō Jihō]. (Journal published in Tokyo by Chikazumi Jōkan, 1899–1903.)

Repentance Record 懺悔録 [J: Zange-roku]. By Chikazumi Jōkan.

"Revelation of the High Treason Incident" 大逆事件の啓示 [J: Taigyaku Jiken no Keiji]. By Itō Shōshin.

Rinsen-ji Regulations 臨川寺家訓 [J: Rinsen-ji Kakun]. By Musō Soseki, 1339.

Sand and Pebbles 沙石集 [J: Shaseki-shū]. Completed by Mujū, 1283. (Translated by Robert E. Morrell as *Sand and Pebbles: The Tales of Muju Ichinen, a Voice for Pluralism in Kamakura Buddhism*. Albany, N.Y.: State University of New York Press, 1985.)

Sayings of Holy Man Ippen 一遍上人語録 [J: Ippen Shōnin Goroku]. By Ippen, ca. 1751.

Second Defeat of "Correction of the Errors of Buddhist Doctrine" 釈教正謬再破 [J: Shakkyō Seibyū Saiha]. By Ugai Tetsujō.

Seeking the Way 求道 [J: Gudō (later, Shinkai Kengen 信界顕現)]. (Magazine published in Tokyo by Chikazumi Jōkan, 1901–1903.)

Self-Admonishments 自戒集 [J: Jikai-shū]. By Ikkyū, possibly 1455.

Selfless Love 無我の愛 [J: Muga no Ai]. (Magazine published in Tokyo by Itō Shōshin, 1903.)

Sermons on the Ten Good [Precepts] 十善法語 [J: Jūzen Hōgo]. By Jiun. (Translated by John Laidlaw Atkinson as "The Ten Buddhistic Virtues." *Transactions of the Asiatic Society of Japan*, vol. 33, pt. 2, 1905, pp. 159–184; vol. 35, pt. 1, 1907, pp. 33–70; vol. 36, pt. 1, 1908, pp. 9–22. Tokyo: The Asiatic Society of Japan.)

Seven-Article Injunction 七ヵ条の制誡 [J: Shichikajō no Seikai]. By Hōnen, 1204.

Seventeen-Article Constitution 十七条憲法 [J: Jūshichijō no Kempō]. Attributed to Prince Shōtoku, 604. (Translated in De Bary, *Sources of Japanese Tradition* 1 [see Suggested Reading], pp. 47–51.)

A Short History of the Twelve Japanese Buddhist Sects 十二宗綱要 [J: Jūnishū Kōyō]. Translated by Nanjio Bunyiu. Tokyo: Bukkyō-sho-ei-yaku-shuppan-sha, 1886.

Significance of the True Dharma for the Protection of the Nation 護国正法義 [J: Gokoku Shōbōgi]. By Dōgen.

A Skeletal Outline of the Philosophy of Religion 宗教哲学骸骨 [J: Shūkyō Tetsugaku Gaikotsu]. By Kiyozawa Manshi.

Smashing the Wheel of Heresy 摧邪輪 [J: Zaijarin]. By Myōe, 1212.

Songs of the Way 傘松道詠 [J: Sanshō Dōei]. By Dōgen, possibly 1420. Comp. by Omoyama Zuihō, 1747.

Sources for the Essentials of Jōdo Shin Sect Teachings 真宗法要典拠 [J: Shinshū Hōyō Tenkyo]. By Gōzei, 1784.

Speaking Quietly to a Friend 竊かに知己に示す書 [J: Hisoka ni Chiki ni Shimesu Sho]. By Nakaoka Shintarō.

Spiritual World 精神界 [J: Seishin-kai]. (Magazine published in Tokyo by Kiyozawa Manshi, 1901–1903.)

354 DOCUMENTS

Studies in the History of Zen Thought 禅思想史研究 [J: Zen Shisōshi Kenkyū]. By Suzuki Daisetz.

A Study of Good 善の研究 [J: Zen no Kenkyū]. By Nishida Kitarō, 1911. (Translated by Valdo H. Viglielmo. Tokyo: Japanese Government Print Bureau, 1960.)

Sutra of Good Accomplishment 蘇悉地経 [J: Soshitsuji-kyō (full title: Soshitsuji Kara-kyō 蘇悉地羯羅経); C: Su-hsi-ti-ching; S: Susiddhikaramahatantra-sadhanopayika-patala-sūtra]. *T* 893.

Sutra of Infinite Life (Larger Sukhavati-vyuha) 無量寿経 [J: Muryōju-kyō; C: Wu-liang-shou-ching; S: Sukhāvatī-vyūha]. *T* 360.

Sutra of the Appearance of the Good Doctrine in·[Sri] Lanka 楞伽経 [J: Ryōga-kyō; C: Leng-chia-ching; S: Laṅkāvatāra-sūtra]. *T* 671.

Sutra of the Perfect Net 梵網経 [J: Bommō-kyō; C: Fan-wang-ching; S: Brahmajāla-sūtra]. *T* 1484.

Sutra of the Principle of Wisdom 理趣経 [J: Rishu-kyō (full title: Dairaku Kongō Fukū Shinjitsu Sammaya-kyō 大楽金剛不空真実三摩耶経); C: Li-ch'ü-ching]. *T* 243.

Sutra on Benevolent Kings 仁王経 [J: Ninnō-kyō (full title: Ninnō Hannya Haramitsu-kyō 仁王般若波羅蜜経); C: Jen-wang-ching]. *T* 245.

Systematization of Buddhist Philosophy 仏教哲学系統論 [J: Bukkyō Tetsugaku Keitō-ron]. By Inoue Enryō.

Tales of Times Now Past 今昔物語 [J: Konjaku Monogatari]. By Minamoto Takakuni, probably 11th century. (Translated by Marian Ury as *Tales of Times Now Past: Sixty-two Stories from a Medieval Japanese Collection*. Berkeley, Calif.: University of California Press, 1979.)

Teaching, Practice, Faith, Attainment 教行信証 [J: Kyōgyōshinshō]. By Shinran, possibly 1224. (Translations: partially translated by Shizutoshi Sugihira as "Pure Land Document of the Truthful Doctrine, Work, and Attainment." *The Eastern Buddhist*, 8, no. 3 [Nov. 1957]:27–42; Ryukoku Translation Center, *The Kyō Gyō Shin Shō*. Kyoto: Ryukoku University, 1966; D. T. Suzuki, *The Kyōgyōshinshō*. Kyoto: Shinshū Ōtaniha, 1973; Yoshifumi Ueda, ed., *The True Teaching, Practice, and Realization of the Pure Land Way, A Translation of Shinran's Kyōgyōshinshō*. 4 vols. Kyoto: Hongwanji International Center, 1983–; Kōshō Yamamoto, *The Kyogyoshinsho*. Ube: Karinbunko, 1975.)

Telling Politicians and Religious Leaders 告政治家及宗教家 [J: Koku Seijika oyobi Shūkyōka]. By Kitabatake Dōryū.

Ten Stages of the Development of Mind 十住心論 [J: Jūjūshin-ron]. By Kūkai, 830. (Described by Yoshito S. Hakeda in *Kūkai: Major Works*. New York: Columbia University Press, 1972, pp. 68–75.)

Tetsugen's Dharma Words in Kana 鉄眼仮字法語 [J: Tetsugen Kaji Hōgo]. By Tetsugen, 1691.

Theory That Buddhism Develops the Nation 仏教開国論 [J: Bukkyō Kaikoku-ron]. By Sada Kaiseki.

Theory That Delusion and Disease Have the Same Origin 惑病同源論 [J: Wakubyō Dōgen-ron]. By Hara Tanzan.

Three Years in Tibet 西蔵旅行記 [J: Chibetto Ryokō-ki]. By Kawaguchi Ekai, 1909. India: Chronica Botanica, 1979.

Timely Opinions on the Ecclesiastical World 教界時事 [J: Kyōkai Jiji]. (Journal published in Tokyo by the Shirakawa Party, 1903–1906.)

Treatise on Buddhist Defense of the Nation 仏教護国論 [J: Bukkyō Gokoku-ron]. By Gesshō.

Treatise on Discerning the Real and the Provisional 決権実論 [J: Ketsu Gon-jitsu-ron]. By Saichō, 818–21.

Treatise on Prohibiting the Slander of Giving 禁断謗施論 [J: Kindan Hōse-ron]. By Nichiō, 1624.

Treatise on Protecting the Correct Principles 守護正義論 [J: Shugo Shōgi-ron]. By Nichiō, 1599.

Treatise on the Establishment of the Doctrine of Consciousness Only 成唯識論 [J: Jōyuishiki-ron; C: Ch'eng-wei-shih-lun; S: Vijñaptimātratāsiddhi-śāstra]. *T* 1585.

Treatise on the Establishment of the True Dharma and the Peace of the Nation 立正安国論 [J: Rissho Ankoku-ron]. By Nichiren, 1260. (Translations: Senchu Murano, *Risshō Ankoku Ron or Establish the Right Law and Save Our Country.* Tokyo: Nichiren Shu Headquarters, 1977; Kyotsu Hori, *St. Nichiren's Risshō Ankoku-ron.* Tokyo: Nichiren Shu Overseas Tokyo Propagation Promotion Association, 1992.)

Treatise on the Mahayana Precepts 顕戒論 [J: Kenkai-ron]. By Saichō, 820.

Treatise on the Stages of Yoga Practice 瑜伽師地論 [J: Yugashiji-ron; C: Yü-chia-shih-ti-lun; S: Yogācārabhūmi-śāstra]. *T* 1579.

The True Object of Devotion 観心本尊鈔 [J: Kanjin Honzon-shō]. By Nichiren, 1273. (Translations: Senchu Murano, *Nichiren's Nyorai Metsugo Go Gohyakusai Shi Kanjin Honzon Sho or The True Object of Worship Revealed for the First Time in the Fifth of Five-Century Periods after the Great Decease of the Tathāgata.* Tokyo: Nichiren Shu Seiten Eiyaku Kenkyu-kai, 1954; Kyotsu Hori, *St. Nichiren's Kanjin Honzon-shō.* Tokyo: Nichiren Shu Overseas Tokyo Propagation Promotion Association, 1991.)

Tso's Commentary on the Spring and Autumn Annals 左伝 [J: Sa-den; C: Tso Chuan].

Twenty-four Followers of Shakyamuni 釈氏二十四孝 [J: Shakushi Nijūshikō]. By Gensei.

Ullambana Sutra 盂蘭盆経 [J: Urabon-gyō; C: Yü-lan-p'en-ching; S: Ullambana-sūtra]. *T* 685.

The Unification of Buddhism 仏教統一論 [J: Bukkyō Tōitsu-ron]. By Murakami Senshō, 1901.

Verses in Praise of Amida 弥陀和讃 [J: Mida Wasan (full title: Gokuraku-koku Mida Wasan 極楽国弥陀和讃)]. By Senkan.

Verses in Praise of Crown Prince Shōtoku 皇太子聖徳奉讃 [J: Kōtaishi Shōtoku Hōsan]. By Shinran, 1255. (Translated as ''The Kōtaishishōtokuhō-san by Shinran'' in *Shinshū Seiten: The Holy Scripture of Shinshū*, pp. 247–248. Honolulu: Honpa Hongwanji Mission of Hawaii, 1955.)

Vimalakirti Sutra 維摩経 [J: Yuima-gyō; C: Wei-mo-ching; S: Vimalakīrti-nirdeśa-sūtra]. *T* 474, 475, 476.

Vinaya of Four Categories 四分律 [J: Shibun-ritsu; C: Ssu-fen-lü; S: Dharmaguptaka-vinaya]. *T* 1428.

Vision 展望 [J: Tembō]. (Journal published in Tokyo by Chikuma Shobō, 1946–1978.)

Wandering Sage Ippen 一遍聖絵 [J: Ippen Hijiri-e]. Comp. 1299.

The Way and Its Power 道徳経 [J: Dōtoku-kyō; C: Tao-te-ching]. By Laotzu. (Translated by Arthur Waley as *The Way and Its Power: A Study of the Tao Te Ching and Its Place in Chinese Thought*. London: Allen and Unwin, 1934; Boston: Houghton, 1935.)

The Way to Become a [Real] Person 人となる道 [J: Hito to Naru Michi]. By Jiun, 1773–1774.

Winged Feet of Enichi Temple 恵日羽足 [J: Enichi Usoku]. By Tokuitsu.

Yearnings for the Ancient Chinese Style [J: Kaifūsō]. Comp. ca. 751. (First collection of poetry in Chinese published in Japan.)

Zen: A Collection of Articles. 禅 [J: Zen]. By Suzuki Daisetz et al. Chicago: University of Chicago Press, 1958.

Zen Buddhism and Its Influence on Japanese Culture 禅と日本文化 By Suzuki Daisetz, 1938. (Rev. and repub. as *Zen and Japanese Culture*, Bollingen Series 64. New York: Pantheon Books, 1959.)

Suggested Reading

Anezaki, Masaharu. *Nichiren, the Buddhist Prophet.* Cambridge, Mass.: Harvard University Press, 1916.

Arntzen, Sonja. *Ikkyū and the Crazy Cloud Anthology.* Tokyo: University of Tokyo Press, 1986.

Bando, Shojun. "Kiyozawa Manshi's *The Great Path of Absolute Other Power* and *My Faith.*" *The Eastern Buddhist,* n.s., 5, no. 2 (October 1972): 141–152.

Bodiford, William M. *Soto Zen in Medieval Japan.* Studies in East Asian Buddhism 8. Honolulu: University of Hawaii Press, 1993.

Brown, Delmer M., and Ichiro Ishida. *The Future and the Past: A Translation and Study of the Gukansho, an Interpretative History of Japan Written in 1210.* Berkeley, Calif.: University of California Press, 1979.

Coates, Harper, and R. Ishizuka. *Hōnen, the Buddhist Saint: His Life and Teaching.* Kyoto: Chionin, 1925.

Collcutt, Martin. *Five Mountains: The Rinzai Zen Monastic Institution in Medieval Japan.* Cambridge, Mass.: Harvard University Press, 1981.

Covell, Jon Carter, and Sobin Yamada. *Zen at Daitoku-ji.* Tokyo: Kodansha International, 1974.

———, in collaboration with Sobin Yamada. *Unraveling Zen's Red Thread: Ikkyū's Controversial Way.* Elizabeth, N.J.: Hollym International Corp., 1980.

Davis, Winston. *Japanese Religion and Society: Paradigms of Structure and Change.* Albany, N.Y.: State University of New York Press, 1992. (Kiyozawa Manshi discussed in chapter 5, "Buddhism and Modernization.")

De Bary, William Theodore, ed. *Sources of Japanese Tradition*. Vol 1. New York: Columbia University Press, 1964.

de Visser, M. W. *Ancient Buddhism in Japan*. 2 vols. Leiden: E. J. Brill, 1935.

Dobbins, James C. *Jodo Shinshu: Shin Buddhism in Medieval Japan*. Bloomington, Ind.: Indiana University Press, 1989.

Dumoulin, Heinrich. *Zen Buddhism: A History*. Vol. 2, *Japan*. Translated by James W. Heisig and Paul Knitter. New York: Macmillan Publishing Company; London: Collier Macmillan, 1990.

Eliot, Sir Charles. *Japanese Buddhism*. London: Routledge and Kegan Paul, 1964.

Fields, Rick. *How the Swans Came to the Lake: A Narrative History of Buddhism in America*. Boston: Shambhala Publications, 1981.

Groner, Paul. *Saichō: The Establishment of the Japanese Tendai School*. Berkeley Buddhist Studies Series 7. Berkeley, Calif.: University of California, 1984.

Hakeda, Yoshito S. *Kukai: Major Works*. New York: Columbia University Press, 1972.

Haneda, Nobuo. "The Life of Manshi Kiyozawa." In *December Fan: The Buddhist Essays of Manshi Kiyozawa*, pp. 77–90. Kyoto: Higashi Honganji, 1984.

Hardacre, Helen. *Shinto and the State, 1868–1988*. Princeton, N.J.: Princeton University Press, 1989.

Hirota, Dennis. *No Abode: The Record of Ippen*. Kyoto: Ryukoku University, 1986.

Hori, Ichiro. *Folk Religion in Japan*. Chicago: University of Chicago Press, 1968.

Inoue, Yasushi. *The Roof Tile of Tempyo*. Translated by James T. Araki. Tokyo: University of Tokyo Press, 1975.

Keene, Donald. "The Portrait of Ikkyū." In *Landscapes and Portraits: Appreciations of Japanese Culture*. Tokyo: Kodansha International, 1971. Also in *Some Japanese Portraits*. Tokyo: Kodansha International, 1983.

Kim, Hee-Jin. *Dōgen Kigen—Mystical Realist*. Tucson, Ariz.: University of Arizona Press, 1975.

Kishimoto, Hideo, ed. *Japanese Culture in the Meiji Era*. Vol. 2, *Religion*. Tokyo: Toyo Bunko, 1969.

Kitagawa, Joseph M. *On Understanding Japanese Religion*. Princeton, N.J.: Princeton University Press, 1987. (Kūkai discussed in chapter 11, "Master and Saviour.")

Kiyota, Minoru. *Shingon Buddhism: Theory and Practice*. Los Angeles: Buddhist Books International, 1978.

Kodama, Misao, and Hikosaku Yanagishima. *Ryōkan the Great Fool*. Kyoto: Kyoto Seika Junior College Press, 1969.

Kodera, Takashi James. *Dogen's Formative Years in China: An Historical*

Study and Annotated Translation of the Hōkyō-ki. Boulder, Colo.: Prajna Press, 1980.

Kondo, Tessho. "The Religious Experience of Ippen." *The Eastern Buddhist,* n.s., 12, no. 2 (October 1979): 92–116.

Kraft, Kenneth. *Eloquent Zen: Daito and Early Japanese Zen.* Honolulu: University of Hawaii Press, 1992.

Matsunaga, Daigan, and Alicia Matsunaga. *Foundation of Japanese Buddhism.* 2 vols. Los Angeles: Buddhist Books International, 1974, 1976.

McMullin, Neil. *Buddhism and the State in Sixteenth-Century Japan.* Princeton, N.J.: Princeton University Press, 1984.

Morrell, Robert E. "Jokei and the Kofuku-ji Petition." *Japanese Journal of Religious Studies* 10, no. 1 (1983): 6–38.

———. *Sand and Pebbles: The Tales of Muju Ichinen, a Voice for Pluralism in Kamakura Buddhism.* Albany, N.Y.: State University of New York Press, 1985.

———. *Early Kamakura Buddhism, a Minority Report.* Berkeley, Calif.: Asian Humanities Press, 1987.

Morris, Ivan. "Saigō Takamori." In *The Nobility of Failure.* Tokyo: Tuttle, 1982.

Murakami, Shigeyoshi. *Japanese Religion in the Modern Century.* Translated by Byron Earhart. Tokyo: University of Tokyo Press, 1980.

Nakamura, Kyoko Motomochi. *Miraculous Stories from the Japanese Buddhist Tradition: The Nihon Ryōiki of the Monk Kyōkai.* Cambridge, Mass.: Harvard University Press, 1973.

Nihongi: Chronicles of Japan from the Earliest Times to A.D. 697. Translated by W. G. Aston. Tokyo: Tuttle, 1972.

Reischauer, Robert Karl. *Early Japanese History.* 2 vols. Gloucester, Mass.: Peter Smith, 1967.

Rogers, Minor Lee. "The Shin Faith of Rennyo." *The Eastern Buddhist,* n.s., 15, no. 1 (Spring 1982): 56–73.

Sanford, James H. *Zen-Man Ikkyū.* Harvard Studies in World Religion, no. 2. Chico, Calif.: Scholars Press, 1981.

Sansom, Sir George. *A History of Japan to 1334.* Tokyo: Tuttle, 1974.

Senzaki, Nyogen, Sōen Nakagawa, and Eido Shimano. *Namu Dai Bosa: A Transmission of Zen Buddhism to America.* New York: Theatre Arts Books, 1976.

Suzuki, Daisetsu T. *Shin Buddhism.* New York: Harper and Row, 1970.

Takahatake, Takamichi. *Young Man Shinran: a Reappraisal of Shinran's Life.* Waterloo, Ont.: Walter Laurier University Press, 1987.

Varley, Paul. *The Onin War.* New York: Columbia University Press, 1967.

Watson, Burton. *Ryōkan: Zen Monk-Poet of Japan.* New York: Columbia University Press, 1977.

Weinstein, Stanley. "Rennyo and the Shin Sect Revival." In *Japan in the Muromachi Age,* edited by John Whitney Hall and Toyoda Takeshi. Berkeley, Calif.: University of California Press, 1977.

Yamamoto, Kosho. *An Introduction to Shin Buddhism.* Ube: Karinbunko, 1963.

Yamasaki, Taiko. *Shingon: Japanese Esoteric Buddhism.* Translated by Richard and Cynthia Peterson. Boston: Shambhala Publications, 1988.

Yanagi, Soetsu. "Ippen Shonin." *The Eastern Buddhist,* n.s., 6, no. 2 (October 1973): 33–57.

Contributors

Manabu Fujii is professor of Japanese history at Kyoto Prefectural University.

Daisetsu Fujioka is professor of Japanese history at Shimane Prefectural Women's Junior College.

Takehiko Furuta is a professor at Showa College of Pharmaceutical Science.

Aishin Imaeda is professor emeritus of the University of Tokyo.

Yuishin Itō is professor of Japanese literature at Bukkyo University.

Yūsen Kashiwahara is professor emeritus of Otani University.

Shiki Kodama is professor of history and philosophy at Shimonoseki College of Fishery.

Hitoshi Ōkuwa is professor of Japanese history at Otani University.

Ryū Sakuma is a lecturer at Tokai Gakuen Women's Junior College.

Kōyū Sonoda is a professor at Kansai University.

Kōnen Tsunemitsu (1891–1973) was the publisher of *The Bukkyo Times,* a newspaper devoted to Japanese Buddhist affairs.

Index

Name in **BOLD CAPITALS** indicates biography is included in part 1; name in **bold** type indicates biography is included in part 2. For written works, full bibliographic information, as well as Chinese and Sanskrit translations of titles, can be found in the Documents section of this Appendix.

362

364 INDEX

Collection of Kakusō [Hara Tanzan] (Hara Tanzan), 292
collection of letters to Saichō from Kūkai, 47
Collection of National Polity, 48
Collection of Passages on the Original Vow and the Nembutsu (Hōnen), 63, 67, 69–70, 90, 266, 267, 284
Collection of Poetry Exchanged by Gen[sei] and Yüan[-yun], 279
Collection of the Discussions in Dreams (Musō Soseki), 271
Collection of the Essentials of the Jōdo Sect (Benchō), 266
Collection of Writings on the Chapter of Manifest and Unmanifest (Kakujō), 268
Collection [Telling How] the Nembutsu Invocation Created Good (Chōgen), 264
Commentary on Fa Li's Annotations on the Vinaya of Four Categories (Ting-pin), 16
Commentary on the Meditation Sutra (Shan-tao), 66–67, 137, 267
community ceremonies, 22
Concentration and Insight, 33, 77, 257
Continued Chronicles of Japan (comp. Fujiwara no Tsugutada), 3, 4–5, 6, 8, 9
Correction of the Errors of Buddhist Doctrine (Joseph Edkins), 291
Court Buddhism, 125, 126, 127
Crazy Cloud Collection (Ikkyū), 147, 149–50, 154, 155, 156–57
Critique of the Three Articles of Instruction, A (Shimaji Mokurai), 215

Daien (大円; fl. ca. 1782), 287
Daigo, Emperor (醍醐天皇; r. 897–930), 54
Daikō (大航; fl. ca. 1892), 228
Dainichibō Nōnin (大日房能忍; d. 1194?), 80, 118, 120
Daiseishi Bodhisattva, 74
Daitoku-ji Regulations (1615), 176–80, 183
Daitsū (大通; 1649–1716), 282

"dancing nembutsu," 143–44
Death Registers for Clergy in Days Gone By (Ippen and Shinkyō), 145
Department of Shinto Ritual, 213, 214
Description of the Meditation Sutra (Jōjin), 261
Description of the Teachings of Yūzū Nembutsu (Daitsū), 282
Detailed Accounts of the Spherical Model (Sada Kaiseki), 290
Dewdrops on a Lotus Leaf (Ryōkan and Teishinni), 192
Dharma Words of National Teacher Daitō (Sōhō Myōchō), 270
Diamond Peak Sutra, 257
Diamond Realm, 46, 257
Diary of National Teacher Honkō (Sūden), 277
Discourse on the Awakening of Faith in the Mahayana (Ashvaghosha), 225, 243, 292
Discussion of the Five Teachings and the Ten Sects (Fa-tsang), 31, 265
Discussion of the Pure Land (Hōrin), 284
Discussion on the Teachings of the Jōdo Sect (Benchō), 266
Distinction Between Faith and Reason (Takuan), 178
DŌGEN (道元; 1200–1253), 97, 124, 137, 188, 189, 193; anecdote about, 97–98; birth and early life of, 98; death of, 122; and founding of Eihei-ji, 119–20; his meeting Ju-ching, 99–100; his practice of "just sitting," 100–119; rejection of lay Buddhism by, 120–22; as Tendai cleric, 98–99
Dōhō, Prince (道法親王; 1166–1214), 84
Dōji (道慈; d. 744), 3, 7, 15–16, 255
Dōkyō (道鏡; d. 772), 3, 24
Dōsen (道璿; Tao-hsüan; 702–760), 16–17, 19, 20, 29
Dōshō (道昭; 629–700), 3, 4, 254
Dōshō (道昌; 798–875), 257–58
Doubts Concerning the Bodhisattva Precepts (Kakujō), 268

and early life of, 64–67; *Collection of Passages on the Original Vow and the Nembutsu,* 69–70, 266, 284; conflict surrounding, 70–72; death of, 73–75, 92; exile of, 72–73; as figure of controversy, 63–64; growing influence of, 67–69; and Ippen, 135, 136, 137, 138, 143, 144; and Shinran, 90–92, 93, 94
Hōren (法蓮; fl. ca. 721), 8
Hōrin (法霖; 1693–1741), 283, 284
Hosshin (法進; Fa-chin; 709–778), 21, 22, 23, 25
Hōtan (鳳潭; 1659–1738), 283–84
House of Councilors, 300
Hōzō (法蔵; 905–969), 60, 260
Hsiang-yen (祥彦; fl. ca. 742), 17
Hsing-man (行満; fl. ca. 804), 31, 32
Hsü-an Huai-ch'ang (虚菴懐敞; fl. ca. 1187), 79
Hsüan-tsang (玄奘三蔵; 600–664), 254
Hsüan-tsung, emperor of China (玄宗; 685–762), 16, 154
Huang-lung Hui-nan (黄竜慧南; 1002–1069), 79
Hui-kuo (恵果; 746–805), 45–46
Hymn of Amida's Vow (Ippen), 146

Ichinose Chūtarō (一瀬忠太郎; fl. ca. 1870), 220
Igan Shūtetsu (囲巌宗鉄; fl. ca. 1700), 281
Ii Naosuke (井伊直弼; 1815–1860), 194, 195, 201
I-jan. *See* Itsunen
Ikegami Munenaka (池上宗仲; fl. ca. 13th century), 134
Ikkō Shunjō (一向俊聖; 1239–1287), 136
IKKYŪ Sōjun (一休宗純; 1394–1481), 147, 173–74, 175–76, 189; birth and early life of, 147–49; character of, 147, 148, 149–51; his confrontation with Yōsō, 151–53; death of, 157; his love of attendant Mori, 153–57; portraits of, 157–58
Illustrated Life of the Revered Master of Hongan-ji (Kakunyo),88, 89

Imakita Kōsen (今北洪川; 1816–1892), 220–21, 225, 242, 245
Imperial Academy, 292, 297, 298
Imperial Constitution, 242
Imperial Parliament, 242
In Defense of Buddhism (Mori Shōken), 290
Indications of the Goals of the Three Teachings (Kūkai), 42
Ingen (隠元; Yin-yüan; 1592–1673), 187, 279–80
Inoue Enryō (井上円了; 1858–1919), 230, 231, 235, 295–96, 298, 299
Instructions for the Zen Cook (Dōgen), 97, 117
IPPEN (一遍; 1239–1289), 53, 124, 135; birth of, 136; and "dancing nembutsu," 143–44; death of, 146; enlightenment gained by, 137–39; religious wandering of, 145–46; as sage who discarded everything, 141–43; teachings of, 139–41; as warrior's son, 135–36
Iron Wall and Piece of Cloud (Hōtan), 283
I-shan I-ning. *See* Issan Ichinei
Issan Ichinei (一山一寧; I-shan I-ning; 1247–1317), 269–70
I-shan I-ning. *See* Issan Ichinei
Itō Hirobumi (伊藤博文; 1841–1909), 212
Itō Shōshin (伊藤証信; 1876–1963), 300–301
Itsunen (逸然; I-jan; 1601–1668), 280
Ittō Shōteki (一凍紹滴; 1539–1612), 173–74, 184

Jakumetsu (寂滅; fl. ca. 1235), 3
Japanese, The (magazine), 296
Japanese Spirituality (Suzuki Daisetz), 248–49
Jewel Cave of the Ten Good [Precepts] (magazine), 295
Jien (慈円; 1155–1225), 85, 267
Jihaku Shin (慈柏森; Mori; fl. ca. 1471), 155–57
Jikun (慈訓; 691–777), 4, 21–22, 25, 256